# Iran in the 21st Century

Iran is an ancient country, an oil-exporting economy and an Islamic Republic. It experienced two full-scale revolutions in the 20th century, the latter of which had large and important regional and international consequences, including an eight-year war with Saddam Hussein's Iraq. And now in the 21st century, it confronts issues, experiences and problems which have important implications for its future development and external relations.

In the domestic sphere, the country faces conflicts over national identity and ethnic minorities, democracy and human rights, personal and political freedoms, women's rights, youth culture, full employment, the economy and the use of the oil revenues, and the widening gap between rich and poor. Regarding external affairs, there are more or less severe problems both in regional and in global relations, headed by the ongoing conflict with the West over Iran's nuclear energy programme.

This book is the first study of Iran at the turn of the 21st century in all the above aspects by leading sociologists, social anthropologists, political scientists and economists in the field of Iranian studies.

**Homa Katouzian** is a social scientist, historian, literary critic and poet. He is the Iran Heritage Research Fellow, St Antony's College and Member, Faculty of Oriental Studies, University of Oxford, and an Honorary Research Fellow in the Department of Politics, University of Exeter, and editor of Iranian Studies.

**Hossein Shahidi** teaches Communication at the American University of Beirut. He was a journalist and journalist trainer for more than twenty years, mostly at the BBC World Service, and Gender and Media Specialist with the United Nations Development Fund for Women (UNIFEM) in Afghanistan (2003–2004).

**Iranian Studies**
Edited by
Homa Katouzian
*University of Oxford*

Mohamad Tavakoli
*University of Toronto*

Since 1967 the International Society for Iranian Studies (ISIS) has been a leading learned society for the advancement of new approaches in the study of Iranian society, history, culture and literature. The new ISIS Iranian Studies series published by Routledge will provide a venue for the publication of original and innovative scholarly works in all areas of Iranian and Persianate Studies.

# Iran in the 21st Century

Politics, economics and conflict

**Edited by
Homa Katouzian and
Hossein Shahidi**

Routledge
Taylor & Francis Group

LONDON AND NEW YORK

First published 2008
by Routledge
2 Park Square, Milton Park, Abingdon, Oxon OX14 4RN

Simultaneously published in the USA and Canada
by Routledge
270 Madison Ave, New York, NY 10016

*Routledge is an imprint of the Taylor & Francis Group,
an informa business*

Typeset in Times New Roman by
Newgen Imaging Systems (P) Ltd, Chennai, India
Printed and bound in Great Britain by
Antony Rowe Ltd, Chippenham, Wiltshire

*British Library Cataloguing in Publication Data*
A catalogue record for this book is available
from the British Library

*Library of Congress Cataloging in Publication Data*
Katouzian, Homa.
    Iran in the 21st century : politics, economics and confrontation /
Homa Katouzian and Hossein Shahidi.
        p. cm. – (Iranian studies ; 3)
    Includes bibliographical references and index.
    1. Iran – Social conditions – 1997 2. Iran – Politics and government –
1997– 3. Iran – Economic condition – 1997– I. Shahidi, Hossein, 1953–
II. Title. III. Title: Iran in the twenty-first century.
    HN670.2.A8K39 2007
    955.05'44–dc22                                              2007008685

ISBN10: 0–415–43558–7 (hbk)
ISBN10: 0–415–43559–5 (pbk)
ISBN10: 0–203–93977–8 (ebk)

ISBN13: 978–0–415–43558–1 (hbk)
ISBN13: 978–0–415–43559–8 (pbk)
ISBN13: 978–0–203–93977–2 (ebk)

# Contents

# Figures

# Tables

# Notes on contributors

**Hamid Ahmadi** is Professor of Political Science at the Faculty of Law and Political Science, and a senior researcher at the Center for Middle Eastern Studies, University of Tehran. His published works include 'Unity within Diversity: The Foundations and Dynamics of National Identity in Iran', *Critique*, 14.1, 2005, and the following books in Persian: *Irano-Saudi Relations during the Pahlavi Era* (2007); *Con-societal Democracy and Political Stability in Divided Societies, the Case of Lebanon* (2007) and *Ethnicity and Ethnopolitics in Iran* (2006).

**Ali M. Ansari** is Professor of Iranian History at the University of St Andrews and Associate Fellow of the Middle East Program with reference to Iran, at Chatham House. His published works include *Iran, Islam and Democracy: The Politics of Managing Change* (2nd edition, 2006); *Modern Iran* (2nd edition, 2007) and *Confronting Iran, the Failure of US Foreign Policy and the Roots of Mistrust* (2006).

**Mehdi Askarieh** is the Radioactive Waste Disposal Assessment Manager at United Kingdom Nirex Limited (Nirex). He also chairs the international management boards of the OECD Nuclear Energy Agency's Thermochemical Data Base (TDB) and Sorption Project. His published works include *Topical Report on Post-closure Criticality Safety Assessment* (1998); *Nirex 97: An Assessment of the Post-closure Performance of a Deep Waste Repository at Sellafield, Overview* (1997) and 'The Potential Impact of Oil and Other Non-aqueous Phase Liquids (NAPLs) on the Long-term Management of Radioactive Wastes', *Proceedings of the 9th International Conference on Radioactive Waste Management and Environmental Remediation* (2005).

**Touraj Atabaki** is Professor of Social History of the Middle East and Central Asia at Leiden University and Senior Research Fellow at the International Institute of Social History, currently focusing on historiography of everyday life and comparative subaltern history. His recently published works include *The State and the Subaltern, Society and Politics in Turkey and Iran* (ed., 2007); *Iran and the First World War: A Battleground of the Great Powers* (ed., 2006); *Men of Order, Authoritarian Modernization in Turkey and Iran* (co-ed. with

Erik Jan Zürcher 2004) and *Beyond Essentialism. Who Writes Whose Past in the Middle East and Central Asia?* (2003).

**Farhad Atai** is Associate Professor of International Relations, University of Tehran. His books and articles include *Art and Culture in Post-Soviet Central Asia* (1998); *The United States and the World in the 21st Century* (in Persian, 2007); 'Nationalism and Nation-States in Central Asia and the Caucasus', *Central Asia and the Caucasus Review*, 44, winter 2004; 'Iran and the Newly Independent States of Central Asia', in *Iran and Eurasia*, eds, Anoushirvan Ehtesami and Ali Mohammadi (2000); 'State-Managed Art and Culture: The Case of Central Asia under the Soviet Union', in *Culture, Society, and Politics in Central Asia*, ed., P. Khosla (1999) and 'A new Outlook in Turkey's Regional Policy', *Middle East Quarterly*, 5, 18, Autumn 1999.

**Farideh Farhi** is an independent scholar and Affiliate Graduate Faculty of political science at the University of Hawai'i at Manoa. She has taught comparative politics at the University of Colorado, Boulder, the University of Hawai'i at Manoa, the University of Tehran and Shahid Beheshti University. Her published works include *States and Urban-Based Revolutions in Iran and Nicaragua* (1990) as well as numerous articles and book chapters on comparative analysis of revolutions and contemporary Iranian politics and foreign policy.

**Hassan Hakimian** is Senior Lecturer in Economics and Associate Dean at Cass Business School, City University (London). He specializes in Development Economics with reference to Iran and the Middle Eastern economies. He is the author of *Labour Transfer and Economic Development* and co-editor of *The State and Global Change*, and *Trade Policy and Economic Integration in the Middle East and North Africa*. He has published in various academic journals and acted as consultant to international institutions and aid agencies. He is the editor of the Routledge Series '*Political Economy of the Middle East and North Africa*'.

**Ahmad R. Jalali-Naini** is Chair of the Department of Economics at the Institute for Management and Planning Studies, Tehran, Iran. He has taught graduate macroeconomics, monetary theory and finance. His research interest and work covers monetary and exchange rate policy, banking risk analysis and business cycle studies, particularly in MENA countries. He has served as Director of Financial Markets in Energy at the International Institute for Energy Studies and as Director of Foreign Exchange Studies at the Institute for Monetary and Banking Research, Central Bank of Iran.

**Massoud Karshenas** is Professor of Economics at the University of London (SOAS), and a fellow and member of the Board of Trustees of the Economic Research Forum for Arab Countries, Turkey and Iran (ERF). His numerous published works include *Oil State and Industrialization in Iran* (1990); *Industrialization and Agricultural Surplus: A Comparative Study of Economic*

*Development in Asia* (1995) and *Social Policy in the Middle East: Political, Economic, and Gender Dynamics* (ed. with V.M. Moghadam, 2006).

**Homa Katouzian** is the Iran Heritage Foundation Research Fellow, St Antony's College and Member, Faculty of Oriental Studies, University of Oxford and Honorary Research Fellow in the Department of Politics, University of Exeter. He is the editor of *Iranian Studies*, Journal of the International Society for Iranian Studies. His recently published works include *Iranian History and Politics, the Dialectic of State and Society* (paperback edition, 2007); *Sadeq Hedayat, His Work and His Wondrous World* (ed., 2007); *Sa'di, the Poet of Life, Love and Compassion* (2006) and *State and Society in Iran, the Eclipse of the Qajars and the Emergence of the Pahlavis* (paperback edition, 2006).

**Azadeh Kian-Thiébaut** is Professor of Sociology and Gender Studies, University of Paris 7 (Denis Diderot) and a researcher at CNRS-monde iranien et indien. Her recently published works include, *La République islamique d'Iran: de la maison du Guide à la raison d'Etat* (2005); *Famille et mutations socio-politiques* (ed. with M. Ladier-Fouladi, 2005); 'Mahmoud Ahmadinejad, la césure', *Outre-Terre, Revue française de géopolitique*, 16, 2006; 'L'Iran: menace ou modèle pour le monde musulman?', *Questions internationales*, 25, 2007 and 'Le féminisme et l'islam, Les conservateurs iraniens face aux mouvements des droits des femmes', *La vie des idées*, 2007.

**Saideh Lotfian** is Associate Professor of Political Science and Associate Dean for Research at the Faculty of Law and Political Science, University of Tehran, and has taught at Boston University and the University of Iowa. She has been a member of the Pugwash Council since 2002, was a visiting researcher at Stockholm International Peace Research Institute in 1995 and Visiting Iranian Fellow at St Antony's College, University of Oxford in 2003. She has written many articles on non-proliferation and nuclear disarmament in the Middle East, security of the Persian Gulf and Central Asia and foreign and defence policies of Iran.

**Trita Parsi** is Adjunct Professor of International Relations at Johns Hopkins University SAIS in Washington DC. He is the author of *Treacherous Alliance – The Secret Dealings of Israel, Iran and the United States* (2007).

**Ahmad Sadri** is Professor of Sociology and James P. Gorter Chair of Islamic World Studies at Lake Forest College. He is the author of *Max Weber's Sociology of Intellectuals* (1994) and three books in Persian.

**Mahmoud Sadri** is Professor of Sociology at Texas Woman's University and the Federation of North Texas Area Universities. His published works include *Migration Dynamics: A Theoretical and Substantive Reader* (with Mohsen Mobasher, 2003); *Reason, Freedom, and Democracy in Islam: The Essential Writings of Abdolkarim Soroush* (with Ahmad Sadri, 2000); 'Weber and the Stroussian Charge of Relativism', *Rethinking Sociology Series* (with Ahmad Sadri, 2007); 'Premonitions of Interfaith Dialogue', *Interreligious Insight*,

January, 2006 and 'Sacral Defense of Secularism', *Intellectual Trends in 20th Century Iran* (2003).

**Djavad Salehi-Isfahani** is Professor of Economics at Virginia Tech. He was Assistant Professor of Economics at the University of Pennsylvania (1977–1984) and visiting faculty at the University of Oxford (1991–1992). He has served on the Board of Trustees of the Economic Research Forum (2001–2006), a network of Middle East economists based in Cairo, where he has been a Research Fellow since 1993, and on the Board of the Middle East Economic Association. He is the co-author of *The World Oil Market* (1991) and has edited *Labor and Human Capital in the Middle East* (2001).

**Hossein Shahidi** is Assistant Professor of Communication at the American University of Beirut and assistant editor, social sciences, of *Iranian Studies*. He was a journalist and journalist trainer (1979–2001), mostly at the BBC World Service, and Gender and Media Specialist with the United Nations Development Fund for Woman (UNIFEM) in Afghanistan (2003–2004). Apart from writing extensively for the broadcast and print media on Iran, Central Asia and the Arab world, he has written a detailed account of the establishment of the BBC's Persian Service and its conduct during the conflict between Iran and Britain over the nationalization of Iranian oil. He is the author of *Journalism in Iran: From Mission to Profession* (2007).

# Preface

It had been increasingly felt within the circles of the academic profession of Iranian studies that an extensive if not comprehensive study of the social, economic and cultural problems facing Iran, conducted with the utmost intellectual detachment and objectivity, was long overdue and had to be addressed by members of the profession. To this end, an advisory programme committee which was formed consisting of Ahmad Ashraf, Ali Banuazizi, Hormoz Hekmat, Vahid Nowshirvani, Djavad Salehi-Isfahani, Reza Sheikholeslami and me, charged me and Sheikholeslami with arranging a conference on this theme at Wadham College that was also sponsored by St Antony's College and the Oriental Institute, all of the University of Oxford. I took on the task of organizing and coordinating the conference as well.

The international conference entitled 'Iran facing the new century' was duly held at Wadham between 4 and 7 April 2004. It was attended by about 45 guest speakers, chairs and discussants from distances as far apart as Hawaii and Afghanistan. They presented papers and partook in discussions on Iranian national identity, domestic economic problems and issues, Iran's foreign and regional relations, issues regarding reforms and political development, the position of women, the Iranian Diasporas, etc.

From the earliest conception of the conference it had been intended that its proceedings should be gathered in final drafts and edited by Hossein Shahidi and myself for publication as a book, a book which both because of its subject and in view of the prominence of its authors is likely to become a standard text for the relevant academic courses. However, Trita Parsi's contribution was later added to the collection. I should also point out that the last article was presented to another conference, the annual conference of the Iranian Economic Association on economic history and Iranian economic history held in early December 2004 in Tehran. They asked me to be the keynote speaker and I was otherwise engaged. They then suggested that I send them the paper and it would be presented by someone else, and as it turned out by Hossein Shahidi, to whom I am grateful both for this and for acting as joint editor of this volume. Since the paper had been written in English, I thought it would be appropriate to include it in this volume as a critical view of issues arising both from economic history and especially from the economic history of Iran.

It is because of the great importance of the matter that I mention last the extremely generous financial support of the Persian Cultural Foundation, without which nothing like the scale and distinction of the conference could have been attempted let alone achieved. And all the more so because not only is Dr Akbar Ghahary, the Foundation's Managing Director, terribly keen on the promotion of Persian and Iranian studies, but, equally helpfully, he does so with good humour, the minimum of fuss and no undue intervention in the running of the programmes and projects which he supports. He therefore deserves a large vote of thanks and a big round of applause from all those who are involved in this process, be they lay or academic.

Homa Katouzian
2007

# 1 Introduction

## Iran in the 21st century – politics, economics and conflict

### Homa Katouzian and Hossein Shahidi

Iran has emerged from the 20th century having experienced two massive revolutions, two world wars, a movement for independence and democracy which began with the nationalization of Iranian oil and ended with the coup d'etat of August 1953, and a long war with Iraq. In the meantime the Qajar monarchy gave way to the Pahlavi dynasty, and the latter to an Islamic Republic.

A century ago the Constitutional Revolution aimed at the establishment of government based in law in place of Iran's traditional arbitrary rule (*estebdad*), and ended up with a constitution which promised not only lawful but also democratic government. Virtually the entire urban society rose up against the state, including landlords, merchants, the ulama and the common people, the peasantry not having an independent presence in the Revolution. No social class resisted the Revolution, and the small number of ulama who advocated Islamic government (*mashru'eh*) did not manage to attract a sizable public following.

Yet the Revolution's triumph in 1909 led to growing chaos rather than law, order and democratic government, for chaos had been the traditional Iranian society's response to the fall of the state. The intrusion of World War I and the warring forces into the country worsened the state of chaos but it was not its cause; nor did the end of the war result in a normal state either in politics or in society. Chaos was not only in the provinces but more effectively in the capital, in the centre of politics, in the parliament, in the government, in the press and in the streets. The 1919 Anglo-Iranian Agreement was intended to bring stability to the country and prepare the ground for modernization within the framework of constitutional monarchy. But Iranians saw this as a British attempt to turn Iran into a protectorate and their solid opposition prevented its application and implementation.

All roads to the normal functioning of constitutional government having thus been blocked, the country's choices were either disintegration – as had happened many times in its long history – or a strong government which would stamp out chaos and impose order and discipline. This was achieved by the 1921 coup which brought Reza Khan to power with some help from British military officers and diplomats on the ground, although the British government had had no previous knowledge of it. The relative security and stability which this brought within a couple of years was appreciated by a growing number of propertied and modern social classes who provided the principal base and legitimacy for Reza Khan's successful bid in 1925 to abolish the Qajars and establish his own monarchy in 1926. Even the ulama acquiesced in the establishment of the Pahlavi regime.

It was in the first decade of Reza Khan/Reza Shah's rule, 1921–1931, when the chaos was stamped out everywhere and the foundations for modern industry and public institutions were laid. This was a decade of growing dictatorship, but in the decade which followed, government reverted back to the traditional Iranian arbitrary rule in a modern guise. By the time the Allied troops entered Iran in 1941, there was little political legitimacy and social base left for the Shah, the landlords having been alienated because of encroachments on their property and the elimination of their political influence; merchants, also for the same reasons as well as the government's strong *étatist* policies; the ulama, for attacks on religious culture and institutions; ministers and the civil service, for having no executive power at all; and modern intellectuals, for the absence of freedom and human rights.

The abdication of Reza Shah did not result in democracy but once again in chaos in the centre as well as in the provinces, in line with Iran's age-old traditions. At one stage riots were organized by the royal court and leading establishment politicians during which the prime minister's own house was ransacked and looted. There were revolts in Azerbaijan, Fars and elsewhere. The Tudeh party at first attracted many young and younger modern Iranians who longed for democratic government, but its approval of the revolt in Azerbaijan under pressure from the Soviet Union lost it much support. And later, when it became an orthodox Stalinist party, it lost its popular base despite enjoying a strong militant membership.

It was the movement for the nationalization of Iranian oil led by the National Front which attracted the Tudeh's erstwhile popular base and more. It began in the late 1940s following an official attempt to extract from the Anglo–Iranian Oil Company concessions to rectify the 1933 oil agreement. This agreement was highly unpopular and the strongest reason why most Iranians believed, although unfairly, that Reza Shah had been a British agent. The nationalization of Iranian oil quickly became symbolic for a campaign to rid the country of British interference in its politics, the adoption of a non-aligned foreign policy and the promotion of democratic government.

Thus Iranian politics was made up of three opposing tendencies: the Tudeh party which depended on the Soviet Union and favoured a totalitarian regime; the Shah and conservatives who wanted a strong regime and sought Western support; and Mosaddeq and the popular movement who believed in parliamentary democracy and non-alignment. But the situation was far from stable since the conservatives and Tudeh were both busy trying to eliminate their other two rivals, and Mosaddeq's government did not try hard enough to check rebellious and chaotic activities. On the other hand, the failure to settle the oil dispute with Britain and the loss of oil revenues resulting from the international boycott of Iranian oil led to the deterioration of the economic and political situation. Eventually the American and British governments managed to organize and enable Mosaddeq's conservative opponents to stage the coup d'etat of August 1953.

The decade 1953–1963 was a period of growing dictatorship somewhat comparable to the first decade of Reza Shah's rule, although its last three years witnessed a power struggle from which Mohammad Reza Shah emerged triumphant. In 1955 the Shah dismissed General Zahedi's loyal government in a bid to strengthen his own personal rule, but until 1960 the parliament still had a certain amount of independence, although it was dominated by the landlords, and its members had to have the Shah's approval. In the meantime, the Consortium oil agreement and American foreign aid returned the flow of foreign exchange which enabled the Plan Organization to implement the second Five Year Plan, but corruption and the 'open doors' foreign trade policy led to the economic crisis of 1960.

Ali Amini's loyal government of 1961–1962 intended to reduce the Shah's executive powers, curb corruption and implement a land-reform programme. It had America's blessing and managed to make a beginning with land reform, but the combined opposition of the Shah, the second National Front and the Tudeh party forced it to resign. The fall of Amini considerably strengthened the Shah who in January 1963 put a six-point social and economic reform programme, described as the White Revolution, that included land reform and women's suffrage to referendum. The landlords felt unhappy for loss of economic as well as social power, the ulama were alienated for the same reasons as well as the Westernizing trends, and the urban public was restless owing to lack of freedom and political participation. The result was the revolt of June 1963 led by Ayatollah Khomeini; the revolt was suppressed, and the Ayatollah was later exiled to Turkey and eventually Iraq.

From the mid-1960s until the late 1970s power was concentrated entirely in the Shah's hands rather like the second decade of his father's rule. The growth and then explosion of the oil revenues greatly strengthened the state vis-à-vis the public as well as foreign powers. There was a high growth rate throughout the period although differences in income and welfare increased both between town and country and within the urban sector itself. The total absence of freedom and participation coupled with Western, especially American, support for the Shah convinced the public that he was no more than a puppet who was implementing the policies of imperialism. This led to very strong feelings against both the Shah and the West even in the upper classes of society. Therefore, when in 1977 a limited degree of freedom was allowed, largely in response to criticisms from the West, there was a massive revolt which ended in the fall of the state in February 1979.

Just like the Constitutional Revolution and the traditional Iranian revolts before it, the 1979 Revolution was a revolt of the society against the state. No social class or political party defended the regime, and towards the end, men and women of the highest orders of society joined the massive demonstrations against it. Islamic, traditional and modern, liberal, democratic and Marxist–Leninist, they were bound together only by the objective of removing the Shah and bringing down the state. It was therefore natural that in the chaos that followed the declaration of the Islamic Republic, not only various political parties and trends, but also various social classes and groups should come into conflict with one another over what was to replace the fallen regime. The result was extensive as well as intensive civil conflict, the monopolization of political power by the Islamists of the Revolution and the widespread emigration of the persecuted and disenchanted.

The war with Iraq which was started by Saddam Hussein in 1980 was a double-edged sword. It led to great human sacrifice, physical destruction and financial losses, but it also helped consolidate the new Islamic regime – led by Ayatollah Khomeini representing *velayat-e faqih* or guardianship of the jurisconsult – to the exclusion of all other political tendencies. Ayatollah Khomeini's death in 1989, a year after ceasefire with Iraq, was followed by the succession of Ayatollah Khameneh'i to spiritual leadership, a period of reconstruction under President Rafsanjani, and the emergence of conflict within the ranks of the Islamists themselves. All being Islamists, the President represented the pragmatic tendency; the Assembly of Experts and the Council of Guardians of the Constitution symbolized the conservatives; while the radical fundamentalists and the revisionist reformists stood at either end of the spectrum.

Mohammad Khatami's surprise election as president in 1997 led to an upsurge of reformist activity. There was more freedom of expression, greater observance of legal processes, higher regard for human rights, less cultural pressure on women, and a certain amount of normalization in regional and foreign relations. Yet the eight years of Khatami's presidency saw the consolidation of anti-reformist factions, the slowdown of the pace of reform, the division of reformists into various tendencies and the loss of the early optimism for political reform and development. Finally, there appeared to be almost a complete reversal of the reformist trends with the shock electoral victory in 2005 of President Ahmadinejad who was close to the radical fundamentalist tendencies.

Such was the background in brief of Iranian history, politics and society when Iran arrived at the 21st century. In the domestic sphere, the country faces conflicts over national identity and ethnic minorities, democracy and human rights, personal and political freedoms, women's rights, youth culture, full employment, the economy and the use of the oil revenues, and the widening gap between rich and poor. Regarding external affairs, there are more or less severe problems both in regional and in global relations, headed by the ongoing conflict with the West over Iran's nuclear energy programme.

The question of national identity or what makes an Iranian has been a source of conflict, disagreement and tension since the 1920s. In her chapter, 'Crafting a national identity amidst contentious politics in contemporary Iran', Farideh Farhi argues that in the past century Iranians have been energetically vacillating between extremes of contentious Islamism and secularism, pre-Islamic and Islamic imagination, and avid anti-imperialism and absorption in global trends, leaving them with 'tired bodies and souls'. According to Farhi, the latest phase of this experience is the Iranians' disappointment with the reform process that emerged in the Islamic Republic, and which led them to find 'solace in their private homes and selves'. They were not helped by 'platitudinous' efforts to forge a 'Janus-faced national identity as children of both Cyrus the Great *and* Mohammad'. This is a direct reference to the Nobel Laureate Shirin Ebadi, who, according to Farhi, was declared by the 'sanguine Norwegian guardians of global political correctness' as an example of the possibility of being acceptable as a Muslim, a democrat, a liberated (wo)man, a proud Iranian with pre-Islamic heritage, and at peace with the world, all at the same time.

Farhi sets herself the task of answering a set of questions: Can the 'mantra' exemplified by the Ebadi case be believed by those who are meant to be the 'carriers of these multiple identities'? Can the Iranian body-politic survive, with its 'habitual self-mutilation through the expunging of substantial parts of itself'? Have Iranians 'lost yet another opportunity for a story/narrative' that makes them feel good about themselves as a collectivity? Is 'the bipolar pull of extremes' their story, as well as their fate?

Farhi maintains that Iran cannot achieve social and political cohesion and stability 'without a narrative that connects, at least loosely, all sectors of the society to a somewhat commonly acceptable recent history'; that there needs to be an understanding of the century-long tension between 'autocratic/theocratic/ arbitrary rule and democracy/chaos, and Iran's relationship to the outside world'; and that this tension needs to be resolved gradually.

She points out that the national/ethnic question has become more complicated in the Islamic Republic, with the 'two conflicting and incompatible conceptions of sovereignty, authority and legitimacy that exist in the Islamic constitution', and laws that allow 'arbitrary clerical rule and fail to protect basic freedoms'. These factors have created common ground among those seeking political reform and those seeking equitable laws for ethnic and religious minorities, including the Sunni Muslims. Externally, 'engagement with the world and promotion of democracy at home have become inextricably linked in the Iranian political discourse'.

Hamid Ahmadi discusses the foreign policy implications of the Iranian–Islamic duality in his chapter, 'The dilemma of national interest in the Islamic Republic of Iran'. Ahmadi argues that the concept and practice of national interest in contemporary Iran has been affected by the supra-national outlook of the Islamic Republic's constitution and the structural dualism embedded in its political system. According to Ahmadi, the Islamic Republic's Constitution gives more weight to concern for the Islamic world in Iran's foreign policy, and can therefore be considered more as an Islamic internationalist charter than a document which delineates the guidelines for a foreign policy based on the national interest of a nation-state. The state structure, for its part, includes two conflicting components: the traditional Islamic system of *velayat-e faqih*, and the modern presidential system.

Ahmadi identifies three approaches to foreign policy under the Islamic Republic: 'rejecting the whole concept of national interest as an anti-Islamic notion'; 'justifying the idealistic foreign policy of the Islamic Republic as one which serves Iran's national interest'; or reducing national interest to a combination of the necessity of pursuing a realist foreign policy and 'the importance of maintaining the Islamic nature and values of the system'. The practical result has been a cycle of rise and fall of realism, pursued 'somehow' by the Foreign Ministry, and idealism promoted by the traditional power structure. The conflict, argues Ahmadi, was best exemplified in the controversies over Salman Rushdie in 1989 and the opposition to US–Iran rapprochement in 2001, and will not be resolved as long as the structural dualism exists.

In the chapter that follows, 'From multilingual empire to contested modern state', Touraj Atabaki further discusses the issues arising from the multi–ethnic nature of the Iranian society. Atabaki points out that six changes of the Iranian capital between 1500 and 1800 CE – Tabriz, Qazvin, Isfahan, Mashhad, Shiraz and Tehran – each brought about because of the assumption of power by a different ethnic community, and policies of forced resettlement and sedentarization of large nomadic tribes, have resulted in metropolitan centres with ethnically and religiously mixed populations. Although conflicts among these communities have not been uncommon, says Atabaki, 'not a single city has ever disintegrated because of ethnic or religious diversity.'

In more recent times, centralization of state power, further forced migration and resettlement of nomadic tribes, and rapid urbanization and industrialization have caused 'more ethnic dislocation', in particular creating large concentrations of Azerbaijanis in Tehran and many other big cities, 'dominating the local economy'. At the same time, the expansion of education and communication has contributed to a more homogeneous culture. Movements for varied degrees of autonomy for the country's ethnic minorities have been defeated, especially the ones among Iran's largest non-Persian speaking communities, the Azerbaijanis and the Kurds.

Atabaki reviews the rise and fall of the idea of Iranian Azerbaijan joining the Republic of Azerbaijan after the disintegration of the Soviet Union and concludes that while Iran has so far avoided the fate of the Ottoman, Russian and Soviet empires, the fate of its ethnic composition and its territorial integrity may depend, more than on any other factor, on the introduction of reforms in the country's political structure.

Mahmoud Sadri and Ahmad Sadri, writing about 'Three faces of dissent' in con- temporary Iran, examine two by-products of rapid urbanization and industrializa- tion: the emergence of 'expressive and traditionalist discourses of dissent', as distinct from the 'cognitive face' that is 'produced and disseminated, for the most part, by professional intellectuals: university professors, authors, journalists, and the clergy'. They argue that the expressive discourse 'usually takes immediate (e.g. audio-visual, demonstrative) forms with amorphous and intractable practi- tioners, who pose an immediate – even if ephemeral – threat to social order'. They describe one example of such discourse as found in the graffiti by Tehran youth groups who call themselves Rap or Heavy Metal – not always closely related to the Western concepts of the two terms – and are known by their Western hair and clothing styles. The two groups are confronted by the Basij, or mobilization, youth groups affiliated to the Revolutionary Guards.

According to the authors, one manifestation of the traditionalist discourse of dissent is in 'the heterodox mass religiosity of Persianate Shi'i Islam that continues to defy the yoke of official interpretation'. Examples include two religious sites dating back to the days before the Islamic Revolution: Jamkaran, in the vicinity of Qom, which received its mythical status through a dream in the middle of the 20th century, and Astaneh Ashrafieh, a popular mausoleum on the Caspian coast. These sites have been approved by the Islamic Republic and are provided with urban and transport services.

However, the government does not appear to favour the establishment of new holy sites, such as one that became the base of a spontaneous cult in the industrial city of Mobarakeh, Isfahan province, in 1993, when a housewife 'witnessed blood that she took to be that of Imam Hossein (Prophet Mohammad's grandson) bubble from underneath a brick on her earthen oven'. The cult was soon suppressed and its shrine demolished by the security forces. The authors explain the popularity of the cult by highlighting the growth of a community of impoverished immigrant workers facing alienation, humiliation and despair who live near Mobarakeh and are barred from fully participating in civic celebrations in the city, including mourning processions marking Imam Hossein's martyrdom. As for the reason behind the suppression of the cult, the authors argue that while such manifestations of mass religiosity would have been ignored by the secular, pre-Revolution regime, for a government based on religion they present 'a drain on scarce resources of legitimacy'.

Given the legal and social inequalities between men and women in Iran, women have been in the forefront of issues facing the Islamic Republic. The development of gender relationships in Iran since the 1979 Revolution is examined by Azadeh Kian-Thiébaut in her chapter, 'From motherhood to equal rights advocates: the weakening of patriarchal order'. She argues that while the Islamic Republic's legal system deprived women of their civil rights and institutionalized gender inequality, it also created an incentive for women to devise new strategies against traditionalist values and divine justifications for segregation policies. These included increased participation in the public sphere in spite of the patriarchal system and gender inequality, and questioning the patriarchal family founded on gendered roles and male domination, resulting in the weakening of patriarchal order and male domination in both public and private spheres.

Kian-Thiébaut further argues that women also refute patriarchal logic by establishing a new relationship with their children that is no longer founded on authority but on dialogue and persuasion. According to Kian-Thiébaut, youths' individualization, their resistance against totalitarian thought and forced Islamization, their aspiration to modernity and their demands for all-out social, political and cultural change are outcomes of a permissive type of education and new educational values adopted by their parents, especially their mothers. The stake is to construct a new relationship with the political power that would account for the profound changes that have occurred within the family institution.

The most important single issue facing Iran in its external relations is the continuation of the cold war between the United States and the Islamic Republic. In 'Iran and the US in the shadow of 9/11 – Persia and the Persian question revisited', Ali Ansari presents an analysis of 'the dialectical nature of US–Iran relations', especially following the 9/11 terrorist attacks on the US and President Bush's State of the Union address in January 2002, in which he classified Iran as a member of the 'Axis of Evil'. Ansari argues that the 9/11 events fundamentally altered the nature of US foreign policymaking, 'away from the bureaucratic rationality of the past and towards a charismatic justification with a revolutionary message'. During the same period Iran was following the opposite course, with a tendency for 'a routinization of the revolution, and more towards rationalization and the international order'. As a result, Iranian policy makers, steeped in American international relations theory, who had been seeking to engage the 'realist', were disconcerted to discover 'the revolutionary' in the United States.

Ansari defines the ensuing critical tension and a continued failure of communication as 'an epistemological gap' which 'may only be overcome through the exercise of decisive leadership'. Such leadership, however, appears to be lacking on both sides. The nuclear impasse between Iran and the United States indicates that 'neither side has been willing to recognize a cultural and ideological dimension to the construction of interest, or to see their positions as anything but real and rational. The focus on particularities has obfuscated the wider problem of cultural communication and disguised the reality that myth is just as important to US policymaking as it is to revolutionary Iran'.

The collapse of the Soviet Union in the 1990s presented Iran with fresh foreign policy problems regarding the newly independent Muslim countries on and near its borders. Farhad Atai considers Iran's relations with the former Soviet Republics in Central Asia and the Caucasus in 'A look to the north: opportunities and challenges'. Atai says that following the disintegration of the Soviet Union in 1991, Iran was in a unique strategic position with respect to the landlocked countries of the Central Asia–Caspian region with their massive energy resources. The same privileged position created concern in the West and in Russia that the Islamic Republic would be tempted to 'encourage Islamic movements and activities among the predominantly Muslim population of Central Asia, leading to further destabilization of the region'; that the peoples of the region would take Iran as their model to lay the foundations of their new independent states; and that, in the longer term, there would appear 'an Islamic block, with a population of 300 million, from the Mediterranean to the Indian Ocean'.

In practice, Iran's level of influence in Central Asia and the Caucasus has been relatively small, resulting from 'a rational and positive course of action', an important element of which has been the recognition of Russia's influence and interest in the region. Iran has been advocating unity and economic co-operation in Central Asia based on a common history and culture rather than radical Islam. Atai argues that all states in the region can benefit from long-term economic, political, and cultural relations with Iran which can be 'a moderating element' following '9/11 and the rise of extreme and violent Islamic radicalism – like that of the Taliban – in the region'.

The closely interrelated subjects of Iran-Israel relations and Iran's nuclear programme are discussed by Trita Parsi, Saideh Lotfian and Mehdi Askarieh.

In his chapter, 'Israel–Iranian relations assessed: strategic competition from the power cycle perspective', Trita Parsi tries to explain the state of Iranian–Israeli relations in the post-Cold War era – early to mid-1990s – from the perspective of Charles Doran's power cycle theory, which depicts the relative power of a state in relation to that of other states in its system. According to the theory, 'states follow a cyclical path of growth, maturation, and decline that mainly stems from uneven rates of internal economic development'. Power is calculated for each state on the basis of population, GDP, per capita GDP, energy consumption, military expenditure and military size. A state's ability to exercise its power without consuming it, described as the state's 'role', is granted to it by the other members of the system.

Parsi observes that both before and after the 1979 Revolution Iran has believed that its size, population, educational level and natural resources have destined it to be the most powerful nation in the region and that it should play a leadership role in regional affairs that reflects this perceived reality. Since the end of the Iraq–Iran war, however, Iran has gradually reduced its role aspirations and the definition of its national security environment to encompass only the Persian Gulf and Caspian Sea and not the greater Middle East. Parsi further argues that according to the power cycle theory, 'within this area, any order that would subjugate Iran to the domination of any other Middle East power would be unstable due to Iran's long-term rejection of such a role-power discrepancy'.

Israel, by contrast, has steadily expanded its role aspirations because of its insistence that it must dominate its environment militarily in order to avoid the destruction of the Jewish state since peace, based on the Muslim world's voluntary acceptance of Israel into the region, is impossible to achieve. Iraq's missile attacks on Israel during the war over Kuwait made Tel Aviv 'painfully aware of its vulnerability' vis-à-vis 'the outer circle' of countries in the region, including Iran.

According to Parsi, at the height of the US invasion of Iraq, Iranian officials privately communicated with US officials and called for the post-Saddam order of the Middle East to be discussed at a conference attended by all regional countries (i.e. an Iranian acceptance of Israel's participation). He argues that this may constitute a realization that, on the one hand, Iran cannot exclude Israel from regional decision-making (just as Israel failed to exclude Iran), and on the other hand, that Iran, unlike Israel, in the long run does not need to isolate Tel Aviv in order to achieve its role objectives. Parsi concludes that while 'Iran's role withdrawal may reduce tensions between the two states in the short run, the taming of the Israeli–Iranian rivalry will not occur until a corresponding role modification takes place in Tel Aviv as well'.

Discussing Iran's 'Nuclear policy and international relations', Saideh Lotfian places 'the immediacy and seriousness of Israel's unconventional weapons capability' and 'the need for a strategy to deal with unanticipated threats such as a US–Iran military confrontation' at the top of the list of the main factors which have been influencing Iranian attitude towards the nuclear weapons question. The other factors include the threat posed by Pakistan's nuclear weapons capability, the prestige and relative importance accorded to new nuclear states in international politics, the ineffectiveness of the non-proliferation regime, and the inadequacy of major arms control agreements as constructive instruments of foreign policy.

Lotfian argues that the Iranians' viewpoints on a peaceful nuclear energy programme are affected by two factors: the need for a new energy policy aimed at improving energy efficiency and making Iran's energy future more dependable and safe; and the need for seeking new energy sources to reduce reliance on environmentally damaging traditional sources such as oil. She emphasizes that support for and opposition to a military nuclear capability have existed across the political spectrum, both among the conservatives and the reformists. The arguments for and against are 'never mutually exclusive', nor has any individual been consistently associated with one view or another. She describes the public debate over the issue as 'a good sign' against the background of 'political expediency, disorganization and the lack of public debate on major foreign policy issues' in Iran in recent years.

Lotfian concludes that while Iran cannot afford to develop a military nuclear capability for reasons including US and international pressure and prohibitive costs, Iranians are not likely to abandon the option of building a civilian nuclear infrastructure, believing that their compliance with the NPT, proven by the IAEA inspections, will deter a US military strike against the Bushehr reactor. Lotfian ends her article by declaring her 'personal anti-nuclear bias', which forces her 'to advocate the acceptance of international treaties that ban nuclear weapons in the hope of gradually achieving the goal of complete elimination of all destructive biological, chemical, nuclear and radiological weapons being stockpiled by states in their persistent search for security'.

Presenting a 'case for sustainable development of nuclear energy', Mehdi Askarieh traces Iran's nuclear programme to its inception well before the Revolution. The programme was started by the Shah in 1974 as one of the components of an ambitious plan for the optimum utilization of diverse energy resources – oil, gas, hydro and nuclear – to ensure a flexible system of energy supply and preserve national hydrocarbon reserves as long as possible. A second reason for the nuclear programme was the country's rapid industrialization and the need for nuclear technology as a means of enhancing its level of technological development.

Askarieh notes forecasts of significant increases in global energy consumption in the next 50 years and presents economic, technological, environmental and social argument in support of nuclear energy – which 'produces about 17 per cent of the world's electricity'. He also discusses widespread concerns about nuclear energy, including the safety of nuclear installations, the ultimate disposal of long-lived radioactive waste, nuclear energy's potential to help reduce greenhouse gas emissions, the economy of the whole fuel cycle, and the non-proliferation of nuclear weapons. He finds the industry 'at something of a crossroads at the beginning of the second nuclear century'. In the absence of satisfactory solutions to such problems, 'nuclear energy is likely to decline, at first slowly, in importance. Yet, if it can be demonstrated that nuclear energy does address these concerns it is likely that there will be strong new growth in nuclear power'.

The economy and matters arising from social and economic problems and policies are covered in the last four chapters of the collection. 'Managing oil resources and economic diversification in Iran' by Massoud Karshenas and Hassan Hakimian is a critique of the Islamic Republic's economic performance. Karshenas and Hakimian argue that after a succession of oil booms and busts, external war, trade sanctions, and heightened strife within the state since 1979, Iran's political outlook seems opaque to most observers and the economic record is equally lacklustre with many Iranians experiencing a considerable regression in their living standards by regional and international standards. The power struggle within the state and Iran's ability to live off its oil rent have delayed 'the largely overdue modernization of Iran's ailing economy'.

Having presented a broad overview of Iran's economic performance over the last two decades and identifying its structural features and continued weaknesses, Karshenas and Hakimian discuss possible models of oil revenue utilization and their economic and political implications, to highlight ways in which structural reforms can lead to diversification of the economic structure away from dependency on the oil sector in the long term. The approach they call for is 'to restructure the utilization of the oil industry to achieve true decentralization of economic decision-making and pave the way for political reform'.

Another call for reform is made by Ahmad Jalali-Naini, writing on 'Capital Accumulation, Financial Market Reform and Growth in Iran: Past Experience and Future Prospects'. Jalali-Naini argues that to attain a sustainable and high economic growth rate, Iran needs to invest heavily in infrastructure, human capital, new equipment and technology and develop the social and institutional foundations that support the economic process. With the labour supply expected to rise at a fairly rate during the next decade, Iran can face 'higher rates of unemployment and increased incidence of poverty, particularly amongst the younger population, with unpleasant social consequences' if it fails to achieve 'a reasonably robust growth rate.'

Jalali-Naini says while Iran has the potential to join the rank of high income developing countries, it faces a number of major challenges, chief among which is the development of socio-economic institutions to reduce uncertainty and transaction costs, thereby encouraging greater participation and effort by non-governmental entities. Acknowledging the importance of policy issues such as the efficiency of the labour market, the educational system, and trade policy, Jalali-Naini discusses the composition of Iran's gross domestic fixed capital formation, the cost of capital, investment and growth, and policies that can improve mobilization of resources and the efficiency of investments. He lists Iran's main difficulties in achieving and maintaining high growth rates as: maintaining higher saving and investment rates; raising economic efficiency; pursuing balanced macroeconomic policies; and rethinking industrial policies and promoting non-oil exports.

Discussing in his chapter, 'Human resources in Iran: potentials and challenges', Djavad Salehi-Isfahani says that in the last 30 years the global economy has come to depend more on human than physical capital, and that for Iran creating human capital is much harder than physical capital. According to Salehi-Isfahani, human capital is widely distributed among individuals and is therefore less responsive to planning and government directives. He identifies 'Iran's rigid labour markets' as the largest obstacle to the development of its human resources, and regards their reform as a principal challenge facing Iran in the new century. The main task would be to shift rewards from unproductive skills, such as rote memorization and test-taking skills, to productive but hard-to-test skills ranging from a specific skill, such as writing, to more general skills such as character, confidence, creativity and ability to work in teams.

Salehi-Isfahani also notes favourable developments on the demographic front that bode well for the long-term economic growth, including the decline in fertility which started in the mid-1980s. This, he argues, not only helps reduce the future growth of the labour force but also provides a tremendous opportunity for economic growth by allowing the ratio of adults to children to rise dramatically for the next 20 years. Another encouraging trend has been an impressive and widely distributed increase in educational attainment for men and women in rural and urban areas. Higher education and lower fertility together provide 'evidence of a significant change in the role of the Iranian family in the economy, from the traditional units of survival and procreation to agents of growth'.

In his concluding chapter, 'The significance of economic history, and the fundamental features of the economic history of Iran', Homa Katouzian considers the fundamental and long-term issues that face Iranian society and political economy. Having discussed the significance of economic history in general, he highlights the basic concepts and categories affecting the economic history and political economy of Iran in the 20th century. And, in line with his earlier works on the subject, he shows how the receipt of substantial oil revenues by the state determined and distorted the strategy for economic development and created a rentier class who benefited from the oil bonanza without making commensurate contributions to economic growth and welfare. It promoted a culture of high consumption amidst extensive poverty and deprivation, a tendency which seems to have returned since the early 1990s.

Katouzian's theory of 'the short-term society' goes further and discusses the short-term nature of Iranian history and society, the fact that the composition of social classes changed from one short-run to the next, that power and riches were temporary and insecure, that property was not a right but a privilege, and that life itself was at the will of arbitrary rulers and their officials. One important result of Iran's historical sociology thus briefly described was the virtual impossibility of long-term saving and therefore capital accumulation. Iranian society still contains many of these historical features and unless they are seriously addressed and reformed it is unlikely to enjoy sustained political, economic and social development in the long run.

# 2 Crafting a national identity amidst contentious politics in contemporary Iran[1]

*Farideh Farhi*

## Introduction

It is perhaps no exaggeration to suggest that the crafting and re-crafting of national identity through actions of authorities and/or political mobilization and struggle has been a national preoccupation in modern Iranian history. This is not to imply that Iranians and their political leaders, going through the global process of modernity, have been any more or less creative than others in the world in reinventing their 'national' selves. However, a case can be made that in the 20th century Iranians have been afforded,[2] or have produced, more opportunities to recreate themselves in a bombastic and dualistic fashion, energetically vacillating between extremes of contentious Islamism and secularism, pre-Islamic and Islamic imagination, and avid anti-imperialism and absorption in global trends.

The result of these century-long Manichean struggles, some would argue, is tired bodies and souls. Having recently mustered youthful energy, yet again, to attempt the transcendence of these contentious identities, by taking refuge in a constitutionalism that could make cohabitation of these so far conflicting identities not only possible but also mutually reinforcing, many people in Iran seem to have packed their bags after their disappointment with the reform process and are finding solace in their private homes and selves.[3] An editorial in the *Sharq* newspaper goes so far as to suggest people's rejection of not only political leaders and their contending ideas, but also political and civil society altogether.[4]

In this midst, salutary efforts to reject epic-making politics, based on the presumed 'heroic' efforts of individual political leaders, and develop respect for gradualism (*à la* Khatami) are by now apparently disdained while attempts to forge, almost mechanically, a Janus-faced national identity as children of both Cyrus the Great *and* Mohammad (*à la* Shirin Ebadi, walking proudly on a global stage), already seem more platitude than possibility.[5] True! The sanguine Norwegian guardians of global political correctness have declared that it is both possible and acceptable to be a Muslim, a democrat, a liberated (wo)man, a proud Iranian with pre-Islamic heritage, and at peace with the world, all at the same time. But can those who are now ordained as carriers of these multiple identities also believe this mantra? Is the time over for a body politic whose regenerative capacity seems to be in habitual self-mutilation through the expunging of substantial parts of itself? Or have we Iranians already lost yet another opportunity for a story/narrative that makes us feel good about ourselves as a collectivity? Is the bipolar pull of extremes our story, as well as our fate?

This paper attempts to dwell on these questions by mulling over the roots and direction of the latest attempt to create gradually a territorially based and yet inclusive civic national identity; an identity that posits a territorially satisfied state, defined as a set of institutions, residing fairly, if not entirely happily, in a home of multi-vocal, sometimes cantankerous and even antagonistic, people who nevertheless see themselves as a family.

The main points of the paper are several. First, rather non-controversially, it posits the importance of understanding the stories and narratives 'we' tell about 'our' selves and nation in the search for political stability and popular legitimacy. My presumption is that without a narrative that connects, at least loosely, all sectors of society to a somewhat commonly acceptable recent history, social and political cohesion and stability will remain a far-flung aspiration. Second, it argues for the understanding of two clusters of stories that have remained fundamental and intricately interrelated in Iranian politics for more than a century, revolving around the tension between autocratic/theocratic/arbitrary rule and democracy/chaos and Iran's relationship with the outside world. Both of these clusters were reiterated by the nature of the revolution Iran experienced a quarter of a century ago. To be sure, the way they manifest themselves at any given historical moment has varied. For instance, in the past year, the question of Iran's relationship with the outside world has served as the context or crucial backdrop for a more limited and technical discussion of whether Iran should sign the 93+2 Additional Protocol to the Nuclear Non-Proliferation Treaty (NPT). The fundamental question about the proper relationship between democracy and arbitrary rule has also served as fuel for almost every confrontation that has occurred between non-elective and elective bodies in the past few years.

As a country that in the past century has experienced two revolutions, the end of two dynasties, exile of several kings, quite a few periods of popular mobilization, several attempts at igniting lasting parliamentary democracy, two rounds of international sanctions, and foreign occupations without colonization, it can safely be said that Iranians have long been quite preoccupied with these two clusters of issues and have tried every conceivable means for a cathartic or spectacular resolution of grand issues of democracy and national sovereignty. But despite a turbulent century, resolution of key concerns via spectacular grand events has not been forthcoming. The third and final point of this paper, therefore, is that the contentious politics of the past decade in Iran must be seen not only as yet another endeavour at resolving the tensions associated with these two clusters that are intricately connected to questions of national identity but also as an attempt at resolving them in a different fashion, involving gradualism.

Periods of contentious politics in modern Iran – during the constitutional era, in the immediate post-WWII period, and around 1979 – have been crucial in shaping collective answers to the questions of 'Who are we?', 'What are we?' and 'Who are they?', offered by political entities making public claims on each other and on the polity as a whole. There is no reason to think that this latest period of highly contentious politics is any different. The purpose of this paper is to offer a few tentative ideas about what it means for Iranian national identity if indeed it is true that the idea of gradual reform (and moderation) has taken hold of popular and elite imagination and, more importantly, daily conduct against the backdrop of a century of revolutions (and momentary excesses).

In pursuing this discussion, I am acutely aware of arguments about the 'short-term' nature of Iranian society; a society in which, in the astute words of Homa Katouzian, 'both continuity and change tend to be short-term phenomena...due to the absence of an established and inviolable legal framework, which would guarantee long term continuity'.[6] I am also aware of the implications of this argument for exaggerated vacillations in Iranian national identity. If history is indeed 'a series of connected short runs rendering cumulative change difficult',[7] then drastic and dramatic alterations of national identity in successive short terms should not come as a surprise. But the point of this essay is to explore the possibilities this awareness about Iranian history – an awareness not only present in Katouzian's essay but also implicit and even sometimes explicit in the contemporary gradualist discourse – offers for the development of a more steady, if not steadfast, national identity.

In the following sections, these possibilities are explored through three sets of discursive transformations: (1) The transformation of the national question into an ethnic challenge; (2) The transformation of Islam/pre-Islam dichotomy into a confrontation between popular sovereignty and patrimonialism; and finally (3) the transformation in the way 'Iran' sees itself in the world.

## Territorial Iran and transformation of the national question into an ethnic challenge

National process of identity assertion, argues Charles Tilly,[8] in general emphasizes two main ideas: (1) The world's population divides, and ought to divide, into historically formed, connected, coherent, and relatively homogenous nations; (2) Nations should correspond roughly to states, and vice versa. Tilly also emphasizes the importance of contentious politics and what he calls the creation, deployment, and alteration of contentious *repertoires* in the formation of identities people assume as they make collective claims. Such an assertion should of course be of no surprise to students of Iranian nationalism. There have been many different iterations of Iranian national identity, including linguistic, territorial, ethnic, and religious. But, as Firouzeh Kashani-Sabet points out, what is perhaps unique to the Iranian struggles for staking a claim on national identity 'is the way in which the varying emphases on these complementary but often competing articulations of nationalism has transformed Iranian politics in radical ways'.[9] In other words, Iranian politics has not only been contentious at particular historical moments, but the contention has also led to stark choices and radical swings in terms of national identity. If at one time language was the primary defining characteristic of the modern Iranian, at another juncture religion became the principal marker of Iranianness. And the struggle continues.

At the same time, it is important to note areas in which the so-called Iranian national project has been successful. It could safely be said, for instance, that in 2004 Iran confidently portrays itself as a territorially satisfied nation-state, confirming one of the most persistent themes – territorial integrity – in Iranian nationalism. This is a noteworthy development considering the fact that, as in many other countries, the initial impetus for nationalism began with patriotic yearnings and lamentations over the loss of Iranian territory.[10] As Iran faced other challenges to its frontiers and its natural resources, nationalist ideology inspired both populist activism and state directed policies to assure the delimitation of a territory that can 'from now on' be called Iran and defended with passion. This satisfaction with what Iran looks like on the map ('a sitting cat') has taken out of contention an important element of Iranian identity. Most importantly, it has given the Iranian state its most important mission: the defence of Iranian territory.

The Iranian revolution of 1979, with its internationalist pretensions, unsettled this formulation but only momentarily. To be sure, with Iraq's invasion of Iran, the defence of Iranian territory, now declared 'sacred' and in need of Shi'i values and methods of war (i.e. martyrdom) was pursued tenaciously to make a statement about Iran's resurgent Islamic/revolutionary identity.[11] But, as the 'first modern war in which Iran did not lose territory,' it also became a double-edged statement about continued Iranian territorial steadfastness in addition to the confirmation of the Islamic identity that had made this sacred defence of 'Iran' possible. The revolution might have constituted a break in the socio-cultural sphere, but not in terms of Iran's territorial understanding of itself. In this sense, political Shi'ism ironically became a mechanism to confirm rather than negate Iran. The determination with which Islamic Iran defends the claim over the two Tunb and Abu Musa Islands, set in motion during Mohammad Reza Pahlavi's reign, must also be seen in the light of this 'settled' territorial understanding; a settlement that in the current Islamic Republic discourse interestingly finds its justification in the rejected monarchic past and hence should presumably not be perceived as either political or questionable.[12]

This essentially settled territorial self-understanding has also prevented Iran from acting ambitiously once its surrounding nation-states began to fall apart, a fact that presumably continues today in Iranian government's behaviour and official statements regarding Iraq. To be sure, Iran did enter Iraqi territory in 1982, but in official ideology the entry was not based on any specific territorial claim (contrast this with Iraq's specific claim to Khuzestan). It was presented as a buffer needed to prevent Saddam from re-entering Iran or a bargaining chip. More significantly, the cries of 'War, war until victory' and 'The road to Jerusalem passes through Baghdad' were bellowed more as discursive claims in the ideological battle for the ascendancy of an abstract Islam in the world without any concrete reference to the expansion of the Iranian territory. Even today, while non-Iranians, including Iraqis, may worry about Iranian influence, they do not fret over its territorial ambitions. The contrast between Iran and Turkey in the wake of the disintegration of the Soviet Union and now possibly Iraq is instructive and reflective of Iran's territorial satisfaction. In official discourse, Iran of course worries about its porous borders in Sistan and Baluchistan, Kermanshah, Kurdistan, and Khorasan but these worries have become part and parcel of 'technical' border problems, involving the familiar terrain of human, drug, merchandise and weapons smuggling; that is, law enforcement problems, nothing more, nothing less.

If territorial irredentism has mostly disappeared from the Iranian national discourse, the 'national question' has remained but its shape has become part of the contest. It is discussed less as a threat to Iran's territorial integrity and presented more as an 'ethnic' challenge, along with many other challenges by 'women', 'the youth' and so on, in the struggle to build a responsible state that treats all its citizens equally. The Revolution and post-revolutionary war with Iraq again did much to transform the fear of 'ethnic separatism' into a political challenge over how to respond to the demands of ethnic minorities for equal citizenship rights. They brought into the limelight more hyphenated Iranians, including Arab–Iranians, confirming their existence, their inclusion in the Iranian Islamic community, their contribution to the body politic, and their suppression. But by acknowledging their sacrifices on the side of 'Iran', the war also confirmed their legitimate claims to equal citizenship.

More significantly, however, it was elite competition and the movement for gradual political reform that has sprung from this competition that reiterated these claims. So long as elite competition is energetic, and ethnic voices stand to gain from it by holding aspirations that need to be wooed and satisfied in a competitive political game, the majority of these voices will remain 'insider' voices, notwith-standing the continued persistence of minority separatist utterances.

This assertion should not come as a surprise. As a thoroughly modern phenomenon, as elsewhere, the 'national' question in Iran, as a question of identity, rights and civil and democratic liberties, finds its roots in the construction of the modern state: that is, in the policies of territorial centralism and construction of a uniform Iranian national identity, pursued by force by the first Pahlavi state from 1926 to 1941, and then, after a short lull, again by the second Pahlavi state and continued up to 1979. The Iranian Revolution and the downfall of the monarchy effectively did nothing to change this dynamic. It re-imposed the extant system in some places, such as Kurdistan and Turkaman Sahra, with brute force and even more coercion, ironically again using transnational Islam to confirm Iran as a national project. As Abbas Vali points out, in the case of Kurdish nationalism it was precisely the process of construction of the modern nation-state in Iran that actually transformed the very character of Kurdish politics, from tribal rebellions to the politics of rights and identity.[13]

Identity is not just what defines a person, or a larger collectivity. It also insists on the experience of the subject, especially his or her experience of oppression and the possibility of a shared and more authentic alternative: an alternative that in the words of Charles Taylor allows individuals or collectivities to seek ways of being that are somehow truer.[14] As such, it defines the rights, liberties and obligations of a person, or collectivity within a society. Given Iran's recent history and the intricate relationship between the construction of the modern Iranian state and the crushing of independence movements among the Kurds, Azeris,

Baluchs and Turkamans, the 'national' question will continue to remain significant in Iran not merely as a question of national identity and national rights but also as a constant reminder of the deficiencies and shortcomings of the citizenship, democracy, and democratic political process within the juridico-political framework of Iranian sovereignty.[15]

In effect, what we may be witnessing in Iran is a gradual, and yet significant, change of focus on the nature of the crucial problem confronting various collectivities co-existing under the same political rubric. The problem can be seen less as one of identity – who is an Iranian? – and more as one of institutions – how can the Iranians of all colours and hues build a common political life and effective institutions of government? Implicit in this shift of focus is the separation of cultural identity from national identity. Depending on one's point of view, this can be considered an auspicious transformation at many levels. It can eventually open the way for the gradual resolution of a contradiction that, according to Abbas Vali, was initiated in the 1906 constitution between conditions of political sovereignty, derived from the collective will of the Iranian nation, and of citizenship, derived from the constituent elements of Persian ethnicity, allowing other ethnicities to enter the political process as citizens of the state only if they were prepared to deny certain aspects or defining elements of their identity.[16] Through the transformation of the national question into an ethnic question within a competitive political framework, the state will in due course be robbed of its main weapon for its assertion of national identity: the linkage of ethnic/minority cultural identity to national security/sovereignty and questions of territorial integrity. Eventually, 'ethnic/cultural issues' can no longer be easily excluded from the realm of everyday 'domestic' politics. They will become (and have indeed increasingly become) part and parcel of the political process, no longer lending themselves to a military 'solution'.

To be sure, the national/ethnic question has become a bit more complicated in the Islamic Republic with the two conflicting and incompatible conceptions of sovereignty, authority and legitimacy that exist in the Islamic constitution.[17] But it is precisely because of this explicit contradiction that the 'ethnic' question (along with the rights of the religious minorities including the Sunnis that intersect with ethnic minorities) has become one of the very important arenas in which democratic and civil liberties and the struggle to build effective institutions converge on one another. In this new discursive terrain, the stakes are clear. The struggle is as much about competing interpretations of Islam as it is about the democratization of the state, expansion of civil society and the creation of a legal order and anti-democratic opposition to it. The popular quest for democracy and civil society challenges the doctrine of *velayat* and questions its legitimacy. The more impetus the popular political process to democratize gains, the more it will absorb the national question within it.

This absorption is buttressed by the fact that the essence of legal problems facing ethnic minority problems in Iran is not that there is a body of discriminatory anti-ethnic legislation. There is little such legislation (the comparison with anti-Kurd legislation in Turkey for instance is noteworthy). Minority political movements in Iran essentially face the same obstacles confronted by other pluralistic, secular or religious movements for reform: that much of the law in the Islamic Republic permits arbitrary clerical rule and fails to protect basic freedoms. Constitutional provisions establishing rights of expression, association, and pursuit of cultural interests are rendered impotent by clauses that give primacy to ambiguous Islamic interests, with non-elective bodies having the right of defining those interests on the spur of the moment. This creates common interests among forces of reform and aspirations of ethnic minorities in the pursuit of equitable laws.

Of course, the joining of the popular process in pursuit of specific political objectives, which are rooted in the civil and democratic rights and liberties emanating from the official recognition of ethnic identities in Iran, does not mean the resolution of these problems in any definite fashion. Nothing is guaranteed in an open-ended gradualist political game and objectives may be realized only partially. The only constant is the continuation of an activity called 'politics', which is no longer seen as a series of conspiracies but a process through which individuals and groups in society articulate, negotiate, implement, and enforce competing claims upon another and upon the whole. Nor is there an expectation of a definite moment when the 'victory' of democratic forces and its constituent elements will be announced, guaranteeing the realization of a multiplicity of objectives, including ethnic ones, that are present in the Iranian society. Regarding the ethnic issue, however, the odds are not wholly against the partial realization of objectives, even without a detailed and comprehensive programme for regional administrative autonomy. The democratic forces in Iran and their supporters know that their conception of civil society can only be meaningful if this society is prepared, albeit gradually, to respect national, ethnic, and cultural difference, and honour the political and civil rights of the other. The anti-democratic forces will no doubt use every issue, including the ethnic one, to further the cause of the national security state. But in this struggle, the discursive terrain has already shifted, at least temporarily, the way the Iranian 'we' is being constructed and whether or not its gradual and loose construction will keep people living inside Iran's borders engaged in the construction and maintenance of an Iranian, even if hyphenated, identity.[18]

## After all these years...who are we?

Mohammad Tavakoli-Targhi, in his well-researched and provocative book, *Refashioning Iran*, has shown the crucial role played by the dialogic interaction with India, Europe, and the Arab-Islamic culture in the 18th and 19th centuries in allowing for the displacement of dynastic and Islam-centred chronicles with Iran-centred histories and stories.[19] To recover from a historical amnesia, Tavakoli-Targhi argues, a pre-Islamic Iran was reinvented, with many righteous carriers, in a conscious effort to dissociate Iran from Islam and the Arabs. The lamentation for bygone glories, in turn, prompted a regenerative desire for a better future. According to Tavakoli-Targhi, 'These contemporaneous backward and forward gazings intensified the dissatisfaction with the *present* order of things, a dissatisfaction that informed the discourse of constitutionalism'.[20] More significantly, he argues, through protracted discursive manoeuvres, the Iranian nation or people of Iran (*mellat-e Iran*), was dissociated from Islam and the Creator, anchored in life-giving mother nation, with 6,000 years of presumably uninterrupted history, a mother tongue, and a defined territory.

This attempt at re-fashioning Iranian national identity was of course set upside down with the 1979 Revolution. But the duality itself was not fundamentally changed. Unlike the constitutionalist discourse that re-configured the pre-Islamic past as the age of enlightenment and glory, the revolutionary discourse considered that past as an era of monarchical despotism and oppression. With the intensification of memory wars, the attempts to articulate a popular pre-Islamic heritage remained futile with the effective casting of pre-Islamic Iran as imperial and monarchical. By the time of the1979 Revolution, battle lines were clearly drawn. Pre-Islamic symbolisms and autocracy stood on one side while the 'people' and Islam stood on the other. By ideologizing the past, contemporary politics further deepened the temporal divide separating the pre-Islamic and Islamic Iran. But such stark and clearly political dividing lines naturally begged a reversal in time. In fact, with increased dissatisfaction with the Islamic Republic in the past two decades, the pendulum may be swinging in the other direction. Particularly in the Diaspora, the ancient past has once again become a repository for the expression of anti-clerical, anti-Islamic and anti-Arab sentiments, similar to that of earlier times.[21]

But in the conversation that has been generated inside Iran in the past few years, there are also signs that usual dichotomies are being transcended.[22] One public sign of this transcendence can be detected in the two-volume works of Mohsen Kadivar in which at least nine different interpretations of the notion of *velayat* are presented. His argument in an interview published in the now banned *Khordad* newspaper (in 1999) that the current interpretation of the practice by the Iranian regime amounts to a 'monarchic' interpretation of the *marja'iyat* landed him in jail for more than a year.

Later, in an article by the well-known and now imprisoned post-revolutionary editorialist, Abbas Abdi, in the reformist *Asr-e Azadegan*, a comparison was made between Ali Akbar Hashemi Rafsanjani and the Mohammad Reza Shah, accentuating their common patrimonial ways.[23] In the span of a few years, since the publication of the above works and the recent sit-in by the reformist deputies in parliament, everything that was oblique in Abdi and Kadivar's argument has become explicit. Several years of public and contentious conversation about the autocratic ways of the Islamic Republic has erased the dichotomy between Islam and the monarchy that assured the victory of the Islamic forces in 1979. What was deemed as a real choice between Islam and the monarchy in 1979 is now fused into one single obstacle appropriately named 'Islamic monarchy'. The one-hundred-year constitutionalist struggle that began with the mutual influence of secular nationalist and Islamic discourses and ended in a civil war between the two has now come full circle. Secular nationalists and Islamists can once again be found, but this time in larger numbers, lining together on both sides of the national divide that is being increasingly reconstituted.

The divide is now less focused on 'us' or our 'authentic' national identity and cultural heritage (Islamic or pre-Islamic). Rather, harking back to a century-old divide, it is based on a modern version of the discussion about what kind of rule or institutions Iranian society needs and demands. Indeed, it is only through the tracing of this old contest between arbitrary rule and a society based on rule of law that one can make sense of the current debate about the 'Chinese Model' in Iran.[24] The call for the reassertion of 'autocracy' à la China after a period of fractured politics is of course premised on the argument about the deep Iranian psycho-cultural need for the stern patrimonial rule of a father. The counter relies on the historical argument about the political inability to establish a viable autocracy and the perpetual deterioration of autocracy into arbitrary rule.

What may be different in this new version of divide is the clear articulation and staking of claims as part and parcel of the gradual political process of reform: a process not only spurred by ideological contention but also by the hard realities that most Iranians seem to be physically and psychologically weary of tumultuous or abrupt change. There is also the fact that the legalized institution of *velayat-e faqih* has created an institutional and legal excuse, providing bases for political mobilization and legal claims for change without being against Islam. By giving the institution a legal life of its own, the Islamic constitution of 1979, as amended in 1989, has literally begged the move away from Islamic/anti-Islamic identity politics and towards a gradualist struggle for institutional change.[25]

The result has been the creation of a discursive terrain in which previously existential questions about what constitutes or should constitute Iranian national identity are rather cool-headedly discussed almost as policy options. Clearly the answer to the question of whether 'we' are autocrats (because we ultimately submit to the rule of autocrats) or democrats at heart is not going to be immediately forthcoming either through the imposition of a half-baked version of the Chinese Model or the resistance to it. The point is that by setting up the equation in the policy terrain, provided Iran does not descend into chaos and continues in this path of messy gradualist politics, the potential has been created not only for the transcendence of an essentially existential question (are we Muslims or children of Cyrus or both?) but also for the relegation of grand issues of Iranian politics and political identity to an arena in which policy positions (including support for or opposition to *velayat*) can be ultimately shown to work or not work in terms of their intended objectives and adjusted accordingly. This is an important and, I think, auspicious change in Iranian politics.

## And finally, who are they?

Fundamental changes cannot be merely introspective, particularly in the arena of national identity where so much of who we are is determined by how we see others. A nation, the French philosopher Ernest Renan reportedly said, 'is a group of people united by a mistaken view about the past and a hatred of their neighbours'.[26]

Hatred perhaps is too strong a word but the scapegoating of the neighbouring Arab/Islamic and the neglect of the Arab within can certainly be considered as what was cultivated in the promotion of the Iranian national identity, at a time when even the question of Iran's territorial integrity was not settled. Iran was constituted as a delimited and yet timeless place with links over and beyond the region. It was also imagined as linguistically and ethnically pure despite the obvious variety.

As mentioned above, the Islamic Republic, voluntarily and involuntarily, attempted to invert the extra-regional links and affiliations laboriously developed by Mohammad Reza Shah but the inversion did not translate into love of neighbours. Giving an Islamic veneer to the essentially leftist anti-imperialist stance, the Islamic Republic used antagonistic external relations as a means to buttress its political hold internally. In this way, inversion turned into isolation. 'Neither Western, Nor Eastern' was certainly a nice mantra that appealed to the quintes-sentially modern and century-long struggle of Iranians to become masters of their own house, to stand up to the superpowers of the moment. But Islamic Iran's attempt at non-alignment was immediately turned into a farce because of its inability to get along with neighbours of different colours and hues, from Iraq to Kuwait, Saudi Arabia, Afghanistan and even Turkey.

The solid placement of Iran in the category of the few 'rogue' states did have its purposes however. As many astute Iran observers have pointed out, the particular experience of Iran with revolution, war, sanctions, and estrangement from international community created a shared sense of embattlement in a hostile environment, allowing the post-revolutionary state-builders to portray themselves as the 'true' guardians of Iranian security and shut off debate on foreign policy and security issues and then use national security to foil aspirations for political change.[27] In this process, the hands of hardliners were strengthened by the essentially punishment-oriented nature of external pressures, allowing them to identify proponents of reform as weak on security.

But, with a changed global environment, isolation has an expired purpose. Recent events indicate that external factors and policies have begun to impact on Iranian politics in a different way. This impact goes beyond the usual caveats about the difficulty of avoiding the impact of the Internet, satellite televisions of the exiled opposition and international non-governmental organizations, which are of course influential in this inter-connected world. The impact has to do with the desire on the part of large sectors of post-revolutionary elite as well as the population for Iran to become a 'legitimate' member of the international community and to be connected to larger trends in the global arena. This means that not only many Iranians make efforts to have access to every piece of information that is produced outside Iran about Iran, but also that public debates are generated about these pieces of information. Coming out of isolation and not making an emphatic statement about Iran's national identity is what is at issue.

Added to this dynamic is the basic reality that Iran's neighbourhood has been rather turbulent in recent years and external bellicose statements and actions against Iran are on the rise, making the costs of isolation quite clear. To give a rather obvious example, the 'axis of evil' terminology which came out of the blue with regard to Iran, particularly after Iran's cooperation with the US in Afghanistan, clearly lent itself to the question of 'what does the US have in store for us?', after the first of the 'axis' trio was attacked. Furthermore, it opened the way for an array of opinions about whether a US invasion of Iran is desirable or not. The mere fact that the question was asked in Iran, and let us say, not in Egypt or Saudi Arabia, was the result of external impact. As such, the response to the question remained significant only so long as the external variable remained present. With the continued difficulties in Iraq, even after the so-called handover of sovereignty to local forces, and the exposure that the US may not have the appetite for further invasions, the question has become less significant in the Iranian political discourse.

With the various responses the European and American policy makers have had principally to Iran's nuclear programme, and also due to the activities of domestic forces agitating for human rights, a different kind of discussion about the impact of external factors on Iranian politics has come to the fore, centring on how external forces can help foster effective political institutions in Iran. The issue of Iran's nuclear programme is a particularly interesting one to examine since, given the specific nature of the international demands on Iran, it offers a good case for understanding how international pressures now work their way into Iranian domestic politics.

Initially, given the lack of specific demands within the context of an international forum that Iran considered legitimate, external pressures strengthened the hand of hardliners and weakened Iran's diplomatic apparatus, which was accused by all sides of the political spectrum of being ineffective and short on preventative action. However, as the possibility and need for a compromise with Europe became part of the Iranian discourse, the voices of those pushing for more integration in the international community and using the signing of the Additional Protocol as 'a step in confidence building' turned more assertive. Their position was bolstered by the possibility of improved relations with Western Europe and a realistic assessment of the necessity to work and negotiate with forces and countries that do not necessarily accept the 'axis of evil' assessment of the Iranian regime put forward by the Bush administration.

The agreement that was reached with the European foreign ministers on 21 October 2003 was stunning both in terms of content as well as the manner in which it came about. An important step was taken – a step that many thought too difficult for Iran's contentious and bickering political system to take. While in Iran there was much talk that the Iranian leadership would ultimately 'buckle under' the international pressure and sign the protocol, very few expected the agreement to come about in a such a dramatic manner, with at least a symbolic confirmation of Iran's importance to Europe.

The quick agreement with Europe, however, followed a long period of national conversation that was unusual in many ways both in its frankness about Iran's difficult international position and what could be done about it.[28] In this context, the decision to take the initiative and enter into agreement with the three European states must be seen as a culmination of a heated internal debate, a national conversation so to speak, that at least in its first round was won by those who argued that the signing of the Additional Protocol was a necessary affirmation of Iran's commitment to international obligations and not an abridgement of sovereignty. The reformists and reformist political organizations, such as the Islamic Iran's Participation Front and the Mojahedin of Islamic Revolution, that pushed for the agreement and made the push part of their official position unanimously celebrated the decision while acknowledging that this was just the beginning of a long road and that Iran's troubles were not over yet. In this way, they were able to record the agreement as a victory for reform-oriented ideas, even if those who apparently made the final decision were not generally identified as supporters of reform. Similar dynamics are at work regarding relations with other countries. Improved relations with Egypt, for instance, were again achieved through the public isolation of a vocal group of hardliners, despite the fact that it couldn't have happened without the assent of key players among the hardliners.

Along similar lines, discussions of relations with the United States, once considered taboo, are now commonplace and have become even more specific in terms of open calls for direct relations with the US. Public discussions on relations with the United States no longer dwell on whether, but on how to begin formal relations. More significantly, the question of relations with the United States has occurred within the context of frank discussions about the costs of foreign and security policy choices Iran has made in the past two decades and the extent to which they have adversely affected Iran's economic and political wellbeing as well as its internal drive towards more popular participation.

The result of these public debates has been the rise of powerful sentiments inside Iran, among ordinary folk as well as the elite, who no longer see external forces, identified as 'imperialist' during previous attempts at democratization in the 1950s and 1970s, as an impediment to the internal drive towards democracy. In other words, engagement with the world and promotion of democracy at home have become inextricably linked in the Iranian political discourse. The two key concerns of the Iranian polity in the past century – national sovereignty and democracy – no longer seem at odds in the minds of a significant number of, if not all, Iranians. This is an important change of mood that has come about gradually, allowing many Iranians to begin the process of leaving behind the elevated role given to foreign powers of averting attempts to bring about democracy in Iran (in particular in 1953).

To be sure, harking back to the real or imagined confrontation between internal democracy and imperialism, there are concerns and discussions inside Iran regarding the possibility of the hardliners manoeuvering to strike a 'grand bargain' with powerful external players, particularly the US, of course always involving the mediation of the omnipresent British, allowing the hardliners to placate external hostility to their rule. Such a bargain, in turn, it is argued, would give the Iranian hardliners a free hand to crush domestic dissent and competition. But, given the human rights violations and undemocratic implications of such a deal, neither Iran's domestic political environment nor contentious politics inside other countries would probably allow such a public scenario to materialize. More importantly for our purposes, however, it is the public airing of these issues of historical concern that will hopefully act as the best chance against the repetition of history.

Let me end by suggesting that despite dreams of a Velvet Revolution, neither democracy nor unblemished relations with the outside world will come to Iran overnight. But, given the vibrant nature of democratic agitation in Iran, within various layers of both the state and society, the least the gradualist process has offered Iran is a period of double-edged national reflection focused on institutional inadequacies as well as on limits of identity politics. Whether this period of reflection is sufficient to transform the understanding of political life in Iran from short, frenzied outbursts of emotion associated with identity politics to the tranquil and steady dedication of a lifetime to the building of effective institutions is of course yet to be seen.

## Notes

1 An earlier version of this paper was presented at the conference on 'Iran Facing the New Century' held at Oxford, UK, 5–7 April 2004. I would like to thank Homa Katouzian and Hossein Shahidi for their generous help in revising the paper.

2 The use of the term 'Iranians' is probably not justified here. The proper terminology is 'Iranian leaders,' 'Iranian opinion makers,' and so on, as one could easily argue that the majority of Iranians have managed to combine various elements of their reported national or political identity in their everyday lives without much fanfare or posturing. Note, for instance, the routine appearance of the Quran on the haft sin arrangements for the Iranian New Year. There are usually deep differences between the largely unarticulated and generally porous identities embedded in daily social life and those rather rigid and bounded political identities that become evident through political contention.

3 Evidence of this disappointment can be detected in the precipitous drop in voter turnout (from low to mid 70 percent to low 50 percent) between the 1997 and 2001 presidential elections and 2000 parliamentary elections on the one hand and the 2003 municipal and 2004 parliamentary elections on the other.

4 Mehran Karami, 'Varunegi-ye Siyasi' (Political Inversion), *Sharq*, 22 January 2004:1.

5 For the text of Shirin Ebadi's Nobel Prize speech see www.payvand.com/news/03/dec/1065.html. My point is neither to question Ebadi's admirable statement of who she is, nor her aspiration, which I also share. I only intend to point to the irony that exists in her Nobel Prize speech: the highlighting of precisely the same contending elements of Iran's national identity, constituted as opposite s by a century of highly charged ideological struggle, as a means to overcome the struggle.

6 Homa Katouzian, 'Legitimacy and Succession in Iranian History', *Comparative Studies of South Asia, Africa and the Middle East* 23, 1&2 (2003): 242.

7 Ibid.

8 Charles Tilly, *Stories, Identities, And Political Change*. Lanham: Rowman and Littlefield, 2002, ch. 5.

9 Firoozeh Kashani-Sabet, 'The Evolving Polemic of Iranian Nationalism,' in *Iran and the Surrounding World* edited by Nikki R. Keddie and Rudi Matthee. Seattle: University of Washington Press, 2002.

10 Ibid. and Juan R. Cole, 'Marking Boundaries, Marking Time: The Iranian Past and the Construction of Self by Qajar Thinkers,' *Iranian Studies* 29 (1996): 36–56.

11 For a good discussion of the way war poetry was used to frame the defence of territory within the context of Shi'i values and methods of war see Mohammad Javad

Gholamreza Kashi, *Jadu-ye goftar: zehniyat-e farhangi va nezam-e ma'ani dar entekhabat-e dovvom-e khordad* (The Magic of Discourse: Cultural Consciousness and the System of Meanings in the 2 Khordad Election). (Tehran: Ayandeh Puyan, 1379/2000, pp. 326–334.) As examples, Kashi points to the use of symbols from Karbala, recreation of particular events in the war in the light of Ashura, and the use of sacred Shi'i titles for war operations.

12 This line of argument, or more properly justification, emphasizing continuity with pre-1979 positions as a means to legitimate Iranian post-1979 claims and policies, is not only limited to questions related to the Iranian territory. It is also a favoured strategy, for instance, in justifying post-revolutionary strivings towards the development of nuclear energy.

13 Abbas Vali, 'The Kurds and Their Fragmented "Others": Fragmented Identity and Fragmented Politics'. *Comparative Studies of South Asia, Africa, and the Middle East* 21, 1&2 (2002): 82–94. Vali states that the Kurdish question in Iran is a question of denial of the Kurdish identity by the sovereign power and the Kurds' resistance to this denial. A similar argument can be made regarding others, although a case can perhaps be made that the Kurdish question has proven more muscular and urgent given the persistence of the question in the surrounding countries.

14 Charles Taylor, *Sources of the Self: The Making of the Modern Identity*. Cambridge, MA: Harvard University Press, 1989.

15 For instance, in October 2001, all six Kurdish members of Iran's Parliament resigned in protest at what they described in a letter to the interior minister as 'denial of their legitimate rights' and the central government's failure to address the 'political, economic and cultural rights that they have brought out'. Quoted by Afshin Molavi, http://www.eurasianet.org/departments/culture/articles/ eav041503.shtml. For a different take insisting on the increasing importance of the 'national question,' see Brenda Shaffer *Borders and Brethren: Iran and the Challenge of Azerbaijani Identity*. Shaffer challenges the widely held view in contemporary Iranian scholarship that a broad Iranian identity supersedes ethnic identities.

16 Vali, 'The Kurds and Their Fragmented "Others".

17 Asghar Shirazi, *The Constitution of Iran: Politics and the State in the Islamic Republic*, translated by John O'Hare (London: I.B. Taurus Publishers, 1997).

18 I say 'at least temporarily' because there is no guarantee that the linkage between the resolution of ethnic issues and the political process will occur naturally. Clearly government policies do matter and gradual movement towards a more democratic state is key. Without it ethnic nationalism and even separatism is always a possibility. So far, evidence from the electoral behaviour of minorities suggests a desire to operate within the political system. For instance, since 1997 and until the 2000 parliamentary elections the rate of participation in electoral politics, as well as the percentage of votes cast in favour of reformist candidates have been among the highest in the four predominantly Kurdish provinces, as well as in other ethnic minority provinces. However, during the parliamentary elections of February 2004, the rate of disqualification of candidates by the Guardian Council was also the highest in these Kurdish provinces, as well as in other provinces dominated by ethnic minorities, with the exception of Lorestan. These important figures by themselves do not provide a full picture of the relations between ethnic populations and the central state in Iran. But they do suggest that the minority populations have vested much in the political process. How they will respond to the political process in the future will depend much on the actions of the now unified conservative power structure over the next few years. The government may try to throw money at the problem, in time-honoured authoritarian fashion. But Iran's social problems run deeper that the central state's co-optation abilities. The options facing the central government are either political or coercive, the latter clearly risking separatist reactions. For Iran's Ministry of Interior data on electoral participation in Iran's various elections see www.moi.gov.ir.

19  Mohammad Tavakoli-Targhi, *Refashioning Iran: Orientalism, Occidentalism and Historiography* (New York: Palgrave, 2001).

20  Ibid., p. 135.

21  Note the appalled reaction when Iran announced that it was seeking observer status in the Arab League.

22  The focus on public conversations as distinct from the intricacies of factional politics is intentional here since it is in the latter arena that one can find hope and a latent vision missing in the impasse of factional politics.

23  Abbas Abdi, 'Enqelab 'aleyh-e tahqir (Revolution against Humiliation), *Asr-e Azadegan*, 2 February 2000.

24  For a clear and longing aspiration for the Chinese model see the editorial in *Keyhan* (23 January 2004) by Mohammad Imani. For a discussion of why the autocratic Chinese model will not work for the Islamic Republic see the *op cit* piece by Ebrahim Yazdi in *Sharq* (7 February 2004).

25  This point about the existence of legalized institutions creating oppositional movements to bring about institutional change is well made by Charles Tilly, in comparing racially discriminatory regimes in South Africa, the United States and Brazil. He argues that Brazil, while sustaining as much social and economic inequality by race as the United States, avoided legalizing racial distinctions to anything like the degree of South Africa and the United States. 'In the short and medium runs, the difference surely worked to the advantage of Brazil's black populations. But over the long run stringent racial categories provided bases for political mobilization and legal claims for redress in South Africa and the United States, while in Brazil the very absence of legalized racial categories, statistics, and agencies inhibited black collective action' (p. 68).

26  Quoted in Avi Shlaim, 'A Betrayal of History', *The Guardian*, 22 February 2002. http://www. guardian.co.uk/israel/Story/0,2763,654054,00.html.

27  On this point see Shahram Chubin and Robert S. Litvak, 'Debating Iran's Nuclear Aspirations', *The Washington Quarterly* 26, 4 (Autumn 2003): 99–114.

28  For a discussion of the internal debates that led to the agreement with the three European powers see Farideh Farhi, 'To Sign or Not to Sign? Iran's Evolving Debate on Nuclear Options', in *Iran's Bomb* edited by Geoffrey Kemp (The Nixon Center, March 2004). http://www.nixoncenter.org/ publications/monographs/IransBomb.pdf.

# 3 The dilemma of national interest in the Islamic Republic of Iran

*Hamid Ahmadi*

## National interests: conceptual issues

National interest as a concept of social science does not have a wide range of use, with more limited interdisciplinary application than some other concepts such as identity, security or rationality. It is mostly used in political science in general, and in its international relations sub-discipline in particular. Although the concept did make an appearance in historical and political publications before the 1950s,[1] it found its popularity by the dominance of the realist school of thought in international relations as a distinct discipline of politics in the aftermath of World War II. Hans Morgenthau popularized the concept when he gave it the second place among his six principles of political realism.[2]

According to Morgenthau, 'the main signpost that helps political realism to find its way through the landscape of international politics is the concept of interest defined in terms of power'.[3] Here, the founding father of political realism makes it clear that 'interest' is a rational phenomenon distinct from other concepts and issues such as ethics, ideology and religion. As Morgenthau puts it:

> The concept (interest) provides the link between reason trying to understand international politics and the facts to be understood. It sets politics as an autonomous sphere of action and understanding apart from other spheres, such as economic . . . ethics, aesthetics, or religion.[4]

While power is the main criterion for the definition of interests in politics, economics relies on wealth as its main defining criterion est. Thus, accepting this widely-used formula for interest, one can conclude that the concept of national interest encompasses both power and wealth as its main defining criteria. As such, a policy based on the pursuit of the national interest is one that tends to increase the nation's power and its wealth as a whole.

## The question of national interest in contemporary Iran

Compared with many other issues, such as democracy, civil society, development, identity, political ideas and ideologies, both in general and with respect to the

Islamic and Iranian contexts, there has not been much discussion in Iran about national interest, either as a conceptual-theoretical issue or as a case study in the Iranian foreign policy. This fact applies to both before and after the Islamic Revolution. There are various reasons for this lack of conceptual and theoretical literature on national interest. The main causes in the pre-revolutionary era included the orientation and practice of foreign policy, on the one hand, and the paucity of publications on social sciences, in particular political science publications, on the other.

During this time, it was assumed that the Pahlavi state was mainly pursuing a foreign policy based on Iranian national interest at regional and international levels.[5] Therefore, the issue of national interest was not a problem which the academic and intellectual circles had to examine. On the contrary, because of the preoccupation of the intellectual elite, especially at opposition level, with radical revolutionary ideals, there was a prominent intellectual tendency towards an idealistic foreign policy orientation rather than one based on national interest. However, the few journals devoted to political science, such as *Journal of the Faculty of Law and Political Science* (*Majalleh-ye Daneshkadeh-ye Hoquq va Olum-e Siaysi*), published by the University of Tehran, *International Relations* (*Ravabet-e Beinolmelal*) by the Department of International Relations of the same university, and *World Affairs* (*Masa'el-e Jahan*), a quarterly journal published by the private sector, used to discuss the issue of power politics and national interest in the context of Hans Morgenthau's realist school.

The reason for the lack of any discussion of national interest in the post-revolutionary era, especially in its first two decades, was different. The ideological government established after the fall of Prime Minister Mehdi Bazargan's liberal Provisional Government in 1980, considered the term 'national' to be anti-Islamic. This tendency stemmed not only from the fundamentalist orientation of the ruling system based on the concept of the '*Umma*', or the Muslim community, rather than the 'nation',[6] but also from a long standing rivalry and struggle for political power.

This latter problem had a much longer history, going back to the confrontation between the nationalist and Islamist trends of the early 1950s. The Iranian National Front (INF) as the most important manifestation of nationalism in the Iranian political scene was led by Mohammad Mosaddeq, the Prime Minister who was removed from power by the 1953 Anglo-American coup d'etat.[7] Ayatollah Kashani and his followers, who formed the basic organizational structure of the traditional Islamic trends in the 1960s and 1970s, mostly opposed the National Front. The instrumental use of the term 'national' by the Shah's regime, on the one hand, and the marginalization of the religion in socio-political programs, on the other, deepened the gap between the religious and nationalist factions.[8]

While the common struggle against the Shah brought a degree of harmony and cooperation between the Islamist and nationalist trends in the short period before and after the fall of the Pahlavi dynasty, their different political goals and orientations were to come to the fore later on. Prime Minister Bazargan's provisional government (1979–1980), itself a coalition of religious and nationalist forces, came into conflict with the radical faction led by prominent Shi'ite clergy. National Front leaders, such as the Foreign Minister, Karim Sanjabi, withdrew from the Bazargan government and took an opposite stance vis-à-vis the fundamentalist policies of the Islamic Republic of Iran (IRI). Soon after the National Front's condemnation of the *Qesas* (Retribution) Bill presented by the Shi'ite clergy as the basic feature of Iran's new penal code, Ayatollah Khomeini declared that the organization had committed apostasy. From then on, the term 'national' was considered to be non-Islamic and its use was interpreted as an overt act of opposition to Islam and the Islamic regime. Nationalism had an even worse fate, and was described by Ayatollah Khomeini as being 'against Islam'. Instead of 'national interest', the interests of *Ummat-e Islami* (the Muslim Community) were widely used in the declarations and speeches given by formal and informal decision makers in IRI. In such a socio-political context, some books and many articles[9] were written in praise of Islamic internationalism and the condemnation of nationalism.[10]

## The question of national interest in the IRI: conceptual issues

The problem of national interest cannot be understood clearly without a discussion of the guiding principles of the IRI's constitution on foreign policy. The constitution can be described as the best manifestation of Islamic idealism as far as the question of foreign policy is concerned. No mention of the concept of 'national interests' of Iran is found in the constitution. Only the preservation of the country's 'territorial integrity', to which Article 152 refers as a duty of the state, can be interpreted as a factor of national interest in the constitution. Nevertheless, this is mentioned in the same Article that also declares the defence of the rights of all Muslims as the IRI's foreign policy goals. Article 152 says:

> The foreign policy of the Islamic Republic of Iran is based upon the rejection of the exertion of or submission to all forms of domination, the preservation of the independence of the country in all respects and its territorial integrity, the defence of the rights of all Muslims, non-alignment with respect to the hegemonic superpowers, and the maintenance of mutually peaceful relations with all non-belligerent states.

Since the constitution gives more weight to concern for the Islamic world in Iran's foreign policy, it can be considered more as an Islamic internationalist charter, rather than a document which delineates the guidelines for a foreign policy based on the national interest of a nation state. In fact, the constitution lays greater emphasis on defending the collective interest of the Muslims as a main goal of the IRI's foreign policy. Such Islamic internationalism is one of the general principles of the constitution, as demonstrated in Article 11:

> In accordance with the sacred verse of the Qur'an, 'This your community is a single community, and I am your Lord, so worship Me' (21:92), all

Muslims form a single nation, and the government of the Islamic Republic of Iran has the duty of formulating its general policies with a view to cultivating the friendship and unity of all Muslim peoples, and it must constantly strive to bring about the political, economic, and cultural unity of the Islamic world.

Indeed, chapter 10 of the constitution goes beyond Islamic internationalism and considers support for all oppressed people (*mostaza'fin*) of the world against the oppressors (*mostakbirin)* as one of the IRI's main goals. According to Article 154 of the constitution:

The Islamic Republic of Iran has as its ideal human felicity throughout human society, and considers the attainment of independence, freedom, and rule of justice and truth to be the right of all people of the world. Accordingly, while scrupulously refraining from all forms of interference in the internal affairs of other nations, it supports the just struggles of the *mostaz'afin* against the *mostakberin* in every corner of the globe.

All this emphasis on the importance of Islamic idealism in IRI's constitution does not mean that the Islamic Republic of Iran has fulfilled those principles totally. There are, in fact, some religious considerations according to which Islamic idealism can be superseded by a more realistic foreign policy. Two such principles in Islamic jurisprudence are those of '*maslaha*' (expediency) which is a general Islamic term,[11] and '*hefze beyzeh-ye Islam*' (protecting the citadel of Islam) which has more Shi'ite roots.[12] Both principles imply that under particular conditions some of Islam's basic requirements can be ignored to serve the interests of the whole Muslim community. The Islamic Republic authorities have used these two principles on many occasions, among them the IRI's position with respect to the 1982 Islamic uprising in Syria; the 1988 acceptance of the UN Security Council Resolution 598 that ended the war with Iraq; and the IRI's indifference toward the Chechen Islamic movement in the 1990s.[13] However, these cases cannot be generalized as the basic tenets of the IRI's foreign policy. Despite these and other cases, national interest has not become the guiding principle of foreign policy of the present day Iran. This fact can be better understood by discussing the IRI's foreign policy in the past 25 years.

## National interest and the foreign policy of the IRI

The foreign policy of the IRI can be studied from different points of view. One useful approach for understanding the status of national interest in the IRI's policy is to apply conceptual and theoretical models to the Islamic Republic's performance in the realm of foreign policy. Although different theoretical frameworks have been presented for the explanation and understanding foreign policy,[14] mere concentration on these models cannot help one understand the place of national interest in the IRI's foreign policy. Most of these models have been delineated to explain the influential determinants of foreign policy decision-making and its outputs, either in the domestic or in the international environment. Different conceptual approaches need to be applied to judge whether national interest has been an important factor in the formulation of the Islamic Republic's foreign policy. Conceptual discussions related to the goals and the orientations of each state's foreign policy are more relevant here.

One useful way to explain the foreign policy behaviour of the developing countries would be to focus on their foreign policy goals. Five important goals have been considered for such countries: (1) economic welfare; (2) national security; (3) nation building; (4) state building; and finally (5) regime maintenance.[15] Among these, it seems that national security and regime maintenance, each at a different time, have been the IRI's main foreign policy goals..

As far as national interest is concerned, economic welfare, nation-building and state-building as foreign policy goals, can better serve the interest of a nation. Of course, national security is an important aspect of national interest. However, national security itself is a dependent variable influenced by domestic or inter-national factors. While in most cases a state's national security is threatened by foreign challenges not related to the nature of its foreign or domestic policies, there are cases when the nature and the orientation of the state's foreign policy can lead to the rise of foreign challenges that could threaten its national security. In other words, a country's national security can be challenged as the result of its performance at the international, regional or even domestic levels. In the Iranian case, during the past 25 years, the nature of the Islamic Republic's foreign policy has had an important role in the rise of foreign challenges to its national security. Furthermore, as will be discussed later, the concept of national security here has been rather tantamount to regime security. By pursuing value-laden ends not compatible with its means, the Islamic Republic has continuously instigated harsh reaction from both regional and international actors. Such interaction has led to the emergence and accumulation of security threats that have turned regime maintenance into the most important goal of the Islamic Republic's foreign policy.

The Islamic Republic's foreign policy orientation is another arena in which the question of national interest can be studied. To use Holsti's model of foreign policy orientation,[16] one can say that the Islamic Republic has mostly chosen the non-alignment orientation. Other forms of foreign policy orientation such as neutrality, isolation, and coalition-alliance formation have not been used by the Islamic Republic. Only during regional armed conflicts such as the 1991 Kuwait crisis, the United States' anti-Taliban war in Afghanistan in 2002, and its invasion of Iraq in 2003 has the Islamic Republic taken a neutral stance. However, this non-aligned orientation has been somehow different from what one understands of the non-alignment policy. In other words, the Islamic Republic has had different types of non-aligned orientation in different historical periods.

At least three types of non-alignment are discernible in the last 25 years: mutual non-alignment (1979–1982); conflict-laden non-alignment (1982–1985); and compromising non-alignment (1985–1988, and again in 1997–2003).[17] Mutual non-alignment policy was pursued mostly in the first years of the Islamic Republic, under Prime Minister Bazargan's liberal provisional government, followed by the government of President Bani-Sadr . The rise to power of the radical revolutionaries who ousted President Bani Sadr marked the beginning of conflict-laden non-aligned policy. In this period the Islamic Republic was involved in an armed conflict with Iraq and laid emphasis on exporting the Islamic Revolution, thus trapping itself in a political conflict with the Arab World and the United States. During 1985–1988, the Islamic Republic was engaged in a compromising non-aligned policy in order to reduce the heavy burden of war with Iraq. The failed secret negotiation with the United States (the Iran-Contra Affair) and the final acceptance of the UN Security Council Resolution 598 were the main examples of such compromising policy. The Salman Rushdie controversy marked the beginning of a new era of conflict-laden, non-alignment with the West. A new round of compromising non-aligned foreign policy started following President Mohammad Khatami's election in 1997.

## The dilemma of national interest in the Islamic Republic: contradictory trends

The ebbs and flows of different orientations in the Islamic Republic's foreign policy indicate the existence of contradictory trends regarding the issue of national interest, manifested in the several periods of a realistic orientation. To have a better understanding of this dilemma we have to rely on more common theoretical frameworks for the study of foreign policy. The most popular approach in this area is the famous dichotomy of realism-idealism in international relations. Presented by distinguished scholars such as E. H. Carr,[18] Hans Morgenthau and later Kenneth Waltz,[19] this approach stresses that national interest can only be secured with a foreign policy based on realism rather than idealism. Realism is oriented towards maximizing a state's national power. An idealist foreign policy has a value-laden orientation, in many cases in contradiction with a country's national interest. This idealist policy has been criticized more strongly with regards to the way in which idealist policy makers or political thinkers look for peace and international security.

The Islamic Republic's foreign policy is essentially an idealist one. The main principles of the IRI's constitution on foreign policy, as discussed in the second section of this paper, have a revolutionary value-laden orientation. Not only is the term 'national interest' not mentioned in the Islamic Republic's constitution, but also other tenets of a policy based on national interest, such as Iran's economic development and other related issues, are not considered as foreign policy goals. However, in spite of the fact that the Islamic Republic has generally pursued an idealist foreign policy based on the defence of the Islamic world, especially the Islamic movements, there have been several cases of realistic decision-making in this regard. Tehran's policy regarding the Islamic uprising in Syria in 1982, which subjected the IRI to criticism by many Islamic movements,[20] and the war in Chechnya in the late 1990s and early 2000s are two examples.

However, unlike many other 20th century revolutionary regimes, such as those of the Soviet Union and China, which had a coherent policy of transformation from idealism to realism and the search for national interest in foreign policy, the Islamic Republic of Iran has not demonstrated a coherent and consistent approach. On the contrary, there have been ebbs and flows of idealist and realist orientations during the last 25 years. After a period of idealistic policies, a tendency for the pursuit of a more realistic policy does take precedence, only to be neutralized soon after by the resurgence of the idealistic revolutionary trend. There have been many examples of this pattern in the past.

In the aftermath of the Shah's downfall, Prime Minister Mehdi Bazargan's government pursued the foreign policy of 'passive balance', delineated mainly by Mosaddeq in the 1940s and early 1950s, which sought to keep all foreign forces out of the Iranian political scene. In spite of its idealistic overtones, such a policy could have served Iran's national interest. However, a radical idealistic and value-laden trend protested against Bazargan's foreign policy. Using his meeting with President Carter's National Security Advisor, Zbigniew Brzezinski, in Algeria on 1 November 1979, as a pretext, the radicals effectively forced Bazargan's resignation. The seizure of the US embassy on 4 November 1979 and the capture of its staff as hostages by radical Islamists marked the beginning of an idealist foreign policy based on the defence of the Islamic world. This idealist policy was intensified by the United States' failed military operation in 1982 to free the hostages.

However, the breakout and prolongation of the Iran–Iraq war showed the fruit-lessness of the idealist foreign policy and led to the renewal of a realist foreign policy in 1984. This policy, focused mainly on a rapprochement between Iran and the United States, began to be implemented with Iran's efforts to solve the 1984 Lebanese hostage crisis. The swing to realism was intensified by the secret deal between the United States and Iran that culminated in the visit to Iran by the US National Security Advisor, Robert McFarlane in 1985 and became known as the 'Iran-Contra Affair'. Ayatollah Khomeini's emphasis on the necessity of having political relations with all countries, and the invitation to the German Foreign Minister to Iran signified the beginning of a new era of realist foreign policy. Nevertheless, this did not last long. The rival, idealist political trend took the initiative and disclosed McFarlane's trip to Iran in the Lebanese journal, *Al-Shira'*. The political pressure imposed on the realists by this disclosure was so great that the then Speaker of Parliament, Ali-Akbar Hashemi-Rafsanjani, had to deny his involvement in the Iran-Contra Affair even though he had been its prime mover.

Thus, a new round of idealist foreign policy began in mid-1986 and lasted for almost two years. The beginning of a new wave of anti-Americanism in the foreign and domestic arenas, the deterioration of Iran–Saudi relations because of a dispute over Hajj, and Iran's push for victory in the war with Iraq, which brought about United States and European support for Iraq, were the hallmarks of the new idealism. The support given to Iraq, especially by the United States, on the one hand, and the lack of manpower and financial support for the continuation of war inside Iran, on the other, forced the Islamic Republic to accept the Security Council's Ceasefire Resolution 598 in August 1988. The end of the Iran–Iraq war,

Iran's rapprochement with Europe and Hashemi-Rafsanjani's rise to presidency encouraged many observers of Iranian politics to foresee the final victory of the realist trend in Iran.

However, the expectation for the adoption of a permanent realist foreign policy was not realized. In the midst of Rafsanjani's efforts to normalize Iran's relations with Europe, the Salman Rushdie affair destroyed everything. Ayatollah Khomeini's *fatwa* against Salman Rushdie, the author of *Satanic Verses*, was a partial victory for the idealist trend that considered such a rapprochement a breach of the Revolution's principles. For at least a year, the Rushdie affair influenced every aspects of the Islamic Republic's foreign policy and neutralized all former efforts to end the Islamic regime's isolation. Since Rushdie was a British citizen, Ayatollah Khomeini's *fatwa* had a greater impact on Iran's relations with Europe than with the rest of the world. The irony was that at this time, Mr Rafsanjani had been trying to turn Europe into Islamic Republic's main international partner, a status held in the past by the United States.

In spite of the Rushdie affair and its adverse effects on relations between Iran and the outside world, particularly the West, the Rafsanjani government could not afford to continue its activities without engaging in a new era of realistic foreign policy. Hence, after one year of crisis, Mr Rafsanjani began to normalize Iran's relations with Western Europe. The European countries also considered this rapprochement beneficial to the West in general. This, in fact, was a twin-track policy to which the United States had agreed. Not only the United States, but also Europe had the vision that the normalization of economic and political relations with Iran would moderate Tehran's radical Islamism.

The help provided by international institutions such as the World Bank and the IMF could only fulfil Mr Rafsanjani's economic reform policy that sought to integrate the Islamic Republic into the global market economy. Both Europe and the United States hoped that the IMF and World Bank's medicine of structural adjustment would spill over into the political arena and convince the Islamic Republic to revise its idealist Islamist foreign policy in the region. This approach to regional politics, manifested in the renewal of Iran–Saudi relations, the two countries' cooperation within OPEC[21] and Tehran's informal cooperation in the war for the liberation of Kuwait, convinced the international community that a new era of realism in the foreign policy of the Islamic republic had begun.

However, the economic reform policy was not accompanied by the required political change, either domestically or internationally. In other words, the Rafsanjani administration's policy towards Iran's opposition forces on the one hand, and its approach to the most crucial problem in the Middle East, that is the Arab–Israeli conflict, on the other, remained the same. Tehran's idealist stance towards the Arab–Israeli conflict was devised in accordance with the principles of the Islamic Republic's constitution, which regarded the Palestinian cause as one to which all Muslim countries had to be committed.

The Islamic Republic's position on Palestine was a strong idealistic one, which contradicted its more realistic economic policy and the necessity of improving political relations with the West. Tehran was so idealistic towards the Palestinian cause that it preferred to support fundamentalist Islamic forces such as the Islamic Jihad and Hamas, rather than the Palestine Liberation Organization (PLO).[22] This was reflected in the IRI's reluctance to recognize PLO's 1988 Declaration of Independence or the PLO's acceptance of the United States' three basic conditions for US–PLO negotiations in early 1989.[23] The IRI considered this initiative a betrayal of the Palestinian people in particular and the Muslim World in general.

When the Oslo Peace Treaty was signed between the PLO and Israel, the Islamic Republic's fundamentalist rhetoric against the PLO and the proponents of the peace process intensified.[24] This was accompanied by stronger support for the Islamic forces inside the Occupied Territories. In fact the Islamic Republic was considered by the Clinton administration as one of the few ardent opponents of the peace process. The Israeli government also wanted to put more economic and political pressure on Iran to bring about a change of policy. Therefore, the US policy of economic sanctions against Iran neutralized Rafsanjani's efforts to improve economic and diplomatic relations with the West. European countries were also criticizing Tehran's position towards the Arab–Israeli question and the peace process. In a general assessment, Rafsanjani's foreign policy was not very successful in improving Iran's international standing through economic realism while Iran was pursuing an idealist foreign policy with respect to the most important factor of the Middle East politics, the Israeli–Palestinian peace process.

The emergence of a reform movement following Mohammad Khatami's victory in the 1997 presidential election was the most dramatic change in the Islamic Republic's foreign policy as far as the question of national interest and realism was concerned. While the Rafsanjani government had looked for better relations with the world through Europe, President Khatami and his reformist supporters sought to improve IRI–US relations too.[25] Khatami's controversial interview with CNN and the reformist media's support for a US–Iran political détente implied a decisive trend towards realism and Iran's national interest in the international domain. This desire for realism was so strong that some reformist journalists, and activists, and some academics started to talk about the necessity of a change in the Islamic Republic's position and policy towards the Arab–Israeli conflict and the peace process.[26]

Some positive developments in the foreign policy realm did take place in this period.[27] However, President Khatami's most successful foreign policy arena was regional, rather than international. There were improved relations between Iran and its main regional rivals, especially Saudi Arabia.[28] The attendance of the leaders of the Islamic countries at the 8th summit of the Organization of Islamic Conference in Tehran in December 1997 was a very important diplomatic achievement for President Khatami's realistic foreign policy.[29] However, despite all optimism for the renewal of Iran–Egypt relations in the late 1990s and the early 2000s, no positive initiative was taken.

More important were the relations between Iran and the United States. While the Clinton administration showed its good intentions for a positive dialogue between the two countries and in spite of the formal apology of the United States Secretary of State, Madeleine Albright for the US role in the 1953 coup d'etat, the Khatami government was unable, given the strong opposition from the conservative idealists at the highest echelons of the Islamic Republic, to take the initiative and use this important event to promote Iran's national interest. In addition to this, a new round of fundamentalist rhetoric regarding the Palestinian issue and support for the Islamic fundamentalist Palestinian groups started in 2001. Many radical Palestinian and Middle Eastern Islamists attended the Tehran conferences in support of the Palestinian *intifada* in 2001, 2002 and 2003.[30] And in 2002, the Israelis declared that they had seized weapons sent from Iran for Hezbollah and the Palestinian Authority (the Karine-A Affair). All these events, taken together, frustrated the Iranians and foreign observers who had hoped for a real new era of realism under President Khatami. President George W. Bush's declaration of the 'Axis of Evil', which grouped together Iran, Iraq and North Korea as rogue states, put an end to any hope of a breakthrough in Tehran's foreign policy.

## Structural dualism and the dilemma of national interest in the IRI

The dilemma of national interest in the foreign policy of the Islamic Republic indicates the rise and fall of the realist trend. In fact, we have witnessed a cycle in this regard: after a short period of realism in foreign policy and the rise of a new trend towards serving the national interest, a conflicting idealism emerges and places major obstacles in front of the realist trend. The ebb and flow of idealism versus realism can be observed in the entire history of the Islamic Republic. Before explaining the cause of this problem, it should be pointed out that, basically, there have been three approaches to the question of national interest in the Islamic Republic of Iran.

1   Rejecting the whole concept of national interest as an anti-Islamic notion which contradicts the basic principles of Islamic constitution in the realm of foreign policy. The traditional conservative trends and the traditional followers of *velayat faqih* have followed this approach.
2   Justifying the idealistic foreign policy of the Islamic Republic as one which serves Iran's national interest. This approach presents an ideological interpretation of national interest that is compatible with the regime's foreign policy. Some Islamic academics use this approach and consider, for instance, the foreign policy of the Islamic Republic towards the Arab-Israeli conflict and the peace process as a policy which theoretically is adaptable to one based on Iran's national interest.[31]
3   Reducing national interest to a policy based on both the necessity of pursuing a realist foreign policy on the one hand, and emphasizing the importance of maintaining the Islamic nature and values of the system on the other.[32] This approach is essentially a contradictory one insofar as it wishes to integrate national interest with ideological, Islamic values.

A general assessment of the history of the Islamic Republic's foreign policy and the arguments of the three existing approaches towards the question of national interest reveal that national interest has been seen as equal to the interest of the political system. Three critical examples, that is, the resolution of the hostage crisis in 1981, the acceptance of the Security Council Resolution 598 to end the Iran-Iraq War in 1988, and the acceptance in 2003 of the IAEA's Additional Protocol that would impose tighter controls on Iran's nuclear programme, show that whenever the whole existence of the political system has been in real danger, the issue of national interest has become important.

Another subject that requires an explanation is the dilemma of the cyclical rise and fall of realism and idealism. Many factors may be presented to explain this problem, but the basic argument of this paper is that the structural dualism embedded in all aspects of the Islamic Republic of Iran is the main reason behind the dilemma of national interest in its foreign policy. This structural dualism stems from the fact that the Islamic political system is based on a dual power structure manifested in its constitution. This two-dimensional power structure, the traditional Islamic system of *velayate faqih*, on the one hand, and the modern presidential system, on the other, are in conflict with each other. While the traditional power structure was mainly concerned about ideological and religious principles of Islam, the modern power structure was essentially looking for the administration of the society and the government.

In practice, this modern structure has become mainly oriented towards a realist foreign policy, in contradiction with the value-laden concerns of the traditional structure. When the constitution was ratified and passed by the Experts' Assembly (*Majlis-e Khobregan*) in 1980, it seemed that no contradiction would develop. However, as the executive arena of the traditional power structure expanded, the representatives of the spiritual leader, *vali-ye faqih*, tended to intervene in all aspects of politics. Along with this, different pressure groups affiliated with the traditional power structure turned into informal decision-makers in all aspects of politics.

Foreign policy was one of the main arenas of this dualism. During the past 25 years of the Islamic Republic, while the Foreign Ministry, the executive branch of the modern structure in foreign policy, was somehow oriented towards Iran's national interest, the traditional power structure and its affiliated pressure groups promoted an idealist foreign policy and reacted harshly to neutralize all efforts for pursuing a policy based on national interest. The Salman Rushdie case in 1989 and the opposition to the US-Iran rapprochement in 2001 were the best examples in this regard.

The main reason for the traditional power structure's strong reaction against the modern structure's realistic foreign and domestic policies is that the former considers the development of the latter's policies to act against its basic interests and power basis. In other words, the idealist tendency's reaction against realism and its emphasis on the maintenance of the value-laden principles of the constitution are, in fact, aimed at self-maintenance. Therefore, it is predictable that as long as this structural dualism exists, the dilemma of national interest in the foreign policy of the Islamic Republic will not be resolved.

# Notes

1 See, for example, Charles Raymond Whittlesey, *National Interest and International Cartels* (New York, 1946) .

2 Hans J. Morgenthau, *Politics among Nations: The Struggle for Power and Peace* (New York, 1978): 4–15.

3 Ibid., 5.

4 Ibid.

5 See Rouhollah K. Ramazani, *Iran's Foreign Policy, 1941–1973. A Study of Foreign Policy in Modernizing Nations* (Charlottesville, 1975); Rouhollah K. Ramazani, *the Foreign Policy of Iran, 1990–1941. A Developing Nation in World Affairs* (Charlottesville, 1966).

6 Fred Halliday, 'Iran's Foreign Policy since 1979: Internationalism and Nationalism in the Islamic Revolution', in Juan R.I. Cole and Nikki R. Keddie, eds, *Shi'ism and Social Protest* (New Haven, 1986).

7 See Homa Katouzian, *Mussadiq and the Struggle for Power in Iran* (London, 1990).

8 For more details, see Hamid Ahmadi, 'Din va Melliyat: Keshmakesh ya Hamyari?' (Religion and Nationality in Iran: Conflict or Harmony?), in *Iran: Hoviyat, Melliyat va Qowmiyat* (Tehran, 2004).

9 See, for example, Seyyed Mohammad Saqafi, 'Nasionalism Chist?' (What is Nationalism?) in *Tarikh va Farhang-e Mo'aser*, 6–10 (1372–1373/1993–1994).

10 On the books written against nationalism, see Reza Davari, *Nasionalism va Enqelab* (Nationalism and Revolution) (Tehran, 1986); Ali Mohammed Naqavai, *Islam and Nationalism* (Tehran, 1985).

11 See Hamid Enayat, *Modern Islamic Political Thought* (London, 1982): 148–149.

12 For more details see, Said Amir Arjomand, 'Traditionalism in Twentieth-Century Iran', in S.A. Arjomand, ed., *From Nationalism to Revolutionary Islam* (Albany, 1984): 202–203.

13 See David Menashri, *Post-revolutionary Politics in Iran, Religion, Society and Power* (London, 2001): 236, 283.

14 Among them, see Ali E. Hillal Dessouki and Bahgat Korany, 'A Literature Survey and a Framework for Analysis', in Ali Hillah Dessouki and Bahgat Korany, eds, *The Foreign Policy of the Arab State: The Challenge of Change* (Boulder, 1991): 8–25; Steve Smith, 'Theories of Foreign Policy: A Historical Review', *Review of International Studies*, 12 (1986); Lloyd Jensen, *Explaining Foreign Policy* (New Jersey, 1982).

15 K.J. Holsti, *International Politics: A Framework for Analysis* (Englewood Cliffs, 1996): 4.

16 Ibid.

17 See Houman Sadri, 'Trends in Foreign Policy of Revolutionary Iran', *Journal of Third World Studies*, 15, 1 (1998).

18 E.H. Carr, *The Twenty Years of Crisis, 1919–1939* (London, 1946).

19 Kenneth Waltz, *Theory of International Politics* (Boston, 1979).

20 See Umar F. Abd-Allah, *The Islamic Struggle in Syria* (Berkeley, 1983); Rudi Matthee, 'The Egyptian Opposition on the Iranian Revolution', in Juan R. Cole and Nikki Keddi, op.cit: 249–284.

21 Shahram Chubin and Charles Tripp, *Iran-Saudi Arabia Relations and Regional Order* (New York, 1996).

22 See for example, Elie Rekhness, 'The Terrorist Connection: Iran, the Islamic Jihad and Hamas', *Justice*, 15, 1 (1995).

23 The United States' three conditions were: the formal recognition of Israel as a state, the condemnation of terrorism against Israel and the acceptance of the Security Council's Resolution of 242. Yasir Arafat accepted all these conditions in early 1989 and the US–PLO negotiations started afterwards.

24  See Menashri, *Post-revolutionary Politics in Iran*, 264–287; and Mohammad Reza Maleki, 'Iran va Farayand-e Solh-e Khavar-e Miyaneh', in Mehdi Zakeriyan, ed., Arzyabiy-e *Siyast-e Khareji-ye Khatami az Manzar-e Sahebnazaran*, Khatami Foreign Policy as viewed by specialists (Tehran, 2002): 195–200.
25  See Gary Sick, 'The Future of US-Iran Relations', *Global Dialogue*, 3, 2–3 (2001).
26  See Menashri, *Post-revolutionary Politics in Iran*, 290–292.
27  See Anoushiravan Ehteshami, 'Iran's New Order: Domestic Developments and Foreign Policy Outcomes', *Global Dialogue*, 3, 2–3 (2001).
28  Keyhan Barzegar, 'Iran va Arabistane Saudi' (Iran and Saudi Arabia), in akeriyan. op. cit.
29  See Shahreza Abolhasani, *Majmu'eh-ye Asnad-e Ejlas-e Hashtom-e Saran-e Keshvarha-ye Islami* [Collected Documents of the 8th Summit of the Islamic Conference Organization, Tehran 9–11 December 1997] (Tehran, 1999).
30  Maleki, 'Iran va Farayand-e Solh-e Khavar-e Miyaneh'.
31  See for instance, Amir Mohammad Haji Yusefi, *Iran va Israel: az Hamkari ta Keshmakesh* (Iran and Israel: From Cooperation to Conflict) (Tehran, 1383–2004); Amir Mohammad Haji Yusefi, 'Nazariyeh-ha-ye Ravabet-e Beynolmelal va Siysat-e Khareji-ye Iran dar Qebal-e Israel' (Theories of International Relations and Iran`s Foreign policy Towards Israel), *Faslnameh-ye Motale'at-e Khavar-e Miyaneh* (1383–2004); Amir M. Haji Yusefi, 'Foreign Policy of the Islamic Republic of Iran Towards Israel, 1979–2002', *Strategic Studies*, Pakistan (2003).
32  See, for instance, Mohammad Reza Tajik, *Moqaddameh'i bar Esteratezhiha-ye Amniyat-e Melli-ye Jomhuri-ye Islami-ye Iran* (An Introduction to the Strategies of National Security of the Islamic Republic of Iran) (Tehran, 2002): 168.

# 4  From multilingual empire to contested modern state[1]

*Touraj Atabaki*

This study aims to address concerns over Iranian territorial integrity with respect to ethnic identity by examining three interrelated points:

- centre and periphery in Iran
- territorial attachment and the political borders
- ethnic identity and social mobility.

Finally I shall discuss the challenges Iran has been facing throughout the 20th century on maintaining her territorial integrity.

## Introduction

Throughout history, alongside the development of urban life, pastoral nomads and peasant communities gradually formed on the Iranian plateau.[2] These nomads, with their cohesive social structure, mostly dwelt in the mountains, and often embodied quasi-autonomous entities. The nomads were not only in constant contact with peasants and urban dwellers, but many of them were also recruited into the army. The Qezelbash formed the main body of the army under the Safavids (1500–1736), guarding the country's borders against the constant threat of the Ottoman Empire. Nader Afshar (1736–1747) was himself from the Turkmen Afshar nomad tribe and enjoyed the support of the tribal communities. Karim Khan Zand (1750–1779), the founder of the Zand dynasty, was raised as a Lori nomad tribesman, and the subsequent Qajar dynasty was founded by a Turkic nomad tribal chief, Aqa Mohammad Khan. All these men, Isma'il (the first Safavid monarch), Nader, Karim Khan, and Aqa Mohammad Khan, who reigned over Iran from 1500 AD to 1797 AD, utilized nomad tribal forces effectively to neutralize their rivals and maintain the boundaries of their kingdom.

The peasant communities in turn see themselves as direct descendants of a fictitious or real individual who originally founded their community. Such a tight, non-segmented social structure contributed greatly to the cohesiveness of the village community, safeguarding it from alien elements in rural areas. Patrilineality and the practice of patrilocal marriages restrained the intrusion of ethnic and linguistic elements. On the other hand, due to repeated foreign invasions, large segments of the rural population were forced to migrate into the arid zones in the interior of the country.[3]

Cities constituted the most vulnerable components of society. They were the first places to attract migrants and thus became the centres of destructive conflicts as well as productive contacts; they were centres of arbitrary rule, which influenced the political and territorial makeup of the country. Furthermore, the often vast territories governed by Iranians meant the emergence of sophisticated city-based administrative apparatus.[4]

The network of social interaction in Iran has been articulated and coordinated within a unique characteristic form. Such a pattern of interaction can be found to exist in the institution of, what has been called, arbitrary rule. The framework of arbitrary rule also ensured political unity, despite the heterogeneous nature of Iranian society. Furthermore, as Homa Katouzian puts it, the 'absence of functional social classes, which was associated with the transitory nature of private ownership and the state's monopoly of all independent power' increased the potential for high social mobility for every individual regardless of ethnic origin.[5]

## Centre and periphery in Iran

Throughout the 20th century, most of the secessionist movements worldwide have involved, in one way or another, the problem of periphery against centre. The location of the centre in relation to the periphery involves the antagonistic relationship of state to society in Iran, as well as the problem faced by peripheral areas in obtaining greater autonomy from the centre or the central government.

Iran has never had a single city as her permanent centre of political power for any lengthy period of time, unlike neighbouring Constantinople with a rather long history of being the seat of imperial strength. In the 400 years since 1500 AD, Iran has had to contend with several capital cities.

The development of the powerful centralized Safavid state began in the north-western city of Ardabil and later in Tabriz, on the crossroads of ethnic and cultural blending between Iran and the Ottoman Empire. Moreover, Tabriz was – and still is – the capital of Iran's largest ethnic minority community, the Azerbaijani Turks. After Tabriz, Qazvin, with a Turko–Persian ethnic composition, in the heart of the Safavid empire, became the capital city. From Qazvin the capital moved to Isfahan, in the centre with a Persian-speaking majority.

Following the fall of the Safavid dynasty, under the short-lived rule of Nader (1732–1747), Mashhad, in north-east Iran, enjoyed a brief status as Iran's capital. However, when Karim Khan Zand (1747–1790) founded his dynasty, he chose the southern city of Shiraz as power base. Finally, with the rise of the Qajar dynasty, the then insignificant town of Tehran was named as the new capital in 1792.

The immediate consequence of a city being named as the capital was the spectacular rise of its political, social and economic status, followed by a significant rise of the city's population and the complexity of its ethnic composition. In this context, Mashhad might be a noteworthy example, with a population increase of a quarter of a million following of Nader's decision to choose the city as his capital.[6]

A contributing factor to the tremendous and sudden rise of the urban population was first

> the fact that not only the royal family, but its huge entourage of administration and bureaucrats, military personnel and religious leaders filled the capital cities. Second, the majority of the national [nobility and notables] that is landlords and nomad tribal chiefs – seemed to have gathered around the crown. Third, the kings themselves ordered the resettlement and sedentarization of large nomad tribal groups as well as that of ethnic and/or religious minorities in neighbourhood close to the royal residences. All these had immediate impacts both on capital city development and spatial structures within the empire as a whole. [7]

The policy of population dislocation by means of forced migration and sedentarization of the nomads had a tremendous homogenizing effect on the ethnic as well as the religious composition of the empire's subjects. For example,

> the 'Safavids' population policy [of forced migration] included the resettlement of approximately 100,000 [Turkic] nomad tribal families, not to speak of at least 20,000 Armenians and Georgians in the southern precincts of Isfahan. The short rule of Nader Shah affected about 150,000 families. The Zands finally caused approximately 40,000 nomad tribal families to be removed from their traditional areas closer to Shiraz.... Resettlement was accompanied by genuine population policy: new villages were founded, existing villages enlarged and cities were transformed by the addition of new *mahalleh*s (quarters).[8]

The inner-urban quarters were separated along ethnic and religion demarcations and the inhabitants of these quarters regularly interacted with each other across socio-economic barriers. It may be argued that growing cosmopolitan cities which quartered a mixed and fluid population of diverse ethnic and socio-economic backgrounds, at times encouraged an individual sense of neighbourliness, fidelity, allegiance, and most importantly, attachment to territory. In the history of Iranian cities, dissatisfaction, discord, and bloody episodes of *heydari-nem'ati* conflicts between different communities were not uncommon, however, these conflicts never had an ethnic base and not a single city has ever disintegrated because of ethnic or religious diversity. Furthermore, the phenomenon of bilingualism (or even multilingualism) checked the spread of linguistic identity, with its homogenizing policies.

Although the rise of one city as the new capital would lead to the relative decline of the previous capital, especially its population, the new capital was never capable of causing a 'dramatic decay of the predecessor', as has been perceived by some scholars.[9] Each former national capital remained the administrative centre of its respective province; hence it was able to retain much of its economic role and function. In the Qajar era, Iran was divided into the four large *ayalat* (provinces) of Azerbaijan, Khorasan, Fars and Kerman-Sistan, each with its own *vali* (governor) and numerous *velayat* (districts). Later, with the reshuffling of the old provinces, a new province was formed with Tehran as its centre. The 19th century saw the prospering of Mashhad and Tabriz, two cities that functioned sometimes more effectively than Tehran: Mashhad with its special role as a Shi'a centre of pilgrimage and Tabriz as the gateway for European and Russian economic penetration into the interior of the country. Indeed, during the reign of the Qajar dynasty (1790–1925), Tabriz flourished as the predominant commercial centre, as the country's granary, and its second politically important city, the site of the Qajar Crown Prince's court, was Dar al-Saltaneh. During this period, Tabriz proved to be more receptive to outside influences and was a breeding ground for progressive political thinkers, many of whom became leaders of the Iranian constitutional movement of 1905–1911.

## Territorial attachment and political boundaries

Prior to 1900, Iranian borders were predominantly elastic. The Safavid attempt to introduce greater political unity through centralization and institutionalization of Shi'ism created for the Iranians a new, defensive identity in relation to those who lived beyond their borders. For the subjects of Safavid Persia defined themselves not by their own 'national' characteristics, but rather by local exclusion, that is, through a negative definition, comparing themselves with their immediate Sunni Muslim neighbours.

Whatever the case may be for the rise in self-identification and dynastic allegiance which arose in Safavid Persia, the emergence of Persia, as a territorial entity stretching from the Caspian Sea to the Persian Gulf, took on a more concrete shape in the seventeenth and eighteenth centuries with the production of the first semi-modern European maps of the country. The mapping of Iran as such, mainly based on the Safavid territorial achievements, was different from the ancient design of the Persian empire. In the pre-modern period, the Ottoman expansionist threat made the European powers concerned about the boundaries of their fervently hated neighbour. Indeed, it was with reference to such mapping that when in 1736, following the fall of the Safavids the Ottomans seized the north and north-west of Iran, Nadir began to demand the return of those territories, insisting on the persistence of Iran's legitimate frontiers. It is noteworthy that it was not only Nadir who referred to Iran's legitimate frontiers in his clash with the Ottomans. The Safavids' territorial Persia indeed turned out to become a standard reference for all following rulers. Karim Khan Zand and Aqa Mohammad Khan Qajar also came up with a similar call.

During the early 19th century, having been defeated by the Russians in successive wars, in 1813 and 1828, and forced into signing a peace treaty with Britain in 1857, Iran lost part of its north-west, east and north-east territories and was squeezed into its present frontiers. The eastern territory later became part of the newborn Afghanistan and the northern part was annexed by the Russian empire. The fate of the people in the north-west, most of them Shi'a Muslims, then became far more intimately connected with the Russians and the Muslim peoples of the Russian empire than with Iran. It was only during the final days of the First World War that the people of Nakhjivan signed a petition, urging the Iranian government to reunite them with Iran, a call drowned in the post-War uproar.

The process of territorial demarcation and realization of 'international boundaries' through wars and subsequent peace treaties in the 19th century helped shape the growing sense of territorial identity for Iranians:

> shaping boundaries focused attention on territory as the source of Iranian, as opposed to Persian, identity. It promoted land and geography as compelling criteria for Iranian-ness. The 'closed' frontier assembled peoples from varying ethnic background under the unequivocal rule of sovereign for the first time. Whereas before, nature had limited the movement of peoples and local rulers had obscured matters of sovereignty, by the end of the [19th] century new treaties and great-power politics had led to a redefinition of geographical authority and, at the same time, an arbitrary delineation of cultural boundaries. The closing of the frontier went hand in hand with an attempt at centralization by the government. The imperial court had finally recognized that the centre's survival depended on the cooperation of the periphery. As the monarch's domains diminished, Iranians voiced their calls for nationhood. No longer just a *mulk* belonging to the king, but rather a *millat* with invested citizens.[10]

During World War I, in the absence of a powerful state, one might well have expected that Iran, like the Ottoman Empire, would disintegrate into a number of smaller states. Yet Iran managed to preserve its territorial integrity after the war, partially thanks to the Bolshevik revolution which not only thwarted, albeit temporarily, Russian ambitions in Iran, but also made the West give priority to their agenda of an integrated, centralized and powerful Iran as a barrier to the spread of communism in the region.

## Ethnicity, mobility and modernization

It was a dominant paradigm in the 1950s and 1960s amongst social scientists that modernization breaks down traditional loyalties and confronts the individual with new needs and opportunities, depending on individual achievements in harmony with universal criteria.

> As people come to desire the same goals and rewards, they become more similar. Occupational and class differences become the salient social differentiators, displacing traditional solidarities that lose their utility and are reduced to innocuous cultural vestiges; loyalties are transferred from parochial to more encompassing national symbols produced by powerful and irreversible nation-building processes.[11]

Consequently, 'modernization, by socially mobilizing large segments of the population, would increase both the likelihood and tempo of their assimilation'.[12] According to such argument, the urbanization, industrialization, schooling, communication and transportation would lead to ultimate assimilation in the multi-ethnic societies.

> A decisive factor in national assimilation or differentiation was found to be the process of social mobilization, which accompanies the growth of market, industries, and towns, and eventually of literacy and mass communication. The trends in the underlying process of social mobilization could do much to decide whether existing national trends in particular countries would be continued or reversed.[13]

However, the validity of this theory could be challenged if one only examines the lengthy history of practising modernization in today's most advanced industrialized societies. Communal solidarity, ethnic particularism and cultural awareness in these societies have not vanished with the high degree of social mobilization, technological and economical integration, but rather have been modernized, articulated and intermingled with individualism and individual autonomy both being indispensable parts of modern man's perception of civility.

The age of modernity in Europe began with a new era when the basic unit in the structures of modern society was the individual rather than, as with agrarian or peasant society, the group or community. Accordingly, the individualism that was embodied in the liberty and autonomy of the individual provided a new definition embracing the new association between the individual and the polity. According to this new association, the individual in a modern society, in principle at least, was not any more the subject and agent of a particular king or priest, sultan, shah or sheikh, endowed with divine or prescriptive authority. The individual rather acted according to rational and impersonal precepts formulated in laws. The investiture of new juridical and political rights including the right of representation was indeed the conclusion of this new association. The emerging commercial and industrial urban middle class was inextricably linked to this individualism.

However, if in European society the process of modernization was associated with the gradual development and expansion of critical reason compiled by gradual embodiment of individual autonomy, and with the emergence of a civil society, in Iran the reverse was true. There, modernization was embraced by an intelligentsia composed of bureaucrats and military officers, who identified their own interests with those of the state. The rights of the individual and his relationship with the state were of marginal rather than central significance in the eyes of Iranian modernizers and critical reason and individual autonomy seemed to have little relevance. The main reason for such a discrepancy lay in the fact that the development of modern European societies was synchronized with and benefited from the age of European colonialism and imperialism and wars against the Orient. Modernization in the Middle East was a defensive reaction.

The practice of authoritarian modernization in post-First World War Iran was embedded in the perceived failure of the earlier attempts at introducing modernization in the country both from below as well from above. After all, the efforts of the 19th century and early 19th century reformers had not protected the country from occupation by European powers. The setback that the Iranian constitutional movement (1906–1911) suffered in the years before the outbreak of the First World War, the political disintegration and partial occupation of Persia during the war, all of these left the middle classes and the intelligentsia in Iran no other option than to look for a *man of order*, who, as an agent of the nation would install a centralized, powerful (though not necessarily despotic) government capable of solving the country's growing economic as well as political problems, while at the same time safeguarding the nation's unity and sovereignty.

Where social egalitarianism, liberalism and romantic territorial nationalism had inspired the earlier generations of intellectuals in their efforts to initiate change and reform throughout the country, for the post-war intelligentsia more preoccupied with the ideas of modern and centralized state building, political authoritarianism and linguistic and cultural nationalism became the indispensable driving forces for accomplishing their aspirations.

Despite the diversity of their political views, what singled them out from the previous educated or learned individuals was the model of society, which they took for granted. The European model of society presupposed a coherent entity, by definition organized around the distinctive concepts of *nation* and *state*. They were convinced that only a strong centralized government would be capable of implementing reform, while preserving the nation's territorial integrity. Likewise, they believed that modernization and modern state building in Iran would require a low degree of cultural diversity and a high degree of ethnic homogeneity. Along with ethnic and linguistic diversity, the existence of classes, too, was rejected.

Only when the country fulfilled the pre-conditions for a nation state as defined by the nationalists, when 'empirically almost all the residents of a state identify with the one subjective idea of the nation, and that nation is virtually contiguous',[14] could they realistically cherish hopes of safeguarding territorial integrity and gaining a respected place in the world. Some even argued that *Emruzi budan*, literally meaning being contemporary or modernized, would be attainable only when an 'ideal dictator' had set up the country for a social revolution by retaining power and concentrating his political authority through 'banning the press, dismissing the parliament, and restricting the power of the clerics'.[15] It was no surprise that such calls would soon find adherents in societies with a long record of arbitrary rule, although it has to be said that there were always those among the modernist intelligentsia who rejected this solution. In Iran it was Mosaddeq who during a session of the Iranian parliament in October 1925, warned the deputies with the following words:

> Today you Deputies of the Majlis wish to make a shah of Sardar-e Sepeh, Reza Khan. The honorable gentleman is now not only Prime Minster, but also the Minster of War and the Commander-in-Chief of the armed forces. Today after twenty years of widespread bloodshed, our country is about to enter a phase of retrogression. One and the same person as shah, prime minister, minister of war, and the commander-in-chief? Such a thing does not exist even in Zanzibar.[16]

Reza Shah's policy of centralizing government power and implementing modernization was in a sense a reaction to this widely-felt need for authoritarian reform. The process of political and cultural centralization, flavoured with secularism, westernism and meritocratism, generally enjoyed the support of many members of the intelligentsia, especially those with progressive and left-wing leanings. Persian periodicals such as *Kaveh* (1916–1922), *Farangestan* (1924–1925), *Iranshahr* (1922–1927) and *Ayandeh* (1925–1926), which dominated the ideological environment of the time, were pioneers in publicizing and promoting these policies. Kazemzadeh argued in an editorial that the society should be liberated from the yoke of the clerics by getting rid of religious superstitions, separating religion from the state, and accepting religious principles in accordance with the parameters of modern times.[17] Taqizadeh, the editor of *Kaveh* believed that salvation from long lasting misery was only possible by submission to the Western civilization: 'Iran must be westernized outwardly as well as inwardly, physically as well mentally'.[18]

> By absolute submission to Europe, through adaptation and promotion of European civilization, with no reservation or condition one could hope that our country would eventually become prosperous.[19]

The editor of *Ayandeh*, Mahmud Afshar, in an editorial entitled *Gozashteh – Emruz – Ayandeh* (Past–Present–Future), expresses concern for Iranian unity, before displaying his perception of modernization in the following terms:

> What I mean by Iran's national unity is a political, cultural and social unity of the people who live within Iran's present-day boundaries. This unity includes two other concepts, namely, the maintenance of political independence and the geographical integrity of Iran. However, achieving national unity means that the Persian language must be established throughout the whole country, that regional differences in clothing, customs and such like must disappear, and that *moluk al-tavayef* (the local chieftains) must be eliminated. Kurds, Lors, Qashqa'is, Arabs, Turks, Turkamans etc. shall not differ from one another by wearing different clothes or by speaking different languages. In my opinion, unless national unity is achieved in Iran, with regard to customs, clothing, and so forth, there will always be the possibility that our political independence and geographical integrity will be endangered.[20]

And by way of eliminating ethnic divisions and fostering national unity, he adds:

> Thousands of low-priced attractive books and treatises in the Persian language must be distributed throughout the country, especially in Azerbaijan and Khuzestan. Little by little, the means of publishing small, inexpensive newspapers locally in the national language in the most remote parts of the country must be provided. All this requires assistance from the state and should be carried out according to an orderly plan. Certain Persian-speaking

tribes could be sent to regions where a foreign language is spoken and be settled there, while the tribes of that region, who speak a foreign language, could be transferred and settled in Persian-speaking areas. Geographical names in foreign languages or any souvenirs of the marauding and raids of Genghis Khan and Tamerlane should be replaced by Persian names. The country should be divided from an administrative point of view if the goal of national unity is to be achieved.[21]

Thus, even before Reza Shah became monarch, the blueprint for the future execution of reforms and changes throughout the country was already in place.

During his twenty-year rule (1921–1941) Reza Shah achieved with absolute consistency the realization of most of the demands voiced by such intellectuals as Kazemzadeh, Taqizadeh and Afshar. His policy of authoritarian modernization gradually changed Iran's traditional social as well as political setting. New institutions were founded, among them: a national standing army based on a programme of universal male conscription and extensive reserve units; a secular education curriculum; a literacy programme, reading and writing in the dominant language, Persian, reducing linguistic differences; a secularized juridical system; and a national monetary system. Moreover, a centralization policy that included such harsh and disruptive measures as forced transfer and settlement of tens of thousands of nomads was pursued to achieve greater national uniformity. However, within a couple of years of his accession, Reza Shah's dictatorship was evolving into autocracy and soon afterwards it turned into arbitrary rule. While some intellectuals were forced to accept political retirement, there were others who were imprisoned or executed. Only a few could find shelter in exile, unable to witness the fulfilment of their aspirations.

Reza Shah's policy of authoritarian modernization during the 1920s and 1930s with the motto – 'one country, one nation' – was not too dissimilar to attempts by previous monarchs to rewrite the parameters of ethnic identity in Iran. Forced migration and resettlement of nomad tribes continued with even greater force, this time in order to eradicate the power of tribal chieftains who were perceived as posing a threat to Reza Shah's modernization programme. Encouraging a homogeneous urban society was seen as the formula for modelling the image of a modern Iranian citizen. Constructing the modern nation state was based on the assumption of unity and homogeneity and the nation state itself changed to become a viable entity.

Furthermore, the well-known enduring social mobility, a characteristic of Iranian social dynamic, remained in place alongside growing anti-ethnic/anti-tribal social polices, contributing to a rapid growth of economic mobility in society. Therefore, a new meritocracy was gradually formed in Iran. Every citizen regardless of his/her ethnic origin enjoyed the right of personal achievement in the newly-established administration, as long as he/she appreciated the state definition of Iran as a modern integrated nation state and submitted to arbitrary rule. There was no dominant ethnic group that held the key positions at the others' expense. The country's cultural unity was considered to be paramount in Reza Shah's brand of nationalism. As a result of the educational reform, the traditional religious *maktab-khaneh* was transformed into the modern primary schools with a curriculum taught in Persian, now Iran's national language.

Meanwhile, it was not permitted to publish books and newspapers in any language other than Persian. Moreover, to achieve greater national uniformity, Reza Shah, at a later date ordered the setting up of a government office called *Sazeman-e Parvaresh-e Afkar* (Organization for the Promotion of Thoughts), with the task of guiding and directing the younger generation toward service to the homeland.[22] As a result, a new Iranian 'high culture' – to use Gellner's terminology – was gradually recast. Here too, the influence of economic imperatives determined cultural and national norms. A modern economy depends on mobility and communication between individuals at a level that can only be achieved if these individuals have been socialized into high culture (i.e. the official culture of the state and its ruler), so as to be able to communicate properly. This can only be achieved by a fairly monolithic educational system. Thus, culture, not community, provides the inner sanctions. The requirements of a modern economy inevitably result in the new idea of the mutual relationship of modern culture and state.[23]

## The question of Azerbaijan

During the 20th century, there were three major revolts in Iranian Azerbaijan aimed at demanding change and reform throughout the country, limiting the central government's authority in the region and thereby instituting a new power structure based on a greater measure of local participation. These attempts all ended in complete failure. The first endeavour, Khiyabani's revolt, dates back to the 1920s, the chaotic years following the First World War; the second under the patronage of the Soviet Union, was made by the Azerbaijan Democratic Party led by Ja'far Pishevari in 1945–1946; and the third came in the immediate years following the Islamic Revolution of 1979.

Khiyabani, a preacher calling for radical reforms, lived for a time under the rule of Tsarist Russia, but he was much more strongly influenced by social ideas that had originated in 18th century Europe. Although staunchly opposed to Iran's centralized administration, he was also committed to preserving the country's territorial integrity and to the establishment of Iranian nation state, rather than to independent or even autonomous rule in Azerbaijan. In this area, his political demands did not go beyond seeking a fair distribution of executive powers between the central government and local authorities throughout Iran.

Indeed, an undertaking to introduce political reforms throughout the country from the capital, as compared with more regional initiatives, was one of the main issues dividing the Iranian nationalist-reformist camp. If by launching their campaign for reform from Tabriz rather than Tehran, Khiyabani and his comrades were playing down the central government's functions, others in the reformist camp wholeheartedly felt that any initiative which decreased the role of the capital would directly or indirectly weaken and thereby endanger the country's integrity. The two sides were so divided on this issue that even Khiyabani's independent stand and his outright refusal to seek any support from foreign powers did not prove adequate in persuading the entire reformist camp to unite under his banner.

Khiyabani's uncompromising policy not only made it impossible for him to negotiate with the central government but he was also unable to coordinate his efforts with other contemporary regional movements in Iran, for example, with Mirza Kuchik Khan, the leader of the rebellion in Gilan. When Mirza Kuchik Khan called for the formation of a popular front with the purpose of restoring the constitution in Iran, Khiyabani went so far as to compare him to Vosuq al-Dawleh:

> What is the difference between you and Vosuq al-Dawleh? He wants to rule Iran with the assistance of the British forces and you would do the same with the backing of the Russians.[24]

Finally, the central government put an end to Khiyabani's days by appointing Mokhber al-Saltaneh Hedayat as governor of Azerbaijan in August 1920. Mokhber al-Saltaneh reached Tabriz in September and within one week of his arrival, on 12 September, the Cossack Brigade[25] was deployed to take control of all the strategic points throughout the city. In a short time, the Cossacks had achieved their objectives and fifty Democrats had been killed, including Khiyabani. The central government's authority was unambiguously re-established over the whole region.[26]

Although Khiyabani's power was short-lived, he exercised an important influence on political thought and attitudes in Iran, especially with regard to reformist trends. His initiative to set up his government as an alternative to the central government's authority in Azerbaijan caused a major split in the reformist camp. While the modern tendency within the *Nahzat-e Melli* (Popular Movement) was towards playing down the central government's functions and granting more autonomy to the provinces, the traditional current in reformist politics was still wholly committed to establishing a strong, centralized (not necessarily despotic) government in Iran. The suppression of Khiyabani's revolt can be taken as a sign of the widespread vigour and legitimacy which this traditional current still enjoyed.

Twenty-five years later, Pishevari, a revolutionary communist, while maintaining that he had learned a lesson from Khiyabani's tragic end, prepared to lead another regionally based movement in Azerbaijan. As a Marxist-Leninist who had spent years in the communist movement, Pishevari not only considered Iranian Azerbaijanis to be a separate nation, but also insisted on championing the Bolsheviks' rallying cry of 'the right of nations to self-determination, the right to secede and form an independent state'. Pishevari's understanding of autonomy clearly went beyond merely demanding a greater degree of local participation in regional legislation and administration, while remaining within the borders of an established sovereign state. Furthermore, Pishevari belonged to the generation of communists who not only believed in the right of the communist camp to intervene internationally in the internal affairs of associated political parties, but also never hesitated to seek direct assistance from the communist camp. In Pishevari's eyes the Soviet Union, as the leading communist power, was not in the

same category as other great powers such as Britain or the United States, who were mistrusted by Iranians because of their interventions in Iran's internal affairs.

Undoubtedly, not everybody within the political spectrum of liberals, not even all communists, shared these attitudes with Pishevari. Since the beginning of the 19th century, foreign intervention in Iran's internal politics had been a constant threat. To be identified with a foreign power, in the long run at least, worked against a statesman's chances of political success. Thus, it was difficult even for many members and cadres of the Tudeh party to give their unconditional support to the measures taken by Pishevari's Democratic Party. Consequently, in view of what was perceived to be Pishevari's unambiguous involvement with, and dependence on, the Soviet Union, one is obliged to question the extent to which his movement for autonomy was indigenous. Of course, there were numerous local grievances which have been referred to above, but such grievances alone would never have been an adequate cause for the autonomous government to employ such menacing, provocative language in its dealings with the central government or to adopt such drastic measures as it did – even to the extent of breaking off all ties with Tehran.

Far from what Pishevari had expected, Soviet backing for the Azerbaijani Democrats' call for autonomy had, in the end, rather negative consequences. The existence of the then Soviet Socialist Republic of Azerbaijan – bearing the same name as the Iranian province of Azerbaijan – made many Iranians wary that what really lay behind the Soviet policy was nothing less than the desire eventually to annex the Iranian Azerbaijan. In the face of this lurking suspicion, many politically active Iranians who were generally in favour of greater autonomy for the provinces were reluctant to lend their unconditional support to the Azerbaijani Democrats. In their minds, Pishevari's call for regional autonomy was associated with the nightmare scenario of Azerbaijan's secession from Iran. Furthermore, the fact that the Azerbaijani Democrats in many cases adopted an imprecise terminology with regard to autonomy and ethnic issues only added to the confusion and ambiguity which surrounded their policies in the public's eyes.

Similarly, on their home ground in Azerbaijan, the Democrats' policy of relying on Soviet support appears to have gradually alienated the Azerbaijanis from their autonomous government. Here, too, the spectre of secession engendered widespread anxiety that for the foreseeable future all ties with Iran would be cut, leading to irreversible economic and cultural losses for Azerbaijan. Consequently, despite the government's implementation of many attractive educational, electoral, and especially the large-scale land reforms, their policy makers clearly did not manage to win and hold on to genuine popular support, as is attested by the autonomous government's swift collapse when challenged militarily by Tehran.

Following Prime Minister Ahmad Qavam's early diplomacy to settle the 'Azerbaijan Crisis', the central government launched its final attack against Azerbaijan in late November 1946, while Pishevari was still threatening:

> Our people have sworn an oath to preserve, at whatever cost, the liberties which they have won... We have stood by our word, and those who wish,

by force of bayonets, to trample our freedom under foot, whoever they may be, will be pounded by the strength of the people's biceps and driven back. This is my final word: *Ölmak var, dönmak yok*! (Death, yes; retreat, no!)[27]

Pishevari later changed his tone and called on all 'Iranian brothers…to stand up and fight to safeguard liberty and democracy in the country'. He promised 'to crush the attack of the reactionaries' in order to 'make it possible for the Iranian nation to liberate itself'. The declaration ended with a series of patriotic exclamations: 'Long live Iran's independence'.[28]

On 12 December 1946, just one year after it had been established, the Democrats' rule in Azerbaijan came to an end. Ironically, this was the date on which anniversary celebrations were set to take place in commemoration of 'the glorious day when the government of the province had been placed in the hands of the people'. The Iranian army had prepared itself to face stiff resistance from the Democrats over an extended period of time,[29] but, to everyone's surprise, the army did not encounter any serious barriers to establishing its authority in the province. There were only a few isolated cases of Azerbaijani armed resistance.[30] However, according to some descriptions, what was supposed to be 'the army of liberation was a savage army of occupation'.[31] As a result, during the early days of chaos, following the arrival of government troops in Azerbaijan, many lives were lost and a mass migration to Soviet Azerbaijan took place.[32]

## Islamic revolution and the question of ethnic minorities

Following the fall of the Azerbaijan Autonomous Government of 1945–1946, and in the years following World War II, as Iran's geopolitical location and national resources made the West become aware of the importance of her territorial integrity, the country went through a major socio-economic transformation. The process of rapid urbanization and industrialization caused some degree of ethnic dislocation throughout Iran. In the capital, Tehran, as in almost all the country's big cities, Azerbaijanis formed a strong community, dominating the local economy. Tehran's Azerbaijani population even exceeded that of Tabriz, a most populous Azerbaijani city.

Furthermore, the expansion of education and communication for the most part contributed to a more homogeneous culture in Iran. This tendency towards homogeneity on the social, political and cultural level may be seen to have culminated in the Islamic Revolution of 1979. Except for Kurdistan's calls for regional autonomy within Iranian frontiers, one could not find a serious political challenge with either an ethnic or religious flavour during the Revolution. However, the popular consensus during the anti-monarchical movement of 1978–1979 was by no means an indicator of the disappearance of provincial resentment in Iran.

The early stance of the Islamic government on the question of ethnicity and ethnic diversity was demonstrated during the vociferous debates over the country's new Constitution in the Assembly of Experts (*Majlis-e Khobregan*). Article 15 of the Constitution acknowledges Iran's ethnic diversity and the ethnic communities' fundamental rights to preserve their distinctive identities and cultures:

> The official language and script of Iran, the lingua franca of its people, is Persian. Official documents, correspondence, and texts, as well as textbooks, must be in this language and script. However, the use of regional and tribal languages in the press and mass media, as well as for teaching of their literature in schools, is allowed in addition to Persian.[33]

Following the ratification of the Islamic Republic's Constitution, Ayatollah Khomeini in a statement addressed the ethnic minorities' question in Iran in the following words:

> Sometimes the word minority is used to refer to people such as the Kurds, Lurs, Turks, Persians, Baluchis, and such. These people should not be called minorities, because this term assumes that there is a difference between these brothers. In Islam, such a difference has no place at all. There is no difference between Muslims who speak different languages, for instance, Arabs or Persians. It is very probable that such problems have been created by those who do not wish the Muslim countries to be united.... They create the issues of nationalism, of pan-Iranism, pan-Turkism , and such isms, which are contrary to Islamic doctrines. Their plan is to destroy Islam and the Islamic philosophy.[34]

However, if the call for regional autonomy was absent in the revolutionary uproar during the Revolution, except from the Kurds, social and political unrest in Iran with an ethnic flavour was often registered in its aftermath. There were revolts in Kurdistan and Turkaman-sahra in early 1979 – which in the Kurdistan case lasted for another six years – and political unrest in Khuzestan and Baluchistan in mid 1979. The most intense political unrest came in regions with a majority of Sunni Muslim population, one of their main objections aimed at the Constitution's provision that, as in the previous constitution, Twelver Shi'sm was to be Iran's official religion. However, when in late 1979 to early 1980 news of uproar from Azerbaijan reached Tehran, the capital reacted to the reports anxiously. With a predominant Shi'ite population, Azerbaijan greatly contributed to the revolutionary Islamic leadership. The question that then dominated the central government's mind was the extent to which the political unrest in Azerbaijan had been flavoured with ethnic issue.

On 25 February 1979, only days after the seizure of power by the new revolutionary regime, the Muslim People's Republican Party (MPRP) (*Hezb-e Jomhuri-ye Khalq-e Mosalman*) was set up in Tabriz, with Ayatollah Kazem Shari'atmadari's implicit endorsement. In its first declaration the new party announced that its objectives included the establishment of an Islamic, multi-party democracy, and maintaining Iran's territorial integrity. As a tendency outside the mainstream Islamic establishment, the MPRP launched its political campaign with reservation on the plebiscite organized by the government for April 1979 that was to determine the nature of Iran's political system. While the referendum called on the people to choose between the Islam republic and the monarchy, the MPRP argued that the public should be given more choices. The referendum was held in disregard of such reservation and the electorate overwhelmingly voted for the establishment of an Islamic republic.

Following the April referendum, the writing of the country's new Constitution was put on the government's agenda. Although the ruling clerics had already promised a constituent assembly with 500 members, Ayatollah Khomeini opted for a 73-member Assembly of Experts. The MPRP objected at this point, arguing that the Assembly of Experts could not be a broadly-based, representative institution replacing the Constituent Assembly, with members representing the MPRP and its sympathizers from Azerbaijan and other parts of Iran; both Ayatollah Shari'atmadari and the MPRP boycotted the referendum for the Constitution in December 1979. The main objection raised by the moderate Ayatollah Shari'atmadari and the MPRP centred on the adoption of the concept of *velayat-e faqih*, or the guardianship of jurist consult, which according to them contradicted the sovereignty of the nation. Here too, there was no indication of ethnic issues and the rights of ethnic minorities in Iran.

Following the referendum for the new Constitution, with a dramatic decline in the number of votes cast, compared to the earlier one for the nature of the political system in the country,[35] the streets of big cities in Azerbaijan, particularly Tabriz, turned into the scene of bloody confrontation between the supporters of Ayatollah Shari'atmadari and those of Ayatollah Khomeini, both camps dominated by native Azerbaijanis. The Tabriz unrest lasted for another two months, during which period government offices were intermittently occupied by the rival forces. Finally, when the political confrontation reached the military establishment, Ayatollah Shari'atmadari intervened personally; he issued a statement that disassociated him from the MPRP, and put an end to the chaos in the city.

Contrary to later political assessment by some academics or political activists,[36] the ethnic dimension was neither absent nor all-pervasive in the 1979 Tabriz unrest. Ayatollah Shari'atmadari's moderate position, insisting on a clear distance form Ayatollah Khomeini's revolutionary clericalism, attracted supporters not only in Azerbaijan but also throughout Iran. In the early days of the revolution Ayatollah Shari'atmadari's stance offered an appropriate shelter to all those who found themselves in an uneasy indenture with Ayatollah Khomeini.

It is interesting to note that during the revolutionary days and in their immediate aftermath, with Azerbaijan and the rest of the country passing through a relatively non-conventional period, one could not find any reference to the activities of the old Azerbaijan political societies and organizations such as the Azerbaijan

Democratic Party which still had an office across the border in Baku. There was even no attempt to commemorate historical events such as the formation of the Azerbaijan Autonomous Government (December 1945) or to honour its leader, Ja'far Pishevari. The activities of those advocating the upholding of Azerbaijani cultural awareness were limited to the publication of periodicals such as *Yoldash* (Comrade), *Inqilab Yolunda* (On the Revolution's Path), *Yeni Yol* (New Path), and *Varliq* (Entity) with limited circulation, mainly amongst the veteran Marxists and ex-Marxists. Indeed, it was the latter group who during the same period formed the Azerbaijan Society and attempted to introduce the notion of self-determination in the revolutionary discourse.[37]

The outbreak of the war with Iraq in 1980, which lasted for eight years, had far reaching consequences for cultural harmony in Iran. Forced migration and population dislocation refashioned the Iranian identity within the national territory. For the Iranian establishment, the dominant ideology of war was Shi'ite Iran against Sunni Iraq. The Azerbaijani Shi'ites, therefore, turned into forerunners of the war. However, by the end of the war in 1988, and the during the period of 'reconstruction' and partial liberalization under President Rafsanjani, the notion of ethnic rights gradually entered into the general discourse of individualism, individual autonomy and citizenship which was the preoccupation of the reformist circles. Such contributions became even more transparent during President Khatami's term, exposing an interconnection between the issues of citizenship and individual rights, including the rights of ethnic minorities in contemporary Iran. However, the most dramatic episode during this period was the fall of the Soviet Union and the emergence of eight republics on the northern frontier of Iran.

## The end of the Soviet era

At the turn of the millennium and in a world coming out of the Cold War, the international political setting had dramatically been altered. Across Iran's northern frontiers, instead of a great Tsarist/Soviet power, with which Iran had become accustomed to live over the previous two centuries, a number of small independent states had emerged, some of them home to majority population with corresponding ethno-linguistic groups within Iranian territory. Calls for unity of the people who share a common language but live under different national flags are occasionally heard, utilizing the familiar Eurocentric ethno-linguistic discourse where 'ethnicity and language become the central, increasingly the decisive or even the only criteria of potential nationhood.'[38] For example, in the newly formed Republic of Azerbaijan, some political groups and intellectual circles initiated a campaign advocating the establishment of a greater Azerbaijan. To attain this goal, once again the call was raised for the provinces of Iranian Azerbaijan to secede and unite with the Republic of Azerbaijan.

In June 1989, during a congress in Baku that brought together academics, artists and trade unionists, the '*Azerbaijan Khalq Jebhesi*' (The People's Front of Azerbaijan, PFA) was formally established. In a programme that was adopted during the party founding congress reference was made to the PFA's chief goal of abolishing all political barriers obstructing the development of cultural and economic ties with Iranian Azerbaijan:

> The People's Front supports the restoration of ethnic unity of Azerbaijanis living on both sides of the border. The Azeri people should be recognized as a united whole. Economic, cultural, and social ties between our divided nations should be restored. All obstacles to the creation of direct human contacts (visits to relatives and friends) should be abolished.[39]

With ethnic violence spreading throughout the Caucasus and the crisis of Nagorno-Karabakh leaving the Azerbaijanis with a feeling of being ignored or even humiliated by Moscow, the call for solidarity between all Turkic people of the region, particularly the Azerbaijanis, became the main item on the PFA's agenda. The political temperature was further raised when Gorbachev decided to send the Soviet Army to the Caucasus to bring back together the pieces of the empire's jigsaw. In its weekly gatherings in *Maydan* (the largest square in Baku and known as Lenin Square, that once had been the site of official parades), the PFA often invited individual Azerbaijanis from Iran to ascend the stone podium and address the huge crowds about the bitter pages of their history, their division and their heartfelt longing to change the status quo and rejoin each other. During these gatherings, one of the most popular calls was for repealing the Tukamanchai Treaty of 1828 that had set the Araxes River as the new border between Iran and Tsarist Russia, splitting the northern and southern parts of the Province of Azerbaijan from each other.

The call for unification was somewhat realized during the last days of 1989, when a crowd of Azerbaijanis from the Nakhjivan province dismantled and crossed the frontier posts and installations that had been dividing them from Iranian Azerbaijan. On the Iranian side of the border, the event was observed cautiously, with enthusiasm and compassion being confined to the frontier settlers who had family ties in the north. Nevertheless, for some circles in Baku, the event provided an analogy with the recent fall of the Berlin wall. The border-crossing episode received wide media coverage in the West and for a few days the whole world became familiar with the euphoric crowds burning the frontier's military installations and clipping the barbed wire. In another corner of Azerbaijan, in the Lenkaran region, the Azerbaijanis also adopted the Nakhjivani practice. Free passage across the Iranian border soon became a common event. The Iranian government's response was a cautious welcome to Shi'ite brothers and sisters from the north, whose experience was seen in a religious, rather an ethnic context. On the other hand, Moscow dispatched some provocateurs and agitators to the region to distribute pictures of Ayatollah Khomeini, in an attempt to provide justification for its march towards Azerbaijan in order to halt the spread of 'fundamentalist Islam' within its borders.

The Soviet Army's assault on Baku in January 1990, although successful in halting the rapid political change in Azerbaijan, was unable to turn back the clock. In September 1990, with martial law still in force, an election for a new Supreme

Soviet was conducted. During the election campaign, the PFA raised the demand for the two Azerbaijans' unity, albeit more cautiously than before, calling for closer cultural and economic ties with 'southern Azerbaijan'.

In the Caucasus, the economic hardship of the last year of Soviet rule was exacerbated with wide-ranging ethnic conflicts. The most momentous of these conflicts erupted between two neighbours, Armenia and Azerbaijan over Azerbaijan's largely Armenian-inhabited autonomous region of Nagorno-Karabakh, a quarrel that eventually developed into military confrontation. Ill-equipped Azerbaijani troops suffered a series of humiliating defeats when confronting successive Armenian military offensives against Azerbaijan frontier cities. While Moscow was standing by her historical ally, Armenia, Azerbaijan turned to neighbouring countries for help. However, neither Iran nor Turkey was willing to jeopardize its relations with Moscow.

The failure of the August 1991 coup in Moscow left the Azerbaijan's former local communist power elite, led by President Ayaz Mutallibov, in total disarray. An appeal for independence which had been made in late August was formally ratified on 18 October 1991, with Mutallibov still acting as president. Nevertheless, the political chaos that was spreading all over the country forced the president to resign and a new presidential election was held in June 1992. Abulfazl Elchibäy, a former political prisoner, became the first elected president of the independent Azerbaijan Republic.

Although Elchibäy's presidency did not last more than a year, his programme which included opposition to Azerbaijan's membership in the Commonwealth of Independent States (CIS), close relations with Turkey, and ignoring Tehran, while exhibiting a desire for extended links with the Azerbaijanis in Iran, caused some mistrust and power re-alignment in the region. For many Iranians, his pro-Turkish nationalistic stance and his aspiration to form a greater Azerbaijan were nothing less than a replication of the old Soviet-style scenario. Except for some small nationalist circles in the diaspora, Elchibäy's call for a greater Azerbaijan was not enthusiastically received among Iranian Azerbaijanis. Yet, abhorrent as the idea of breaking away from Iran, and therefore being denied access to a potentially huge market may have been, one should not underestimate the effect that a neighbouring country might have on a bordering province, especially when the peoples of both regions have a common language and culture. The call for more cultural rights, including the right to have a bi-lingual national colloquium in Azerbaijani as well as in Persian, has become increasingly prominent in Iranian Azerbaijan.

During Elchibäy's year-long presidency, the newborn Republic of Azerbaijan faced widespread economic as well as military crises. Unable to address the worsening military situation in Nagorno-Karabakh and the declining domestic economy in Azerbaijan, Elchibäy was left with no option but to abandon power and leave the capital for his birthplace, Karaki, a small village in the east of Nakhjivan.

The tragic end of Abulfazl Elchibäy's short rule in Baku was simultaneously marked with the elevation of Heidar Aliev to the presidency in June 1993.

Among the factors that eased the return of Heidar Aliev to power, one could certainly refer to the disillusionment that the Azerbaijanis felt with Elchibäy's pro-Turkey policy. In the end, Turkey's support for Azerbaijan turned out to be not much more than an emotional liaison.

In contrast to his predecessor, Heidar Aliev unequivocally displayed his displeasure with any 'greater Azerbaijan' scenarios from the early days of holding office. Even before becoming President of Azerbaijan, during his office as President of the Autonomous Republic of Nakhjivan, Aliev made a visit to Iran and made pilgrimage to the shrine of the Imam Reza in Mashhad. His restrained policy towards Azerbaijan's neighbouring countries turned out to be more durable and profound than might have been expected.

## Reformist period and regional activism

During the eight years war with Iraq, with the exception of a few ethnically oriented armed groups based beyond the western Iranian frontiers and functioning in the border regions, one finds no trace of any references to the ethnic challenges threatening Iranian territoriality or any call for practising ethnic identities in an individual or collective form. However, by the end of the war, when the dichotomic culture of the war gradually faded away, writing on Iranian multiple identities and ethnic groups' rights became an intellectual enterprise engaging a large number of ethnic minorities' intelligentsia. In such a context, even writing ethnic history has developed into a persuasive political project, shaping a significant and unbroken link with each ethnic group's constructed past, aiming to fill the gap between the ethnic group's origin and its actuality.

The most articulated manifestation of such interlacing was the rapid increase of the number of books and periodicals published in ethnic languages since 1990. According to a survey during the presidencies of Rafsanjani and Khatami, the number of books published in Azeri-Turkish reached 460 titles with a circulation of 920,000 copies. During the same period there were 78 periodicals published either in Azeri-Turkish or Azeri-Persian bilingual. For the Kurdish language these figures reached 708 titles of books with a total circulation of 1,416,000 copies and 21 periodicals.

The development of a culture of reform during Khatami's first presidency term to a large extent changed the mental mapping of activism in Iranian Azerbaijan and Kurdistan. In the case of Kurdistan this change manifested itself in adopting a new course of protest, from armed confrontation to non-violent action ensuring the Kurds' civil rights. Published in different cities of Iranian Kurdistan and Azerbaijan and distributed through legal means, the publication of non-clandestine literature in Kurdish and Azerbaijani with a profound non-political accent, presented an insightful ethnic culture in the region. In the majority of this literature the amplified presentation of vernacular non-religious culture is not only a challenge to the Iranian government's general attitude on religiosity, but it also fashions a type of communal solidarity underlined more than anything else by a sense of Azerbaijani-ness or Kurdish-ness. In other words, these publications have developed into a manifestation of the juxtaposition of the individual and its autonomy with the aspiration of promoting a collective identity distinguishing the Azeris and Kurds from the neighbouring peoples.

Another means of communication in the public space is the emergence of Kurdish and Azeri televisions and internet sites. With a rather short history, the Kurdish television broadcasting from outside the Iranian frontiers has become the dominant form of communication, spreading news and political analysis throughout the region. The Kurdish television channels can now be received by satellite dish, a device strictly forbidden in Iran. In addition to these television channels there are dozens of radio stations, all except one broadcasting from Iraqi Kurdistan. Some even broadcast their programmes in both Persian and Kurdish and exclusively address the Iranian Kurds. Finally one should refer to the inception of Internet Cafes in the urban centres which, by providing connection with Kurdish web logs, are gradually becoming one of the most popular entertainments for the Kurdish youth. In the case of the Azeris however, the domain of all these means is very limited, but it is prevailing.

The consequence of such development is a change in the mental mapping of activism. If in the old days the agencies in political movement were exclusively monopolized by political elites which in their multiplicity were enlightened individuals or political institutions, in the new development the traditional landed tribal or elites have been replaced by a new generation of individual with university degrees, a cultural and symbolic capital and dozens of cultural societies, trade unions and guild organizations whose demands are far from claiming political autonomy or even seceding from Iran and joining the Republic of Azerbaijan or the Iraqi Kurdistan. What brings all these new activists together is a pursuit of improving living conditions and enjoying the freedom to practise their culture as the Azeris and the Kurds practising in northern Iraq or the Republic of Azerbaijan by non-violent means rather than taking up arms in the mountains.

## Conclusion

To conclude this paper, I would like to recall the final question that *Newsweek* magazine's Carroll Bogert put to me in an interview in 1997: 'Can one expect that one day the dogs of ethnic strife begin to bark in Iran?'[40] My immediate reaction was that 20th century Iran had so far succeeded in avoiding the fate which had befallen the Ottoman, Tsarist and later the Soviet empires, and that its different ethnic groups had been getting along. Nonetheless, one should not overlook the fact that the fate of Iran's ethnic compositions and its territorial integrity may depend, more than any other factor, on the introduction of reforms in the country's political structure.

With the conclusion of Khatami's term of office, a government whose broadly reformist agenda had allowed an informal expression of ethnic identity, and the election of the Khomeinist radical Ahmadinejad, one should expect that government to adopt a less conciliatory stand against the ethnic minorities' demand for equal cultural rights. On the other hand, the development of ethnic activism in Iran seems at present to depend on the inception of reforms in the country's political structure. Individual rights as well as collective rights for a non-discriminatory inclusion and access to economic opportunities, political participation, or cultural status, including recognition of the mother-tongue, either on an individual basis or through some pattern of group proportionality are part of this process. If these processes are gradually realized they could ensure the sustainability of existing borders, although nothing is quite eternal.

## Notes

1 I am grateful to Homa Katouzian, Houchang Chehabi and Hossein Shahidi for their insightful comments and helpful editing of this article.
2 On nomads and tribes in Iran see Lois Beck, 'Tribes and the State in Nineteenth- and Twentieth-Century Iran', in *Tribes and State Formation in the Middle East*, ed. Philip S. Khoury and Joseph Kostiner (Berkeley: 1990); Richard Tapper, *Pasture and Politics. Economics, Conflict and Ritual among Shahsevan Nomads of Northwestern Iran* (London, 1979).
3 Nader Afshar Naderi, in Shahrokh Amirarjomand (ed.), *Iran, Elements of Destiny* (New York, 1978): 230.
4 Ibid.
5 Homa Katouzian, 'Arbitrary Rule: A Comparative Theory of State, Politics and Society in Iran', *British Journal of Middle Eastern Studies*, 24 (1997): 53.
6 Ibid.
7 Ibid., 161.
8 Ibid.
9 Ibid.
10 Firoozeh Kashani-Sabet, 'Fragile Frontiers: The Diminishing Domains of Qajar Iran', *IJMES*, 29 (1997): 227.
11 Milton J. Esman and Itamar Rabinovich (eds), *Ethnicity, Pluralism, and the State in the Middle East* (Ithaca, 1988): 14–15.
12 Walker Connor, 'Nation-Building or Nation-Destroying?' *World Politics*, 14 (1972): 323.
13 Karl Wolfgang Deutsch, *Nationalism and Social Communication: An Inquiry into the Foundations of Nationality* (Cambridge, 1953). Quoted in Walker Connor, 'Nation-Building or Nation-Destroying?'.
14 J.J. Linz and A. Stepan, *Problems of Democratic Transition and Consolidation, Southern Europe, South America, and Post-Communist Europe* (London, 1996): 25.
15 *Farangestan* (1924), nos. 4 and 5.
16 From a speech by Mosaddeq during the session of parliament on the change of dynasty, 31 October 1925.
17 *Iranshahr* (1923), no. 1.
18 *Kaveh* (1920), no. 1.
19 Ibid.
20 Mahmud Afshar, 'Aghaz-nameh', *Ayandeh* (1925), no. 1.
21 Ibid.
22 Hossein Makki, *Tarikh-e Bist Saleh-ye Iran* (Tehran, 1983): 412–413.
23 Ernest Gellner, *Nation and Nationalism* (Oxford, 1983): 140.
24 Gerigor Yaqikiyan, *Showravi va Jonbesh-e Jangal, Yaddasht-ha-ye Yek Shahed-e 'Eyni* (Tehran, 1984): 137.
25 For a comprehensive study of Khiyabani's revolt, see Homa Katouzian, 'The Revolt of Sheikh Mohammad Khiyabani', *Iran*, XXXVII, 1999, reprinted in Homa Katouzian, *Iranian History and Politics* (London and New York, 2003). The Cossack Brigade

formed in 1879 was composed of Iranian troops. Under Russian officers, it soon came to enjoy a reputation for military discipline, rigidity and brutality. The most notorious example of the Brigade's intervention occurred in 1907, when under the command of the Russian colonel Liakhov, it bombarded the *Majles*. Russian control over the Cossack Brigade ceased following the collapse of the Tsarist empire in 1917, but the Brigade continued to exist and, indeed, provided Reza Khan with military support to launch his *coup d'état* in 1921. Reza Khan then merged the Brigade with the Gendarmerie as part of his reorganization of Iran's national army. F.O. 371/2762, Memorandum on the Persian Army, 1907.

26 F.O. 371/4927. In his memoirs, Mokhber al-Saltaneh (*Khaterat*, 318) says that the Sheikh was found and killed by Cossacks in an exchange of fire, but he also mentions a suicide note by the Sheikh, although he does not vouch for its veracity. According to Bristow, the British Consul in Tabriz,: 'The Sheykh was discovered in his hiding place and shot by Cossacks.' See: F.O. 371/ 1278, 15 September 1920.

27 *Azerbayjan* (1946), no. 357.

28 *Azerbayjan* (1946), no. 366.

29 Wash. Nat. Arch., 891.00/12–2346, 23 December 1946.

30 Among such minor cases was the vague resistance organized by the *Komiteh-ye Enteqam* (Revenge Committee) in a suburb of Tabriz; Mohammad Ruzegar, *Khaterat* (unpublished memoirs). In an interview with the author, Mohammad Ruzegar described the resistance as 'purely unprompted' and denied any possible link between the above-mentioned group and the Azerbaijan Democratic Party leadership.

31 W.O. Douglas, *Strange Land and Friendly People* (New York, 1951): 45.

32 In accounts of the Democrats, reference is made to more than 10,000 casualties, whereas semi-official reports of the Iranian government estimate the number of dead at 800. On the other hand, a British source cited by the US Embassy in Tehran gives the number of killed Democrats as 421. For the Democrats' account, see: Azerbaijan Demokrat Ferqahsi, *Azadliq Yolunun Mubarizlari*, 2 (Baku, 1969): 5. The Iranian government estimate has been reported in *Khandani-ha*, no. 36, 24 December 1946. The American Embassy's report has been classified under Wash. Nat. Arch. 891.00/1–1547, 15 January 1947.

33 *The Constitution of the Islamic Republic of Iran*, Tehran, Islamic Consultative Assembly (no place, no date): 33.

34 British Broadcasting Corporation (BBC), Summary of World Broadcasts, Middle East and Africa, 19 December .

35 While in the referendum for the nature of the political system in the country Tabriz contributed with 718,368 votes, in the second referendum the number of cast votes was 389,063.

36 See, for example, Brenda Shaffer, *Borders and Brethren. Iran and the Challenge of Azerbaijan Identity* (Cambridge, 2002): 96–97.

37 The Azerbaijani Society was founded among others by Javad Hey'at, Hamid Notqi, Hossein Ali Katebi and Mohammad Ali Farzaneh.

38 Eric Hobsbawm, *Nation and Nationalism since 1780, Programme, Myth, Reality* (Cambridge, 1990): 102.

39 *The Caucasus and Central Asian Chronicle*, 8 (1989): 7–10.

40 Carroll Bogert, 'They all Get Along', *Newsweek* (May 26, 1997): 31.

# 5    Three faces of dissent

Cognitive, expressive and traditionalist discourses of discontent in contemporary Iran

*Mahmoud Sadri and Ahmad Sadri*

Three climates of contrarian discourse have thrived in post-revolutionary Iran. By far the most noticed and privileged among these is the cognitive discourse articulated by intellectuals. Meanwhile, the expressive discourse of the peer-group networks, and the traditionalist discourse developed by heterodox charismatic movements remain obscure to most observers. Cognitive discourses of dissent articulated by intellectuals mould the 'public opinion' and pave the path of organized collective action and social change. They embody deliberate and conscious resistance of what Robert Ezra Park called 'the public'. Expressive and traditionalist discourses of dissent, on the other hand, reflect the temperament of Park's 'crowd'. Far from sober responses to oppression, they signify improvised and chaotic but tremendously effective reactions to repression. Their sparse articulation, their episodic resurgence (during football celebrations, sectarian revolts, and other occasions for spontaneous collective action), their dependence on visual and emotional means of expression, and their evanescence make them even more elusive and invisible to the investigative gaze. Nevertheless, as expressive and traditionalist discourses of discontent embody the needs and aspirations of vast segments of the population, they are indispensable to an adequate understanding of political culture in contemporary Iran. They contain energies that can, in time, fuel full-fledged dissident movements.[1] We must not forget that the Revolution itself started not as a rational extension of the cognitive revolutionary discourse analyzable in purely political, organizational, cultural, economic, or military terms but as largely spontaneous collective action that proved unpredictable not only to Western analysts but even to its own leaders and participants. The Iranian Revolution, thus, sprang forth and gathered force in opposition to seemingly minor provocations, harvesting tremendous energy out of every measure taken for its suppression. Only after the Revolution had already started was the cognitive component made salient, causing the articulation of demands and selection of heroes and leaders.[2] None of this is intended to belittle the role of cognitive discourse, which has been and continues to be central to opposition politics in Iran. Hence, we will start this study with a brief taxonomy of cognitive discourses of the opposition in contemporary Iran before moving on to the expressive and traditionalist discourses.

## Cognitive discourses of dissent: intellectual fault lines

Three spectrums of political discourse, already present in pre-revolutionary Iran, have dominated the intellectual discourse in the last twenty-five years. They include religious orthodoxy, religious reform, and secular critique. Intriguingly, discourses that were affirming of the status quo during one era emerged as critical in another and vice versa.

The chart below articulates representative movements in each strand and traces their developments in three successive periods.

Cognitive discourse is best known to the social scientists and historians because it is produced and disseminated, for the most part, by professional

*Table 5.1* The three spectrums of political discourses from pre-revolution to 21st century Iran

|  | *Before 1979* | *1979–2004* | *2004 onwards* |
|---|---|---|---|
| | **Quietist traditional Islam:** | **Empowered heterodoxy as the reigning theocracy:** | **Empowered and state sponsored ultra-orthodoxy:** |
| **Religious orthodoxy and heterodoxy** | *Seminaries in Qum, Najaf and Mashhad* | *Velayat-e Faqih* | *Mo'talefeh and Ansar-e Hezbollah formations* |
| | **Radicalized political heterodoxy:** | **Suppressed orthodoxy:** | **Apolitical orthodoxy:** |
| | *Khomeini and his lieutenants* | *Khat-e Feqahat* | *Hey'at and Khaneqah religiosity* |
| | **Liberal reading of Islam:** | **Political reform movement:** | **Radical 'Anti-movement'* reform:** |
| **Religious reform and innovation** | *Nehzat-e Azadi* | *Hajjarian, Khatami* | *Disenchanted reformists: Ganji, Webloggers* |
| | **Radical reading of Islam:** | **Intellectual reform movement:** | |
| | | | **Reformed (post-Khatami) reform:** |
| | *Mojahedin-e Khalq* | *Dissident political Theology: Soroush, Shabestari, Kadivar* | *Neo- Melli-Mazhabi: Sazegara* |
| | **Liberal nationalism:** | **Liberal secularism:** | **Liberal secularism:** |
| **Secular critique** | *Jebhe-ye Melli* | *Jebehe-ye Melli, reconstituted* | *Jomhouri Khahan* |
| | **Laic critique:** | | **Radical secularism:** |
| | | **Radical laicite:** | |
| | *Radical secular and anti-clerical critique* | *Underground circles, 'little magazines'* | *Advocates of Philosophical enlightenment* |

Note

* Michel Wieviorka, *The Making of Terrorism*, translated by David Gordon White (Chicago, 1988): 3–23.

intellectuals: university professors, authors, journalists, and the clergy. Intellectuals remain the focus of attention in Iran. They are heard and heeded far more attentively than is the case in Western countries. Not a month goes by without a major article or book appearing on the role of intellectuals in the destiny of the country. Much has been written on this issue and no doubt more will be written. For the time being, however, we will forgo further discussion of this issue in favour of highlighting the other two discourses that are usually neglected in the study of dissent in Iran.

## Expressive discourses of dissent: graffiti wars

Expressive discourse usually takes immediate (e.g. audio-visual, demonstrative) forms. Its practitioners, unlike the proponents of cognitive discourse, are more amorphous and intractable and, as such, pose a greater immediate – even if ephemeral – threat to social order. An example of expressive discourse is found in the work of competing graffiti crews[3] such as 'Rap' and 'Heavy Metal' and their common opponents: the state-sponsored vigilantes that comprise the 'mobilization' militia known as 'Basij' that are affiliated with the Revolutionary Guards.

The baby-boom generation of the early years of the Revolution and the war with Iraq does not remember – or care for – the experiences and beliefs that are at the core of the regime's claim to legitimacy. This is particularly true of the progeny of the urban middle classes, despite the fact that the regime celebrates the events of the Revolution and the war, and expands on revolutionary axioms such as the defiance of imperialism and protection of Iran's Islamic identity on posters and murals in public spaces,[4] and fills walls with slogans and quotations from the revolutionary leaders.[5] There is nothing to indicate that this saturation of the public space with the hegemonic political discourse reaches its intended audience. Neither can one avoid the evidence of resistance to this kind of propaganda on the streets of the country. One such form of resistance is the practice of 'striking type'. Due to the strict dress code of the Islamic Republic, a rebellious youth subculture based on slight alterations of appearance and mannerism in defiance of state sanctions has emerged and thrived in Iran. This form of symbolic resistance to the cultural hegemony of the state ideology is known, rather innocuously, as '*teep zadan*' or striking type. It involves adhering to alternative styles of grooming that amount to a subtle stylistic revolt against the state-sanctioned norms of correct appearance in public. These outward modifications involving hairstyle and outfit are modest and almost invisible to the uninitiated. And yet, in their subtlety, they are glaringly obvious to the native eye. Two among many 'styles' that have appeared in the last two decades are *Rap* and *Heavy Metal* that reached the height of their popularity in the mid-1990s in Tehran. This does not mean that other youths who do not 'strike type' are type-free. Those who try but do not succeed to strike a type are contemptuously called 'Javaad', a common Islamic name in Iran, used in this context to imply that the person concerned is not 'hip', or is a 'country bumpkin'.

In stark contrast to the affluent urban youths, the state-sponsored Basij represents the ideological nemesis of the 'type-striking' middle-class youths. However, they 'strike' their own type by sporting army khakis, plaid Kaffiahs, and adolescent beards. They are often seen stopping and inspecting cars driven, mostly, by their middle-class counterparts, and searching them for illegal substances and/or illicit relationships.

Iranian Rap bears little resemblance to the American inner-city Rap subculture. The Iranian Rap, in terms of its preferred tastes and ideals, is more like a cross between the spirit of the 'flower children' of the 1960s and the clean-cut, 'preppie' look for boys (blue jeans, T-shirt, and so on) and, for girls, tighter than usual outfits while exposing a fair amount of hair beyond the mandatory scarves. Basij members are scandalized by the use of their Kaffiahs as headdress by the Rap girls. Rap groups usually scrawl the names of their favourite bands and peace signs in their graffiti.[6] The Rap subculture takes a minimalist position toward the hegemony of the Islamic government and its supporters. It expresses a desire to be left alone to have clean fun. It does not valorize excessive sexual behaviour or the use of drugs and other illegal behaviour.

There is slightly more to connect the Heavy Metal fans in Iran to their Western counterparts. They are radically opposed to the sanctioned model of behaviour for the youths in Iran and appear contemptuous of the conformism of the Rap lifestyle. The most important item in the accessories of female Heavy Metal fans is army boots. Male fans sport leather outfits but hide tattoos, piercing, and razor blade-inflicted scars.[7] Heavy Metal stakes its claim to the position of the 'cool' anti-establishment, anti-heroic rebellion. The contest between Heavy Metal and Rap continues on the walls of Tehran, although the1990s was the heyday of this rivalry. A particularly telling occasion arises when rival Rap and Heavy Metal crews share the same space on a wall, extolling their own groups and lambasting their rivals with the use of slogans and insignia. One such graffiti on Ba Honar, formerly Niavaran, street in the north of Tehran, near the former royal palace, appeared as a pastiche of Islamic revolutionary slogans: '*The cult of Metal, struggling to escape the material and spiritual domination of Rap: Pure Metal.*'

Obviously those who strike the same types are likely to hang out together, listen to the same music and attend the same 'mixed parties' – uttered in English, the word denotes gender inclusive gatherings. Regardless of what music is played or what type is struck in a party or whether alcohol, drugs, or illicit sex are involved, going to a 'mixed party' is treated as a form of juvenile delinquency by the vice squads. 'The Bureau for the Promotion of Virtue and Prohibition of Vice' attends to minor offences of the affluent youth gangs, pursuing and apprehending them, confiscating their paraphernalia, summoning their parents, and setting up public forums aimed at educating and warning the youths against the temptations of Western music, mores, and life styles. There is no doubt that occasional criminal activity including drug abuse is also associated with the underground music gangs. However, it is doubtful that the association is as strong as the authorities suggest. The Bureau's educational posters for the edification of the high school and college youths feature literalist, alarmist, and mostly incorrect interpretations of the Western Heavy Metal and Rock groups' lyrics and insignia.[8] For example, the poster describing the type of deviance promoted by the band 'Kiss' interprets their facial make-up as a sign of their homosexual life style.

Local graffiti crews from Tehran's affluent, northern neighbourhoods usually compete and occasionally clash with the Basijis, who come either from the city's impoverished neighbourhoods or from amongst the youths with limited prospects for educational success in any neighbourhood.[9] The lines of the symbolic war between the youth gangs and the Basij are thus drawn. (For profiles of an affluent gang member and an Islamic vigilante gang member see Appendix I.) The Basijis also participate in the graffiti war. Their crews roam the city at night and produce hastily scrawled or spray-painted slogans and stencilled portraits of the revolutionary leaders, replete with grammatical and syntactic errors.[10] What is remarkable in the expressive discourse of dissent (whether of the Rap or Heavy Metal variety) is the subjugation of the political content to artistic form (Figures 5.1 and 5.2).

*Figure 5.1* Gang graffiti from Rap and Heavy Metal. Photograph by Ahmad Sadri.

*Figure 5.2* Gang graffiti from religious vigilantes and Rap gangs. Photograph by Ahmad Sadri.

There can be little doubt that the elusive and mostly illegal graffiti of dissent is in response both to the Basij graffiti and to the officially commissioned gigantic murals and slogans that dominate the public space.

## Traditionalist discourses of dissent: charismatic heterodox cults[11]

One of the manifestations of the traditionalist discourse of dissent in Iran is the heterodox mass religiosity of Persianate Shi'i Islam that continues to defy the yoke of official interpretation. As such, it epitomizes the universal phenomenon of the autonomy of mass religiosity from the strictures of the official religion. This autonomy can shade into deliberate defiance of the official fundamentalist interpretation of Shi'a Islam that has functioned as the state religion in the past quarter of a century in Iran. The fiercely traditionalist (or Velayati) interpretation of esoteric Shi'ite tradition is one example of the rejection of the politicized religion in Iran. Depending on its amenability to political exploitation, popular religiosity has been tolerated by the ruling theocracy. 'Jamkaran', a 'blessed site' in the vicinity of Qum, received its mythic status through a dream in the middle of the 20th century. The same is true of another popular mausoleum in the north of Iran. The state appears to approve the sanctity of these sites and their putative holy state by paving roads and facilitating transportation and congregations at these sites. But it seems to disapprove of further supernatural claims leading to the establishment of new 'holy' sites. The present study concentrates on the case of the spontaneous cult that grew around a supernatural experience in the central city of Mobarakeh (population 37,000, Isfahan province). Within 21 days of its founding, on 1 July 1993, this cult was suppressed and its shrine was demolished by the security forces dispatched from the nearby state capital, Isfahan. On that day, the security forces clashed with the protectors of the makeshift shrine built on the site of the alleged miracle in the house of an elderly couple who were already under house arrest in Isfahan (Figures 5.3 and 5.4). The events of Mobarakeh were briefly reported in the Iranian opposition press and flashed across the international wire services and radio broadcasts. Of course, most of the news and analyses were based on rumours as the security forces immediately closed all communication to the town. Our extensive interviews with the participants and witnesses of the event conducted in August 1993 revealed distinct groups ranging from believers to bystanders, sceptics, and detractors around the central

*Figure 5.3* Revolutionary Guard officer preventing pilgrims from approaching the site of the burnt oven in Mobarakeh. Photograph by Mahmoud Sadri.

*Figure 5.4* Prophetess of Mobarakeh with her husband under house arrest in Isfahan.
Photograph by Mahmoud Sadri.

figures: the illiterate elderly woman who had the 'vision' and her husband, a
retired security guard, who shared part of the experience.[12]

The vision was experienced by the 59-year-old Soghra Aminpour who witnessed
blood that she took to be that of Imam Hossein, (Prophet Mohammad's grandson,
the 'lord of martyrs', according to Shi'a belief) bubble from underneath a brick on
her earthen oven, where she was performing a private ceremony in commemoration
of 'Ashura'.[13] She also noticed that two of the candles she had kindled in honour
of the occasion had melted in the form of an open palm, another sacred symbol
signifying the severed hand of Imam Hossein's brother, Abbas. This observation
led to the transformation of the oven and the kitchen of Mrs. Aminpour into a
shrine for the people who heard about her experience. The religious authorities
and the security forces treated the miracle with attitudes ranging from mild
incredulity to open hostility. The official condemnation of the vision of Soghra
Aminpour as false and heretical two weeks later by the top clergy of Isfahan
(Appendix IV) set the stage for the final assault on the cult and the razing of
the shrine that led to riots that left downtown Mobarakeh in ruins. More than one
hundred casualties and three hundred arrests were reported (for a detailed
chronology of the events of Mobarakeh see Appendix II). Mrs. Aminpour and her
husband were still under house arrest in Isfahan as they were interviewed by the
authors in the presence of representatives from the security forces. Mrs. Aminpour
appeared intimidated and nervous but did not waver on the authenticity of

her vision.

> By God, we don't fabricate lies. I lighted the candles. It was dusk already.
> I kept saying: O Hossein, we desire to come to 'Karbala',[14] and let these
> who are prisoners of war [Iran–Iraq war of 1980–88] be, I mean, be freed.
> So the war comes to an end. With this intention I kept calling on Hossein.
> All of a sudden (breaks into tears, has trouble forming words for a few
> seconds) all of a sudden my heart shook. I said (raises her voice, as if
> reliving the experience) O Zahra[15] your Hossein has appeared in the oven.
> As I was saying O Zahra, O Zahra, your Hossein is in the oven, all of a
> sudden I saw blood bubbling from under the brick. I kept reciting the
> 'salavat'.[16] I was then hit with a wonderful fragrance of rose water; as if
> there was a light in the kitchen; more than the candles [could account for].
> Inside the oven too was bright. I came to the door of the kitchen and called
> out to Haji.

Soghra's husband who is a '*noheh khaan*' or a cantor of dirges in the mourning
services of the neighbourhood also bore witness to the veracity of the vision:

> Yes, I was preparing my lines when I heard my wife calling out to me. I said
> what is the matter? Did you get scared in the kitchen? Then, as God is my
> witness, I swear to Imam Hossein himself, as I entered the kitchen, the fragrance
> overwhelmed me . . . . When I came in I saw a streak of blood that had trickled
> down the side of the oven and had moistened an area the size of a plate on
> the dirt floor of the kitchen. I saw a couple of fresh drops of blood bubble
> from under the brick. I started shaking. I said let's go. This is some kind of a
> miracle. Don't tell anyone. I kept making her swear not to tell anyone and she
> kept making me swear I would not tell anyone.

But, in time, everyone found out and the elderly couple's house was overrun by
the pilgrims. Soghra continued:

> The next day, I said let me go get the brick. But I swear by the Mecca that
> I have visited twice, and to my frequent pilgrimages to 'Sham' (Damascus,
> Syria) and Mashhad (in Iran, the site of the 8th Shi'a saint, Imam Reza) no
> matter how much I tried I could not detach the brick from the tile (because
> of dried blood). I came to pick the water from inside the oven, as God is my
> witness, I saw a black piece of cloth around it (the basin), this size (holds her
> hands a foot apart) I had not placed this cloth in the oven when I put the water
> in. When I removed the water I noticed the other pair of candles had melted
> into the form of a palm of a hand with five fingers. We had every intention
> of keeping this a secret but our grandchildren had gone into the kitchen and
> had learned about the affair. The third day my son had let it slip in *ta'zieh*

(the passion play ceremonies). All of a sudden, we saw by four o'clock the neighbours came in droves. Some five million people began to come to my house. Then we tried to control the crowd but couldn't.

According to the local police, within hours the entire earthen oven was hauled away due to the popular belief that anything that comes in contact with a miracle becomes holy and thus curative. This also caused the plundering of the cloths of anyone who claimed to have been cured at the site by other pilgrims. The chief of local revolutionary guards, Mr. Shafi'i, reported that the entire oven was literally ingested in the ensuing frenzy. He himself witnessed a man chewing on a chunk of clay from the oven the size of a piece of 'gaz' (nougat).

The sociological question is: how did this obscure vision become a national phenomenon within days of its inception? We can plot the position of believers according to their dedication to the vision on a series of concentric circles. The nucleolus features Soghra and Haji, their children, grandchildren and relatives. Then come the neighbours, a select group of whom ended up running the day-to-day affairs of the shrine. A typical figure in this circle would be Ali Iranpour, the barely literate *me'mar* (master builder), one of the six artisans and small businessmen of the neighbourhood who formed the board of trustees of the shrine in order to handle the routine affairs and devotional offerings of the pilgrims that started to pour in almost immediately after the vision was publicized. The process by which he was brought into the second circle of believers is described below:

We went to lay electric lines in a house and we noticed the commotion. We asked what was happening? The guy said there had been a miracle around there. We came down from the electric pole and went there but saw no remnants of the oven. We asked Haj Hossein what is going on? He said: go get a block of ice [for the pilgrims] I'll tell you later what is going on. Later he told me such a thing has happened. Now they have deluged and destroyed my house. They have taken parts of the [oven] to the revolutionary guards' headquarters for dusting and such things. He said we are told to shut the door of this place... The kitchen was small, two metres by three metres. I saw the roof was about to collapse (from the pressure of the pilgrims). I said let's get together and erect a wall. They said how do we go about it? I said you should go to the city hall and get a permit for a door... Congregations kept coming day in and day out, day and night. It had become a twenty four hour affair... We stuck around for a couple of days, till they called us over to the city governor's office. He appealed to the neighbourhood. He was very upset. We were all pulled into this... Whoever would come for a visit would get addicted. My own business suffered. I had to get some plumbing done for my own house but I couldn't. I would come home for a couple of hours and then I would go back to the shrine. I would be pulled back on account of love, devotion, and faith. These people were wailing and beseeching so, the way they would moan 'Hossein, Hossein' well, anyone in our shoes [would have been affected], particularly in this neighbourhood.

Then there is the circle of the 'Bagheris' a notorious self-mutilating *qameh zan* religious congregation (who hit themselves on the head with blades during the Ashura mournings for Imam Hossein), who seem to have appeared on the site of the kitchen and played a decisive role in the defence of the shrine in the ensuing clashes. Although the Ashura mourning was over, the Bagheris seem to have performed their self-mutilating rituals and spurred on the enthusiasm of the crowd of pilgrims and spectators. They were reported to have announced that they wanted their blood mixed with the miraculous blood from the oven. The fourth circle consisted of the people of the marginal and impoverished neighbourhood of *Rossi-ha* (literally meaning 'the people of clay' in reference to the newly built poor section of the town) who found a cause to celebrate their lowly neighbourhood and to take pride in the miracle that had visited it. They seem to enthusiastically have advocated the cause of their neighbourhood's 'healing oven'. The fifth circle comprises pilgrims, particularly the sick and the invalids, some five hundred of whom were found tied by the neck to the wall of the kitchen, awaiting a healing miracle when the security forces stormed the shrine. Most of these had come from neighbouring towns but some had travelled hundreds of miles in open trucks and chartered buses from as far as Yazd, in central Iran, and Tabriz, in the north-west. The next group comprises the bystanders and the gapers from other parts of Mobarakeh who maintained a non-committal attitude towards the events of the *Rossi-ha* neighbourhood. Many among this group questioned the vision of blood and candle wax. As a rule, the residents of the more affluent neighbourhoods of the city were more dismissive of *Rossi-ha*'s oven miracle. The educated classes and the intellectuals (regardless of their neighbourhood) adopted a similar attitude. Embarrassed by the mass frenzy, they disparaged the reports of spontaneous healings as proof of their fellow citizens' incurable superstition. But they agreed with local residents and the authorities that violent suppression of the cult by the forces from Isfahan was wrong. A typical figure in this circle would be Mr. Abbas Ahmadi, a local poet who satirized the cult in a widely circulated poem (Appendix III). In the outermost circle we place the regional clerics who not only doubted the authenticity of the 'miracle' but found it threatening to what they considered their monopoly of religious sentiments. Some of them, including the town's *Imam Jom'eh* (official leader of the Friday prayer), asked the cult leaders to play down their claims or to remain silent about them. Other clergy from the nearby Isfahan disparagingly dubbed Soghra Aminpour, her husband, and the adherents of the cult *ajelleh-ye johhal va a'aze-e avaam* (the most ignorant among the ignoramuses and the most common among the common people). The high clergy of Isfahan finally issued a fatwa denouncing the miracle (Appendix IV) and legitimizing the final assault of the Isfahan security forces on the shrine. Obviously, the most hostile group to the cult of the oven were the commanders of the troops dispatched to put an end to what they considered to be a false miracle and a threat to the peace and security of the region.

But it must be borne in mind that the clergy and the security forces of the city of Mobarakeh were uniformly opposed to the physical suppression of the cult. Indeed, a cleric (Mr. Asadi) and a lay seminary student (Mr. Moosavi) who were both residents of the *Rossi-ha* neighbourhood, proved crucial in sanctioning and defending the 'miracle of the oven'. Initially reluctant to be identified with the bloody fiasco, they finally agreed to be interviewed. They described the events leading to the phenomenon of the *Rossi-ha* miraculous oven and explained how some local government officials seemed to initially tolerate or even celebrate the miracle of Mobarakeh. They repeated the rumours that a pinch of the mud from the oven was taken to heal the paralysed hand of the Supreme Leader, Ayatollah Khameneh'i. Asadi and Moosavi bitterly complained of the unnecessary force exercised by the haughty commanders of the security forces. The leaders of the Mobarakeh Revolutionary Guards had also considered the incident as a nuisance but had gone no further than monitoring the events by planting informants among the cult members. They agreed with the local clergy and townspeople that a violent suppression of the cult was an unnecessary escalation.

At the beginning of our interviews, the local witnesses were understandably diffident. But after a few days some of them actually flagged down our car and volunteered to offer their eyewitness accounts of the events of the 21 July 1993. They accused the commander of the security forces from Isfahan of reckless bravado in the face of the crisis. He was reported to have marched up and down the neighbourhood waving around the fatwa (religious decree) of the Isfahan clergy and threatening to destroy everything that stood in his way. They reported that he had refused to give enough time for the evacuation of the sick and the invalids, ordering the lobbing of tear-gas canisters among the worshippers, whereupon an unfavourable wind had blown the noxious gases back at the troops who had come under a barrage of rocks from the shrine. The escalation of the hostilities led to the final assault on the shrine. Live ammunition was used against the remaining pilgrims and blade beaters. While the security forces were taking over the site and bulldozing the shrine in the mistaken belief of having quelled the riots, bands of blade beaters redeployed to the centre of the town and led the crowds who attacked and set ablaze government buildings, banks, and vehicles. Most of the above account was corroborated by the local commander of the Revolutionary Guards.

As we stated earlier, supernatural claims like the miracle of the oven in Mobarakeh are not rare. But these events rarely explode into the public consciousness. It was reported that the site's alleged number of miraculous healings had exceeded those reported at Iran's holiest site, the mausoleum of the Eight's Shi'ite Imam in Mashhad. This may not be unusual for new outbursts of religious effervescence. And yet no other site of miraculous cures would have been attacked and razed to the ground in pre-revolutionary times. Our interviews with security personnel in Isfahan revealed that the events of Mobarakeh had engendered new vigilance by the security forces to nip in the bud similar religious outbursts. At the time of our research a man claiming to commune with the occulted Imam (the Shi'ite Messiah) was under house arrest in Isfahan.

What was special about Mobarakeh? What other sociological factors contributed to its phenomenal prominence as a site of healing and its final reduction to rubble under the assault by government forces?

*The larger context*:  The name of Mobarakeh is synonymous with rapid industrial modernization in Iran. The city is surrounded by advanced iron ore mining and smelting mills as well as communication industries – some of which operate with foreign (mostly Italian) involvement. However, these industries are highly mechanized, which means they hardly recruit their labour force from the poor neighbourhoods of Mobarakeh. In the midst of this apparent modernization and industrialization and the conspicuous consumption of some residents of the city, the impoverished immigrant workers of *Rossi-ha* faced alienation, humiliation, and despair. It is not surprising if under these conditions they would become more susceptible to the comforts of folk religion and magical beliefs.

*Class and status:* The first waves and the more central circles of believers around the miracle consisted of day labourers and marginal workers of the *Rossi-ha* neighbourhood, the members of its congregational procession (*dasteh*) and their families. The inhabitants of *Rossi-ha* were seen as poor upstarts and were barred from fully participating in civic celebrations: their '*dasteh*' was not even allowed to march to the central religious enclosure ('*Hoseinieh*') during the festival of Ashura. Also, there were insinuations that the *Rossi-ha* neighbourhood was tainted with criminal ill repute. Sardar Mohajer, the acting commander of the security forces of the province of Isfahan, shared this view: '*Rossi-ha* is a kind of place that is well known for all kinds of misdemeanours and crimes. Most of the rogues and scoundrels reside in this neighbourhood'. But the miracle had apparently changed all that. The last became the first as the rumours of healing powers of the site put Mobarakeh on the map and patients in search of miraculous healing began to arrive at *Rossi-ha* from all over the country. However, the sceptics continued to see this as nothing more than a symptom of the deficiency of health care in the country. Mr. Ahmadi, the local satirist of the events of Mobarakeh, referred to this phenomenon in his poem:

> *To make up for the scarcity of medicine in this country*
> *The ashes of an oven have become medicine in 'Mobarakeh'.*

The more cynical observers (interviewed in the offices of the city's police) went for an even more reductionistic explanation of the events: that they were engineered to drive up the prices of soft drinks and confections sold by the vendors to the pilgrims. Be that as it may, it seems that the resentment of the underclass and lower classes in *Rossi-ha* and their perceived sense of inferiority may have spurred their enthusiastic embrace of the miracle and their fierce defence of it against outsiders.

*Order and orgiastic practices:*  Our interviews revealed that the proliferation of intensely emotional blood rituals was cause for alarm among the official clergy and security apparatus of Mobarakeh even before the events under discussion here. One of these practices is the grisly ritual of 'blade beating' or *qameh zani* during which mourners lacerate the skin of their head with machetes and bleed profusely on their white shrouds as they walk in processions. The religious establishment as a whole takes a grim view of this practice as it violates the Islamic injunction against self-mutilation and goes against the holiness codes that instruct avoiding such bodily fluids as blood. In the years following this incident, the Supreme Leader of the Islamic Republic issued a formal fatwa against blade beating. But even the combined forces of religious authority and law enforcement have not been able to eradicate the practice. According to the top cleric of the town (the leader of Friday Prayers), nine out of thirteen processional congregations of Mobarakeh practised blade beating before the events of July 1993. After the 'miracle of the oven' two more congregations joined the practice. The same soft- spoken clergyman related his own sensible advice to the security forces intent on a military solution to the problem of the cult:

> I told them: these are blade beaters, hitting their own heads with machetes!
> They won't be impressed by your batons. You have to resolve this peacefully.
> But they would not listen.

To add insult to injury, passion plays (*ta'zieh*) that are also discouraged and declared scandalous by the official clergy (because they include acting, music, and public entertainment) were performed on the site of the makeshift shrine. The immediate access to the experience of the holy in the various guises of passion plays, blood orgies performed by blade beaters, and the frenzy of direct miracles of healing seem to have entirely cancelled out the normal and official religiosity during the 21 days of the Mobarakeh miracle.

But why the violent suppression? The pre-revolutionary, Imperial regime ignored similar periodic manifestations of mass religiosity with the disdain of a secular officialdom. But a theocracy could ill afford to allow such a drain on the scarce sources of its legitimacy. Iran's Islamic regime, heir to a massive charismatic revolution, has been attempting to 'routinize' the charisma of its departed leader[17] in legal and social forms. The regime successfully channelled religious fervour to mobilize the youths during the Iran-Iraq war. It continues to do so by organizing events such as the 'Jerusalem Day' (the last Friday in the fasting month of Ramadhan) and sanctioning the less politicized religious and political anniversaries, gatherings and festivals often broadcast on national radio and television. Although the Friday prayer leader of each city is appointed from among the trusted clerical hierarchy, the government goes out of its way to synchronize the political messages delivered in the sermons in various cities through the Centralized Office of Friday Prayers. It must be obvious that the kind of religious 'effervescence'[18] that animated the events and eventually inspired the riots of Mobarakeh would not be tolerated by such a system. The eruption of the 'holy' outside the officially sanctioned venues could pose a direct challenge to the regime and would, at any rate, deplete the reservoir of religious sentiments that the ruling clergy hope to harness for their own ends.

## Conclusion

The defeat of the Khatami phase of political reform in Iran due to the intransigence of Iran's clericocracy has ushered in a new era of conspicuous silence in the Iranian public square. It would stand to reason that in the current impasse the energies that were once spent in political reform would back up and spill over into the triple fields of contrary discourses discussed above. The steep decline of voter participation in the recent municipal and parliamentary elections has eroded the legitimacy of the system rendering it more fragile and, hence, susceptible to rapid deterioration in the face of the kind of volatile collective action that brought down the monarchy a quarter of a century ago.

Post-reform ethos is remarkably similar to the pre-revolutionary disposition: brooding, passive, even submissive at first glance, the public sphere is rife with cryptic acts of defiance. Disparate disturbances, quelled with overwhelming force, once proved to have been tremors that ushered in cataclysmic quakes of the Revolution. Today's cognitive utopias challenging the ideology of the Islamic Republic and episodic contrary outbursts may carry a similar portent.

## Appendix I

The following profiles, based on several interviews, flesh out the drama of graffiti wars and the crews behind them:

*Abouzar*   is named after an early Islamic warrior, popular with the 'radical chic' intellectuals in pre-revolutionary Iran. He has adopted the name 'Nozar', a pre-Islamic name popular with his peer group. His father, a former executive in the Mayor's office in Tehran, now works in a lucrative semi-governmental corporation. The family lives in one of the most affluent neighbourhoods of northern Tehran. Abouzar gets arrested with some regularity for such minor offences as sporting ostentatious Western attires and accessories, and for public association with the opposite sex. His father has told him that he will not bail him out if he gets into serious trouble. He has many friends among a Rap youth gang but does not admit to participating in the graffiti war. His class and status conform to the general view that the 'rebels without a cause' of the Islamic Republic are the children of the upper crust of the Iranian middle classes. This case also illustrates the fact that many of the families that are ideologically committed to the Islamic Revolution have failed to reproduce themselves ideologically.

*Saleh*   was interviewed while standing with his comrades in front of a cooperative store belonging to the Revolutionary Guards. His father is a greengrocer. He belongs to the Islamic vigilante corps of the Basij. He is seventeen-years old but still a junior at a vocational high school. His professional ambitions are quite modest. He hopes to join the police force one day and trusts membership in Basij will help pad his resume when he applies for the police academy. After some hesitation he invited one of the authors to join one of their planning meetings in the '*Container*' (pronounced in English). It is, literally, a large metal shipping container that is furnished and decorated with flags and pictures of martyrs of the war. The Container is located a few blocks away from Abouzar's house on a busy square in the north of Tehran. Saleh believes that Rap and Heavy Metal are fronts for American neo-colonial corruption. He feels bad that the Basij is publicly identified, solely, with enforcing the prohibition of *monkarat* (acts that are forbidden in Islam). He is also somewhat embarrassed that his high school friends, including some 'Rap' adherents, know of his association with the Basij. As Saleh described his activities with some excitement, there was bantering among his friends. His direct commander, a youth in his early twenties, volunteered with a straight face that Saleh was very committed to patrolling the stretch in front of the girl's high school. Saleh blushed and appeared hurt by the joke that was made at his expense. In an attempt to regain his poise he launched into a commentary on political figures who were soft on corruption and he appeared to slander the powerful clergyman and former president, Ali-Akbar Hashemi Rafsanjani, and his family. The next day he approached the authors and asked them to destroy the pictures and the tape of the interview. But his commander intervened to dismiss his request on the grounds that Saleh must learn to keep his mouth shut in front of the 'reporters'.

## Appendix II

### *Partial chronology of events of the cult of Mobarakeh*

| | |
|---|---|
| 1 July 1993<br>(Moharram 10, 1414) | The paranormal experience of Mrs Aminpour. |
| 4 July 1993 | Public revelation of the experience.<br>Crowds gather and ransack the site in their enthusiasm for blessed and curative objects. |
| 5 July 1993 | Mr Aminpour is taken to the police station and made to sign a pledge to end the affair.<br>The first meeting of Mr and Mrs Aminpour with the town's Imam Jom`eh. |
| 6 July 1993 | The second meeting with the Imam Jom`eh.<br>The second pledge is given to the police to end the affair. |
| 8 July 1993 | At the request of the town's governor the seven-member board of trustees is convened to care for the pilgrims and manage the devotional offerings.<br>A name is devised for the site, *Ra`sol-Hossein*, meaning the Severed Head of Imam Hossein; banners and signs are installed throughout the town to guide the pilgrims. |
| 19 July 1993 | The official high clergy of the city of Isfahan (the capital and administrative centre of the province) after meeting with the couple issues a public notice denouncing the authenticity of the miracles of the oven. |

|                    | A satirical poem lampooning the events of Mobarakeh is widely distributed with the apparent approval of the officials. |
|--------------------|---------------------------------------------------------------------------------------------------------------------|
|                    | The security council of the town is convened with the participation of the municipal authorities, Revolutionary Guards and the Imam Jom'eh. A decision is made not to resort to violence. |
| 20 July 1993       | The security council of the province is convened in Isfahan and apparently leans toward a more forceful approach. |
|                    | Some five hundred anti-riot police are dispatched from Isfahan to Mobarakeh. Their mandate is to bring the affair to an end; they take position around the site. That night they turn away some two thousand pilgrims. |
| 21 July 1993       | Hostilities commence at around 7 A.M. Some three hundred believers clash with the security forces. Tear gas and bullets are used. A fire ensues. Most of the people leave the site and regroup at the main street of the town. They ransack the local government and revolutionary offices and banks. They also burn a police van. Some three hundred and sixteen people are arrested, and one hundred are wounded. Some are hospitalized with serious bullet wounds. The situation is declared under control at 11.20 A.M. |
|                    | At 1.00 P.M. the local Revolutionary Guards take over from security forces. An 'Extraordinary Situation' ('situation red') is declared. |
| 24 July 1993       | The security situation is downgraded to yellow. |
| 28 July 1993       | The security situation is downgraded to grey. (Field research conducted between 10–14 August.) |
| 24 August 1993     | The projected end of the extraordinary situation. |
| (Safar 28, 1414)   | The projected date of the end of house arrest for Mr and Mrs Aminpour. |

## Appendix III

***Translation of the satirical poem lampooning the cult of Mobarakeh, released on 19 July 1993, the day the official denunciation of the authenticity of the 'miracle' was published***

IN THE NAME OF THE EXALTED ONE

Every so often, a bunch of charlatans and opportunists exploit the emotions of the gullible and plain people. They tend to take advantage of people's devotion to 'the family of infallibility and purity' (the Prophet and his family) and the chief of the martyrs (Imam Hossein). They profit from the spectacle they have created and laugh at the simpletons whom they have deceived. The recent events in Mobarakeh are a case in point. I composed the following poem as soon as I heard of the false rumours but waited until it was denounced by the religious and official authorities (before releasing it to the public). Since 'Mokram' the poet from 'Habib Abad' also fought against superstitions I address this poem to him.

*'Mokram'*[19] *rise up, arrive in Mobarakeh.*
*Observe what is happening in Mobarakeh.*

*Watch right now from the house of 'khooli-ye-asbahi'.*[20]
*Miracles have emanated in Mobarakeh.*

*The ruin of an oven has become the gateway of wishes.*
*God's hand has become manifest in Mobarakeh.*

*Hossein has abandoned the soil of Iraq.*
*He has travelled from Karbala to Mobarakeh.*

*A light has appeared that looks like,*
*Now a banner, now the sword of 'Zolfeghar',*[21] *in Mobarakeh.*

*From the blessings of the ashes of the oven,*
*Two hundred people a day have been healed in Mobarakeh.*

*To make up for the scarcity of medicine in this country*
*The ashes of an oven have become medicine in Mobarakeh.*

*The doctors' offices everywhere are boarded up.*
*Because of the cure-all clinic that has been raised in Mobarakeh.*

*In the stampede of the crowds, through the work of miracles,*
*Quite a few people have lost their lives in Mobarakeh.*

*It is rumored that crowds have started to move like flash floods;*
*From near and far; in mornings and in evenings, toward Mobarakeh.*

*A crowd that is beyond enumeration and census.*
*A crowd like the one in the desert of 'Mena', in Mobarakeh.*

*He who denounces it will be transfigured,*
*Into a four-legged animal, publicly, in Mobarakeh.*

*From Isfahan and Shiraz and Yazd and Qom,*
*Travellers arrive, as pilgrims and mourners, in Mobarakeh.*

*Don't bother whether it is true or false,*
*Some people's wishes are being fulfilled in Mobarakeh.*

*Some people's business is booming,*
*Under the assumed name of beggars in Mobarakeh.*

*An enterprising bunch are striving in this midst,*
*Engaged in profit taking and buying and selling, in Mobarakeh.*

*There should be a season's market and a common market,*
*And a variety of winter and summer foodstuffs in Mobarakeh.*

*Through the lies of a wretched destitute woman,*
*An entire people have gone astray in Mobarakeh.*

*Were there not enough men so that the [Imam];*
*Would have to appear to a 'woman' in Mobarakeh?*

*Not even the elder of Khomein [Ayatollah Khomeini] claimed such a feat.*
*Maybe there has been a splitting of the Red Sea in Mobarakeh!*

*O illiterate people! What has happened to your reason?*
*If the Divine shall be incarnate, why on earth in Mobarakeh?*[22]

*O noble nation, to what extreme will you follow superstitions?*
*Behold the abyss between the age of atom and yourselves, in Mobarakeh.*

*O people of science and knowledge and culture and revolution,*
*Satan has lain a groundwork in Mobarakeh.*

*People in the slumber of ignorance and charlatans at work,*
*So that they could benefit from us in Mobarakeh.*

*Last year the three-headed snake*[23] *performed miracles.*
*This year God's mercy has appeared in Mobarakeh.*

*O God let not the hand of CIA slip out of its sleeve,*
*Along with trickery and deception in Mobarakeh.*

*O 'Ahmadi' be fearful of the people's wrath.*
*If you were to come to town, come in disguise to Mobarakeh.*

Abbas Ahmadi, Mordad 28, 1372 (21 July 1993)

## Appendix IV

### *Translation of the text of the clerical denunciation of the 'miracle' of Mobarakeh, released on 19 July 1993*

IN THE NAME OF THE EXALTED ONE

In the wake of what has happened in the martyr-raising town of Mobarakeh – and it is rumored that there has been a miracle there – some have claimed that they have been cured of various diseases. Hence, it has become necessary to appraise the Muslim people about a few facts.

First: There is no doubt that a spiritual relationship with the family of the Messenger – the family of infallibility and purity, may God's Greetings be upon them – and appealing to them whether in their life or after their passing is a source of special blessings. Denial of their supernatural assistance (*karamat*) and special attentions (*tavajjohat*) as a result of appeals by the faithful would indicate lack of knowledge and insight concerning those exalted souls.

Second: It has been the constant recommendation of the religious leaders and Imams not to accept anything without obtaining sufficient rational and authoritative proof, and not to be swayed by rumors and manipulations. This, too, is a positive and definite principle.

Third: Concerning what has transpired in Mobarakeh, comprehensive investigations, on a case by case basis, have convinced us of the falsehood and of the claims that have been made in different quarters.

Accordingly, we expect the Muslim and vigilant citizens to act with more prudence and caution and to deny the opportunity to those who use such claims to weaken people's convictions and faith. There is a danger that the enemies of the Revolution, too, will benefit from such events to condemn our ever-vigilant people as simpletons who can be misled by the slightest provocation and excited by the flimsiest rumours. This will certainly bring harm to Islam and the glory of the Islamic Republic.

May God almighty guide all of us to the path of true understanding of Ashura, Karbabala, and the sacred blood of the martyrs? Peace be upon those who heed the guidance.

| signed: | signed: | signed and sealed: |
|---|---|---|
| SEYED JALALEDIN TAHERI | SEYED KAMAL | FAGHIHI ISMAIL HASHEMI |
| Mordad 4, 1372 | Mordad 4, 1372 | Mordad 4, 1372 |
| Moharram 28, 1414 | Moharram 28, 1414 | Moharram 28, 1414 |

## Notes

1  The distinction between 'crowd' and 'public' still rings true despite the hyperbole of its defenders: Gustave Le Bon, *The Crowd: A Study of the Popular Mind* (New York, 1960); Gabriel Trade, in Terry Clark (ed.) *On Communication and Social Influence*, (Chicago, 1969); Robert Park, *Crowd, the Public and other Essays* (Chicago, 1975); Elias Canetti, *Crowd and Power* (New York, 1978) and the vehemence of its detractors: Ralph Turner and Lewis Killian, *Collective Behavior* (New Jersey, 1957). Common ground is now claimed by the proponents of 'Collective Behavior Theory' and the advocates of 'Social Movement Theory'; heirs to the crowd versus public debate. Recently, 'Critical Mass' theories have persuasively argued that that the behaviour of the crowd has a local 'logic' of its own that involves perceived 'thresholds' of action, as well as 'hidden scripts' and 'private preferences'. Charles Kurzman, *The Unthinkable Revolution in Iran* (Boston, 2004): 130–134.

2  Charles Kurzman opens his eloquent study of Iran's 'unthinkable revolution' with words that encapsulate this idea: 'In just one hundred days, protests would bring down the Iranian monarchy. Demonstrations would multiply into the millions. Strikes would spread and shut down the economy.' Kurzman, *The Unthinkable Revolution in Iran*, 1.

3  Graffiti research has bloomed into a bustling cottage industry with contributors ranging from archaeology and history to literary criticism and urban anthropology. Ronaldo Castellen, *Aesthetics of Graffiti* (San Francisco, 1978); Jeff Ferrel, *Crimes*

*of Style: Urban Graffiti and the Politics of Criminality* (New York, 993); Craig Catleman, *Getting Up: Subway Graffiti in New York* (New York, 1982); Russel Potter, *Spectacular Vernaculars: Hip-Hop and the Politics of Postmodernism* (Ithaca, 1995); Jane M. Gadsby, 'Looking at the Writing on the Wall: A Critical Review and Taxonomy of Graffiti' (unpublished master's thesis, 1995); however, comparative and cross-cultural research is still relatively rare in this area: Jennifer Brown, 'The Writing on the Wall: The Messages in Hungarian Graffiti', *Journal of Popular Culture* (Fall, 1995); Ivor Miller, 'Creolizing for Survival in the City', *Cultural Critique* (Spring, 1994); Sojin Kim, *Chicago Graffiti and Murals: The Neighborhood Art of Peter Quezada* (Jackson, 1995); Monica Smith, 'Walls Have Ears: A Contextual Approach to Graffiti', *International Folklore Review* (1986); Even less frequent are cross-cultural political studies of graffiti and murals: Kenneth J. Grieb, 'The Writing on the Walls: Graffiti as Government Propaganda in Mexico', *Journal of Popular Culture* (Summer, 1984).

This project grew out of our interest in graffiti and murals that saturate public spaces in Iran. We suggest that these images and messages reflect the discourses of legitimation and dissent in post-revolutionary Iran. Studying and tracing them to their authors led us to nuanced polemics of discontent that litter the political culture of a country struggling with legitimation and social change. The present study is based on a research project that the authors conducted in the mid-1990s in Tehran.

4  This genre is akin to what in the former Soviet Union was dubbed 'Socialist Realism'. The use of state-sponsored murals in public space is rare in the West but it still enjoys wide popularity in developing countries, due to its immediacy and its appeal to less-educated masses (Kenneth Grieb, 1984).

5  Portraits of Ayatollah Khomeini, his successor, Ayatollah Khameneh'i, and other members of the clerical establishment such as Mr Rafsanjani are prominently displayed. In addition, the themes of defiance of imperialism and promoting the Islamic identity are prominently featured as mainstays of the Islamic Republican virtues.

*Anti Imperialism*   in particular anti-Americanism is still prevalent though less visible than in the past two decades. The 'death to the USA' mural on Karim Khan Street in central Tehran that replaces the stars on the US with sculls and its stripes with bomb trajectories is the only one of its kind that has survived throughout the last 25 years of the Islamic Republic. After the death of Ayatollah Khomeini, in order to emphasize the continuity of the leadership, the mural was adorned by a quotation from the present spiritual leader, Ayatollah Khameneh'i: 'We will never compromise with the USA.'

A majority of the murals feature themes concerning the martyrs of the Revolution, terrorism, and war. Here are some examples: 'Martyrdom is a great and auspicious lesson for the students of the school of monotheism,' 'The blood of the martyrs conveys an eternal lesson in resistance to the world,' 'The Secret to true survival is in annihilation' and so on.

*The Islamic Code of Dress*   is enforced with varying degrees of seriousness, including periodic crackdowns on the increasingly lax levels of observance. Official and semi-official notices and slogans extol the virtue of modesty of dress for women. The following is a sample of such slogans from the streets of Tehran:

> *'Veil for a woman is like the petals for a flower.'*
> *'Having a virtuous wife indicates the good fortune of the husband.'*
> *'Practicing modesty of dress is an indication of free thinking among*
> *    Moslem woman.'*
> *'Woman in veil is like pearl in its shell.'*
> *'Woman's immodesty is a sign of man's lack of honor.'*

Most governmental and semi-governmental agencies and foundations, such as the Martyrs' Foundation, the Ministry of Culture and Islamic Guidance, local municipal authorities and even banks commission murals featuring martyrs or leaders of the Islamic Revolution. Most of these emphasize the themes of continuity and persistence of the identity of the Islamic Republic through the unbroken chain of its leaders. One mural on Sadr highway, for example, declares: 'Khomeini: The flag that you unfurled we will never lay down.' The mural depicts Ayatollah Khomeini along with two assassinated leaders, Rajai and Bahonar, handing the flag to the present spiritual leader, Ayatollah Khameneh'i.

6  Here are some graffiti in this genre from the streets of Tehran: 'Greetings to Love', 'You are mine,' 'Love Kids', 'Only Buns', 'Fear of Love'. The ubiquitous 'peace' sign is an icon of the Rap groups in Iran.

7  Some graffiti read: *'Slayer, season in the abyss, fuck Rap, EAF, NAPALM'* – *'RAM', 'MET,' 'Metallica'.*

8  The following are titles of some of these 'educational' posters we saw at the central office of the vice police strategically located in the vicinity of Sa`i park in the North of Tehran : 'Bon Jovi', 'ACDC', 'Nirvana', 'Pink Floyd', 'Sodom, Iron Maiden', 'Anthrax', and 'Kiss'. The exhibit also includes confiscated T-shirts, heavy metal rings and other paraphernalia. The 'educational posters' of the moral police include cautionary tales about the decadent practices of these groups that include animal and human sacrifices on stage.

9  In some northern neighbourhoods, entire walls are filled with such graffiti. One anti-vigilante graffiti reads: *'Basij (Militia)* = *the stuff of corruption, Basij* = *the vagabond and the loiterer'.*

10  The following are some examples of such Basij graffiti: *'The Hezbollah, they are the victorious', 'Hezbollah does not accept compromise', 'Shame on you, you the refuses of Satan. You are international prostitutes, who have crawled in your holes. Don't you know that the lesson of martyrdom is not a lesson in terror?' 'This movement will continue until all these remaining rotting roots are dissolved, O God O God, until the appearance of the Mahdi* [Prophet Mohammad's 12th descendant, known as the Hidden Imam] *keep and protect Khomeini.'*

11  The authors wish to thank Akbar Faryar and Emad Afrough, students at Ahmad Sadri's doctoral seminar on Sociology of Religion at the Tarbiat Modarres University in Tehran for their valuable assistance in conducting interviews and negotiating access to the area and informants. We also wish to thank Tarbiat Modarres University for facilitating our travel to the region.

12  In conducting these interviews and the appertaining field work, we took our cue from Clifford Geertz, 'Religion as a Culture System', *The Interpretation of Cultures* (New York, 1973) and Robert Wuthnow, *Rediscovering the Sacred: Perspectives on Religion in Contemporary Society* (Grand Rapids, 1992). Both emphasize the use of observable cultural materials: texts, sermons and discourse to develop an 'adequate sociology of religious culture' that articulates the 'dramaturgical and communicative function' of religion in culture.

13  Concerning the background belief structure of this cult, the annual ritual drama of the tragedy of Karbala, 681 AD, during which Hossein and a group of his supporters were killed by the forces of the Caliph, Yazid is celebrated by the Shi'a Muslims in the form of passion plays, processions, dramatic recitations of the calamities of Karbala and discursive orations. Scholarly investigations have, so far, focused on specific aspects of the phenomenon that include the following: dramatic value of the Shi'a passion plays or Ta'zieh: Peter Chelkowski, *Ta'ziyeh, Ritual and Drama in Iran* (New York, 1979); the theological doctrine of redemptive suffering: Mahmoud Ayoub, *Redemptive Suffering in Islam* (The Hague, 1978); and episodic biographical recollections of participants: Roy Mottahedeh, *Mantle of the Prophet* (New York, 1985). A comprehensive study, however, remains to be undertaken.

14  The site, in today's Iraq, of the battle in which Imam Hossein was killed and where his mausoleum is located.

15 The heroic sister of the martyred Imam Hossein who endured captivity after his martyrdom.

16 Ritual salutations to the prophet and his family.

17 Max Weber, 'Social Psychology of World Religions', *From Max Weber* (New York, 1946): 297.

18 Emile Durkheim, *Elementary Forms of Religious Life* (New York, 1995): 298.

19 The name of a famous satirist who lampooned popular beliefs and superstitions of the local communities.

20 The reference is to a villain in the popular recitations of the aftermath of the massacre of Karbala. He kept the severed head of the martyred Imam in an oven overnight so that he could collect a bounty.

21 The reference is to the sword of Ali, subject of great adoration and narrative embellishment in Shiía popular culture.

22 The above four lines enraged all the citizens of the town, regardless of their opinion concerning the ëmiracleí.

23 The reference is to another popular rumour of miraculous healing.

# 6 From motherhood to equal rights advocates

## The weakening of patriarchal order

*Azadeh Kian-Thiébaut*

This paper is largely based on my field works in Iran from 1994 to 2004 and combines qualitative and quantitative methods. I conducted my first qualitative survey (open-ended interviews with a sample of 100 mothers) in Tehran, Isfahan and their poor suburbs from 1994 to 2000.[1] The quantitative survey, which is a result of the collaboration between Monde Iranien (CNRS), the French Research Institute in Iran and the Statistical Centre of Iran was conducted in 2002 with a sample of 6,960 urban and rural households in all 28 provinces.[2] The sample was composed of 30,714 individuals, including 7,633 women 15 years and older and married at least once, and 6,154 single youths, 15–29 years old, who lived with their parents: 3,437 boys and 2,717 girls. The questionnaire contained 150 questions on individual characteristics of household members (age, sex, marital status, economic activity, literacy, level of education, spare time, etc.), household characteristics (revenue and spending, etc.), women's specificities (relations with husband and children, awareness of rights, opinion concerning free choice, women's access to work, political responsibilities, etc.), and youths' specificities (opinion concerning marriage and marital life, relations with parents, etc.).[3]

Based on the results of the quantitative survey, I then chose a sample of 50 married women in Hormozgan (in the south), Sistan and Baluchistan (in the south-east), Golestan (in the north-east) and Tehran provinces, and conducted open-ended interviews. The funding for the survey was provided by the French Ministry of Foreign Affairs, the French Research Institute in Iran, CNRS, the University of Paris III-Sorbonne Nouvelle and the Statistical Centre of Iran.

The paper argues that the application of the Shari'a in the aftermath of the Revolution deprived women of their civil rights and institutionalized gender inequality. Paradoxically, however, it has triggered new forms of strategies within the female population, who increasingly reject traditionalist values and divine justifications for segregation policies. Women realize this strategy on the one hand through their increasing presence in the public sphere that challenges patriarchal system and gender inequality,[4] and on the other hand by questioning the patriarchal family founded on gendered roles and male domination. The result is the weakening of patriarchal order and male domination in both public and private spheres. Women also refute patriarchal logic by establishing a new relationship with their children that is no longer founded on authority but on dialogue and persuasion. Youths' individualization, their resistance against totalitarian thought and forced Islamization, their aspiration to modernity and their demands for all out social, political and cultural change are outcomes of a permissive type of education and new educational values adopted by their parents, especially their mothers. The stake is to construct a new relationship with the political power that would account for the profound changes that have occurred within the family institution.

## Patriarchal logic and modernity

The Iranian Revolution has led to important changes in political, social, economic and demographic structures. Amongst the institutions, family has undergone the most tremendous change in terms of legislation, its dynamics and the relationship between its members. In the aftermath of the Revolution, the Family Protection Law of 1967 and its amendments, which among others granted women the right to divorce and to child custody after divorce and increased the minimum age of marriage for girls from 9 to 13 and later to 18, was abrogated and the Islamic law was implemented. Marriage as the foundation of the 'sacred family institution' is encouraged, especially among the youths; the minimum age of marriage for girls was lowered to 9 (it was recently increased to 13 years), and important limitations were set for women in matters of divorce, child custody, and so forth.

The Islamist ideology denies women individuality, autonomy and independence. It perceives women as family members whose rights and obligations are defined in relation to their male relatives. The model stipulated by the Shari'a according to which 'matrimonial harmony' is founded on male domination is likely to reinforce authoritarian family relationships and to lead to differentiation of feminine and masculine roles. Childbearing, childrearing and housework thus become women's main functions.

By implementing the Shari'a and 'Islamizing' the family institution, the political and religious elite attempted to reconcile society and the patriarchal state. This attempt failed, however, especially because women have adopted new attitudes thereby challenging the Islamic laws and institutions. The change in women's attitudes is due to various factors: increasing urbanization, higher literacy rates for women, higher education for young women, and women's increasing social, cultural and economic activities.

Through modernization policies, the Islamic state intended to restructure women's lives without questioning the patriarchal family structure. The policies, however, had unintended results for the power elite. In post-Revolutionary Iran, urban areas saw a rapid growth. The number of towns has increased from 373 in 1976 to 614 in 1996, 47 of them with more than 100,000 inhabitants, as against 23 before the Revolution. As a result, the majority of the population (65 per cent) now lives in urban areas. To contain rural exodus, rural areas have been modernized. The majority of villages now have road, electricity (88 per cent in 1996), drinking water (71 per cent in 1996), schools, and dispensaries. Although the Islamic regime did not succeed in curbing rural-to-urban migration, the gap between town and country has narrowed, as illustrated in literacy rates among the younger generation in both urban and rural areas: across the country as a whole, 93 per cent of the age group 6–24 are literate (97 per cent of males and 96 per cent of females in urban areas; 93 per cent of males and 83 per cent of females in rural areas).

With the readoption by the government of family planning and birth control policies in 1989, the birth rate has diminished sharply. The results of the first national census of the population under the Islamic Republic (in 1986) had revealed a total increase of 15 million in the population since 1976, when the last national census was conducted under the Shah. The annual population growth rate thus averaged 3.9 per cent, one of the highest in the world. The economic crisis, the lack of resources to respond to the needs of the young generation (in education, health, employment, etc.) forced the government to adopt projects to diminish this birth rate, despite clerical opposition and the pro-birth traditions in Islam. The annual population growth rate is now 1.2 per cent, and the average number of children per family is now 2, as against 7.2 before the Revolution, and over 70 per cent of Iranian women now use contraceptive devices. Urbanization, a better education and the increasing participation of women in the job market have also led to the increase in the average age of marriage for women from 19.75 before the Revolution to 23. The crucial importance of women's education is also illustrated in the number of their children. The results of our quantitative survey show that literate mothers 15 years and older have given birth to 2.5 children against 6.4 for illiterate mothers. Amongst the literate mothers, a correlation can be established between the level of education and the number of children born alive: 3.1 for primary level education against 1.4 for university level education.

Women are also increasingly pursuing higher education. In 1978–1979, out of 175,000 university students, 54,000 (or 31 per cent) were women. In 1996, the country had 966,970 enrolled students, 393,609 (or 41 per cent) were women. In 1998–1999, for the first time since women entered university in 1939 (five years after the creation of Tehran University), 52 per cent of the admitted students were women. Their percentage was 62 in 2002–2003. Contrary to pre-Revolutionary Iran, when educated women were not necessarily involved in economic activity after graduation but rather used their credentials as cultural capital to serve their matrimonial strategies, women now tend to work after graduation. Increased urbanization, change in the social structure and life styles, rise in expectations and generalized demands of various social strata for a higher standard of living along with high rates of inflation have dramatically lowered the purchasing power of families and led to increasing women's economic activity. According to the 1996 census, 13.4 per cent of women aged 15 and over (or 1,671,000 individuals) were officially active: 16.7 per cent in the agricultural sector, 34.5 per cent in industry and 48.8 per cent in the services sector. In urban areas, 76.7 per cent of women were active in the services sector, 21.2 per cent in industry and 2.1 per cent in agriculture. In rural areas, 53 per cent of women were active in industry, 36 per cent in agriculture and 11 per cent in the service sector. Of these women, 55.5 per cent worked in the private sector, 40 per cent in the public sector and 4.5 per cent in the cooperative sector (Table 6.1).[5]

*Table 6.1* Percentage of active women 10 years and over according to the type of employment (1996)

| Type of employment | Urban areas | Rural areas |
|---|---|---|
| High cadres and directors | 3.9 | 0.4 |
| Specialists | 46.0 | 0.4 |
| Technicians | 6.8 | 0.7 |
| Office employees | 10.0 | 0.6 |
| Service employees | 5.9 | 2.5 |
| Agriculture, forestry, fishing | 1.7 | 30.7 |
| Handcrafts | 17.3 | 50.1 |
| Machine operators and drivers | 1.1 | 0.5 |
| Unskilled workers | 3.3 | 6.5 |
| Other | 4.0 | 7.6 |

Source: *Vizhegi-ha-ye ejtema'i va eqtesadi-ye zanan dar iran* 4: 159.

To the material needs which force women to work are added cultural, social and psychological factors that enhance women's drive to participate actively in the public sphere:

*Cultural Aspirations*   Women who wish to maintain the modern culture of their social group against the regime's forced Islamization policies place a high value upon higher education for their children, the learning of a foreign language (usually English), opening to the outside world and cultural and artistic activities as guarantors of their children's future. With the increasing privatization of the educational system, which attests to the Islamic state's gradual withdrawal from this field, the high costs of children's education are entirely borne by their parents. To this are added the high costs of extra-curricular activities that can no longer be borne by one salary (father's). Women's professional activity thus became necessary and forced them to seek a paid occupation in order to fulfil what is usually considered to be the state's social function.[6]

*Aspiration to Autonomy*   Economic independence which had also provided women with some autonomy vis-à-vis their husbands or parents (for single women) has become an integral part of their identity.

*Psychological need to self-assertion*   Some active women are daughters of or married to well-to-do men and do not need their salaries to maintain their standard of living. With the increase of women's resistance against segregationist laws some of these well-to-do women developed a need to participate in social and economic activities and now seek jobs.

Although over half of women active in the formal sector are highly educated, they are seldom given decision-making posts. Among the active women in our survey, 18 per cent work for the public sector, 40 per cent of whom are highly educated against 20 per cent for men.

According to official statistics, the highest number of women holding responsibilities are found in the Ministries of Education (40 per cent), Health (12.5 per cent) and Mines and Metals (11.9 per cent). If we exclude the Ministry of Education, then only 5.3 per cent of the active women in this sector possess directorial or managerial posts (see Table 6.2).

In addition to active women in the formal sector of the economy, a growing number of women are active in the informal sector but the official statistics do not account for the activities of these women who declare themselves as house-wives. These women are usually much less educated than their counterparts in the formal sector of the economy, and are almost exclusively active in occupations that are considered as 'natural' extensions of their housework tasks: dressmakers, hairdressers, caterers, janitors, housekeepers, carpet weavers, petty traders. Through their revenue-earning work, however, they have acquired financial independence and participate actively in the household expenses. Women's professional activity, which is likely to lead them to economic independence and intellectual autonomy, enables them to compete with men's traditional authority (financial and intellectual) and to challenge it both within the family institution and in society. It will undoubtedly introduce a radical change in the traditional balance of power or 'matrimonial harmony founded on men's domination'. This in turn leads to

*Table 6.2* Number and percentage of women active in the public sector with managerial and decision-making posts (1997)

|  | *Number* | *Percentage* |
| --- | --- | --- |
| Presidency | 93 | 8.2 |
| Ministry of Housing | 40 | 7.0 |
| Ministry of Energy | 00 | 00 |
| Ministry of Education | 37,653 | 40 |
| Ministry of Culture and Islamic Guidance | 36 | 3.6 |
| Ministry of Industry | 15 | 5.2 |
| Ministry of Foreign Affairs | 05 | 2.8 |
| Ministry of Health | 341 | 12.5 |
| Ministry of Telecommunications | 01 | 1.1 |
| Ministry of Agriculture | 36 | 1.8 |
| Ministry of Defence | 00 | 00 |
| Ministry of Justice | 36 | 2.7 |
| Ministry of Economy & Finance | 131 | 7.0 |
| Ministry of Road & Transport | 22 | 1.6 |
| Ministry of Higher Education | 66 | 7.7 |
| Ministry of Labour | 02 | 1.4 |
| Ministry of Interior | 32 | 1.7 |
| Ministry of Commerce | 03 | 1.7 |
| Ministry of Cooperatives | 03 | 1.7 |
| Ministry of Oil | 00 | 00 |
| Ministry of Mine & Metals | 19 | 11.9 |
| Ministry of Jihad for Reconstruction | 18 | 2.2 |
| Total | 38,555 | 34.7 |

Source: *Vizhegi-ha-ye ejtema'i va eqtesadi*, 7: 295.

tensions between husbands and wives. For this very reason, men prefer not to authorize their wives to work unless women's revenues are absolutely needed.

To these revenue-earning women are added 5.5 million others who work in family enterprises without pay. The country has over one million family enterprises (carpet weaving, dairy products, etc.) with a 6,600,000 active population, 84 per cent of whom are women. In Kohgiluyeh and Boyrahmad, Bushehr, Ilam, Markazi and Kermanshah provinces, the entire active population in this sector are women.

In our survey, 45 per cent of active women worked for free for a member of their family and 40 per cent of them were illiterate. Likewise, from the active women in our survey 11 per cent had a second job, 73 per cent of them working for a member of their family without pay.

Iran's new social, demographic and cultural reality combined with women's increasing awareness has led them to question the enforced laws that promote gendered relations within the family and submit women to men's control. It has also contributed to women's autonomization and individualization.

Despite the country's overall modernization, regional disparities are significant both in terms of uneven structural developments and women's perceptions that are closely related to their real life experiences.[7] Women's social, cultural and demographic behaviour in tribally based communities such as those in Baluchistan remain traditional. Open-ended interviews with a sample of Baluchi women in Zahedan and observations in this province showed that women's subordination to men and to the family structure is believed to be vital to the community's unity and survival and that women largely endorse such a belief. In this region, the rate of early marriage is high; the age difference between husband and wife is very important; and the rate of polygamy is also very high. Although the younger generation is overwhelmingly literate, as opposed to their parents' generation, the level of young girls' education remains very low and they usually stop going to school after puberty. They remain at home to preserve their chastity, and while waiting for suitors to arrive, they do the housework.

The following tables drawn from the results of our quantitative survey illustrate such disparities.

## Marriage and divorce

As Table 6.3 shows, the average rate of early marriage (under 15 years) among ever-married women 15 years and older in our survey was 16 per cent. The rate was the highest among Baluchi speakers (32 per cent) and the lowest among the Gilaki speakers (0.56 per cent).

As Table 6.4 shows, the average rate of consanguineous marriage at the first marriage is 21.1 per cent for women and 22 per cent for men. The highest rate (45 per cent) belongs to Baluchi women and men (52 per cent). Gilakis have the lowest rate for both women (13 per cent) and men (15 per cent). The rate is

*Table 6.3* Rate of early marriage (under 15 years) among ever-married women 15 years and older by local and ethnic language (2002)

| Local and ethnic language | Rate |
| --- | --- |
| Baluchi | 32 |
| Azeri | 28 |
| Lori | 23 |
| Arabic | 18 |
| Persian | 15 |
| Kurdish | 15 |
| Turkaman | 8 |
| Mazandarani | 7 |
| Gilaki | 0.56 |
| Average | 16 |

Source: Statistical Centre of Iran, National Centre for Scientific Research (France), French Research Institute in Iran, *Socio-Economic Characteristics Survey of Iranian Households 2002* (Tehran, 2003): 80.

*Table 6.4* Rate of consanguineous marriage at the first marriage among ever-married women 15 years and older, by local and ethnic language (2002)

| Local and ethnic language | Rate |
| --- | --- |
| Baluchi | 45 |
| Arabic | 38 |
| Turkaman | 33 |
| Lori | 26 |
| Persian | 22 |
| Mazandarani | 18 |
| Azeri | 16 |
| Kurdish | 17 |
| Gilaki | 13 |
| Average | 21 |

Source: *Socio-Economic Characteristics Survey of Iranian Households*: 82.

38 per cent for Arab women and 37 per cent for Arab men, 33 per cent for Turkaman women and 30 per cent for Turkaman men, 26 per cent for Lori women and 27 per cent for Lori men, 22 per cent for Persian women and 24 per cent for Persian men, 18 per cent for Mazandarani women and 19 per cent for Mazandarani men, 16 per cent for Azeri women and 17 per cent for Azeri men, 17 per cent for Kurdish women and 16 per cent for Kurdish men.

Crucial changes in the family institution, and the weakening of parental authority also entail a decline in arranged marriages and an increase in marriages based on free choice. The rate of marriage based on free choice is 53 per cent for women aged 15–19, 55 per cent for women aged 20–24, 46 per cent for women aged 25–29, against 33 per cent for women aged 40–44, 23 per cent for women aged 45–49, 17 per cent for women aged 60–64, and 11 per cent for women aged 65 and over.

The rate of divorce in our survey was very low owing to the fact that several divorcees had remarried. But it is noteworthy that domestic violence and maltreatment were the most important causes of divorce (28 per cent) followed by drug addiction (9 per cent) and sterility (9 per cent). Among divorced women, 40 per cent of Arabic speakers, 35 per cent of Lori speakers and 33 per cent of Azeri speakers mentioned violence and maltreatment inflicted on them by their husbands as the major causes of divorce. As for men, 50 per cent of divorced Mazandarani men also mentioned the same causes as the major reason for their divorce, declaring themselves to have been victims of domestic violence and maltreatment, followed by Lori men (35 per cent) and Arab men (27 per cent).

## Opinion poll

The opinion poll we introduced for the first time in a major survey taken by the Statistical Centre of Iran shows that profound changes which have occurred in the lives of Iranian women as a consequence of a modernizing society and an increase in women's awareness are about to weaken traditional perceptions concerning men's authority in the family institution and the patriarchal order founded on male domination.

As Table 6.5 shows, 90 per cent of women are for free choice. The rate is 94 per cent for literate women (99 per cent for women with a high-school diploma or with university education) and 84 per cent for illiterate women.

*Table 6.5* Opinion of ever-married women 15 years and older on the equality of rights between men and women concerning free choice, by local and ethnic language (2002)

| Local and ethnic language | Rate |
| --- | --- |
| Baluchi | 53 |
| Arabic | 88 |
| Turkaman | 100 |
| Lori | 85 |
| Persian | 95 |
| Mazandarani | 97 |
| Azari | 83 |
| Kurdish | 95 |
| Gilaki | 94 |
| Average | 90 |

Source: *Socio-Economic Characteristics Survey of Iranian Households*: 160.

## Housework and childcare: women's exclusive responsibility?

Women also question the gender division of labour within the family. As Table 6.6 shows, only 30.5 per cent of women think that housework is women's exclusive responsibility. The rate is 19 per cent for literate mothers and 42 per cent for illiterate ones. Among women with higher education, only 5 per cent believe the housework to be women's responsibility.

Concerning childcare, only 15 per cent of women in our survey believe it is women's exclusive responsibility (see Table 6.7). The rate is 9 per cent for literate women and 5 per cent for highly educated women.

*Table 6.6* Rate of ever-married women 15 years and older who think that housework is women's exclusive responsibility, by local and ethnic language (2002)

| Local and ethnic language | Rate |
| --- | --- |
| Baluchi | 63 |
| Arabic | 51 |
| Turkaman | 23 |
| Lori | 45 |
| Persian | 20 |
| Mazandarani | 29 |
| Azeri | 27 |
| Kurdish | 34 |
| Gilaki | 29 |
| Average | 30.5 |

Source: *Socio-Economic Characteristics Survey of Iranian Households*: 168.

*Table 6.7* Rate of ever-married women 15 years and older who think that childcare is women's exclusive responsibility by local and ethnic language (2002)

| Local and ethnic language | Rate |
| --- | --- |
| Baluchi | 48 |
| Arabic | 35 |
| Turkaman | 04 |
| Lori | 39 |
| Persian | 01 |
| Mazandarani | 09 |
| Azari | 16 |
| Kurdish | 18 |
| Gilaki | 12 |
| Average | 15 |

Source: *Socio-Economic Characteristics Survey of Iranian Households*: 168.

## Women's access to education

Although the official ideological discourse depicts women mainly as mothers and wives, and until 1993 women's access to several university majors such as management, engineering and law was prohibited, young women's quest for education continued and they increasingly enrolled in universities. The active presence of young women in education, made possible thanks to the expansion of schooling in urban and rural areas, led the older generation, overwhelmingly illiterate, to tremendously value women's education. Many poor and illiterate respondents in the qualitative survey attribute their inferior status in the family and society to their lack of educational credentials, which they believe also prevented them from becoming autonomous from their fathers or husbands. They therefore advocate their daughters' education as a crucial means to their empowerment. As Table 6.8 shows, 86.5 per cent of our respondents believe that men and women should have equal access to education. The rate is 81 per cent for illiterate women, 92 per cent for literate women, and 98 per cent for highly educated women.

## Women's access to work

The civil code which legally determines the relationship between men and women grants excessive privileges to men on the grounds that the economic function is the main attribute of men. In other words, men's authority over women in both the public and the private spheres is recognized and sanctioned by law because men are perceived as having an economic function. For this very reason, if women succeed in assuming economic functions outside the family institution, the Islamic laws on the subject would also be questioned. Many Iranian religious authorities now acknowledge women's economic activity outside the household

*Table 6.8* Opinion of ever-married women 15 years and older on the equality of rights concerning equal access to education, by local and ethnic language (2002)

| Local and ethnic language | Rate |
|---|---|
| Baluchi | 60 |
| Arabic | 77 |
| Turkaman | 96 |
| Lori | 81 |
| Persian | 90 |
| Mazandarani | 87 |
| Azeri | 89.5 |
| Kurdish | 92 |
| Gilaki | 88 |
| Average | 86.5 |

Source: *Socio-Economic Characteristics Survey of Iranian Households*: 160.

but continue to consider housework and childcare as women's main responsibility. The Islamic Republic's Supreme Leader, Ayatollah Ali Khameneh'i, argues:

> Islam authorizes women to work outside the household. Their work might even be necessary but it should not interfere with their main responsibility that is child-rearing, child-bearing and housework. No country can do without women's work force but this should not contradict women's moral and human values. It should not weaken women, nor compel them to bend or to stoop low.[8]

However, in order for a woman to work, she needs her husband's authorization if he pays her alimony. Moreover, only the financial and economic dimension of women's activity is recognized to the detriment of its social dimension. This is clearly stated by a traditionalist:

> Islam prefers that women take care of housework ... But if the husband's earnings are not enough to meet his family's needs then his wife is authorized to work in order to complete her husband's earnings provided that her work corresponds to her condition as a woman and that she maintains her chastity. If the costs of marital life prevent a young man from getting married, then woman's work outside the family becomes even compulsory in order to enhance marriage which is the tradition of our Prophet.[9]

The traditionalist's resistance to women's financial independence can be explained by the fact that women's status depends on the control they can exercise on their property and their labour power.[10]

Women in Iran, especially those belonging to the middle classes, increasingly join the work force, and matrimonial and family relations undergo change as and when women have access to a better education, economic independence and social participation. As Table 6.9 shows, in our survey, 77 per cent of women are for

*Table 6.9* Opinion of ever-married women 15 years and older on women's equal access to work, by local and ethnic language (2002)

| Local and ethnic language | Rate |
| --- | --- |
| Baluchi | 48 |
| Arabic | 53 |
| Turkaman | 73 |
| Lori | 74 |
| Persian | 80 |
| Mazandarani | 66 |
| Azeri | 78 |
| Kurdish | 86 |
| Gilaki | 90 |
| Average | 77 |

Source: *Socio-Economic Characteristics Survey of Iranian Households*: 160.

men and women's equal access to work. The rate is 71 per cent for illiterate women, 81 per cent for literate women, and 88 per cent for highly educated women.

## Political activity and decision-making positions

Although women's participation in politics, especially as voters, saw a sharp growth in the 1997 and 2001 Presidential, 1999 local, and 2000 legislative elections, women's representation in national political institutions remains slim (13 women MPs in the 6th parliament and 12 in the 7th, and none in the other institutions) and overwhelmingly limited to the kin of the power elite. Moreover, although women massively voted for reformist candidates hoping that they would implement change in their legal status and condition, women's issues are largely absent from debates between reformers and conservatives. Despite fundamental differences in their views, a consensus exists among them to perpetuate male domination and the patriarchal system. According to some reformers the question of women and their legal and citizenship rights is not intertwined with the building of democracy and therefore does not constitute an urgent issue for democracy ideologies.[11] Likewise, the law continues to consider women as minors and places them for life under the guardianship of their fathers or husbands. Although the 13 female members of the 6th parliament were gender-conscious and quite active in proposing motions to ameliorate women's status (modification of the civil code, facilitating women's access to divorce, sending female students abroad, or increasing the minimum age of marriage for girls from 9 to 18), only a few legal changes have been implemented. The Guardian Council disapproved these laws arguing that they were incompatible with Islam. Finally, the minimum age of marriage and the age of penal responsibility for girls was increased to 13. President Khatami excluded government intervention to promote women's status arguing that the development of civil society inevitably would contribute to satisfying women's demands and would provide women with the means to transform their demands into laws.[12] Despite the crucial role played by women in his election and re-election in 2001, he conceded to conservative pressures by refusing to nominate women ministers in his second cabinet.

The persistence of gender inequality during Khatami's presidency and the 6th parliament dominated by reformers largely disillusioned women activists who had supported Khatami and the reformers, and has widened the gap between the female population and the state. Jamileh Kadivar, a member of the 6th parliament from Tehran, criticized Khatami and argued: 'We know that nominating one or two women ministers will not resolve women's problems, yet we are convinced that such nominations could have had positive social and cultural consequences'.[13] Likewise, Akram Mansurimanesh, a member of the 6th parliament from Isfahan, declared: 'President Khatami's refusal to nominate women who are more competent than male ministers humiliates the entire female population'.[14] Faced with severe criticisms about these women parliamentarians, President Khatami contented himself by saying that he was sorry. Women's disillusionment with reformers has further radicalized women activists who withdrew temporarily from the political sphere, as illustrated by their lack of mobilization in the 2004 legislative and the 2005 presidential elections. These women now exclusively rely on their own efforts to promote women's status and the equality of rights.

The policies of the Islamic state remain ambiguous with regard to women. As Zahra Shoja'i, President Khatami's advisor in women's affairs, argued:

More than two decades after the Revolution, we still ignore the Islamic Republic's doctrine with regard to women. We lack a global programme concerning women. It is not the four principles of the Constitution, Ayatollah Khomeini's sermons or the history of women at the advent of Islam that can lead us to conceive a global programme![15]

This doctrinal ambiguity does not only concern women. Its roots should be examined in the very foundations of the Islamic regime which claims to be both republican and Islamic. Its republican component praises gender equality, while its Islamic component advocates gender inequality. For this very reason, women's fate is intertwined with the fate of the Republic.

The thrusting aside of women from national politics, however, has led many ordinary women to believe that political decision-making is the function of men. Another major impediment to women's participation as candidates in national political activity is the politicization of debates during national elections to the detriment of women's issues and demands. Nonetheless, women's growing quest for gender equality has also led women to discover politics as a powerful agent towards implementing change in their status. As a result, in some parts of the country, where women are either more politicized or more educated, women's involvement in politics and in decision-making government positions is now accepted. As Table 6.10 shows, 53 per cent of women in our survey agree with equal access for women and men to political activities. The highest rates belong to Kurdish-speaking women (with 62.5 per cent) and Persian-speaking women

*Table 6.10* Opinion of ever-married women 15 years and older on women's equal access to political activity, by local and ethnic language (2002)

| Local and ethnic language | Rate |
| --- | --- |
| Baluchi | 23 |
| Arabic | 28 |
| Turkaman | 23 |
| Lori | 45 |
| Persian | 59 |
| Mazandarani | 41 |
| Azeri | 51 |
| Kurdish | 62.5 |
| Gilaki | 54 |
| Average | 53 |

Source: *Socio-Economic Characteristics Survey of Iranian Households*: 161.

(with 59 per cent) and the lowest rate belongs to Baluchi and Turkaman-speaking women (23 per cent). While the traditional attitude of Baluchi women with regard to politics follows their general views on other issues, Turkaman women's understanding of politics as an essentially male-oriented activity is contradictory to their more egalitarian views, as illustrated in other tables. Concerning women's opinion on the equal access for men and women to decision-making government positions, the average rate is 52 per cent (see Table 6.11), with the highest rate belonging to Kurdish-speaking women (64 per cent) and the lowest belonging to Baluchi speakers (23 per cent).

My interviewees suggest that women's involvement in politics should start at the local level where elections are less politicized and women can better identify with the issues that are more related to the everyday life of the population. Educational level and age preconditions constitute another impediment to women's candidacy in national elections where candidates should be 30 to 75 years old and have at least a high-school diploma. The majority of literate women 30 years and older are therefore excluded from national elections as 56 per cent of them have only primary-level education. In local elections, however, primary-level education is sufficient.

As Table 6.12 shows, 69 per cent of women in our survey are in favour of equality in decision-making positions at local level. In terms of the spoken local language the lowest rate belongs to Baluchi women (33 per cent) and the highest rate belongs to Kurdish women (77 per cent) followed by Persian (73.5 per cent).

Women's increasing approval of women's participation in local politics is closely related to their experience in the 1999 municipal and local council elections which led to the rise in women's representation, especially in rural areas. As Table 6.13 shows, there were only 7,276 female candidates out of a total of 333,000; 11 per cent of these women were elected, 6.4 per cent in urban areas

*Table 6.11*  Opinion of ever-married women 15 years and older on women's equal access to decision-making posts, by local and ethnic language (2002)

| Local and ethnic language | Rate |
| --- | --- |
| Baluchi | 23 |
| Arabic | 25 |
| Turkaman | 21 |
| Lori | 47 |
| Persian | 54 |
| Mazandarani | 38 |
| Azeri | 54 |
| Kurdish | 64 |
| Gilaki | 58 |
| Average | 52 |

Source: *Socio-Economic Characteristics Survey of Iranian Households:* 161.

*Table 6.12*  Opinion of ever-married women 15 years and older on women's equal access to decision-making posts at local level, by local and ethnic language (2002)

| Local and ethnic language | Rate |
| --- | --- |
| Baluchi | 33 |
| Arabic | 59 |
| Turkaman | 64 |
| Lori | 59 |
| Persian | 73.5 |
| Mazandarani | 57 |
| Azeri | 71 |
| Kurdish | 77 |
| Gilaki | 69 |
| Average | 69 |

Source: *Socio-Economic Characteristics Survey of Iranian Households*:161.

*Table 6.13*  Number and percentage of women candidates in the local and municipal council elections (1999)

| Total | Per cent | Urban | Per cent | Rural | Per cent |
| --- | --- | --- | --- | --- | --- |
| 7,276 | 2.2 | 4,688 | 7.2 | 2,588 | 1.0 |

*Table 6.14*  Number and percentage of women elected in the local and municipal councils (1999)

| Total | Per cent | Urban | Per cent | Rural | Per cent |
| --- | --- | --- | --- | --- | --- |
| 783 | 10.8 | 300 | 6.4 | 483 | 18.7 |

Source: *Vizhegi-ha-ye ejtema'i va eqtesadi*, 7: 293–294.

and 18.7 per cent in rural areas (see Table 6.14). The overall rate for those elected (120,000 out of 333,000) as a proportion of the candidates was 35 per cent.

Likewise, despite an average 20 per cent drop in the rate of voters' participation in the 2003 municipal and local elections (49.96 per cent), compared to the 1999 elections (64.42 per cent), and although the number of candidates saw a decrease from 333,000 to 220,000, women's representation saw an 80 per cent increase.

## Permissive education and child centredness: protest against patriarchy

The emergence and expansion of child centredness is undoubtedly one of the most crucial aspects of change in post-Revolutionary Iranian families. Several factors can explain the predominant position of children within the family. First, the Revolutionary movement weakened the traditional hierarchical order, which was founded on patriarchal authority and paternalistic monarchy. The weakening of the traditional model of the family allowed youths' massive participation in the Revolution, in spite of the opposition of many parents, especially those belonging to middle and upper-middle classes. The youths participated in a political movement which also reflected the conflict between generations. The triumph of the Revolution with the youths as its major players further weakened parental authority. Revolutionary changes led to the emergence of a new value system among the youths. Opposed to the traditional value system, the youths first substituted ideological authority emanating from the religious leadership of the Revolution or political leaders of the radical leftist groups (depending on political–ideological trends) for parental authority. Marriages founded on free choice as opposed to those arranged by parents or elders were one example of this trend. This type of marriage, which became very fashionable among middle class youths in the aftermath of the Revolution was to the detriment of traditions and was guided by political–ideological considerations, as opposed to matrimonial strategies founded on social and cultural considerations predominant before the Revolution. In pre-Revolutionary Iran and according to traditional cultural precepts, the groom had to be better educated, much older, with a higher social and economic status than the bride. Marriage was thus supposed both to promote the wife's upward social mobility and to strengthen patriarchal authority and male domination.

The tremendous increase in literacy rates among children and youths of lower class origins is another factor that has contributed to the weakening of parental authority and the strengthening of youth's authority within their families. Their level of education is much higher than their parents who are often illiterate or barely literate. This provides the children and youths with important authority within their families as illustrated in the 1997 presidential elections. Those who had not yet attained the voting age (set at 16) accompanied their illiterate parents to the polls to make sure that the name of Khatami, the youths' candidate, would appear on the ballot. Many university students went back to their towns or villages to campaign for the moderate presidential candidate. Their political influence was tremendous, given the prestige and respect that educated people enjoy among the uneducated.

The post-Revolutionary power elite, although elderly and traditionalist, did not openly oppose the youths' new value system. On the contrary, they actively participated in the weakening of parental authority that could have hindered the youths' ideologization. Moreover, with the beginning of the Iran–Iraq war (1980–1988), the authorities needed volunteers and mobilized all the ideological state apparatus, media, Friday prayers, or mosques to encourage the youths to go to the war. Because many parents were against their sons' mobilization for war efforts, the weakening of parental authority served the regime.

Parental authority was also weakened as a result of the state's ideological intervention in the family sphere and its attempts to control families through information that it tried to obtain from school children on the mode of life and values of their parents. The aim was to ensure the state's ideological hegemony over society by controlling the values transmitted to children by their parents. The educational system was in charge of the Islamization campaign. Hand-picked teachers asked pupils questions on their parents' way of life and behaviour: whether they prayed or fasted during the month of Ramadan, whether they watched foreign movies, drank alcoholic beverages or gave mixed parties, whether mothers were veiled etc. A lot of these innocent children caused trouble to their parents, some of whom lost their jobs, while others were even arrested. Faced with this state policy of forced Islamization, parents who did not adhere to the predominant state ideology had no choice but to encourage their children to lie, thereby further losing their authority over children. On the other hand, these children are exposed to two contradictory value systems: one propagated at schools and the other by their family and social and cultural milieu. A 36-year-old Isfahani state cadre and a mother of two sons, argues: 'I try to transmit my values to my children but they are very contradictory with the ones propagated by the school system. For example, they receive a religious education at school but once at home, they realize that their parents do not respect religious precepts. The crusade launched by the school system against satellite programmes is another example. But, in fact, we do have satellite at home and my children like to watch these programmes. These contradictions have led to the youths' split personalities.'

Although methods used by the state did not result in respect for state authority by children and youths, they did contribute to the questioning of parental authority by children and to the emergence of a schizophrenic identity among them, leading to an unprecedented identity crisis among the youths.

Child centredness and the weakening of parental authority accelerate the process of individualization among the youths who develop individual strategies vis-à-vis other members of the family. Through the means that parents, especially mothers, have provided to their children, they have facilitated their entrance to the modern world, and have encouraged them to internalize western values thereby opposing the regime's forced Islamization policies. Mothers who are more than ever in charge of their children's education have rejected the authoritarian type of education (high control, low support) opting for permissive education, which consists of low control and high support of children. It is through their intervention in their children's education, which is one of the rare spheres where women's contribution is recognized by the authorities and their own husbands, that frustrated mothers do invest themselves entirely. One of the implications of child centredness is the intensification of conflict between tradition and modernity, which marks more than ever the Iranian society. Permissive education leads children to enjoy an unprecedented individual freedom within their families. They gain autonomy and construct an individualized identity.

The adoption by mothers of permissive education seems to be a form of protest against patriarchy. They react against the patriarchal system and values and norms propagated by the Islamic regime, which is reinforced by laws. It also illustrates the rejection by Iranian parents of the civil code and the penal law based on Islamic laws that consider children as their parents', especially their father's, belongings. According to Article 1179 of the civil code, parents are entitled to punish their children physically. Likewise, according to Article 220 of the penal law, if a child is killed by his father or his grandfather, the murderer will only pay the blood money to the heirs of the child, and might, upon a court's decision, be imprisoned for a short period.[16]

Our survey illustrates the predominance of permissive education and the rejection of laws by the majority of Iranian mothers. Out of the 7,640 mothers in our sample only 162 or 2 per cent declared using violence and physical punishment against their children; 385 or 5 per cent declared themselves author-itarian, against 4,827 or 63 per cent who said they had opted for discussion and persuasion (see Table 6.16); and 2,100 or 27.5 per cent had opted for their children's freedom of decision-making along with parental advice (see Table 6.15). It is interesting to note that 2,998 or 39 per cent, of the mothers in our survey were illiterate, but only 3 per cent of them had physically punished their children. No mother with higher education declared inflicting violence and physical punishment.

As Table 6.15 shows, from amongst the mothers who declared having opted for their children's freedom with parental advice, the highest rate belongs to the Turkaman (46 per cent) and the lowest to the Baluchi (14 per cent). As Table 6.16 shows, the highest rate among those who have opted for the discussion and persuasion method belongs to the Arabic speakers (71 per cent) and the lowest rate to the Baluchi speakers (50 per cent).

*Table 6.15* Rate of mothers 15 years and older who have opted for their children's freedom with parental advice, by local and ethnic language (2002)

| Local and ethnic language | Rate |
| --- | --- |
| Baluchi | 14 |
| Arabic | 18.5 |
| Turkaman | 46 |
| Lori | 24 |
| Persian | 30 |
| Mazandarani | 22 |
| Azeri | 29 |
| Kurdish | 24 |
| Gilaki | 24 |
| Average | 27.5 |

Source: *Socio-Economic Characteristics Survey of Iranian Households*: 172.

*Table 6.16* Rate of mothers 15 years and older who have adopted discussion and persuasion method, by local and ethnic language (2002)

| Local and ethnic language | Rate |
|---|---|
| Baluchi | 50 |
| Arabic | 71 |
| Turkaman | 50 |
| Lori | 60 |
| Persian | 64 |
| Mazandarani | 67 |
| Azeri | 63 |
| Kurdish | 66 |
| Gilaki | 61 |
| Average | 63 |

Source: *Socio-Economic Characteristics Survey of Iranian Households:* 172.

Permissive education has led to the establishment of a dialogue between parents and children and the parents' respect for their children's opinion. The outcome is the rejection by the youths of obedience to authority and the emergence of a political and cultural counter-weight to authoritarian rule. This new reality has gained momentum in the public sphere where the concepts of tolerance, dialogue and freedom have gained tremendous popularity while authoritarianism and violence along with the institutions that generate them are rejected.

## Conclusion

Post-revolutionary Iranian society has undergone tremendous structural, demographic, social and cultural change. Despite the persistence of regional disparities, modernization policies implemented by the Islamic Republic have led to a sharp increase in urbanization, have narrowed the gap between urban and rural areas, and have made possible the access of the overwhelming majority of the population to education and health facilities, electricity, drinking water, roads, etc. This in turn has led to a change in lifestyles and a rise in expectations and demands of the population. The change, however, has had the most crucial ongoing impact on women who are reassessing modern values and behaviour, restructuring their lives, questing for autonomy, aspiring to equal rights and opportunities, and forming new identities. Iranian women who do not perceive themselves exclusively as mothers and wives but also as individuals now challenge patriarchal family order founded on male domination and the Islamic laws and institutions that tend to enforce patriarchy and gendered relations within both the public and the private spheres. Women who play a key role in the education of their children have also challenged patriarchal order by adopting modern educational values, including dialogue and respect for their children's opinion. Mothers' permissive type of education has contributed to youths' individualization and autonomization, their rejection of violence, their aspiration to tolerance and the weakening of patriarchy. One of the most important political outcomes of this all-out change is the increasing demand for the establishment of a democratic system and the rejection of the patriarchal political order which has proved incompatible with the socio-cultural realities of post-Islamist Iranian society. Despite important impediments to women attaining authority and power, the potential for democracy is increasing because women are using the outcomes of modernization from the perspective of women's rights and opposing gendered social relations. They contribute tremendously to the emergence of a democratic system whose prerequisite is the separation of religion and state.

## Notes

1  The results of this survey are published in Azadeh Kian-Thiébaut , *Les femmes iraniennes entre islam, Etat et famille* (Paris, 2002).
2  The sampling frame used was adopted from the one which resulted from the 1996 National Census of Population and Housing conducted by the Statistical Centre of Iran. Each statistical unit is a cluster composed of almost thirty households drawn randomly. A total of 232 urban and rural clusters were thus selected as the sample.
3  According to the general findings of our survey, average size of the household is 4.4 members, literacy rate of the population 6 years and over is 81 per cent: 86.5 per cent for men and 76 per cent for women, average age at the first marriage is 26 for men and 23 for women, rate of arranged marriage is 55.6 per cent for women and 42 per cent for men, and 19.5 per cent of mothers are active. The tables are available on the website of the research group Monde Iranien, CNRS: www.ivry.cnrs.fr/iran.
4  See among others: Azadeh Kian-Thiébaut, *Les femmes iraniennes entre islam, Etat et famille*; 'Women and the Making of Civil Society in Post-Islamist Iran', *Twenty Years of Islamic Revolution, Political and Social Transition in Iran since 1979* (Syracuse, 2002), 4: 56–73; 'Women and Politics in Post-Islamist Iran: The Gender Conscious Drive to Change', *British Journal of Middle Eastern Studies*, XXIV (1997): 75–96.
5  Statistical Centre of Iran, *Vizhegi-ha-ye ejtema'i va eqtesadi-ye zanan dar iran 1365–1375* (The Social and Economic Features of Women in Iran, 1986–1996) (Tehran, 2000), 4: 155–159.
6  According to Article 30 of the Constitution, the government should provide people with free education up to the end of high school and even university.
7  I would like to express my deep gratitude to Soqra Haj-Seyyed-Javadi, Nasrin Eftekhari, Mir Fallah Nasiri and Susan Rafi'i of the Statistical Centre of Iran; Mr Sotudehniya, Foruzan Marzuqi, Mr Akbari, Mr Jalali, Mr Malekza'i, Mr Garshasbi, Isma'il Hashemi, Mr Asgari of the Organization of Planning and Budget in Hormozgan, Sistan-Baluchistan, Golestan and Tehran provinces; Jean During, Dominique Torabi and Babak Pourasadollah of the French Research Institute in Iran; and Mahnaz Yazdani.
8  From Ayatollah Khameneh'i's sermon on 16 December 1992. *Cheshmeh-ye Nur*, (Tehran, 1995), 9: 269.
9  Seyyed Javad Mostafavi, *Behesht-e Khanevadeh* (Qom, 1995), I: 117.
10  For a discussion, see R.L. Blumberg, 'A General Theory of Gender Stratification', *Sociological Theory* (1984): 23–101.

11  See among others: Abbas Abdi's interview 'Rawshanfekri-ye dini va masa'el-e fawritar az masa'el-e zanan', *Zanan*, LVIII (2000): 38.
12  Khatami's interview with *Zanan*, XXXIV (1997): 2–5.
13  See Jamileh kadivar's interview with *Siysat-e Ruz*, CXV ( 2001).
14  See Akram Mansurimanesh's interview in *Zanan*, LXXIX (2001): 12.
15  Mahbubeh Abbasqolizadeh's interview with Zahra Shoja'i, Tehran, Spring 2001. I am grateful to Mahbubeh Abbasqolizadeh who provided me with the text of this interview.
16  Shirin Ebadi, *Hoquq-e Kudak* (Tehran, 1992), 3: 58–59, 12: 190, 12: 194–195.

# 7  Iran and the United States in the shadow of 9/11

## Persia and the Persian question revisited

*Ali M. Ansari*

The aide said that guys like me were 'in what we call the reality-based community', which he defined as people who 'believe that solutions emerge from your judicious study of discernible reality.' I nodded and murmured something about enlightenment principles and empiricism. He cut me off. 'That's not the way the world really works anymore,' he continued. 'We're an empire now, and when we act, we create our own reality. And while you're studying that reality – judiciously, as you will – we'll act again, creating other new realities, which you can study too, and that's how things will sort out. We're history's actors...and you, all of you, will be left to just study what we do.'[1]

In a recent trip to Europe, the new US Secretary of State, Condoleezza Rice, sought to heal the wounds which had emerged over the US decision to overthrow Saddam Hussein. She found a receptive Europe, anxious to avoid the rifts of the past and keen to accentuate the positive. In the aftermath of the elections in Iraq, there was even room for some agreement on how best to deal with Iran and her ambitions for a nuclear programme. Everyone agreed that Iran was not Iraq, and, by all accounts, the Bush administration appeared content to allow the Europeans to pursue their negotiations with a view to resolving 'Iran' through diplomatic means. Indeed, it now seemed that far from sitting on the sidelines – waiting for the negotiations to fail – the United States had agreed to actively support the EU negotiations with offers of their own. Yet behind all the smiles, there was an air of discontent and barely disguised disagreement. The Americans were proving reluctant partners and their rediscovered faith in diplomacy, and the UN for that matter, seemed less a result of deliberate policy and more a consequence of its absence.[2] What the Bush administration lacked in detail it nonetheless made up with 'vision', and Rice's characterization of Iran as a 'totalitarian' state not only highlighted differences in appreciation between the US and her European allies of the reality of Iran but, perhaps more significantly, also marked a distinct shift in emphasis within the United States itself. The State Department was clearly under new management, and the diplomatic ambiguity of the past, along with the flexibility this afforded, had been replaced with theological certainty.[3] It reflected a broader shift in US policy approaches since 9/11, away from 'traditional' realism and towards an ideological construction of international relations driven emphatically by myths.[4]

This paper is an investigation of the dialectical nature of US–Iran relations looking in particular at relations since the 9/11 terrorist attacks and the Iranian responses to President Bush's State of the Union address in January 2002, which classified Iran as a member of the 'Axis of Evil'. The paper argues that the events of 9/11 fundamentally altered the nature of US foreign policymaking, away from the bureaucratic rationality of the past which had been understood under the rubric of a 'realist' interpretation of international relations, towards a charismatic justification with a revolutionary message.[5] This transformation of US attitudes stood in marked contrast to the tendency in Iran for a routinization of the Revolution, and more towards rationalisation and international order. That this process of *normalization* was being encouraged at the very time that the founder and guardian of the global order was engaged in a radical transformation of its relationship with that order – with a view to changing it – resulted in a critical tension and a continued failure of communication which may be defined as an epistemological gap,[6] a gap which may only be overcome through the exercise of decisive leadership. Iranian policymakers, steeped in American international relations theory, have been seeking to engage the 'realist', and have been disconcerted to discover the revolutionary.

## Foundation myths

Throughout the 1990s, Iranian leaders had been grappling with the issue of the United States. Ever since the Hostage Crisis in 1979, diplomatic relations had been severed, and officially at least, the United States had imposed a series of embargos on the Islamic Republic with a view to bringing the Revolution to heel. Nonetheless, in the absence of formal, 'real' relations, both Iran and the United States retained a very real presence in each other's political life, which took on mythic proportions. While American politicians may have been reluctant to indulge in the rhetoric of the 'Great Satan', there is little doubt that the experience of the Hostage Crisis and the subsequent Iran-Contra affair placed Iran in a category all of its own as far as US policymakers were concerned.[7] This emotive element within US attitudes towards Iran may have been vigorously denied by the bureaucratic rationalists within successive US administrations, but it was increasingly apparent to outside observers who were struck by the depth of the animosity. Indeed, this was not simply a popular antipathy but one which affected many members of the Washington elite and transcended party politics. Democrats bemoaned the fall of the Carter presidency and noted with some bitterness that Iran's revolutionaries appeared determined to sabotage Carter's re-election prospects by very deliberately holding the hostages until after President Reagan's inauguration.[8] Meanwhile Republicans were to prove equally unforgiving over the debacle of the Iran-Contra affair, which added criminal proceedings to the indignity of political embarrassment.

Indeed, while American politicians were to emerge from the 1980s with their prejudices affirmed, in Iran the harsh reality of war was beginning to temper the ideological zeal of the revolution. The new president, Ali Akbar Hashemi Rafsanjani, seemed to be inaugurating a period of 'pragmatism', and it was apparent that a cadre of hitherto marginalized *ancien regime* diplomats and intellectuals were being reconciled to the Islamic Republic, with a view to encouraging a rational reconstruction of international affairs.[9] This was, to be sure, an incremental process which laboured under the diplomatic fiasco that was the Rushdie Affair, but there is little doubt that Rafsanjani was seeking a routinization of the Revolution. A number of institutes and think tanks were established, with government support and funding, staffed in large part by International Relations experts trained in the United States, with a view to producing a rational (and 'realist') interpretation of the international order, and more specifically, of the United States.[10] The conclusion they unsurprisingly drew, true to their training, was that the United States was a rational international player who pursued its 'interests'. These 'interests' were somewhat simplistically defined in economic and/or geopolitical terms. Any sense of cultural or ideological determination in American foreign policy was dismissed as methodologically unsound, a view reinforced by those very bureaucratic rationalists who populated the US policymaking establishment – ideology was quite obviously something *others* had. Thus, among the strategies to engage the United States which circulated in the early 1990s was one which sought to position Iran, ironically, as an 'island of stability' within a region that, after the fall of Soviet Union, was, to all intents and purposes, increasingly unstable. This strategy was, however, unsustainable for the very reason that the Soviet Union was no longer a threat, so it was decided to seek engagement on economic terms. This suited the mercantile world view of the Rafsanjani administration which actively encouraged the notion that Iran was 'open for business'. While anticipating domestic criticism from hardliners in the regime, Rafsanjani was less prepared for the cool reception from the United States to the various economic enticements on offer.

Both offers lay in the oil sector, thought by many to be Iran's main source of economic leverage. In the first place, Iranian policymakers sought to capitalize on their geopolitical position as a transit route for oil and gas out of the Caspian basin towards the Persian Gulf, emphasising, with much justification, the economic sense of running pipelines through Iran, as opposed to Turkey and/or Russia, a route which could take advantage of the extensive pipeline network already constructed throughout the country, and which, it was argued, could be a force for stability throughout the wider region as countries became interdependent through the network. The second strategy was to target the United States directly by offering US oil companies, in this case Conoco, a stake in Iranian oil development. Not only did these offers come to nothing, they resulted in a remarkable reaction, which saw the United States seek to circumvent the Iranian pipeline offer by heavily underwriting the expensive alternative routes, including in this case, a dubious (on geographical as well as political grounds) route through Afghanistan, and by the imposition of extensive sanctions through both executive order and legislation (the Iran Libya Sanctions Act – ILSA), which sought to introduce secondary sanctions on any foreign company investing in the Iranian oil and gas sector. There is little doubt that Iranian policymakers were somewhat perplexed by this reaction, but they were comforted by the fact that this was a Democratic administration and, as such, traditionally beholden to the Israeli lobby. President Clinton's decision to block the Conoco contract following intense pressure from the American–Israeli Public Affairs Committee (AIPAC) and his announcement of further sanctions at a meeting of the World Jewish Congress seemed to confirm this suspicion. Moreover, the Clinton administration's antipathy towards Iran had already been revealed by the imposition of 'Dual Containment', and, of course, the appointment of Warren Christopher as Secretary of State in 1993. It was an open secret that Warren Christopher, as a result of personal experiences during the Hostage Crisis, was no friend of Iran. Iranian 'realists' were therefore reassured that this was an anomaly born from Democratic prejudice, and that one had to wait for the Republicans to bring back pragmatic realism (a view reinforced by the Republicans in opposition). After all, in a curious effort to emphasize continuity over change (i.e. *normalization*), even the Shah had had difficulty with Democratic presidents. This was nonetheless a wilful if convenient misreading of the political situation in the United States. Attempts to broker a deal with the first President Bush in 1991–1992 had foundered on the potential embarrassment of the 'October Surprise' revelations, as well as the President's knowledge of the Iran-Contra affair, suggesting that the problem of Iran was not a party political issue in the United States. While the Clinton administration's cautious initial welcome to the Taliban takeover in Kabul in 1995 hinted to those who cared to notice that America's problem was not with radical (revolutionary) Islam.

## Khatami

One person who recognized the depth of the problem confronting Iran was Seyyed Mohammad Khatami, who understood that 'realism', far from representing the scientific objective reality its proponents proclaimed, was itself constructed by and a product of distinctive cultural values and prejudices. If Iran was unable to communicate its message, however tempting, to the United States, this was perhaps because the cultural assumptions were different and while the words may be the same, the meaning imparted was not:

> In its contemporary, complex forms, information technology represents one of the highest achievements of modern culture which uses its control over information to solidify its domination of the world. Thus, inquiry into the nature of the information world is inseparable from uncovering the nature of modern civilization itself. And until we address this important question we will not be able to muster the confidence and wisdom to understand our relationship to modern civilization. Otherwise, we will live in a world whose rules have been set by others, at the mercy of circumstance, not as masters of our fate....The flood of information in our age saturates the

senses of humanity so extensively that the ability to assess and choose is impaired even among Westerners who are producers of information, let alone us who have a peripheral role in the information world. Electronic information is the brainchild of modern civilization. Thus, the power of today's information-based mass culture is tied to the legitimacy of the values of Western civilization for which the information revolution counts as the most prominent achievement....[11]

Khatami, a student of Western philosophy, was likewise seeking an engagement with the West, but the tool at his disposal, the means by which he intended to deconstruct the US hegemony,[12] was not the 'analytical' method of the Anglo-Saxon tradition, but the hermeneutic philosophy of the continent:

True dialogue will only be possible when the two sides are genuinely aware of their roots and identity, otherwise the dialogue of an imitator who has no identity, with others, is meaningless and is not in his interest.[13]

In other words, material 'interest' could neither be communicated nor sustained outside a common cultural framework. Khatami's first systematic attempt to broach this problem was in his interview on CNN in January 1998, where he stressed the commonality of interests between the Islamic Republic of Iran and the United States while acknowledging areas of disagreement. It would be fair to say that the initial reaction from the United States was confused. They had been caught off guard, were unclear what it all meant, and consequently not sure how to respond. For all the discussion of the Pilgrim Fathers and Alexis de Tocqueville, Khatami nonetheless provided some distinctly practical suggestions about how to proceed:

There is a bulky wall of mistrust between us and American administrations, a mistrust rooted in improper behaviour by the American governments. As an example of this type of behaviour, I should refer to admitted involvement of the American government in the 1953 coup d'etat which toppled Mosaddeq's national government, immediately followed by a $45m loan to strengthen the coup government. I should also refer to the capitulation law imposed by the American government on Iran.[14]

Tentative steps were taken to address this 'wall of mistrust' a few months later and, encouraged by different types of sporting diplomacy, there was a sense in some quarters that Khatami's dialogic offensive had made a modest breach in the wall. Nevertheless, despite the greater receptiveness to Khatami's message in Europe, there was little sign, beyond a sympathetic hearing, that the Western bureaucratic elites took him seriously. There is nothing to suggest for example that Khatami's proposition of a Dialogue of Civilizations was anything but a genuine attempt to engage and communicate meaningfully with the West. Unfortunately, the vast majority of his interlocutors regarded him as little more than a well-meaning 'philosopher–president', whose intellectual meanderings were to be tolerated rather than understood. It is important to recognize that Khatami's detractors in this respect were not only his ideological opponents, domestically and abroad (those who, it may be argued, espoused a theological absolutism), but those for whom 'ideology' was a term of abuse and merely the consequence of an unkempt mind. This somewhat dismissive perspective was in some ways more damaging to Khatami, for while its proponents may have had much in common with Khatami with respect to the ends to be achieved, they disagreed sharply on the means to be used. Khatami's natural allies, both at home and abroad, therefore found it difficult to take him seriously, and his inability to secure his political agenda at home only served to confirm this view of him as woolly and ineffectual.

Indeed, by the time the Democratic administration of President Clinton stooped to take up the gauntlet thrown down by Khatami in 1998, the political situation in both countries had taken a turn for the worse. Despite a triumphant election victory in the Majlis (February 2000), domestic pressures faced by Khatami were mounting and Iranian policymakers were becoming increasingly frustrated at the failure of his policy of engagement to yield concrete results. There were as yet no dramatic economic gains, despite a series of high profile visits to the EU, while in the US itself the campaign season had begun in earnest. The consequence of these developments was that the unprecedented apology by the new Secretary of State, Madeleine Albright, in March of that year for US involvement in the overthrow of Dr Mohammad Mosaddeq went largely unheeded in Iran.[15] Instead it was argued that it would be imprudent to negotiate with an administration which may not be in power following the November elections. In any case, pointed out the 'realists', a Republican administration would be easier 'to do business with'.[16]

## The Bush administration and 9/11

This suggestion was of course not without its merits. Charting the developments in US–Iran relations throughout the 1990s, few would have disagreed with the view that the Clinton administration had on balance done enormous damage to the possibility of rapprochement. It was under Clinton, after all, that the policy of dual containment had been developed and implemented; sanctions policy had been extended to include secondary sanctions; and, crucially, US policy towards the Middle East had become intimately tied to the desires of Israel in a way that was inconceivable under the first President Bush. On the other hand, it was President Reagan who had explored contacts in what was to emerge as the Iran-Contra scandal, and there were tantalizing hints that had he won a second term, he would indeed have instructed his pragmatic Secretary of State, James Baker, to investigate an opening towards Iran. This was pure speculation of course, verging perhaps on wishful thinking, and it completely omitted to account for the fact that it had been a Republican Congress which had bound Clinton's hands with respect to the sanctions on Iran. Nonetheless, Iran's realists confidently predicted that a Republican victory in November 2000 would continue where

Bush senior had left off, with a pragmatic 'interest' based foreign policy dominated by that most traditional of US interests, oil. The nomination as Vice President of Dick Cheney, with his links to the oil services company, Halliburton, which was rumoured to have business interests in Iran, appeared to confirm this view, as did the comments of European businessmen and civil servants. Only one concern served to sour this generally rosy picture: the assumption that the Republicans would be so ruthless in pursuit of their vision of US interests that security and economic advantages would far outweigh any desire to see political reform in Iran. This, ironically enough, was a charge that the Democrats had levelled at the Europeans, accusing them of lacking principle in dealing with Iran and putting economic interests first. With a Republican presidency, such idiosyncrasies could be put aside, although some Europeans were undoubtedly worried at the potential competition that American companies represented. From the Iranian perspective, a Republican victory would confirm the veracity of the realist methodology by removing the anomaly that was Clinton; provide an avenue for detente, which, it could be admitted, Khatami's dialogue had facilitated if not opened, and by extension enhance the prestige of the 'pragmatists'.

However, much to Iranian consternation, the election of George W. Bush in November 2000 did not provide the opportunities some had predicted, in large part because it took the Bush administration some considerable time to settle into the job of government. The momentum of the last few years, however slow, was now halted while the new administration officials took up their posts. While Iranians waited to see what would emerge, the indications were proving less than auspicious. The President himself seemed disinterested in foreign policy, espousing what some considered to be the traditional conservative tendency towards isolationism, although the extent to which this was being taken was viewed with genuine concern in some European capitals, especially with respect to the Arab–Israeli Peace Process.[17] More seriously, however, were the people Bush was appointing to positions of importance on Middle Eastern affairs. Indeed, a number of officials had been involved and, as in the case of Elliot Abrams, convicted for their part in the Iran-Contra scandal, while others such as John Bolton were noted for their zealous, even ideological adherence to a particular world view.[18] Still, the decision to host the Taliban in Washington with a view to developing an oil and gas pipeline from Central Asia through Afghanistan could be considered indicative of the new ruthless realism at work. If the Bush administration could work with the Taliban, went the recycled argument, then economic interests predominated over ideology. As noted above, however, the decision to work with the Taliban, had previously been investigated by the Clinton administration, with a view to circumventing the economically rational choice of Iran, and could be more convincingly presented as an ideologically determined decision. In sum, the advent of a new Republican presidency did not fill the realist mould carefully crafted by Iranian analysts – however hard they tried.

Then the events of 9/11 took place. It is in periods of crisis that tensions expose themselves, and 9/11 was no exception. While Americans struggled to come to terms with what had happened and provide an explanation, the tensions between those who sought to 'judiciously study discernible reality' and those who wished to 'create' their own realities came to the fore. What had hitherto been a trend (albeit a clear one where Iran was concerned) now began to dominate. But it was by no means clear in the first months after the 9/11 attack that this particular world view would succeed in establishing its hegemony over US foreign policy. In Iran, on the other hand similar internal tensions were resulting in an unprecedented expression of sympathy which was greeted with some incredulity in the United States. Indeed, some US commentators noticed that there was considerably more public sympathy from Iran than from many of America's allies in the region. There was a moment, indeed, when it appeared that the ideological facade with respect to Iran was about to crack, especially when the rash attempt to blame the 9/11 attacks on radical Shi'as (the ubiquitous Hezbollah) was blatantly contradicted by the facts.[19] Khatami sought to capitalize on this moment by delivering Iranian assistance to the emergent US war against the Taliban. He had assiduously cultivated the cultural framework in which trust could now be contemplated. Now it was time to convert this into a concrete reality by exploiting the obvious coincidence of interests in Afghanistan, and by all accounts Iranian assistance to the coalition both during and after the Afghan war, was not insignificant. Khatami was able to deliver because reformists and pragmatists (conservative or otherwise) within Iran likewise enjoyed a coincidence of interests and real merits in pursuing this policy. Hardliners in Iran were less easy to convince.

Their counterparts in the United States were similarly less than enthralled by the tentative detente, and steps were taken to derail the potential rapprochement. As one Conservative commentator has noted, 'from the perspective of Bush and the neocons, the US has been at war with Iran since 1979 and the time [had] come to settle the score'.[20] A delegation of Israelis was dispatched to Washington to remind the Bush administration of the obvious dangers of the Islamic Republic, a perspective that was enthusiastically amplified by neoconservatives within and around the government, who rushed to the airwaves to accuse Iran of harbouring al Qaeda operatives. There was indeed some confusion in Iranian circles about the presence or otherwise of Al Qaeda, and the final admission that Al Qaeda members had escaped across the border and were now in Iranian prisons did not do much to assuage suspicions of complicity and their conversion into fact in an American consciousness traumatized by 9/11.[21] More conclusive, however, as far as the US administration and their Israeli guests were concerned, was the sudden and timely capture of the Karine A, a ship loaded with weapons for the Palestinian Authority. As the Israeli authorities and Prime Minister Sharon in particular made the most of parading the captured weapons, happily emblazoned with Persian lettering, they were initially confronted by an air of diplomatic incredulity. Not only was the timing of the find highly convenient, but even analysts ill disposed to the Islamic Republic found it remarkable that a regime hitherto experienced in shipping arms and munitions overseas should choose to do this particular delivery via slow boat journey around the Arabian Peninsula. Caution was eventually thrown to the wind when even the sceptics concluded that the source of the shipment was, at the very least, the 'rogue elements' in the regime determined to undermine Khatami. For those who had never been convinced by the 'totalitarian' description of Iran, here was the ready alternative: Khatami, the author of dialogue of civilizations, was not really in charge. Either way the explanation fits the prejudice, and by the beginning of 2002, Khatami's domestic and international policies were in tatters.

Much ink has been spilt debating the causes and consequences of Bush's State of the Union address on 29 January 2002, especially with regard to the inclusion of the theological motif 'Axis of Evil', a phrase which was to have political reverberations, particularly in Iran. Yet the speech is probably as interesting for what it did not include, and it is striking that 'al Qaeda' merited one, almost marginal, mention, and Bin Laden, none at all.[22] It was as if the war in Afghanistan signalled the end of one chapter, and that now it was time to move on – to other targets. The reaction in Iran to this abrupt hardening of American attitude is revealing in both indicating the plurality and sophistication of views with regard to the United States, and the sheer bewilderment of many Iranian analysts who discovered that the real world did not match their *realist* assessment.[23] Even ordinary Iranians who could agree with Bush's criticism of the 'unelected minority' found it difficult to recognize themselves as part of an unholy alliance with Iraq and North Korea.

To be sure, there were some recognizable, if regrettable, reactions. The Supreme Leader, Ayatollah Khamene'i , immediately responded with characteristic rhetoric of his own, noting that 'The Islamic Republic of Iran is proud to be the target of the rage and hatred of the world's greatest Satan', while hardliners, particularly in the Revolutionary Guards, sought to exploit the event by imposing a state of emergency.[24] Despite the absence of formal relations, America had never left Iran. The 'Axis of Evil' ensured that it returned to centre stage. The spectre of America had been realized; regular politics, frequently subjected to doses of American interference (real or imagined), was now put on hold; the nation united against the 'foreign threat'; and conspiracies were amplified.[25] Politicians, meanwhile, became engrossed in the problem of 'who lost America?' Indeed, far from launching diatribes against the United States, Majlis deputies turned their attention to the alleged ineptitudes of the Foreign Ministry.[26] Others, in their eagerness to absolve the United States of such 'irrational' behaviour, could see instead the hand of 'Perfidious Albion'.[27] According to the reformist deputy, Hojjat-ol Islam Alisaghar Rahmani-Khalili:

> By taking such a stance, George Bush is trying to test public opinion. And when the public opinion would correspond to his, he would then act. [The] European Union and a number of Asian and European countries have criticized Bush's position describing it as inappropriate and wrong. Only England has supported Bush. England is behind those crises created in our country and the outside movements that support them. England is the one who motivates America to act brutishly. We must discover England's footprint in these events. In truth, England is the one who fuels events.[28]

While hardliners relished the possibility of further antagonism, reformist politicians along with their pragmatist allies were desperate to discover the realist core at the heart of American rhetoric. Grasping at straws, they were encouraged by the apparent discomfort in the United States at the implications of Bush's comments. The 'realist' old guard in the State Department and Congress, clearly shaken, had sought to soften the rhetoric and even hinted at the possibility of dialogue, a prospect seized upon by reformists.[29] As one reformist journalist commented:

> There is no rational strategic explanation for refusing to hold talks with America. The sooner Iran begins to hold public and official talks with America, the sooner it will be able to further its own interests. However, the longer Iran postpones the talks, the greater the losses it will incur. In fact, if we had started to hold official talks publicly a few years ago, we would not have faced many of the problems in the bilateral relations between the two countries. Postponing the talks means that Iran has hardened its position. Eventually, Iran and America will have to negotiate. The longer such talks are postponed, the greater the losses Iran will incur and this will primarily serve America's interests.[30]

Ironically, efforts at a public dialogue were to be rapidly overtaken by news that a number of private initiatives appeared to be under way. The precise nature of these initiatives, secret and sensitive as they were, is likely to remain clouded for some time, but according to leaks in the Iranian press, it appeared as if the Chairman of the Expediency Council, Hashemi Rafsanjani, had been exploring the possibilities of a 'grand bargain' with the United States.[31] In retrospect, this may have been an attempt by the arch-realist in the Iranian establishment to broker a deal with like-minded ruthless realists in the United States. Rafsanjani's problem, however, was that this move was unlikely to win him friends among the hardline conservatives (who eagerly anticipated his failure), nor among reformists who suspected Rafsanjani's definition of 'interest' to be narrowly centred on issues of mutual security and stripped of any association with human rights and democracy. Indeed, Rafsanjani's gambit revealed a significant flaw in this particular realist conception. It failed to take into account the changes in political culture among Iranians (or, for that matter, within the United States). Neglecting the democratic imperative, it lacked a moral core and, with supreme irony, handed the moral high ground, on a platter, to the neoconservatives. 'Realists', whether in the US or Europe were, quite clearly, unprincipled. In Iran, indignation was rife.[32] This indignation was fuelled by calculated leaks from the hardliners, such as Ayatollah Jannati's unsubtle response to an apparently 'clever' question from an AFP reporter, 'Rafsanjani is not involved in this, but a number of associates are involved in it'.[33] To further muddy the waters, it was unclear who was involved in the negotiations, and which particular factions were represented. In the United States, despite initial rejections, it was later revealed that old Iran-Contra networks were being revitalized, along with all the usual suspects – leading some in Iran to conclude that the neocons were reassuringly realist to the core, while in Iran, Rafsanjani's association with the conservatives led people to conclude that despite all the harsh rhetoric, this was an initiative with widespread conservative backing. The more damning conclusion drawn by many reformists was that, for all the rhetoric, America was quite happy to deal with Iran's 'unelected minority'.[34] Anti-Americanism, like anti-Iranianism, was rapidly becoming a bipartisan affair.

Indeed, contrary to their political leanings, it was the reformists who were protesting that now was not the time to begin negotiations with the United States, while the conservatives increasingly stewed in the embarrassment of further revelations and sought to stifle debate.[35] Ultimately, each tried to outdo each other in their repeated denial of any desire to open a dialogue while public opinion reacted with characteristic irritation at the obvious lack of any progress.[36] The end to this steady debasement of political life came with an intervention from the Leader, Ayatollah Khaméneh'i, urging all parties to desist from further debate. The comment proved highly counterproductive and took the public obsession with the United States to the point of ridicule. The head of Tehran Justice Office, Abbas Ali Alizadeh, a medium-level cleric of moderate education, on apparently no authority or initiative but his own, abruptly announced, via a judicial decree broadcast on State television, that henceforth, any discussion about negotiations with the United States would be considered a criminal offence.[37] Quite apart from the insight it provided into the means by which Iran's 'autocracy' operated, this proved a highly unusual intervention – the Judiciary, let alone regional branches, had not been in the habit of issuing decrees – which took many Iranians by surprise. Shock, however, very rapidly gave way to ridicule as some conjectured that perhaps the decree applied only to Tehran, and that discussions could continue outside the province of Tehran. By the next morning, however, farce gave way to anger as Majlis deputies lined up to lambast the hapless Alizadeh and his 'ignorance' of the law.[38] Even President Khatami was moved to condemn the Judiciary's actions:

> I am surprised with all the fuss made over a matter that has not yet happened. More or less all those who speak about talks with America are either opposed to them or agree that now is not the time for such talks. Why must we create the impression that this is the time for talks? I follow the political system's overall policies. Let us not do anything that will threaten the country's interests and dignity and the system's overall policies. Then somebody announces that whoever negotiates has committed a crime, as if people are queuing in Iran to talk to America, and we have to stop them by force or through the judiciary. What kind of behaviour is this? We must be wise and run this country with intelligence, and God Willing, we are blessed with intelligence.[39]

## Conclusion

Despite all the ridicule, the hardline conservatives were in effect able to put an end to any suggestions of a detente with the United States. Within months, the Judiciary moved, with great secrecy and to the ill-disguised frustration of the government, to arrest individuals involved in polling public opinion with a view to assessing the public reaction to any dialogue with the United States.[40]

Despite the nuanced nature of the responses – Iranians remained on the whole distrustful of US intentions but thought dialogue a positive and worthwhile step – the hardliners dismissed the entire exercise as psychological warfare intended to weaken the revolutionary resolve of the Islamic Republic. Ayatollah Jannati reiterated the revolutionary dogma to a weary public, stressing that antagonism against the United States remained a *raison d'etre* of the state.[41] As an exercise in maintaining the status quo, it revealed a continued absence of decisive leadership in the Islamic Republic, and popular frustration was increasingly making itself felt.[42] Others openly directed their criticism at the Leader himself, lamenting his inability to seize the initiative on this issue, despite the urging of advisers.[43] Indeed, a sympathetic view of the United States and its policies remained among the general public and some reformist politicians all the way up to the Iraqi invasion, with few tears shed for the fall of the Baathist regime.[44] Even among intellectuals, articles discussing US policy continued to define it in terms of realism and rationality, whether in critiquing a prospective war in Iraq or explaining it.[45] Indeed, having absorbed one understanding of realism, Iranians were now digesting another which explained that the policy of regime change was simply an extension of the realist interpretation of international relations which regarded the world as essentially lawless.[46] Few, if any, commentators within Iran were willing to concede a cultural paradigm for the determination of what constituted US interests, in part perhaps because in acknowledging the ideological aspect of US foreign policy, one conceded ground to the ideological hardliners in Iran itself, and paradoxically fed the logic of structural determinism.[47] Iranian realists had all the difficulty of communication with the new American idealism, and none of the reassuring conviction of their ideological compatriots. Dismissive of Khatami, they had no alternative strategy to deconstruct the 'wall of mistrust', while Iranian hardliners relished its construction. The Bush administration, for its part, settled into the political comfort of prejudice and myth, increasingly employing theological motifs which would unsettle their compatriots, but resonate with their opponents. As the current nuclear impasse indicates, neither side has been willing to recognize a cultural and ideological dimension to the construction of interest, or to see their positions as anything but real and rational. The focus on particularities has obfuscated the wider problem of cultural communication and disguised the reality that myth is just as important to US policy making as it is to revolutionary Iran. Perhaps Iran had exported her revolution after all?

## Notes

1  Recounted by Ron Susskind, 'Without a Doubt', in *The New York Times*, 17 October 2004.
2  See, for example, National Security Council member, Bob Blackwill, quoted in the *Financial Times*, 16 March 2004, 'Washington Hardliners wary of engaging Iran'; Guy Dinmore: 'Bush has a vision for the Greater Middle East but not a policy.' The notion that US policy towards Iran, inasmuch as it exists, has failed is of course not new, see, for example, S. Chubin and J.D. Green, 'Engaging Iran: A US Strategy', *Survival*, vol. 40, no. 3, Autumn (1998): 153–169.

3 Contrast Rice's comments with those of Richard Armitage after the State of the Union address in 2002, 'The axis of evil speech was a valid comment [but] I would note there is one dramatic difference between Iran and the other two axes of evil, and that would be its democracy. [And] you approach a democracy differently... I wouldn't think they were next at all.' Richard Armitage quoted in the *Los Angeles Times*, 15 February 2003.

4 In this paper, 'realism', and the 'rationality' that it implies are culturally defined and determined, and therefore reflect particular interpretation as opposed to general laws. 'Myth' is here used as a concept in the social sciences. See, for example, Paul Ricouer *Science and Ideology in Hermeneutics and the Human Sciences* (Cambridge, 1981): 222–246. My reading of myth draws extensively on Roland Barthes, *Mythologies* (London, 1970).

5 See, for example, Leon Harder, 'Operation Iranian Freedom?' *The American Conservative*, 25 April 2005: 3–4; '...the neocons are more entrenched in the power centres while the realists have been cleansed from the CIA and other government agencies....'

6 As Philippe Sands notes in *Lawless World: America and the Making and Breaking of Global Rules* (London, 2005): xi, 'The rules which were intended to constrain others became constraining of their creators.'

7 See, for example, W. Beeman, 'Double Demons: Cultural Impedance in US–Iranian Understanding', *Iranian Journal of International Affairs*, Summer–Fall (1990): 319–334.

8 For details of this interpretation, see Gary Sick, *October Surprise: America's Hostages in Iran and the Election of Ronald Reagan* (London, 1992).

9 The notion of 'national interest' became more prominent in discourse, see, for example, Hossein Seifzadeh 'Estrateji-ye Melli va Siyasatgozari-ye khareji' (National Strategy & Foreign Policy-Making), *The Journal of Foreign Policy*, vol. VII (1994): 705–722.

10 See the editorial in the *Tehran Times*, 23 February 1993, which boldly proclaimed now to be the time for 'realism'. There was also an attempt to out-intellectualize and out-rationalize the West, which often took some striking turns. For example, one of the key proponents of this movement, Mohammad-Javad Larijani, could offer the following assessment of the Islamic Republic: 'While an Islamic society is not at ease with technical rationality, it finds itself quite in harmony with the authentic one. Therefore, Islamic modernity goes far beyond historical modernity and is basically a post-modern phenomenon.' 'Islamic Society & Modernism', in *The Iranian Journal for International Affairs*, VII, 1 (1995): 58.

11 See M. Khatami, 'Observations on the Information World' in *Hope and Challenge: The Iranian President Speaks*, A. Mafinezam (trans.) (Binghamton, 1997): 61–71.

12 'Hegemony' is here used in the Gramscian sense.

13 SWB ME/3099 S1/6 dated 11 December 1997, Khatami's speech to the OIC conference dated 9 December 1997. See also BBC SWB ME/3339 MED/2 dated 23 September 1998, President Khatami addresses Iranian expatriates in the USA, dated 20 September 1998: 'the first rule of dialogue... is to know yourself and identity. The second rule is to know the civilisation with which you want to maintain a dialogue....'

14 BBC SWB ME/3120 MED/5 dated 9 January 1998, CNN interview dated 8 January 1998.

15 The importance of the myth of Mosaddeq to contemporary Iranian political culture can hardly be exaggerated. See, for example, the Persian periodical *Nameh*, 25, Mordad 1382/August 2003, special issue on the 50th anniversary of the Coup; or the previous year's issue, Mordad 1381/August 2002, special issue on 'National Unity', in which the spectre of Mosaddeq looms large.

16 The notion (myth) that 'conservatives' are easier 'to do business with', would in turn be replicated by the Europeans. The standard mantra of this myth is the argument, 'Only Nixon could go to China.'

17 For a traditional conservative critique of the neoconservative agenda see, Pat Buchanan, 'No End to War' in *The American Conservative*, 1 March 2004.

18 Abrams was initially appointed National Security Council Staff Chief for 'Democracy, Human Rights, and International Operations', before moving up in 2002, to become Special Assistant to the President and Senior Director on the NSC for SW Asia, Near East and North African Affairs. See David Corn, *Elliot Abrams. It's Back! The Nation*, 2 July 2001; Terry J. Allen *Public Serpent: Iran Contra Villain Elliot Abrams Is Back in Action in These Times*, August 2001; *The Return of Elliot Abrams* at: *www.tompaine.com/feature.cfm/ID/6895*, 11 December 2002; see also *Iran-Contra, Amplified www.tompaine.com/feature2.cfm/ID/8625* 18 August 2003.

19 It was noticeable, for example, that the standard chants of 'death to America' at Friday's prayers were suspended; see the interesting reflection on the attack and Iranian sympathies for Americans in M. Hajizadeh 'Aqazadeh-ha' (Their Excellencies' Sons) (Tehran, 1381/2002): 143–146. Popular sympathy for the United States continued, see *Aftab-e Yazd*, 5th Esfand 1382 / 24 February 2004: 5.

20 Leon Hardar 'Operation Iranian Freedom?', 4; see also A. Killgore, 'Neocons "Concentrate on Promoting US–Iran War"', in *Washington Report on Middle East Affairs*, March 2005: 32–33.

21 The US Special Envoy for Afghanistan, Zalmay Khalilzad, publicly made the claims on 18 January 2002, see Iran Press Service 18 January 2002, www.iran-press-service.com/articles_2002/Jan_2002/afqanestan_iran_qaeda_18102.

22 See www.whitehouse.gov/news/releases/2002/01/print/20020129–11.html; the 'terrorist underworld' highlighted by President Bush was limited to *Hamas, Hezbollah, Islamic Jihad*, and for good measure *Jaish-e-Mohammad*.

23 See commentary in *Nowruz*, 2 February 2002, BBC SWB Mon MEPol. For an interesting exception to the standard line (albeit written abroad), see G. Qoreishi and M. Soleimani, 'Iran va Amrika: Bazi-ye na-tamam' (Iran & America: The unfinished game), *Aftab*, 2, 15, Ordibehesht 1381/April–May 2002: 14–21, J. Kheirkhahan (trans.).

24 *Khamenei calls Bush 'thirsty for human blood'* AFP, 31 January 2002. See, for example, BBC SWB Mon ME1 MEPol, *Nowruz* website, 18 March 2002, on continuing calls by conservatives for a declaration of martial law.

25 See, for example, BBC SWB Mon ME1 MEPol, IRIB, 12 July 2002, *Demonstrators support Khamene'i, call for trial of 'fifth columnists'*; also, *Etemad*, 29 Mordad 1381/20 August 2002: 2. There was, of course, plenty of public scepticism, see the reader's comment, *Aftab-e Yazd*, 25 Ordibehesht 1381 / 15 May 2002: 11.

26 See Elahe Koulaee's comments in *Nowruz*, 24 Ordibehesht 1381/14 May 2002: 2; also *Aftab-e Yazd*, 21 Khordad 1381/11 June 2002: 1.

27 The alternative was of course Israel, despite the best attempts of overseas observers, see A. Sheikhzadeh, Iran va Emrika: taqabul ya tafahum (Iran and America: confrontation or understanding), *Aftab*, 2, 17, Tir-Mordad 1381/July–August 2002: 16–25.

28 ISNA website, 2 February 2002, BBC SWB Mon MEPol.

29 Majlis deputies welcomed the possibility of inter-parliamentary talks following comments by Senator Joe Biden, *Hambastegi* website, 16 March 2002, BBC SWB Mon MEPol. Ahmad Zeydabadi quoted in ISNA website, 16 March 2002, BBC SWB Mon MEPol; See also Jala'ipour's comments in *Bonyan*, 18 March 2002, BBC SWB Mon MEPol. See, for example, *Nowruz*, 31 Ordibehesht 1381/21 May 2002: 1.

30 Ahmad Zeydabadi quoted in ISNA website, 16 March 2002, BBC SWB Mon MEPol; See also Jala'ipour's comments in *Bonyan*, 18 March 2002, BBC SWB Mon MEPol.

31 *Nowruz*, 19 Ordibehesht 1381/9 May 2002: 5.

32 For a later analysis of these developments, see Guy Dinmore, 'Washington Hardliners wary of engaging with Iran', *Financial Times*, 16 March 2004.

33 See the detailed analysis of the various claims in *Nowruz*, 26 May 2002, BBC SWB Mon MEPol.

34 See Armin's comments in *Nowruz*, 24 Ordibehesht 1381/14 May 2002: 2, and Rafsanjani's reply in *Nowruz*, 25 Ordibehesht 1381/15 May 2002: 2; see also Guy Dinmore 'Washington Hardliners wary of engaging with Iran'. Financial Times, 16 March 2004. See also K. Royce and T.M. Phelps 'Secret Talks with Iranian', *Newsday.com*, 8 August 2003.

35 Mirdamadi, the Head of the Majlis National Security Commission, had been at the forefront of the charge that 'conservatives' had initiated unauthorized talks, see, for example, *Entekhab*, 23 May 2002, BBC SWB Mon MEPol. He was charged with putting the country's national security at risk by the head of the Tehran Judiciary, Alizadeh! See *Resalat* website, 27 May 2002, BBC SWB Mon MEPol.

36 See Mohajerani's comments in *Bonyan*, 14 Ordibehesht 1381/4 May 2002: 2; for public frustration, see *Aftab-e Yazd*, 25 Ordibehesht 1381/15 May 2002: 11; Comment by Habibollah Asgarowladi, 15 June 2002, BBC SWB Mon MEPol.

37 *Nowruz*, 5 Khordad 1381/26 May 2002: 1.

38 *Nowruz*, 6 Khordad 1381/27 May 2002: 1–2; Editorial in *Hadis-e Qazvin* 2 June 2002, BBC SWB Mon MEPol. See also Mehdi Karrubi's press conference, *Nowruz*, 12 Khordad 1381/2 June 2002: 1–2; *Hayat-e No*, 12 Khordad 1381/2 June 2002: 1.

39 *Hayat-e No* website, 1 June 2002, BBC SWB Mon MEPol. See also *Nowruz*, 19 Khordad 1381/9 June 2002: 7; *Hayat-e No*, 11 Khordad 1381/1 June 2002: 1.

40 For details, see *Mardomsalari*, 18 Dey 1381/8 January 2003: 4/9; there was some evidence of Ministry of Information collusion, see *Entekhab* website, 24 December 2002, BBC SWB Mon ME1 MEPol; *Bahar*, 19 Dey 1381/9 January 2003: 1; it was indeed February 2003, before the Judiciary provided details to President Khatami, ISNA website, 2 February 2003, BBC SWB Mon ME1 MEPol.

41 See Jannati's speech, IRIB, 8 November 2002, BBC SWB Mon ME1 MEPol.

42 See, for example, the reader comment, *Aftab-e Yazd*, 17 Shahrivar 1381/8 September 2002: 5, 'In my opinion America has provided the greatest help to Muslims and Iran...'; also reader comment, *Aftab-e Yazd*, 28 Azar 1381/18 December 2002: 5; see also a critique of the 'myth' of America, see Bana S 'Bar gharari rabeteh bah amrika: faseleh gereftan ba romantism-e siyasi' (Establishing links with America: moving away from political romanticism), *Aftab*, Farvardin 1382/April 2003: 84.

43 'Letter of Sholeh-Saadi to Khamenei' December 2002 www.web.peykeiran.com/iran/news/ir_news_92.asp

44 For details, see the editorial in the magazine, *Aftab*, Farvardin 1382/April 2003, along with the interview with Habibollah Peyman. For Elahe Koulaie's criticism of bias of Iranian television against the Americans, see Tehran Times website, 7 April 2003, BBC SWB Mon ME1 MEPol. There was of course a certain amount of anxiety in official circles about the rapidity of the fall of Iraq, *Hayat-e No*, 16 Shahrivar 1381/7 September 2002: 1; *Aftab-e Yazd*, 25 Ordibehesht 1381/15 May 2002: 11; see President Khatami's press conference, *Jaam-e Jam* 28 August 2002, BBC SWB Mon ME1 MEPol. Discomfort at US policies gradually emerged after the war, see R. Mostaqim, 'Iranian Reformers Back Hardliners against War', Inter Press Service News Agency, 2 April 2003. See also the concerns expressed in the Editorial in 'Jang va Ghodrat menhaye Mardom' (War and power without the people), *Jame'eh No*, 2, 15, Ordibehesht 1382/April 2003: 1–2, these views were reflected in the tone of the rest of the special issue.

45 Among observers of US policy that continued to be translated into Persian were the standard-bearers of 'realism', whether as proponents or critiques. See, for example, N. Chomsky, 'Tahlil-e Eqdam Bush dar Araq' (An analysis of Bush's actions in Iraq), *Aftab*, 3, 21, Azar 1381/November–December 2002): 84–85, M. Malekan (trans.); A. Bigdeli 'Amrika: Ostoreh ta Vagheyat' (America: myth to reality), *Jame'eh* No. 2, 13, Esfand 1381/March 2003: 27–28.

46  See, for example, in this vein, F. Fukuyama, 'Mohafezeh-kari-ye Emrakayi' (American conservatism), *Aftab*, 3, 22, Dey-Bahman 1381/January–February 2003: 88–89, M. Malekan (trans.); particularly pertinent to this interpretation is the following article: G. Nassri, 'Tammoli marafat shenakhti bar falsafe-ye siyasi-ye Habbs va mabna-ye qodrat va amniat dar'an (An Epistemological Meditation on the Political Philosophy of Hobbes), *Etele'at Siyasi-Eqtesadi*, vol. 16: 177–178 Khordad-Tir 1381/June–July 2002: 18–31.

47  A view which panders to the *inevitable* 'clash of civilisations'. This perspective was admirably critiqued by Abdolkarim Soroush in *The Three Cultures in Reason, Freedom and Democracy in Islam: Essential Writings of Abdolkarim Soroush*, M. Sadri and A. Sadri (eds and trans) (Oxford, 2000): 156–170. See also Richard Bulliet, *The Case for Islamo-Christian Civilisation* (New York, 2005).

# 8 A look to the north

## Opportunities and challenges

*Farhad Atai*

The collapse of the Soviet Union caught the world by surprise. The people of Soviet Central Asia may have been just as unprepared for the collapse, if not more so, than the rest of the world. It was the developments in the western republics of the Soviet Union neighbouring Europe that eventually led to the collapse. The 'Newly Independent Republics' of Central Asia neither expected nor were ready for independence when they were catapulted to the international arena as new nation states.

Immediately after the collapse, the question was how to deal with what was left of the fallen empire. Outside Russia, it seemed that the West's concerns were mainly with nuclear facilities left in Kazakhstan, and the spread of radical Islam in Central Asia and the Caucasus, while it hoped to exploit the newly emerging economic possibilities in Eastern Europe, the Caucasus, and Central Asia.

As early as 1991, attempts at denuclearizing the former Soviet republics got under way. Subsequent to the adoption of a bill in Washington proposed by senators Sam Nunn (Democrat) and Charles Lugar (Republican), the Security Assistance Program was introduced. It mandated the US Department of Defense to allocate $400 million of its 1992 budget to bring about the destruction of nuclear weapons in the newly independent states of the former Soviet Union. The annual allocation of funds continued through 1995.[1] Kazakhstan, as the only nuclear power in Central Asia, was directly affected by policies in the West, which aimed at denuclearizing the former Soviet republics. After independence, Almaty was faced with a crucial decision, viz.

> Remaining a nuclear state afforded her prestige in the region along with threats of becoming the target of nuclear attacks and international sanctions in case she decided to pursue a nuclear proliferation policy.
>
> Forgoing the nuclear option would, among other things, bring her promises of considerable Western financial and technical assistance.

Almaty opted for the second alternative. Through 'Project Sapphire' in 1993, Kazakhstan's government agreed to transfer to Oakridge, Tennessee, close to 600 Kg of nuclear materials. There were further plans for the destruction of tactical nuclear weapons left over from the Soviet era and/or placing them under the operational command of Russia.[2] In separate agreements with the United States, Russia and China, Kazakhstan was assured that she would not become the target of nuclear attacks. On 26 July 1994 she signed the Safeguard Agreement with the International Atomic Energy and in April 1995, Kazakhstan's president, Nursultan Nazarbayev, reported to the UN Secretary General that the transfer to Russia of all transcontinental ballistic missiles and the destruction of all underground nuclear warheads at Semipalatinsk nuclear test site had been completed.[3] Western concerns about proliferation of nuclear weapons in Central Asia were thus alleviated.

## Radical Islam

The concern here was that the Islamic Republic of Iran would be tempted to take advantage of the arising circumstances, and encourage Islamic movements and activities among the predominantly Muslim population of Central Asia, leading to further destabilization of the region. Another concern was that during this crucial juncture when the Central Asian people were about to lay the foundations of their new independent states, the Islamic Republic might be taken as a model. Yet another long-term concern, though less elaborated on and expressed, was the possible emergence of an Islamic block with a population of 300 million that would spread from the Mediterranean Sea to the Indian Ocean. It is ironic that the real threat of radical Islam that eventually emerged in the region in the form of the Taliban phenomenon, and remains a major security issue, came not from Iran, but from Afghanistan. It has become clear that the collaboration of the US intelligence, the Saudi government's money and ideology, and Pakistani military's logistical support in creating, and training the Mujahedin against the Soviet occupation of Afghanistan were responsible for the creation of Talibanism. President George W. Bush's policies and posture towards the Muslim world have only exacerbated the situation.

As the region opened up to the outside world and more contacts became possible, the preoccupation with the Islamic threat reduced to a considerable extent, only to re-emerge in the mid-1990s. Until then, it was assumed that the West did not have vital strategic concerns in Central Asia. It was even argued that the West had only 'negative interests' in that region; i.e. as long as there was no major upheaval in the region leading to the destabilization of Central Asia, the West would be content.[4]

## Iran and Central Asia

The developments of 1992 placed Iran in a unique and privileged strategic position unmatched by that of any other country. This was due to various factors, the most important of which are the following:

- The Central Asia–Caspian region emerged as one of the world's richest regions in oil and gas reserves. It was initially estimated that the Caspian region with 57.1 trillion cubic metres of gas (excluding that of Russia) has the richest reserves in the world and with 59.2 billion barrels of oil,[5] it has the third largest oil reserves on the globe, after the Persian Gulf and Siberia. By 2010, the republics of Kazakhstan, Turkmenistan, Uzbekistan and Azerbaijan were estimated to produce five million barrels of oil per day.[6] The overly optimistic estimates of gas and oil in the Caspian region were later reduced to one fifth of that. Nevertheless, the Caspian region remains as an energy-rich region having some 3–4 per cent of the world's reserves. In 2002, the region's production reached 1.6 million barrels per day. That is almost equal to the annual production of Brazil, South America's second largest oil producer. It is estimated that by 2010 the countries of the Caspian Sea region will produce between 3 and 4.7 million barrels per day.[7]

- The newly independent states of Central Asia are land-locked with no access to open seas. They depend on their neighbours for transporting goods and commodities to and from the outside world.
- Iran is the bridge linking the world's two largest oil and gas reserves – the Persian Gulf and the Central Asia–Caspian regions. 'With 2000 miles of shore on the Persian Gulf, Iran is the shortest, and the most economical route for transportation of oil and gas from the Central Asia–Caspian region to Japan, and the Far East. The network of Iran's gas pipelines is already linked with Azerbaijan and Turkmenistan. A pipeline that can connect Kazakhstan and Turkmenistan to this network is at least four times shorter and cheaper than the proposed pipelines to the Mediterranean and the Black Sea.'[8]

## The Iranian government's view of Central Asia

After the breakdown of the Soviet Union the Iranian government also looked to Central Asia with interest. The Iranian view of the potential interests in the region proved as naive as those of the Western governments. Iran's hopes and concerns were as follows:

- A hope that with the disappearance of the Soviet Union, the Muslim peoples of the region would follow Iran's footsteps and turn their newly-formed governments into Islamic republics.
- A concern that soon emerged was one with security. The dispute in the Nogorno–Karabakh region between Azerbaijan and Armenia resulted in thousands of refugees at Iran's northern border. The civil war in Tajikistan was a further cause for concern. In the spring of 1992, Iran's deputy foreign minister for research and training, in his address to China's Institute of International Relations, warned, 'the emergence of a handful of undeveloped and poor states that continuously face the threat of rebellion and drought would severely affect the security and stability of the borders of the neighbouring countries'.[9]

Interestingly enough, it seems that, unlike the other governments, the Islamic Republic's initial concern was not economic. Iran's perception of, and policy toward, Central Asia has evolved over the past years. It has gone through various stages. The first stage can be characterized by the belief that the people of Central Asia would be inclined to go back to their roots and hopefully create their own Islamic states. In 1992, in an editorial in *Central Asia and the Caucasus Review*, the Iranian foreign minister hinted at such a desire:

> The true cultural identity in this region of the world is a combination of valuable Islamic principles and ancient national traditions amongst these peoples... With the rich history of this region in mind, we are determined to provide the means for Central Asia and the Caucasus to once again join the main current of world culture and civilization.[10]

It was assumed that this would be the natural consequence of the changing geopolitics of the region, rather than a result of any particular initiative by the Islamic Republic of Iran. In his speech to China's Institute of International Affairs, the Iranian deputy foreign minister explained:

> With the breakdown of the Soviet Union, the region's subsystem has been altered completely. The Middle Eastern subsystem was such that, politically and culturally, Iran stood at its periphery. That subsystem had basically an Arabic character, its main economic feature being the presence of huge oil reserves, a strategic commodity; whereas the recent developments have exited Iran from the Middle Eastern system and entered her into a new subsystem that includes the newly independent states of Central Asia and the Caucasus. The main feature of this subsystem, from an economic and cultural point of view, is its being non-Arabic and lacking any transactable strategic commodity at the international level, such as oil.[11]

This belief was greatly reinforced by an almost total lack of knowledge about the region, its emerging governments, and the wishes of its peoples. With little insight into the nature of the developments in Central Asia, the Islamic government offered verbal support to trends and groups that were not necessarily in harmony with Iran's interests. An example of this was the support offered to the government in Tajikistan that took power after independence. Though labelled Islamic, it was in fact an awkward coalition between Islamists and a group of intellectuals and academicians. The excesses carried out by that regime alienated a great number of Tajiks and brought to power the secular government in Dushanba that has an anti-Islamic attitude and opposed Tajik nationalist tendencies. It later turned out that the main support for the 'Islamic regime' came from the Saudi government, whereas Iran's involvement with that regime did not go beyond verbal support.

The second stage came with the realization that the peoples of Central Asia, and especially their governments, were not enthusiastic about an Islamic state. This became increasingly apparent as diplomatic and commercial contacts between Iran and Central Asia developed.[12] Furthermore, the Russians – who still exert considerable political power in the region and see it as their own backyard – would not tolerate the creation of such states in their former south.

Finally, the perception has evolved into a realistic one according to which the priority in the region should be given to maintaining peace and security, with an emphasis on economic and cultural cooperation. This was reiterated by Foreign Minister Velayati in his address at the seminar on 'Security and Foreign Policy in Central Asia and the Caucasus' in January 1996 in Tehran:

> The Islamic Republic of Iran is convinced that her security lies in preservation of peace and tranquility in the region and it is in this context that her policies vis-à-vis the Persian Gulf, the neighbouring countries, and Central Asia evolve.[13]

A very important aspect of this policy has been the recognition that Russia's influence and interest in the region cannot be ignored. This is an important point worth elaborating. Having been isolated on the international scene, mainly because of the US efforts and European acquiescence, Iran looked to Russia – a former superpower and still the major power in the region for support. At the Iran-o-Russian Roundtable held in Moscow in October 1995, the deputy foreign minister spoke of 'the dawn of a new era of greater co-operation and friendship' between the two countries. 'The recent thrust of the Iran-o-Russian bilateral relations', he said, 'though in an embryonic stage, channelled events toward the right direction... The road ahead seems stable and steady'. Referring to 'Russia's intransigence in face of international pressure and Iran's insistence on maintaining her "special relations" with Russia', he noted, 'Russia and Iran have rejected the groundless accusations of Washington, resisting the spread of unwarranted approaches on the international scene'.[14] This, it seems, has meant avoiding actions and comments that may annoy Moscow. Thus, President Hashemi Rafsanjani, addressing the conference on 'Security and Foreign Policy in Central Asia and the Caucasus', held in Tehran in the summer of 1996, noted:

> Many of their needs are in Russia. Railroads, industries, communications, and their academic expertise are in Russia. [Outside] powers and governments should not attempt to create conflicts between them and Russia. We must try lest the sincerity between them and Russia disappears. The United States, for example, should not, for the sake of her own presence [in the region], think of severing their relations with Russia. Here is not the place for this sort of competition... They must work with them so that gradually their dependence on Russia would be reduced. This is what Iran is doing.[15]

The Iranian government's position on Bosnia–Herzegovina may also be an indication. Even though Russia was by far the most important backer of the Serbs, Iran decided to turn a blind eye on Moscow and blame others as the culprit in the Bosnian tragedy. More recently, the Islamic Republic of Iran's policy towards Chechnya has been cited as another example of Iran trying to appease Russia. Iran has maintained that the problem of the Chechens is an internal one within the Russian Federation and hence, not an international matter.

## Impediments to forging long-term relations with Central Asian countries

Despite relative success, Iran has faced a number of obstacles, both internal and external, to forging a long-term relationship with her neighbours:

In the early years, especially, there was an absence of modern ways of promoting Iran's policies in the region; the Islamic Republic's major tool in gaining influence in Central Asia in those years was sending books in Persian script to the region – and that mainly to Tajikistan – despite the fact that very few people in Central Asia can read any script other than Cyrillic. This was in sharp contrast to Turkey, for instance, that broadcast eighteen hours of satellite programmes daily all over Central Asia, founded many schools in those republics, and in 1992–1993 alone offered scholarships to over 7000 students from the region to study in Turkish universities and other vocational and educational institutions.[16]

This, in turn, was a symptom of another problem. Having gone through a revolution only a decade earlier, Iran was yet to formulate a comprehensive foreign policy. Preoccupation with domestic issues as well as the ideological weight of the Revolution prevented Tehran from forging a long-term policy, congruent with its national interests, towards the rest of the world, including Central Asia. This has meant vacillations and repeated policy changes resulting in confusion. A case in point is the frequent changes in Iran's export and import policies. After the break-up of the Soviet Union Iranian entrepreneurs managed to gain a foothold in the food and clothing markets of Kazakhstan, Turkmenistan, and Gyrghizistan. The severe currency policy adopted by Tehran in 1995 wiped out most of Iranian commercial presence in Central Asia in a matter of months.

Yet another very important obstacle to the implementation of Iran's policy toward Central Asia has been the environment in which the country's private sector has had to operate. In spite of the fact that economic cooperation has been seen by Tehran as a vital tool in Central Asia, the political will to support the Iranian private sector in the region has not been forthcoming. Iran's economic activities in the region have not enjoyed the support of the government. This, once again, is in sharp contrast to Turkey, where from soon after the Soviet collapse, Ankara enthusiastically encouraged and supported the Turkish private sector's involvement in the region.

There were other factors that hampered Iran's efforts to gain her objectives in the region. One such factor had to do with Iran's image problem. There was a view that the presence of the Islamic Republic in the region was a source of instability, both through backing of radical Islam and through providing a model of government for the predominantly Muslim peoples of Central Asia. Iran's image in the world as an outlaw state that condones terrorism and Islamic fundamentalism was mainly a product of the US and the Western media that have had their own agenda vis-à-vis the Islamic Republic.[17] Yet, increasingly, the rest of the world, including Central Asia, depended on and had its views shaped by these media. This, of course, had as much to do with Iran's own neglect of its image as it did with the Western media.

Yet another obstacle has been the political antagonism between the United States and Iran since the Islamic Revolution terminated the US's privileged position in the country. The United States has used its power and influence against Iran, such as in blocking Iran's initiatives in the Nogurno-Karabakh dispute and blocking the National Iranian Oil Company's membership in the Azerbaijani oil consortium in spite of Iran's legitimate and logical right to be a partner in the enterprise.

## The Caspian Sea

Since the collapse of the Soviet Union, the Caspian Sea has become an important issue, affecting the relations of the countries of the region. The Caspian Sea region includes the littoral states – Iran, Turkmenistan, Kazakhstan, Russia and Azerbaijan – and also Uzbekistan, which, even though not a littoral state, has one of the region's highest gas reserves.

Prior to the collapse of the Soviet Union, the Sea was shared between its only two littoral states, the Soviet Union and Iran. The two countries' relations in the Caspian were governed by 1921 and 1940 accords. The first accords between Iran and Russia were signed in 1723 in Saint Petersburg and the northern Iranian town of Rash. The Turkamanchai treaty that was signed between the two in 1828, after Iran's disastrous defeat in the Caucasus, took away Iran's shipping rights in the Caspian. The 1921 treaty with the revolutionary government of the Soviet Union gave back that right. In theory, the two had the right to use all parts of the Sea together. In practice, the Soviet Union maintained a naval force, whereas Iran didn't. Iran limited itself to the southern part of the Sea. While both the Soviet republics of Azerbaijan and Kazakhstan did produce oil, there was no off-shore drilling in the Caspian Sea. Fishing, especially caviar, was the main economic activity in the Sea, and both Iran and the Soviet Union benefited from it.

After the break-up, and the emergence of the new independent states, at Iran's initiative the Organization of Caspian States was formed. It has had thirteen ministerial-level meetings since it began work in 1992. The signing of the Environmental Convention of the Caspian in 1995 has been an achievement for the organization. Finding a solution to the legal status of the sea has proved a lot more difficult. It has been the subject of debate since the collapse of the Soviet Union and the emergence of the newly independent states. Iran's position has been that the legal status has not changed and should still be governed by the 1921 and 1940 treaties. Therefore, the new littoral states should share the Sea.

Initially, most of the littoral states, including the Soviet Union, held the same position. As the prospects of extraction of oil and gas became clearer in the Caspian Sea region, both on and off shore, the countries benefiting most from oil opted for dividing the Sea. This would particularly be advantageous to Azerbaijan and Kazakhstan who can drill for oil off their shores in the Caspian. The practical involvement of Western companies in the Caspian Sea region's oil and the political pressure by the United States forced Russia to abandon its position. The consensus is moving toward dividing the seabed, while sharing the surface.

This would be the worst solution as far as Iran is concerned; the best caviar of the Caspian Sea is near its southern shore within Iran's territorial waters, while oil and gas reserves are close to Kazakhstan, Azerbaijan and Turkmenistan. Despite Iran's objections, the division of the Caspian Sea seems set to go ahead anyway. As the division becomes more and more a reality, talks are focused on the percentage of the sea that each of the littoral states takes. If the two northernmost points of its borders (Astara in the west to Hassanquli in the east) were connected, with 832 kilometres of shore on the Caspian, Iran would get only 14 per cent of the Sea. Azerbaijan, on the other hand, would get 18 per cent with 760 kilometres of shore. This is because of the concave shape of Iran's shores.

Azerbaijan claims that throughout the Soviet period Iran never crossed the Astara-Hassanquli line and therefore the Sea was in fact divided between the Soviet Union and Iran. It further contends that north of the Astara-Hassanquli was under Soviet control, and in fact, in 1960 the Ministry of Industries of the Soviet Union had divided this northern portion of the Caspian between its four littoral republics. This, claims the Azerbaijani government, amounted to a de facto division and Iran never expressed any objection to this act. In fact, when in 1994 Azerbaijan started explorations in the area Iran did not register any objections. Iran, on the other hand, claims that this was an internal memo between these republics and not a mutually agreed international division.

The question, however, is not just the percentage of the Sea that each of the two countries will get. Azerbaijan has done explorations in the Caspian, but has not as yet started drilling. The issue between the two countries boils down to the Guneshli oil field that is claimed by both Iran and Azerbaijan. Iran has said it would start exploration in the area and Azerbaijan has expressed the desire to actually start drilling. If and when either of these happens, it would become a point of contention between Iran and Azerbaijan.[18]

In May 2003, Kazakhstan, Russia and Azerbaijan signed an accord according to which they divided 64 per cent of the north of the Caspian into three unequal parts along a median line principle. Thus, Russia would get 19 per cent and Azerbaijan would have 18 per cent, and Kazakhstan would have 27 per cent of the Sea. Iran and Turkmenistan, did take part in the meeting, but refused to sign the agreement. This means the development of the hydrocarbon potential in the northern part of the Caspian will go ahead.[19]

## The pipelines

Another important issue directly related to the legal status of the Sea and affecting Iran's relations with her Central Asian neighbours has been the transferring of Central Asia and the Caucasus' energy to the rest of the world. The discovery after the collapse of the Soviet Union of the magnitude of the hydrocarbon reserves in the Caspian region immediately posed a critical question: what are the best routes for the energy to be delivered to consumers in the rest of the world? The existing pipelines pointed north to Russia. This meant the newly independent states of Central Asia and Azerbaijan on the Caucasus would be dependent on Russia to get their oil to the world market. Involvement of Western companies and pressure by Western governments, especially the United States, initiated a number of studies to find alternative routes in order to avoid Russia. The Russian route, known as CPC (Caspian Petroleum Consortium), was the first major pipeline to become operational. With a maximum capacity of one million barrels per day, it pumps oil from Kazakhstan's Tengiz oil fields east of the Caspian via Russia to the Russian port of Novorosisk on the Black Sea.

The governments of the United States and Turkey have been pushing for the Baku–Tiblisi–Ceyhan route that would pump oil from Azerbaijan's oil fields of Baku on the eastern shore of the Caspian Sea via the Georgian town of Tiblisi in the Caucasus to the Turkish port of Ceyhan on the Mediterranean Sea. This is the most expensive among the proposed routes. For it to be economical, Azerbaijan's and Turkmenistan's oil would not suffice: Kazakhstan's oil must also be pumped through this pipeline. Kazakhstan's government has already committed itself to CPC and is heavily in favour of the southern route through Iran to the Persian Gulf (see below). In spite of political pressure by the United States and Turkish governments, the oil companies avoided the project until 2002, when it finally got underway. When completed, it is expected to have a capacity of one million barrels per day.

Given Iran's strategic location as having the shortest and most economical routes for the transfer of the Caspian region's energy, the southern route via Iran has been a favourite of the Central Asian governments and the oil companies. However, the United States sanctions against foreign companies doing business with Iran have prevented the pipeline from being constructed. In spite of that, Iran has managed to enter into 'oil swap' deals with neighbouring Kazakhstan and Turkmenistan. Iran's oil fields are in the south of the country near the Persian Gulf. Domestic consumption, however, is mainly in the north, closer to the Caspian. There is, therefore, a network of pipelines and refineries that pump and process oil from the south to the north of the country. With relatively small cost, Iran has redirected its pipelines from north to south. Via swap arrangements, Iran receives oil from Kazakhstan and Turkmenistan, uses it domestically in the north, and delivers its own oil from the southern fields close to the Persian Gulf on behalf of the two countries. Whereas the construction of pipelines like Bakau–Tiblisi–Ceyhan cost billions of dollars, the cost of redirecting existing pipelines for the oil swap has not exceeded $500 million. The first two phases of the project have been completed and over 120,000 barrels of oil are exchanged through the swap arrangement. The final phase that is expected to be completed in the current year increases the capacity to 500,000 barrels per day.[20]

## Relations with the Central Asian countries

Tajikistan is the poorest of the Central Asian countries. The Russian army still patrols its borders, and it is the only country among the former Soviet republics that still uses the Russian rouble as its currency. Tajikistan has no border with Iran. Yet, a special relationship has developed between the two countries. The fact that Tajiks and Iranians speak the same language has a lot to do with this relationship. Iran's limited involvement in the politics of the early days of independence seems to be a thing of the past. Economic relations between the two do exist but are limited, because of the geographical factor as well as Iran's inability to meaningfully invest in that country. The two countries' relations have developed and continue to expand along cultural lines.

Kyrgyzstan is also a poor country and has no border with Iran. Its small size and economy does not leave much room for expanded economic relations between the two countries. As in Tajikistan, a limited presence of the Iranian private sector can be seen there.

Uzbekistan shares no border with Iran. It is, nevertheless, a very important country in the region, both economically and politically. Uzbekistan's relations with Iran since the emergence of the Independent State have been minimal. Iran's image since the Islamic Revolution as a country that stirs up radical religious sentiments has been a decisive factor. Iran's lack of any action to correct the misperception is to blame. Yet, the main obstacle in the way of establishment of close relations with Uzbekistan has been the Uzbek government. Arguably, of all the former Soviet republics in Central Asia, Uzbekistan has undergone the least amount of political change. The authoritarian state with deep suspicion of foreigners still persists in Uzbekistan.

In the case of Iran, the Uzbek authorities were particularly concerned. The concern seems to have been twofold. One concern, understandably though not justifiably, was a fear of Iran's possible involvement in encouraging religious activism in Uzbekistan. The other concern has to do with the sizeable Tajik population of Uzbekistan. Though an accurate figure is hard to come by, moderate estimates put the number of Tajiks at ten million. That is nearly 45 per cent of the population of Uzbekistan. In fact, almost the entire population of the important cities such as Samarkand, Bukhara and Khiva are Persian-speaking Tajiks.

There has not been a strong nationalist or separatist movement by Tajiks, but the Uzbek government seems extremely sensitive about the issue. The government has forcefully implemented policies of 'Uzbekification' since independence. The concern over Tajiks has been directed toward Tajikistan as well. The mining of Uzbek–Tajik borders by the Uzbek government and the refusal of visas to Tajiks of Tajikistan wishing to visit their relatives in Uzbekistan are examples. Only in the past couple of years does there seem to have been signs of a small change in Tashkent's attitude toward the Islamic Republic of Iran.

Economic relations between Turkmenistan and Iran have been on the increase in the past decade. Turkmenistan realizes Iran's transit value as a neighbour that connects this land-locked country directly to the Persian Gulf and the open seas. The two countries have undertaken and completed a number of joint projects: the 'Friendship Dam', Sarakhs–Mashhad railway, and the transfer of electric power and gas are among them.

Through completion of the railway project, the border town of Sarakhs is connected to the major city of Mashhad in north east of the country. Iran completed the construction of the railway between Bandar Abbas on the

Persian Gulf to Bafq in the north – which was already connected to Mashhad. This means there is now a direct north–south route of about 950 Km that connects Turkmenistan to the Persian Gulf and can serve as the shortest transit route for that country. The capacity of the railway system in Iran needs to be drastically increased in order to fulfil this expectation. A year after the signing of an agreement between Iran and Turkmenistan, the second line of electricity transfer was inaugurated on 23 August 2004. Based on the contract signed between the two countries, Turkmenistan will export $500 million of electricity to Iran in the next ten years.[21]

Iran is also the transit route for Turkmenistan's gas to Turkey. Following the signing of the contract during the short premiership of Nejmeddin Erbakan, Iran and Turkey completed a pipeline that provides Turkey with natural gas from Turkmenistan. The completion of the project was delayed several times, and since its completion the two sides have had to renegotiate the deal because of Turkey's demand that the price be lowered. The oil swap arrangement continues with Turkmenistan and is expected to increase in the coming years. The volume of trade between Iran and Turkmenistan, which stood at about $600 million last year, is expected to reach $1,000,000.[22]

Iran's relations with Kazakhstan, the largest of the Central Asian countries, have evolved more than anything else around energy. Iranian businessmen are active in food and textile markets in Kazakhstan, but their volume is minute compared to that in oil. Oil swap deals continue between the two countries. In June, 2004, Kazakhstan's Prime Minister, Danial Akhmetov, announced that Almaty planned to build two oil terminals in Iran after a lucrative oil swap export arrangement had been concluded with Tehran. The terminals that are to be built by Kazmunaygas and Kaznafta will have a capacity of 1.5 million tonnes of oil annually. Kazakhstan has also been studying a project with the French oil giant, *Total*, for construction of a pipeline through Turkmenistan to Iran.[23]

## Conclusion

There is a great deal of activity by outside countries in Central Asia. Russia still enjoys considerable clout in the region as well as political influence and an economic advantage. Turkey has already embarked on a long-term initiative in Central Asia and the Caucasus. China with a long border with the region and an expanding export capability has not hesitated to lay the foundations for exploiting the commercial and economic opportunities in Central Asia. Finally, the United States has found 9/11 a convenient pretext to extend its military presence and influence in the Caucasus and Central Asia.

Twelve years after the collapse of the Soviet Union, the countries of Central Asia and the Caucasus are becoming better known to themselves and to the outside world. The initial uncertainties about their form of government, currency transfer, tax laws (or the lack of them) concerning foreign investment and their foreign policy inclinations are becoming clear. The outside world has begun to forge its political and economic relations with the region. Iran, too, has by now reached an understanding of the dynamics of the situation to its north. State-to-state deals on trade and on transfer of energy have been struck with Turkmenistan and Kazakhstan. A special relationship has evolved between Iran and Persian-speaking Tajikistan. Uzbekistan still remains an unwilling partner. Iran has looked to ECO as a vehicle for cooperation and gaining influence in the region.[24] However, as long as the member states continue to prefer bilateral economic relations with Russia or the developed countries in the West, ECO's potential as a powerful regional organization integrating the economies of the region remains in doubt.

Despite its tremendous potential, Iran's level of influence in the region remains relatively small. It can be argued that Iran has pursued a rational and positive course of action in Central Asia and the Caucasus. In spite of the presence of radical views among some circles within the Islamic government, Iran has been an advocate of unity and economic cooperation in Central Asia based on a common history and culture rather than radical Islam. Long-term economic, political and cultural relations with Iran can be beneficial to all the states in the region. In fact, in the wake of 9/11 and the rise of extreme and violent Islamic radicalism – like that of the Taliban – in the region, Iran can be a moderating influence.

## Notes

1  Saideh, Lotfian, 'Kazakhstan's Nuclear Status and Regional Security', *Amu Darya*, I (1996): 254.
2  Ibid., p. 247.
3  Ibid., pp. 252–253.
4  See Seyyed Mohammad Kazem Sajjadpur, 'Negaresh-ha-ye Mowjud dar Gharb darbareh-ye Raftar-e Iran ba Jomhuri-ha-ye Shawravi-ye Sabeq' (The West's Views on Iran's Behaviour Toward the Republics of the Former Soviet Union), *Motale'at-e Asiya-e Markazi va Qafqaz*, I (1992): 101.
5  Piruz Mojtahedzadeh, 'Didgah-ha-ye Iran dar Rabeteh ba Darya-ye Khazar, Asiya-ye Markazi, Khalij-e Fars, wa Khavar-e Miyaneh' (Iran's Views on the Caspian Sea, Central Asia, the Persian Gulf and the Middle East), *Ettila'at-e Siasi-Eqtisadi*, IX (1995): 8.
6  See Fereydun Barkeshli, 'Mulahezati Darbareh-ye Esteratezhi-ha-ye Mantaqeh'i-ye Jomhuri-ye Islami-ye Iran' (Some Notes on the Islamic Republic of Iran's Regional Strategies) *Manabe' va Zarfiyatha-ye Eqtesadi-e Asiya-ye Markazi va Qafqaz*, ed. Seyyed Rasul Musavi (Tehran 1995).
7  www.doe.gov/styles/EIAfooterjustu.js
8  Mojtahedzadeh, 'Didgah-ha-ye Iran dar Rabeteh ba Darya-ye Khazar, Asiya-ye Markazi, Khalij-e Fars, wa Khavar-e Miyaneh', p. 8.
9  Abbas Maleki's address to China's Institute of International Affairs in June 1992, in 'Ravabet-e Iran va Jomhuri-ha-ye Asiya-ye Markazi' (Iran's Relations with the Republics of Central Asia), *Motale'at-e Asiya-e Markazi va Qafqeaz, I* (1993)1: 5.
10  *Motale'at-e Asiya-e Markazi va Qafqaz, I* (1992)1: 4.
11  Maleki, 'Ravabet-e Iran va Jomhuri-ha-ye Asiya-ye Markazi', pp. 9–10. Apparently, he had not yet been aware of the huge gas reserves under Turkmenistan and the oil reserves in Kazakhstan and Azerbaijan.
12  Extensive interviews during a six-week stay for a related project in Central Asia in the Autumn of 1994 clearly demonstrated this to the author.
13  The inaugural speech delivered by Dr Velayati at the seminar on 'Security and Foreign Policy in Central Asia and the Caucasus', held at I.P.I.S., Tehran, 14–16 January, 1996.

For the text of the speech, see 'The Constructive Role of the Islamic Republic of Iran in Maintaining Regional Security', *Amu Darya*, I & II (1996): 183–189.

14 Abbas Maleki, Assistant Foreign Minister for Research and Training, addressing the Iran-o-Russian Round-table, 4–5 October 1995, in Moscow. In an obvious reference to the United States, he correctly observed, 'In the so-called new world order, some states have gone as far as redefining the interests of nations and entire continents in terms of their own; for instance, they place the Persian Gulf, the Mediterranean and even the Central Asian states within their "security sphere"'. For the text of the speech, see 'The Prospects of Iran-o-Russian Relations till the Year 2000', *Amu Darya*, I (1996)2: 191–199.

15 President Hashemi Rafsanjani's address to the conference on 'Security and Foreign Policy in Central Asia and the Caucasus', held at I.P.I.S., Tehran, 13–15 January 1995. See 'Jomhuri-ye Islami-ye Iran va Keshvar-ha-ye Jadid ol-bonyad' (The Islamic Republic of Iran and the newly founded states), *Motale'at-e Asiya-e Markazi va Qafqaz*, V(1996): 9.

16 By the end of 1993, over 10,000 students were attending schools in Turkey. See Anthony Hyman, 'Central Asia and the Middle East: the Emerging Links', *Central Asia and the Caucasus after the Soviet Union*, ed. Mohiaddin Mesbahi (Florida, 1994): 258.

17 See Mahmud Sariolqalam, 'Shenakht-e Esteratezhi-ye Amrika Nesbat beh Iran va Khavar-e Miyaneh' (American Strategy in Iran and the Middle East), *Faslnameh-ye Khavar-e Miyaneh*, II (1995)2: 304–305.

18 Personal interview with Dr Seyyed Rasul Musavi, Director of the Centre for Central Asia and the Caucasus, Institute for Political and International Studies, Ministry of Foreign Affairs, Tehran, 28 April 2004.

19 www.eia.doe.gov/emeu/cabs/casplaw.html

20 Amir Hossein Tahqiqi, 'Rah Nazdiktar Mishavad; Enteqal-e Naft-e Asiya-ye Miyaneh az Rah-e Iran', *Jahan-e Enerzhi*, I (2003): 15–18.

21 www. bbcpesian.com (accessed 23 August 2004).

22 *IRNA*, 17 April 2004.

23 *Agence France Press*, 19 June 2004.

24 Economic Cooperation Organization. After the Islamic Revolution, at Iran's initiative RCD – a regional organization whose members were Iran, Turkey and Pakistan – was changed to ECO. After the break-up of the Soviet Union, the Central Asian states were invited to join the organization.

# 9 Israeli–Iranian relations assessed

## Strategic competition from the power cycle perspective

*Trita Parsi*

## Introduction

Iran's foreign policy is believed to have lost much of its ideological zeal after the death of Khomeini. One often-cited exception to this general pattern is Iran's relations with Israel. Tehran's posture on Israel and the Middle East peace process is often explained as a remnant of its revolutionary and ideological past and contradictory to Iran's national interest. However, this analysis neglects crucial systemic changes that occurred in the Middle East after 1991, as well as Israel's willingness to improve relations with Iran at the height of Iran's revolutionary fervour in the 1980s and the Islamic regime's refusal to allow ideological considerations to stand in its way to purchase arms from Israel. Furthermore, it reduces Israel's role in the equation to that of a non-player whose destiny is limited to mere reactions to Iran's ideological designs.

The disintegration of the Soviet Union and the defeat of Saddam Hussein in 1991 eliminated the two common threats that had enabled strong common strategic interests to exist for more than three decades. In addition, the Oslo Accords put the final nail in the coffin of the Peripheral Alliance Doctrine that had guided Israel's foreign policy since the late 1950s and induced the Jewish state to forge close ties with the region's non-Arab states in the periphery – Iran, Turkey and Ethiopia – in order to weaken the Arab inner circle.

So why did relations between Israel and Iran take a sharp turn for the worse after the first Persian Gulf War in spite of Iran's increasingly pragmatic foreign policy and outreach to the US? Why did Israel, who in 1987 had referred to Iran as a 'geostrategic friend', label Iran a 'global threat' in 1992? Why did Iran, who initially declared that it would accept any deal acceptable to the Palestinians, become the principal opponent of the Middle East peace process?

This article attempts to shed light on the nature of Israeli–Iranian relations in the post-Cold War era and to explain the root causes of their state of relations in the early to mid-1990s from the perspective of Charles Doran's power cycle theory. It will discern an often-overlooked strategic logic – rooted in the distribution of power in the region and the rivalry for relative power share and role – that fuels the hostile relations between the two former allies. It is based on secondary sources as well as interviews of Israeli, Iranian and American officials and analysts, conducted in Iran, Israel and the United States between February and October 2004.

## The current debate

Numerous scholars have characterized Iran's Israel policy as radical and contrary to Iran's national interest and point to Iran's ideological orientation as the principal cause of this deviation from a rational and self-interested foreign policy. Menashri argues that Iran has turned the Palestinian–Israeli conflict into a religious issue.[1] Sariolghalam points out that 'remnants of ideological thinking especially towards the United States and Israel' can still be found in institutions dealing with foreign policy.[2] Chubin argues that the clergy's anti-Israeli posture has become a source of legitimacy for the regime, an 'area in which the regime can claim to be principled and unique'.[3]

Takeyh contends that 'Iran's international orientation has undergone a steady yet halting march toward pragmatism', but that policies on key issues such as the Israeli–Palestinian peace process continue 'to derive from a self-defeating ideological calculus'.[4] The alleged underlying ideological (and irrational) sources of Iran's Israel policy are also implicitly referred to by voices in Tehran who criticize the government for being 'more catholic than the pope', arguing that Iran should not be more pro-Palestinian than the Palestinians themselves.[5]

Sobhani goes a step further and posits that Iran and Israel are natural allies and that this alliance is 'a permanent and powerful feature of Iranian–Israeli relations' that has only temporarily been neutralized because of the fundamentalist character of the regime in Tehran. Sobhani believes that their relations will revert to their normal state of being, that is, an anti-Arab alliance, once the fundamentalist regime has fallen and a secular government has been reinstalled in Tehran.[6]

While the ideological dimensions of Iran's foreign policy are accounted for in most studies, Israel's Iran policy is rarely characterized as ideological. Rather, the dangers of Iran's ideological orientation and expansionism are often cited as an explanation for Israeli worries, that is, Israel's Iran policy is seen as a rational response to Iran's ideological and irrational Israel policy. Oftentimes, Israel's response is explained by the notion of a balance of threats: with Iraq defeated and sanctioned, Israel sees Iran as the only country left in the region with an offensive capability that can threaten Israel.[7] Iran's repeated calls for the destruction of Israel do little to ease the fears of decision-makers in Tel Aviv, even though such demands were also made during the years in which Israel tried to revive its alliance with Iran.

With Iran's quest for nuclear technology, which would be able to deter Israel's nuclear capacity, Tel Aviv's concerns and fears were further strengthened. In the early 1990s, Israel started to depict Iran and its nuclear programme 'as a lethal threat to Israel'.[8] Shimon Peres writes in 1993 that Iran is 'insane', that it seeks to destroy Israel, and he points out that the defeat of Iraq has made Iran a strategic superpower[9] (Peres' rhetoric mimics that of Ayatollah Khomeini, who in the 1980s christened the Zionist regime a 'cancerous tumor').[10] Furthermore, Israel's enmity toward Iran is also seen as a response to Iran's support for militant anti-Israeli groups such as Hezbollah and Islamic Jihad.

However, others argue that Israel's perspective is also coloured by the ideology of its military and strategic doctrine. The neo-revisionist school of Zionism as professed by Jabotinsky posits that the non-Jewish world is inherently and permanently anti-Semitic.[11] According to the interconnected strategic ideas of this ideology, Israel will never be accepted in the Middle East, and, as a result, there can never be peace in the region, only victory through the military defeat of Israel's neighbours. Since this strategic doctrine foresees a final battle between Israel and its neighbours as inevitable, Israel is left with no choice but to seek preponderance and military supremacy.[12] Consequently, any country with a potential to become a threat is perceived as a threat, that is, the criteria of what should and should not be perceived as a threat differs greatly from regimes that do not hold the neo-revisionists' worldview, which is deemed fatalistic and apocalyptic by its critics.[13] Aspects of this worldview, in turn, have a significant impact on Israel's balance of threat calculations.

Critics of the Israeli alarmists point out that Iran's nuclear programme was terminated by Khomeini and only restarted in the late 1980s as a deterrent against Iraq and not Israel.[14] (According to one senior Iranian official, Iran deterrence against Israel through its proxies in Lebanon is sufficient, rendering nuclear weapons redundant.)[15] Some Israeli academics criticize what they deem to be an exaggerated Iranian threat picture.[16] Others argue that Israel's quest for supremacy has provoked the Middle East arms race while pointing out that Iran's arms purchases have been exaggerated in the West.[17] The notion that Israel's policy vis-à-vis Iran is determined by the ideological clash between the two countries begs the question of why that same ideology did not prevent Israel from seeking extensive cooperation with Iran in the 1980s.

## Theoretical framework

*The Middle East sub-system*   Realism is the dominating paradigm in international relations. Characterized by its hard-boiled willingness to see the world as it is and study international relations as an objective reality, it lacks normative guiding principles. It deals with what is and not with what ought to be. Using the metaphor of anarchy to describe the international system, realists argue that the only order is that which emerges from competition between states – the system's principal players – under anarchy. Realists posit that states are rational players whose primary purpose is to secure their own survival, irrespective of their internal political make-up. Security, in turn, is achieved by maximizing power.

In the words of Kenneth Waltz, the international system is a self-help system in which a nation's security cannot be ensured except through their own actions.[18] Yet, it is not a world of constant conflict. Stein describes the realist worldview as not necessarily one of perpetual warfare, but of perpetual conflict since crises are recurring and inevitable.[19] Tracing their intellectual lineage to Machiavelli and Thucydides, realists refrain from putting their faith in international law and institutions, arguing that treaties cannot affect the fundamental principles of international relations.

Neo-realism shares the basic assumptions of realism, but takes a systemic approach and emphasizes the structure of the international system and its affect on the interacting units and vice versa. Waltz posits that a system is composed of a structure and interacting units in which the definition of the structure is free of the attributes and the interactions of the units. The manoeuvrability of the states is limited by the structure of the system, which constitutes the setting in which states interact.

Constructivists, on the other hand, contend that international politics is 'socially constructed'. Alexander Wendt writes that the fundamental structures of world politics are social and not material and that these structures shape players identities and interests and not just their behaviour.[20] Unlike realists, who see conflicts as a result of the clash of power and interests, constructivists believe that ideas matter greatly since power and interest do not have effects, apart from the shared knowledge that constitutes them as such. Thus, identities and interests are endogenous to interaction, an idea that differs from the rational–behavioural interpretation in which interests are exogenous.[21]

These theories fit the realities of state-to-state interaction differently from region to region. It is often argued that the Middle East is best explained by the neo-realist or realist paradigm, due to the absence of strong institutions, the lack of a normative framework guiding the interaction of the Middle East states, and the Machiavellian nature of its politics.[22] Furthermore, unlike the European system, the Middle East lacks a consensus on the hierarchy of states, in which states, by and large, seek to increase their relative power only through acceptable, non-military avenues and in which all states have accepted the dynamic of how role should be granted to rising states or withdrawn from declining states.

No such order and normative framework exist in the Middle East. Many of its states are new to statecraft and the system has yet to reach equilibrium; in this case, neither the hierarchy for role nor relative power has been set – everything is up for grabs. There are almost as many would-be hegemonies as there are states in the Middle East. Many states can be characterized as anti-status quo states that actively seek to keep their options open by undermining any possible equilibrium. In addition, the lack of a normative framework, that is, an implicit agreement on the accepted rules of interaction and competition, creates an atmosphere in which states often resort to instigation of instability in neighbouring states and support for terrorist groups and secessionist movements. In short, the gloves are always off in the Middle East.

These factors all make the Middle East suitable for explanation through the power-cycle theory. Doran's differentiation between power and role is essential for understanding the hegemonic driving forces of Middle Eastern states. Furthermore, it explains why smaller states in the Middle East do not let their role aspirations be hampered by their moderate relative power share, since relative power share does not necessarily dictate role distribution.

*The power cycle theory*   Charles Doran's theory puts decision-making about wars in the context of the rise and decline of the relative power of states. Doran argues that states follow a cyclical path of growth, maturation and decline that mainly stems from uneven rates of internal economic development.[23] According to Parsaliti, 'power is an analytical construct – it is not a physical thing that can be directly measured'.[24]

Nonetheless, an index of power can be constructed that includes and reflects commonly recognized measures of state size and development. By employing both economic and military variables, that is, military expenditure, population, GDP, GDP per capita, energy consumption and military size, the relevance of both economic and military power in international relations is reflected, as well as the distinction between 'latent' and 'actualized' power. Power is calculated for each state based on these variables, which are then scored relative to the other states in the system. Although these variables do not account for intentions, technology, WMDs and military reach, they do provide an opportunity to trace the state's evolution relative to the system, that is, the state's surroundings. Although structural changes do not determine the state's foreign policies, they do 'define the environment, the influences and constraints in which foreign policy decisions occur'.[25]

The power cycle depicts the *relative* power of a state, where a state's relative power depends just as much on the power of other states as on its own internal growth and decline. A state can increase in absolute power and yet experience a decline in relative power if its growth is less than the systemic norm. An increase in relative power for one state always corresponds to a decrease in relative power for another state or states. This is the main reason strategic competition for relative power share is endemic to the system.

The theory develops the concept of foreign policy role as representing foreign policy behaviour. It is in the dynamics of state capability and role that we can find the major cause for war. Role is defined as the currency of power in the system and is necessarily systemic; *it is the state's ability to exercise its power without consuming it.* Unlike power, however, role is granted to a state by the other members of the system.

The slope of the relative power (role) curve at any specific point measures the rate of growth of relative power (role) at that specific time. It also represents the state's projection of future relative power (role).[26] The derivative of the cycle reverses from increasing to decreasing or positive to negative at four critical points along the cycle. An abrupt inversion takes place in the path of relative capabilities at each of these infliction points at which the *projection* of relative capability and future interests and role radically change.[27]

Minimizing the discrepancy between a state's relative power and role is instrumental, and a state's failure to adjust to a significant change in its projected future ability to lead and implement statecraft (i.e. role) in combination with the failure of other members of the system to cope and adjust to such a change can cause the collapse of the equilibrium and create a setting out of which a major war can grow.[28] In this study, we will focus on developing the concept of strategic competition, that is, the competition for relative power and role between states that precedes the reaching of critical stages of the power cycle.

*Strategic competition* The case of Germany and Russia.[29] Doran depicts the trauma of role adjustment that accompanies critical changes in relative power and demonstrates why the disequilibrated system between 1885 and 1914 led to massive world war. Competition for relative power share often does not primarily take place at the top of the system. In the case of World War I, Germany's main competitor for power share was tiny and fast-growing Russia at the bottom of the system and not Britain or France.

By the time Bismarck had left the German helm, France, Britain and Austria–Hungary were in substantial relative decline. Underdeveloped Russia was at the bottom of the central system, and Germany was the rising newcomer. None of the declining states was willing to make room in terms of status for Germany, much less for an enhanced foreign policy role.

The mechanisms of balance of power caused ascending states to be viewed as hostile to the security and stability of the system. As a result, leading states tried to offset the rise of any ambitious newcomer. Doran argues that by 'subjugating the rising state to superior power, the balance of power sought to forgo any accommodation with the rising state'. By masking the need for role adjustment, the alliances exacerbated the disequilibria beyond a level that the system could tolerate without causing statecraft to fracture. As long as Germany could anticipate further increase in its relative power, postponed role gratification could be tolerated. But in Germany's peak hour in terms of absolute power growth, 'tiny but faster-growing Russia suddenly forced it into relative decline', argues Doran.

Counter to expectations, it was not France or England that constituted Germany's key competitors for power share in the system, but tiny Russia. By rising very fast, it was Russia, and not Berlin's traditional rivals, that took power shares from Germany and halted its increase in relative power. Similarly, Parsaliti shows that Iraq's key competition for relative power in the early 1990s was not Iran, Iraq's traditional rival, but Saudi Arabia and Kuwait.[30]

*Theoretical development* Strategic competition. The power cycle theory states that competition between states for relative power shares or role is endemic to the system and by definition a zero-sum relationship. Although all states can simultaneously grow in absolute power in an 'expand the pie' fashion, no state can by definition grow in relative power (or role) without the concurrent decline in the relative power of another state or states.

This begs the question of who competes with whom in the system. Although the power cycle theory pictures a Hobbesian state of affairs at some periods along the growth and decline of a state's relative power, its power cycle tends to be parallel, converging, or diverging vis-à-vis those of other states.

Positively aligned or parallel power cycles indicate a state of potential strategic alliance; an increase in one state's relative power tends to coincide with (or stimulate) an increase in the other state's relative power. Converging or diverging power cycles indicate a state of strategic competition – the states compete for the same power share because an increase in one state's relative power coincides with a decrease (or decreased growth rate) in the others' relative power.

Various degrees of relative economic integration and the existence of common threats are factors that determine the alignment of power cycles. This interconnectedness explains why an increase in the relative power of one state does not get dispersed into a proportionate decrease in the relative power of all other states in the system according to their relative power share. Rather, some states suffer a disproportionate decrease in their relative power while others remain unaffected or even benefit from the growth of the other state.

A distinction needs to be made between competition between states seeking the domination of the system (hegemonic competition) and competition purely for relative power share (strategic competition). These forms of competition do not necessarily coincide. Whereas hegemonic competition takes place exclusively at the top of the system and is primarily focused on competition for role, strategic competition can take place between states throughout the system and is focused more on relative power share; (hegemonic contenders aim to possess the largest chunk of relative power in the system, but do not necessarily compete with each other for the same relative power shares).

## Iran, Israel and the quest for domination

*Israeli–Iranian relations 1979–1991*    The fall of the Shah was a major setback for Israel. It weakened Israel's security environment, but did not affect Israel's geostrategic objectives. As a result, although the revolution transformed Israeli–Iranian relations from a quiet entente to intense antagonism on the surface, geopolitical forces quickly compelled Israel to use its Iranian channels to seek clandestine relations with moderates within the revolutionary leadership.[31] Indeed, the Iranian revolution created many complications, but it did not end Israeli attempts to pursue its policy of peripheral alliances.[32] Decision-makers in Tel Aviv viewed Khomeini as a passing phenomenon and focused on maintaining their political access to Tehran for the post-Khomeini era.[33] Israel had invested too much in Iran and could not afford to lose Tehran as a geostrategic partner and a counterweight to the Arabs and Sadat, whose increasingly warm relations with the US threatened Israel's influence in Washington.[34]

During the Iraq–Iran war, Tel Aviv feared that an Iraqi victory would bolster the Arabs and weaken Israel's position. Israel's Foreign Minister Ephraim Evron even sought US cooperation in providing the Iranians with weaponry at the height of the Hostage Crisis.[35] On 28 September 1980, only days after the outbreak of war, Defence Minister Mordechai Zippori publicly offered Israel's assistance to Iran, granted a change in Iran's policy vis-à-vis Tel Aviv.[36] Three days later at a press conference in Vienna, Moshe Dayan urged the United States to forget the past and help Iran keep up its defences. These were not empty promises. Iran's attempt to bomb Saddam Hussein's nuclear facilities in Osirak was conducted with Israeli assistance and intelligence, according to a former Iranian official. The operation failed, however, leading Israel to conduct its own bombing campaign on 7 June 1981, effectively pushing back Iraq's WMD programme more than a decade.[37]

The Jewish state viewed support to Iran as contributing to Israel's security by further splitting the Arabs. A continuation of the war helped keep eyes away from the Arab–Israeli conflict and directed Arab financial and military resources towards Iraq and away from the Palestinians.[38] Israel even offered to help Iran circumvent the US blockade in return for political access.[39]

The two Israeli leaders who in the early 1990s initiated a very aggressive Iran policy pursued a diametrically opposite policy only a few years earlier. In 1987, Yitzhak Rabin argued that Iran remained an ally geopolitically.[40] Shimon Peres, who sought a 'broader strategic relationship with Iran', urged President Reagan to seek a dialogue with Tehran. [41]

This was at the centre of the 'Iran-Contra' affair, in which Israel pressured the US to improve relations with Iran and sell advanced American arms to the Khomeini regime.[42] The affair was initiated by Amiram Nir, a close aide to Shimon Peres, who floated the idea of selling arms to Iran in Washington in the mid-1980s. The idea was rejected by the State Department and the Pentagon, but it found support in National Security Council operatives, Oliver North and Michael Ledeen.[43] (Ledeen, a personal acquaintance of Peres, was convinced by the Israelis to pursue a US opening to Iran.[44] Today, he is one of the most vocal opponents of US–Iran talks and advocates a policy of regime-change in Tehran on the grounds that Iran opposes Israel's right to exist.) Israel's key argument was that Iran would once again become an explicit ally of the two if moderate elements in Tehran were strengthened.[45]

This stands in stark contrast to Israel's policy after 1992, driven again by Peres and Rabin, in which Tel Aviv rejected the very concept of 'Iranian moderates' and opposed any rapprochement between the Unites States and Iran.[46] Indeed, one of the questions that arose from the Iran-Contra affair was Israel's seemingly paradoxical role in strengthening a regime that opposed Israel's existence and Iran's collaboration with a state that it officially sought to destroy.

Recognition of Iran and Israel's common security imperatives existed on the Iranian side as well. Despite Khomeini's ideological opposition to Israel, the revolution had done little to change Iran's threat picture. The Soviet Empire – the 'other Great Satan', according to Khomeini – was even more feared than the US by many of the leaders of the Revolution and was still seen as Iran's main adversary. Thus, notwithstanding the deterioration in relations with Washington, revolutionary Iran conducted a policy vis-à-vis Moscow that in essence was identical to that of the Shah.[47] Ironically, Iran's anti-Western and anti-Israeli revolution strengthened the common Israeli–Iranian threat picture, according to one school of thought in Iran.[48] Indeed, just as Nasser's death had reduced Iran's need for Israel, Saddam Hussein and the Arab block's attack against Iran in September 1980 did the opposite, so the reasoning went.

The competing and eventually prevailing view in Iran propagated by the 'Arabists' in Iran's foreign policy circles declared that Iran could best increase its role in the region by pursuing friendly ties with its immediate neighbours, who were dominated by Arab and Sunni people.[49] The Iraq–Iran war reinforced the notion that Iran could not afford to allow its security to be dependent on any other state, and, as a result, befriending Iran's immediate neighbour was a better policy than weakening them through alliances with remote states.[50] Consequently, the clerics faced a dilemma similar to that of the Shah: in order to mend fences with its Arab neighbours, Iran needed to distance itself from Israel. Unlike the Shah, however, the clerics tried to alleviate some of the Arab animosity vis-à-vis Iran by adopting a very harsh ideological rhetoric against Israel.

Needless to say, Iran's rhetoric against Israel won it few friends in the Arab world during the Iraq–Iran war. On the contrary, the Arabs viewed Islamic Iran as a greater threat than imperial Iran, prompting a consolidation of the anti-Tehran Arab block.[51] But the end of the Cold War brought geostrategic changes to the Middle East that resulted in an intense rivalry between Iran and Israel and reinforced Tehran's pursuit of an increased role through rapprochement with the Arabs and hostile opposition to the Jewish state.

*The end of the Cold War and geopolitical changes in the Middle East*   The geopolitical map of the Middle East was significantly redrawn after the end of the Cold War and Iraq's defeat in the Persian Gulf War. The fall of the Soviet empire improved both Iran and Israel's security environment. For Iran, its powerful and hostile northern neighbour was now weak and disintegrating. From Israel's perspective, the collapse of Syria's principal supporter and arms provider effectively eliminated the Arab military option. 'The collapse of the Soviet Union was a very important event. [...] Soviet backing of its clients in the Middle East, mostly Syria at the time', was eliminated, according to Ephraim Kam, deputy head of the Jaffe Centre for Strategic Studies at Tel Aviv University.[52]

The defeat of Saddam Hussein also weakened a common enemy of Iran and Israel. As can be seen in Figure 9.1, the Persian Gulf War reduced Iraq's relative power in the region from approximately 16 per cent in 1990 to 6 per cent in 1991. The US-led coalition driving Iraq out of Kuwait included several Arab states, which indicated the ultimate defeat of pan-Arabism, an ideology that constituted a threat to both Iran and Israel. Furthermore, the US military intervention served to boost Israel's security. Few Arab states had any remaining doubts as to whether the US would step in militarily to defend its interest and allies in the Middle East.

At the same time, the defeat of Iran's and Israel's enemies left both states unchecked. According to a lobbyist for the American-Israeli Public Affairs Committee, the elimination of the Arab threat to Israel made Iran a relatively greater threat. 'Once you have a scenario in which the Soviet Union is gone, the Arab military option is gone, and you are making peace with the Palestinians, Jordanians and Syrians, what other threats are left? Iran then moves to the top of the list.'[53] According to Jesse Hordes of the Anti-Defamation League, Iran was perceived as using its new-found freedom to strengthen its revolutionary image and its ideological zeal while Israeli intelligence indicated that Iran was developing nuclear weapons and missile delivery systems.[54]

But while Israel saw Iran surpassing Iraq as a threat and rival, the changing geostrategic map of the region did not prompt Iran to see the same threat and rival

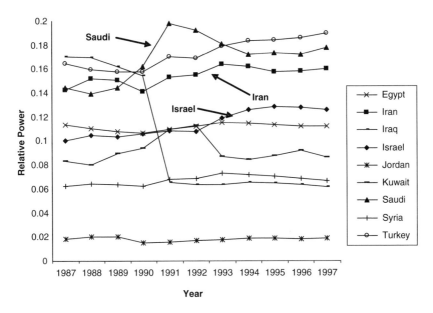

*Figure 9.1* Power cycles: the Middle East region, 1987–1997.

Source: US Department of State, World Military Expenditures and Arms Transfers.

replacement.[55] According to a senior Iranian diplomat who led Iran's negotiations with Iraq both during and after the Iran–Iraq war, the Iranian and Iraqi war colleges continued to consider each other as enemies until the fall of Saddam in 2003. 'I never had the confidence that [the Iraqis] would miss an opportunity to destroy Iran. And they gave me every reason to further believe that'.[56] Whereas the Israelis perceived Iran's rearmament as directed towards Tel Aviv, prompting Rabin to use his first visit to the Clinton White House to change an arms request from tactical F-16s to F-15Es, a strategic bomber aircraft that could reach Iran,[57] Iran's military focus was still on Iraq. The devastating psychological effect of the Iraq–Iran war and Saddam Hussein's continued reign in Baghdad left Iran with little choice.

*Israel's new Middle East*    The threat and rivalry reassessment was part of a greater Iranian and Israeli redefinition of their respective roles and positions in the emerging Middle Eastern order under US hegemony. Although the redistribution of power in the region created three poles in the Middle East – Israel, Iran and Saudi Arabia – who competed for relative power share, the presence of US forces in the region dampened the volatility in relative power fluctuation. As a result, the rivalry turned toward role – the currency of power – since friction between the US and certain regional states served to exacerbate the role–power discrepancy.

Whereas Israel had enjoyed a close alliance with the US, which provided it with strategic importance and avoidance of complete isolation, Iran's isolation had left it with a role deficit. As can be seen in Figure 9.1, Iran was at the top of the system together with Saudi Arabia, Turkey and Israel, yet its role in the region was very limited with many security arrangements designed to further contain and balance the Islamic Republic. Tehran had for more than a decade tolerated the discrepancy between its role and power and accepted postponed role gratification due to the difficulty in improving relations with the US and Arab states at the time of the war. But Iran played a helpful role during the US-led invasion of Iraq in early 1991 and earned positive remarks from key members of the Bush adminis-tration.[58] As a new Middle East order was emerging, Iran believed that the time for its role gratification had arrived; it would be a key player in shaping the new Middle East order and would take on what it considered to be its rightful role in the affairs of the region.

Israel, on the other hand, feared that the US's reorientation toward the Arabs and the possible rapprochement between the US and Iran would leave it isolated.[59] The Iraqi power vacuum was a double-edged sword for Israel. On the one hand, Israel's security environment had improved significantly. On the other hand, the Shamir government's relationship with the US had hit a low due to disagreements over arms sales and Washington's new-found amity with Syria and the Arab states of the anti-Iraq coalition, which diminished Israel's strategic importance to the United States. Furthermore, the Palestinian Intifada and the occupation of the West Bank and Gaza had become increasingly problematic.

By the time the Labour party swept to power in the June 1992 elections, the need for bold action was evident. 'There was a feeling in Israel that because of the end of the Cold War relations with the US were cooling and we needed some new glue for the alliance. And the new glue...was radical Islam. And Iran was radical Islam', according to Ephraim Inbar of the Begin-Sadat Centre for Strategic Studies.[60] Labour's landslide victory enabled it to form a government without the Likud, which provided it with the necessary political manoeuvrability to make major policy shifts. Since Labour lacked ideological attachment to the Palestinian territories, it increasingly came to view the occupation as a threat to the survival of the Jewish State, particularly since the poverty and marginalization in these areas made it fertile ground for the growth of Islamic fundamentalism. Since the Arab neighbours were weak militarily, and the Palestine Liberation Organization (PLO) was on the verge of collapse, Israel's cards were strong, and it could opt to put the peripheral doctrine on its head. A new generation of Labour leaders contended that the growing relative strength of Iran made the periphery the threat and rival, and Israel's long-term security would be better served by befriending the Arab states of the vicinity instead of the non-Arab states of the periphery.[61] According to Ephraim Sneh, member of the Knesset Foreign Affairs & Defence Committee, 'there is the old periphery and the new periphery. The old periphery was aimed to outflank the Arab enemies of Israel. That was the case of Iran at that time. Now we should have a new periphery to outflank Iran'.[62]

Indeed, as can be seen in Figures 9.1–9.3, the redistribution of power after the end of the Cold War caused Iran's and Israel's power cycles to correlate negatively, i.e. they were competing for the same relative power share;. (before 1993, their cycles were either parallel or positively aligned). This new environment prompted

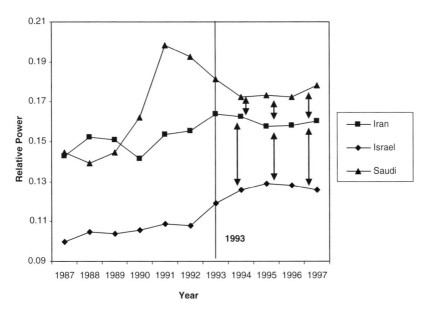

*Figure 9.2* Saudi–Iran–Israel, 1987–1997 (Data from entire Middle East region).

Source: US Department of State, World Military Expenditures and Arms Transfers.

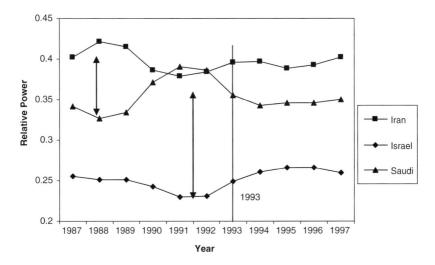

*Figure 9.3* Israel–Iran–Saudi triad, 1987–97.

Source: US Department of State, World Military Expenditures and Arms Transfers.

a rivalry with Iran, which in turn necessitated improved relations with Israel's Arab neighbours, particularly since Iran sought an increased role by playing the Arab street card against the governments of the pro-Western Arab states through its harsh rhetoric and anti-Israel ideology. In addition, by achieving recognition by signing peace treaties with the Arabs, Israel would significantly increase its role by becoming the economic engine of the Middle East that would produce goods for the 200 million-man-strong Arab markets. The Jewish state would lead the development of the region and become its dominant power, which in turn would regain it strategic importance in Washington.[63] This was at the centre of Shimon Peres' vision of 'the New Middle East'.[64] From Israel's perspective, the role to which it aspired came at the expense of Iran, whose isolation and threat depiction – in the view of Israeli and American decision-makers – was believed to be necessary for the success of the peace process and the materialization of Peres' vision.[65]

Peace with the Arabs also came at the expense of Iran's role and standing since Rabin believed that the Israeli population, after years of the Intifada, would be unlikely to believe in a peace with the Arabs unless a greater and more ominous threat – Iran and Islamic fundamentalism – was looming on the horizon. The threat depiction of Iran was needed in order for the Israeli population to adjust to the idea of peace with the Arabs, Rabin reasoned, prompting the sudden Israeli depiction of Iran as a global threat in 1992.[66]

'Rabin played [the Iranian threat] more than it was deserved in order to sell the peace process', according to Ephraim Inbar.[67] Moreover, the Arab states too would be more likely to agree to peace with Israel if they felt more threatened by Iran's fundamentalist ideology than by Israel's policies and nuclear arsenal. In fact, Israel offered many Arab states, particularly the Arab sheikhdoms of the Persian Gulf, protection against possible Iranian aggression. The Israeli gambit was to depict Iran as a threat and contain it in order to conclude peace with the Arabs and establish a new Middle East order in which Iran would 'have no choice but to accept' its own isolation and Israel's leadership.[68] This sheds light on why Israel, who in 1987 had referred to Iran as a 'geostrategic friend', labelled Iran as a 'global threat' only five years later despite Iran's decreasing revolutionary and Islamic zeal.

Israel adopted a very aggressive posture on Iran, echoing Iran's venomous rhetoric against the Jewish state. An intensification in the war of words occurred and Israel initiated efforts to convince the US that its interests were threatened by Iran.[69] The view of Iran as an unredeemable terrorist state became an integral part of Israeli political rhetoric to the extent that any act of terrorism anywhere in the world was automatically blamed on Iran, according to one seasoned Middle East expert.[70] Former Prime Minister Rabin missed no opportunity to stress the 'Iranian danger', Iran's 'dark murderous regime' and the 'turbid Islamic wave' that it produced. Peres followed the same line and even made open threats directed at Iran, stressing that Israel could take action against Iran.[71]

Peres also urged the European Union states to 'stop flirting' with Iran, saying 'the Islamic Republic is more dangerous than Hitler', and that 'Iran is the centre of terrorism, fundamentalism, and subversion'.[72] This stands in stark contrast to

Rabin's view of Iran at the height of Iran's export of Islamic fundamentalism in 1987 when he said the following at a press conference: 'Iran is Israel's best friend and we do not intend to change our position in relation to Tehran'.[73]

*The Iranian response* Iran aspired to be a significant player in the post-Persian Gulf War security arrangement and was initially encouraged by Secretary of State James Baker's indications that it could play a role 'as a major power in the Gulf'.[74] As long as it wasn't excluded, Tehran took a neutral position on the peace process, stating that any accord acceptable to the Palestinians would be acceptable to Iran.

However, the US was not anxious to welcome Iran's rehabilitation in regional affairs. 'The Americans announced that they had opted to keep Saddam [after the Persian Gulf War] in power partly to check and balance Iran. This had a deep impact on the Iranian leadership who realized that the US was willing to go as far as to keep Saddam in power in order to prevent Iran from gaining power and influence', according to a leading reformist intellectual. Iran viewed its non-invitation to the Madrid conference as a major snub and a threat to its role aspirations in the Middle East. Thus, as the geopolitical implications of the Israeli–Arab rapprochement became evident, Tehran switched gears and embarked on a more aggressive regional foreign policy. 'Iran felt that the US didn't want Iran to have a role in regional matters, that it wanted to keep Iran isolated. As a result, the Iranian leadership concluded that Iran must force the US to recognize Iran's role and interest by undermining US policies. This prompted Iran to turn to Palestinian and Lebanese groups that shared the Iranian outlook.' [75]

The Israeli vision of the New Middle East, where Israel would be at the centre economically, was increasingly viewed as leading to Iran's long-term isolation and role deprivation, that is, the acceptance of Israeli hegemony writ into law.[76] Consequently, Iran became the principal opponent of the peace process since it perceived it as cementing its isolation and exacerbating the discrepancy between its role and power.[77]

Iran responded by convening a rejectionist conference in Tehran that coincided with the Madrid meeting, spearheaded by militant and radical Palestinian groups.[78] Tehran increased its rhetoric against Israel and charged Arab governments in support of the peace process of treason, using its Arab street card to undermine the pro-Western Arab governments. On 14 September 1993, the day of the signing of the Oslo agreement, President Rafsanjani accused the PLO of having 'committed treason against the Palestinian people', and that the signing of the historic peace agreement was 'a treacherous step ... with the crippling result of divisions within the Islamic nations of the world'. Rafsanjani condemned Jordanian and PLO leaders agreeing to 'sit at the same table with the Israeli leaders' and repeated the ritual calls for 'jihad' against Israel.[79]

Iran, which in the early 1990s reduced its financial support to Hezbollah and which lacked strong ties and presence in the Palestinian territories, started to reach out and develop relations with rejectionist Palestinian groups after the Madrid conference. Iran's relations with these Sunni groups had until then been very tense, reflective of the Sunni–Shia divide.[80] According to an Israeli diplomat,

'Iranian-sponsored terrorism' against Israel began after its exclusion from the formation of the new Middle East order.[81] According to Itamar Rabinovich, Israel's chief negotiator with Syria under Yitzhak Rabin and Ambassador to the United States from 1993 to 1996, Iran's transition to global terrorism began in 1994 with the bombings of the Israeli embassy in Buenos Aires and a Jewish community centre in Argentina. 'One was a response to the killing of Abbas Moussavi in Lebanon, one was a response to an attack on a Hezbollah camp deep in Lebanon. It became a different ball game. If you can't act against Hezbollah in Lebanon without an Israeli embassy being blown up or a Jewish community centre being blown up in Buenos Aires; this gives you pause. This is a different equation'.[82]

While the Clinton administration feared that dual containment unintentionally could stimulate a rapprochement between Iran and Iraq, the Iranian response was aimed at undermining the Oslo process itself since the perception was that an Israeli–Palestinian peace accord and Iran's isolation went hand in hand. 'The Iranians outsmarted us', commented a leading official in the Clinton administration. 'They had every incentive to oppose [the peace process]. The more we succeeded in making peace, the more isolated [Iran and the rogue states] would become, the more we succeeded in containing [Iran], the more possible it would be to make peace. So they had an incentive to do us in on the peace process in order to defeat our policy of containment.... I can't say that, at the time, we fully understood that that was the consequence'.[83]

Through its actions, however, Iran contributed to its own isolation. Iran's opposition to the Middle East created significant tensions with the EU, while its anti-Israeli position won it few friends in the Arab world. Iran's rejectionist position and its direct or indirect support for anti-Israeli violence confirmed, in the eyes of many, the Israeli argument that Iran was a threat to the stability of the Middle East.

*The 1996 Likud victory: The revival of the Peripheral Doctrine?*    In the spring of 1996, only weeks before the Israeli elections, Israel was shaken by four major terrorist attacks killing 67 and wounding 161 civilians. The bombings had a significant impact on the Israeli public's attitude towards the peace process, paving the way for Benjamin Netanyahu's victory at the polls a few weeks later. Peres believed that Iran was behind the bombings in order to unseat the Labour government and derail the peace process. The Iranians 'are doing whatever they can to bring an end to peace and bring an end to the government that goes for peace.... For that, I have one hundred per cent evidence', Peres said in April 1996.[84] '[Peres] believes till this day that [the terrorist attacks] were ordered by the Iranians as a way to damage the prospects for peace', according to a lobbyist for AIPAC. 'It's not an unreasonable assertion that the Iranians understood that by electing Netanyahu, you would slow down the peace process. And that's exactly what happened'.[85]

Netanyahu, too, recognized that it was Palestinian terrorism that had sealed his election victory, and he feared that its continuation could unelect him as well.[86] The Likud leader adopted a different approach towards Iran and did not repeat the accusations of his predecessors, who 'at every meeting they held, [...] warned about the fundamentalist danger and urged the international community to join forces, bring pressure to bear on Iran, and hurt it in a bid to topple the regime of the ayatollahs'.[87] According to Dore Gold, Netanyahu's foreign policy adviser and UN ambassador, 'there was a sense that perhaps some of the rhetoric of the previous Peres government might have damaged certain relationships in the region'. There was also recognition that Peres' rhetoric had made Israel's neighbours wary of what was perceived as Israeli hegemonic aspirations. 'By talking about the new Middle East and Israel having an economic role, this could have put Egypt on a much more antagonistic footing and we tried to correct that', commented Gold.[88] Furthermore, the new Likud government wanted to clarify that the struggle against fundamentalism, which Peres had made central to his foreign policy, was not a struggle against Islam itself. To alleviate these concerns, Netanyahu argued against the notion that a clash with Islam was inevitable. 'We reject the thesis of an inevitable clash of civilizations. We do not subscribe to the idea that Islam has replaced communism as the new rival of the West', Netanyahu told the US Congress on 10 July 1996.

As the Likud government put an effective freeze on the peace process, it also initiated a re-examination of its relations with Iran. A political source in the Israeli prime minister's office told IDF Radio in late 1996 that the era of dual containment (i.e. the Oslo process) was over and that Israel had changed its approach towards Tehran.[89] The Israeli accounts were confirmed by the Islamic Republic News Agency (IRNA) who reported that the Likud was seeking to settle its political differences with Tehran through the aid of Iranian Jews.[90]

Through these conciliatory measures, Netanyahu sought to avoid any unnecessary provocation against Iran that could lead to more terrorist attacks with unpredictable political consequences. A decision was made at the highest political level to lower Israel's profile on Iran.[91] 'He [Netanyahu] didn't want to use rhetoric that would just antagonize them for no reason', argued Gold. But there were other reasons for Likud's less aggressive tone towards Iran as well. Netanyahu and the Likud were ideologically opposed to the Oslo process and did not conceal their mistrust of the Palestinians. Accordingly, they subscribed to the view that since peace with the Arabs remained highly unlikely, Israeli security was best achieved by forging alliances with the Middle East's non-Arab states, that is, a return to the thinking behind the doctrine of the periphery. Not only was Peres' vision of the New Middle East inherently flawed in their view, but also his strategy of demonizing Iran was against Israel's national interest in the sense that it significantly reduced the possibility of reviving the Iranian–Israeli entente in case of a failure to reach an accord with the Palestinians (which the Likud viewed as next to inevitable). Accordingly, the Likud strategists needed to keep the Iran option alive. 'The Likud tended to be more open to the idea [that] maybe there are residual elements in the revolutionary regime that see things geopolitically the same way as it was during the Shah's time', according to Gold. [92]

Moreover, Israel wanted to avoid a scenario in which Iran and the United States would resume diplomatic ties while Iranian–Israeli relations were still hostile, since improved US–Iran relations under such circumstances could come at the expense of Israel.[93] Finally, from a domestic political perspective, Netanyahu's aim was to turn the Israeli public against the Oslo process and end the 'land for peace' formula. In the words of an AIPAC representative, 'blaming the Iranians for Palestinian terrorism would be counterproductive to his message that terror was coming from the Palestinians'.[94] In short, whereas the Iranian threat depiction served Rabin's efforts to convince the Israeli public to support reconciliation with the Arabs, the very same Iranian threat depiction undermined Netanyahu's efforts to convince Israelis to oppose that very same reconciliation.

From the Iranian perspective, Likud was preferred over Labour for this very reason: an Israel that doesn't pursue the peace process won't need to confront Iran. 'In Iran, the perception was that Likud is not serious about peace, so they do not need a scapegoat [Iran]. Labour, however, needed a scapegoat', explained an Iranian political strategist.[95] As is depicted in Figures 9.1–9.3, Israel's relative power shot up in 1992 and reached its peak in 1995 and 1996. Netanyahu's rise to power and his freezing of the peace process coincided with a reversal in both Iran and Israel's relative power growth; Israel's decline corresponded to Iran's rise. Thus, despite Israeli attempts to lessen friction with Iran, the two countries remained geopolitical rivals in direct competition for relative power share and role.

In the end, the Likud's attempt to reduce tensions with Iran failed. By 1997, Iran announced the production of Shahab-3 ballistic missiles, which put Israel within Iran's reach. In the eyes of many Israelis, the alarmists' exaggerated view of the 'Iranian threat' from the early 1990s started to reflect reality by the mid-1990s. At the same time, Iran increasingly felt sufficiently confident about the doomed destiny of the peace process to adopt a more nuanced policy on Israel.[96] This was crystallized one year later when Iran's new president, Mohammad Khatami, reinstated the policy of accepting any deal agreeable to the Palestinians, including a two-state solution.[97]

## Summary

This study offers an alternative explanation to the prevailing view on Israeli–Iranian relations, which ascribes their poor state of relations to the ideological disposition of the Iranian government (which prevents Tehran from approaching the issue from a rational, realist outlook) and the Israeli government's balance of threat calculations (which necessitate the pre-emption of a nuclear Iran). Although ideological and balance of threat motives certainly may have influenced the policies of the two states, the poor state of Israeli–Iranian relations in the 1990s is not an inexplicable phenomenon doomed to the residual logic of ideology or threat calculations.

Rather, according to the power cycle theory, relations between Israel and Iran took a sharp turn for the worse after the first Persian Gulf War since, at the systemic level, the redistribution of power in the region and the disintegration of the fragile Middle East order created both a strategic rivalry for relative power share and a hegemonic competition for role. At the political level, the manifestation of this rivalry took an untamed form due to the lack of a normative framework for statecraft in the Middle East and the unrealistic role aspirations of the two powerhouses.

The power cycle theory's distinction between role and power is particularly valuable for the understanding of Israeli–Iranian relations due to the collapse of the Middle East order after 1991 and the ensuing process of establishing a new equilibrium in the system, which by nature brings to the surface, and intensifies, rivalries. Both imperial and Islamic Iran have had ingrained in them the notion that Iran's size, population, educational level and natural resources destine it to be the most powerful nation in the region and that it should play a leadership role in regional affairs that reflects this perceived reality. Revolutionary Iran initially aspired to be the leader of the entire Islamic world; the Shah's aspirations for role far exceeded the Middle East geographically, with dreams of establishing Iran as a naval power that guaranteed the security of the Indian Ocean basin. However, since the end of the Iraq–Iran war, Tehran has gradually reduced its role aspirations and the definition of its national security environment to encompass only the Persian Gulf and Caspian Sea and not the greater Middle East.[98] Within this area, any order that would subjugate Iran to the domination of any other Middle East power would, according to the power cycle theory, be unstable due to Iran's long-term rejection of such a role–power discrepancy.

But unlike Iran, where the maturation of the Iranian government has led to a more realistic role ambition, Israel has steadily expanded its role aspirations because of its world view, and insistence on an Israeli military edge. Neo-revisionism, which has dominated Israeli political thinking since the election of Begin in 1977, posits that Israel must dominate its environment militarily in order to avoid the destruction of the Jewish state since peace based on the Muslim world's voluntary acceptance of Israel into the region is impossible to achieve. 'We have to keep the strategic edge regardless. In this region, we have to consider every weapon as if it is directed toward Israel', according to Ephraim Sneh of the Labour party.[99] But while Israel's existence could not be threatened by peripheral countries such as Iran 30 years ago, the Persian Gulf War and the raining of Iraqi scuds over Israeli cities made Tel Aviv painfully aware of its vulnerability vis-à-vis the outer circle, including Iran. In short, the advancement of military technology has vastly expanded what previously would be considered Israel's vicinity and moved the periphery further away. Today, within the construct of the peripheral doctrine, Israeli hawks view Iran as part of the vicinity and non-Muslim India, to which it has forged strong strategic ties as part of the periphery.[100]

At the height of the US invasion of Iraq, Iranian officials privately communicated with US officials and called for a regional security conference dealing with the post-Saddam order of the Middle East, which would include all regional countries (i.e. an Iranian acceptance of Israel's participation). This may constitute a realization that, on the one hand, Iran cannot exclude Israel from regional decision-making (just as Israel failed to exclude Iran), and, on the other hand, that Iran, unlike Israel, in the long run does not need to isolate Tel Aviv in order to achieve its role objectives. Whereas Iran's role withdrawal may reduce tensions between the two states in the short run, the taming of the Israeli–Iranian rivalry will not occur until a corresponding role modification takes place in Tel Aviv as well.

## Notes

1 David Menashri, *Post-Revolutionary Politics in Iran – Religion, Society, and Power* (London, 2001), 262.
2 Mahmood Sariolghalam, 'Israeli-Turkish Military Cooperation: Iranian Perceptions and Responses', *Journal of Political and Military Sociology*, 29 (2001): 293–294.
3 Shahram Chubin, *Iran's National Security Policy: Intentions, Capabilities, and Impact* (Washington, DC: 1994), 60.
4 'Iran and World Bank Loans', Prepared Testimony of Ray Takeyh, 29 October 2003, House subcommittee on Financial Services.
5 David Menashri, *Post-Revolutionary Politics in Iran – Religion, Society, and Power* (London, 2001), 294.
6 Sohrab Sobhani, *The Pragmatic Entente: Israeli-Iranian Relations, 1948–1988* (New York, 1989), 171.
7 Mahmood Sariolghalam, 'Israeli-Turkish Military Cooperation: Iranian Perceptions and Responses', *Journal of Political and Military Sociology*, 29 (2001): 298.
8 Shai Feldman, *Nuclear Weapons and Arms Control in the Middle East* (Cambridge, 1997), 105.
9 Shimon Peres, *The New Middle East* (New York, 1993), 19: 43.
10 Patrick Clawson, Michael Eisenstadt, Eliyahu Kanovsky, David Menashri, *Iran Under Khatami: A Political, Economic, and Military Assessment* (Washington DC, 1998), 33.
11 Ilan Peleg, *Begin's Foreign Policy 1977–1983: Israel's Move to the Right* (New York, 1987), 53.
12 Peleg, *Begin's Foreign Policy*, 53.
13 Interview with Israeli Ministry of Defence official, Tel Aviv, 18 October 2004. 'There is definitely a tendency in Israel [to think the worst] .... Today, the prevailing culture or I would say the mindset of the intelligence industry is to attribute to the enemy almost infinite power and completely underestimate what our strength means to them.'
14 Feldman, *Nuclear Weapons and Arms Control*, 138.
15 Interview with Ambassador Javad Zarif, New York, 1 April 2004.
16 Anoushiravan Ehteshami and Raymond Hinnebusch, *The Foreign Policies of Middle East States* (Boulder, 2002), 123.
17 Yahya Sadowski, *Scuds or Butter? The Political Economy of Arms Control in the Middle East* (Washington DC, 1993), 58.
18 Kenneth Waltz, *Theory of International Politics* (New York, 1979), 121.
19 Arthur Stein, *Why Nations Cooperate: Circumstance and Choice in International Relations* (Ithaka, 1990), 6.
20 Alexander Wendt, 'Constructing International Politics', *International Security* 20, no. 1 (1995): 71–72.
21 J. Goldstein, R. Keohane, *Ideas and Foreign Policy* (Ithaka, 1993), 5.
22 Raymond Hinnebusch and Anoushiravan Ehteshami, *The Foreign Policies of Middle East States* (Boulder, 2002), 18.
23 Andrew Parsaliti, 'The Causes and Timing of Iraq's Wars: A Power Cycle Assessment', *International Political Science Review* 24, no. 1 (2003): 161.
24 Andrew Parsaliti, *Iraq's War Decisions* (PhD Dissertation, Johns Hopkins University, 1998), 28.
25 Parsaliti, *Iraq's War Decisions*, 317.

26 Charles Doran, 'Systemic Disequilibria, Foreign Policy Role, and the Power Cycle', *Journal of Conflict Resolution* 33, no. 3 (1989): 375.

27 Greg Cashman, *What Causes War? An Introduction to Theories of International Conflict* (Lanham, 1993), 269; Parsaliti, 'The Causes and Timing of Iraq's Wars', 270.

28 Charles Doran, 'Systemic Disequilibria', 374.

29 Charles Doran, 'Globalization and Statecraft', *SAISPHERE* (2000): 4–10.

30 Parsaliti, 'The Causes and Timing of Iraq's Wars', 161.

31 Samuel Segev, *The Iranian Triangle* (New York, 1988), 11.

32 The rationale for this foreign policy concept was to weaken Israel's Arab enemies by forming alliances with the non-Arab nations in the region's periphery, such as Ethiopia, Iran and Turkey, who all were wary of Nasserist expansionism and pro-Arab Soviet influence in the Middle East.

33 Interview with David Kimche, former Director General of the Israeli Foreign Ministry, Tel Aviv, 22 October 2004.

34 Gary Sick, *October Surprise* (New York, 1991), 63, 142.

35 Gary Sick, *October Surprise*, 114.

36 BBC, 28 September 1980.

37 Gary Sick, *October Surprise*, 114–115.

38 Interview with Yossi Alpher, senior adviser to former Prime Minister Ehud Barak, Ramat Hasharon, 27 October 2004. Sohrab Sobhani, *The Pragmatic Entente: Israeli-Iranian Relations, 1948–1988* (New York, 1989), p. 150.

39 Gary Sick, *October Surprise*, 70.

40 Sohrab Sobhani, *The Pragmatic Entente: Israeli-Iranian Relations, 1948–1988* (New York, 1989), 149.

41 Victor Ostrovsky, *By Way of Deception* (New York, 1990), 330. Samuel Segev, *The Iranian Triangle* (New York, 1988), 249.

42 Behrouz Souresrafil, *Khomeini and Israel* (England, 1988), 111.

43 Interview with Robert Pelletreau, former US Deputy Assistant Secretary of Defense, Washington DC, 1 March 2004. Nir died mysteriously in a plane crash in Mexico only weeks prior to his scheduled Congressional testimony on his role in the Iran-Contra affair.

44 Segev, *Iranian Triangle*, 137–138.

45 Interview with senior Israeli Ministry of Defence official, Tel Aviv, 31 October 2004. Segev, *Iranian Triangle*, 123. According to Samuel Segev, this sentiment was echoed by a key Iranian contact of the Israelis, Hassan Karroubi, the younger brother of Iran's current Speaker of Parliament, Mehdi Karroubi.

46 Ephraim Sneh, 'Don't Be Fooled: Iran Still Traffics in Terror', *Los Angeles Times*, 4 March 2003.

47 Shireen Hunter, *Iran and the World* (Indianapolis, 1990), 81: 4.

48 Interview with Ambassador Javad Zarif, New York, 1 April 2004.

49 Ehteshami writes that 'disarray in Arab ranks has slowly begun to weaken the grip of the "Arabists" in Iran's politico-religious circles, boosting the hands of the "Persianists" in the establishment who are in favour of developing closer links with Iran's non-Arab neighbours and advocate the creation of an "Iran-first" foreign policy based on an Iranian-culture worldview.' (Anoushiravan Ehteshami, 'Iran's International Posture in the Wake of the Iraq War', *The Middle East Journal* 58, no. 2 (Spring 2004): 188, note 20.

50 Interview with Dr Mostafa Zahrani of the Iranian foreign ministry, Tehran, 7 August 2004.

51 Anoushiravan Ehteshami, *After Khomeini* (London, 1995), 132.

52 Interview, Tel Aviv, 26 October 2004.

53 Interview with Keith Weissman of AIPAC, Washington DC, 25 March 2004.

54 Interview with Jesse Hordes, director of the Anti-Defamation League, Washington DC, 25 March 2004.

55  Interview with Bijan Khajepour, Washington DC, 24 February 2004.
56  Interview with Iranian foreign ministry official, New York, 31 March 2004.
57  Interview with Israeli UN diplomat, New York, 31 March 2004. Interview Ambassador Martin Indyk, Washington DC, 4 March 2004.
58  Kenneth Pollack, *The Persian Puzzle* (New York, 2004), 257–258.
59  Interview with Dan Meridor, former Israeli cabinet minister, Tel Aviv, 27 October 2004.
60  Interview with Ephraim Inbar, Jerusalem, 19 October 2004.
61  Shimon Peres, *The New Middle East* (New York, 1993), 43.
62  Interview, Tel Aviv, 31 October 2004.
63  Interview with Keith Weissman of AIPAC, Washington DC, 25 March 2004.
64  Peres, *New Middle East*, 69.
65  The idea of isolating Iran and excluding it from regional decision-making was adopted by the United States in May 1993 through the so-called Dual Containment policy. Dual Containment was intimately connected to the Middle East peace process, and aimed at isolating both Iran and Iraq in order to enable the Oslo process to succeed. According to a senior Clinton aide, the perception was that Iran needed to be isolated and excluded in order for peace between the Arabs and Israelis to be possible.
66  Interview Ambassador Martin Indyk, Washington DC, 4 March 2004.
67  Interview with Ephraim Inbar, Jerusalem, 19 October 2004.
68  Interview with Israeli UN diplomat, New York, 31 March 2004.
69  World Press, 13 March 1993.
70  Paul White and William Logan, *Remaking the Middle East* (Oxford, 1997), 218.
71  David Menashri, *Post-Revolutionary Politics in Iran – Religion, Society, and Power* (London, 2001), 295.
72  Reuter, 7 March 1996.
73  Agence France Press, 28 October 1987 (From Souresrafil, B., *Khomeini and Israel*, 114).
74  *New York Times*, 6 February 1991.
75  Interview with Dr Ali Reza Alavi-Tabar, a leading reformist intellectual, Tehran, 21 August 2004.
76  Interview with Dr Mostafa Zahrani of the Iranian foreign ministry, New York, 31 March 2004. Mahmood Sariolghalam, 'Israeli-Turkish Military Cooperation: Iranian Perceptions and Responses', *Journal of Political and Military Sociology* (2001): 297.
77  Interview with senior Iranian foreign ministry official, Tehran, 25 August 2004.
78  *Ettela'at*, 11 September 1993.
79  Clark Staten, 'Israeli–PLO Peace Agreement – Cause of Further Terrorism?' *EmergencyNet News Service*, 14 September 1993.
80  Interview with Dr Ali Reza Alavi-Tabar, a leading reformist intellectual, Tehran, 21 August 2004.
81  Interview with Israeli UN diplomat, New York, 31 March 2004. According to a senior American State Department official, the United States shared this perception.
82  Interview, Tel Aviv, 17 October 2004.
83  Interview Ambassador Martin Indyk, Washington DC, 4 March 2004.
84  'Peres: Iran tries to topple my regime', *Reuters*, 8 April 1996.
85  Interview with Keith Weissman of AIPAC, Washington DC, 25 March 2004.
86  Interview Ambassador Martin Indyk, Washington DC, 4 March 2004.
87  IDF Radio, 10 November 1996.
88  Interview, Jerusalem, 28 October 2004.
89  IDF Radio, 10 November 1996.
90  IRNA, 'Likud said to seek understanding with Iran', 24 July 1996.
91  Interview with Zeev Schiff, Tel Aviv, 17 October 2004.

92  Interview, Jerusalem, 28 October 2004.
93  IDF Radio, 10 November 1996.
94  Interview with Keith Weissman of AIPAC, Washington DC, 25 March 2004.
95  Interview with prominent Iranian reformist, New York, 26 February 2004.
96  The correlation is noticeable between intense Iranian animosity towards the peace process and aggressive Israeli pursuit of an accord with the Arabs and unenthusiastic Israeli attitude towards reconciliation with the Palestinians and a more laissez-faire Iranian policy.
97  Interview with Ambassador Nejad-Hosseinian, Iran's former ambassador to the UN, 1997–2002, Tehran, 12 August 2004.
98  Interview with Ambassador Javad Zarif, New York, 1 April 2004.
99  Interview, Tel Aviv, 31 October 2004.
100  This indicates the survival of the strategic logic of the periphery doctrine, albeit adapted to the technological realities of the 21st century. According to Ephraim Sneh, India Azerbaijan and the central Asian states constitute the new peripheral states through whom Israel is weakening Iran.

# 10 Nuclear policy and international relations

*Saideh Lotfian*

## Introduction

In the past 15 years, the United States has repeatedly accused Iran of secretly trying to acquire nuclear weapons.[1] As an essential component of the US campaign against terrorism, the Bush administration has adopted a tougher and less flexible approach to deal with nuclear proliferation in the Middle East. The new policy of counter-proliferation and the pre-emptive use of military and covert force before enemies have acquired weapons of mass destruction is revealed in the National Security Strategy of the United States of America.[2] This way of thinking is increasingly evident in the US efforts to persuade the Board of Governors of the International Atomic Energy Agency (IAEA)[3] that Iran is untrustworthy and is expanding its secret nuclear facilities parallel to a declared nuclear energy programme. For their part, the Iranian leaders believe that the United States is playing a major role in the continuing process of persistent international pressures exerted on Iran to accept the most intrusive IAEA inspections of its nuclear sites.

Due to this dominant perception, many political and military leaders in both the conservative and moderate camps have entered the public debate with their own proposals in support of the nuclear option to counter the heightened level of threat against the Iranian regime. Other commentators have gone as far as suggesting that nuclear weapons could become a useful defence option to deter any states or groups who may have the potential to commit acts of aggression against Iran or its national interests. In this unfolding near-crisis situation, the highest defence priority of the Islamic Republic of Iran is to find a useful way to deal with the most visible and most important element of its current deterrent policy, that is, preventing military attacks on Iranian nuclear facilities, particularly surprise attacks against the Bushehr reactor by the United States or Israel. At the time of writing, the Iranian government insists that it has the right to acquire nuclear technology for peaceful purposes; the United States maintains that the international community must deal severely with Iran as a way of dissuading other states with nuclear ambitions.

The central aims of this paper are to identify the main issues related to Iran's nuclear programme, and present a non-violent way to put an end to this stand-off quickly and efficiently. To address the international implication of this potentially destabilizing war of words between Iran and its adversaries, we should find suitable answers to a number of questions: What are the motivations for the Iranian nuclear programme? Who is involved in the domestic debate on the nuclear issue in Iran? How has Iran's nuclear policy affected its international relations? If international factors are important, which ones matter the most? To what extent is Iran's nuclear programme a function of the nature of Iran–US relations? What are the prospects for change in Iran's existing policy? What would be the practical approach to dealing with nuclear proliferation in the Middle East?

## Iran's nuclear programme, past and present

Iran's nuclear programme started in the 1950s, and a small 5 MW research reactor was built in Tehran with the technical assistance of the United States in 1967. With the help of the rise in oil revenues in the early 1970s, the Shah of Iran was able to invest higher levels of national resources in the military sector of the Iranian economy. By establishing the Atomic Energy Organization of Iran (AEOI), he tried to realize an ambitious goal to generate '23,000 MWe from nuclear power stations'.[4] Iran signed a contract with West Germany's Kraftwerk Union for the construction of the first nuclear power plant in the Persian Gulf port city of Bushehr in 1974. After the overthrow of the monarchy in 1979, Iran's nuclear programme was brought to a halt for five years. The former head of the AEOI, Akbar Etemad, has asserted that the Shah was only interested in peaceful use of nuclear technology and 'considered it absurd, under the existing circumstances, to embark on anything but a purely civilian programme'.[5] Etemad recently revealed that Mohammad Reza Pahlavi had specified that 'he was confident in the superiority of his army over those of the neighbouring states, apart from the Soviet Union'.[6] The Shah did not see the need to acquire nuclear weapons at the time, because he thought such an action would be 'premature and costly', and would 'set the Western powers against' Iran. He did not want to implement any policy which would have inhibited the transfer (to Iran) of indispensable civilian nuclear technology.[7] This does not mean that the nuclear option for Iran was rejected permanently and unconditionally by the Shah. In fact, he believed that 'if within 10, or 15, or 20 years the regional situation evolves (in our disfavour) and this country or that one acquires the atom bomb, then we would have to revise our position. At that time, the nuclear military option would become a priority'.[8] The Iranian *Mehr* News Agency recently interviewed Akbar Etemad who was identified as the chief architect of Iran's pre-Revolution nuclear programme. He reportedly said that he would never have recommended Iran's membership in the Non-proliferation Treaty (NPT) if he had been in a position to decide.[9]

Interestingly, the great powers were even distrustful of the nuclear aspirations of the pro-Western Iranian monarch. Despite the absence of any verified evidence that the international law on the use of nuclear power for civilian purposes had been ignored by the Shah, the Western intelligence organizations assumed that he had a secret plan to embark on a nuclear weapons programme. The Iranian revolutionaries who replaced the Shah in 1979 were highly critical of his grandiose military modernization programme. Immediately after the Revolution, they stopped the Bushehr reactor project. During the war with Iran, the Iraqi forces repeatedly bombarded the site with the goal of destroying the reactor. When the war ended, Iran and the USSR signed the first nuclear cooperation agreement for the reconstruction of the Bushehr facility. In 1995, Iran signed a deal with Russia to rebuild the nuclear reactor and to provide Iran with nuclear technology and expertise.[10] Since then, the US and Israel have been at the forefront of the campaign to draw attention to the possibility of Iran's access to Russian nuclear technology and its capability to develop a clandestine nuclear weapons programme.[11] In reaction to these accusations, the Iranian government officials have been emphasizing the fact that Iran has signed major international arms control and disarmament treaties,[12] whereas Israel is a signatory of only three such agreements: the 1925 Geneva Protocol in February 1969; the Certain Conventional Weapons Convention (CCWC) on 22 March 1995; and the Comprehensive Test Ban Treaty (CTBT) on 25 September 1996. Most importantly, Israel has not signed the nuclear NPT, but has been a member of the IAEA since 1957. Israel began its clandestine programme to develop nuclear weapons in the mid-1950s at the Dimona facility in the Negev desert. Today, it is widely known as a nuclear-weapon state, though it has neither acknowledged nor denied having a nuclear arsenal. Iranians argue that it is unfair to single out Iran or any other state while excluding Israel from the list of states that already possess nuclear weapons or have nuclear ambitions. For instance, there was an international chorus of disapproval when the existence of two nuclear facilities under development for fuel cycle near the Iranian towns of Natanz and Arak were revealed. Yet, the same voices are silent in the case of Dimona and other Israeli nuclear sites.[13]

## Public debate on the nuclear issue in Iran

Few issues have generated as much debate among Iranian policymakers, scholars and politicians as the pros and cons of developing a nuclear programme. Two distinct factions have taken part in the debate regarding the priority that should be accorded to Iran's defence policy and the role of nuclear power as an appropriate means for ensuring Iranian security. Preference for one school over another tends to be determined by one's opinion about a range of core issues. The proponents of the nuclear programme are classified into two groups: those who favour a nuclear option for defence purposes; and those who support a peaceful nuclear programme, arguing that Iran's pursuit of a nuclear power generation programme is legal and economically essential.

The main factors which have been influencing Iranian attitude toward the nuclear weapons question, in a descending order of importance, are as follows:

1  The immediacy and seriousness of Israel's unconventional weapons capability;
2  The need for a strategy to deal with unanticipated threats such as a US–Iran military confrontation;
3  The future of Iraq's weapons of mass destruction programme;

4   The threat posed by Pakistan's nuclear weapons capability;
5   Prestige and the relative importance accorded to new nuclear states in international politics;
6   The ineffectiveness of non-proliferation regime;
7   The inadequacy of major arms control agreements as constructive instruments of foreign policy.

In general, the Iranians' viewpoints on peaceful nuclear energy programme are affected by two factors:

1   The need for a new energy policy aimed at improving energy efficiency and making Iran's energy future more dependable and safe;
2   Faced with growing domestic demand, the need for seeking new energy sources to reduce reliance on environmentally damaging traditional sources such as oil.

These factions are never mutually exclusive; many Iranians have reflected the arguments of one or the other factions in their foreign policy views. Nor can one argue that an individual associated with one way of thinking has been consistent over time. In what follows, I shall summarize the main arguments of the key proponents and opponents of nuclear option in Iran before discussing their policy implications.

## The pro-nuclear faction

The main arguments set forth by the proponents of a nuclear weapons programme for Iran are as follows: First, the majority of the advocates of a nuclear option for Iran say that Iranians should follow a national security policy based on self-sufficiency and deterrence.[14] Given the existence of new nuclear-weapons states (i.e. India, Israel and Pakistan), it is apparent why Iranian strategic thinking has turned to deterrence. Recent history has shown that only the weak challengers will be attacked by the United States. The case in point is Iran's south-eastern neighbour, Pakistan, which was not placed on the list of countries supporting Mollah Omar's Taliban. According to Robert Gallucci, a former United Nations weapons inspector and a CIA consultant on proliferation issues, 'Bad as it is with Iran, North Korea and Libya having nuclear-weapons material, the worst part is that they could transfer it to a non-state group. That's the biggest concern, and the scariest thing about all this – that Pakistan could work with the worst terrorist groups on earth to build nuclear weapons ...'. He warns that 'the most dangerous country for the United States now is Pakistan, and second is Iran'.[15] For Iranian observers, the question is why the United States has not taken a strong action against Pakistan's nuclear weapons programme.[16] Their dominant belief is that the United States will not attack a country that has nuclear capability. Since the Revolution, the United States has intended to destabilize the Iranian regime, and only nuclear weapons could force the Bush administration to accept the right of the Islamic Republic of Iran to exist. Thus, the pro-nuclear arms argument goes, Iran must increase its defence budget and concentrate on a programme for the production of nuclear weapons and missiles, with the goal of keeping up with the new regional arms races. They believe that the non-proliferation regime is already defunct and has gone astray.

As might be imagined, a substantial number of Iran's pro-nuclear observers[17] have been sceptical of the claim that international law will protect weaker and smaller states against foreign aggression. The prevalent view is that international diplomacy is a farce, and Iranian leaders cannot rely on the UN or other powers to protect themselves against US intervention in Iran's internal affairs. Iran is viewed as an isolated country which must create realistic conditions for its military self-sufficiency. To safeguard Iran's territorial integrity, supporters of nuclear power have argued, Iran must be militarily strong. During the 2002 Sacred Defence Week [21–28 September], marking the anniversary of the eight-year war with Iraq, there were wall posters in Tehran proclaiming that 'we are not interested in wars, but we will defend our land'. During the 2004 commemoration week, the slogan was 'defence still remains our goal'. As might be expected, the military planners keep reminding the people that they must be constantly on their guard and vigilant. With no reliable allies, Iranians must help themselves by providing for their own national security.

Second, the nuclear advocates are suspicious of Washington's true intentions. They are convinced that the United States is pressing Iran to forgo the option of developing any type of weapons system which could change the regional balance of power in Iran's favour. While Iranian military power is weakened by the US-imposed sanction regime, regional states are arming at a rapid pace. While the United States is engaged in Iraq and Afghanistan, Iran's pro-nuclear weapons voices say, Iran should pursue a safeguarded enrichment programme to get closer to acquiring nuclear weapons capability. Why, they go on to ask, should the nuclear states be permitted to retain their nuclear weapons and use them as legitimate tools of diplomacy? President George W. Bush's National Security Strategy (NSS) puts more emphasis on 'pre-emption', and threatens the so-called rogue states (e.g. the 'Axis of Evil' states) with the use of military force.[18] These new policy statements of the Bush administration have created a negative image of a nuclear super power, willing to use its nuclear capability to gain global supremacy. The Iranians believe that this link between the forceful disarming of Iraq to a broader doctrine of pre-emption indicates the US intention to change the so-called anti-American regimes in the Middle East. For Iranians the question is whether the US government takes a similar approach in dealing with Iran. Nuclear weapons are no longer viewed as a weapon of last resort (or for deterrence); they are viewed as weapons to be used in a war situation. Nuclear utilization theorists (NUTs) are pushing for the development of a new class of mini-nuclear weapons to deal with regional threats. Once the United States ends its war in Iraq, Washington will turn all its attention to Iran's disarmament, and even regime change. The former president Khatami, who has been publicly supporting Iran's policy of peaceful use of nuclear power, is among the Iranians who argue that Iran must be militarily prepared to defend itself against external sources of security threats. While he has said that nuclear weapons have no place in Iran's defence doctrine, he seems to belong to the group of Iranians who want to turn Iran into a near-nuclear state (like Japan and Germany). He has emphasized Iran's right to acquire nuclear power for peaceful use by saying that 'the nation will not forgive us if we drop nuclear energy from our economic development programme just for hostile attitude of certain countries'.[19] In addition to oil and natural gas, Iran must develop other sources of energy such as nuclear energy to provide the country with the security of a diverse supply of energy. Since Iran has abundant uranium resources that can be used to provide the fuel needed for Bushehr or other, new, nuclear power plants, it should obtain the technology to develop the entire fuel cycle. In fact, Iran has notified the IAEA that it will start extracting uranium ore from its Saghand mine located about 300 miles south of Tehran. This site was inspected by the IAEA in 1992.[20]

Third, most of Iran's neighbours have weapons of mass destruction capability. Given the unstable security environment in which Iran lives, it should change its policy of relying on arms control agreements which have been inadequate to guarantee Iran's national security. Remarkably, an Iranian scholar has presented an extremist view of advocating a policy of secret nuclear build-up in an article which appeared in the quarterly journal of the Centre for Strategic Research.[21] He even asserts that perhaps Iran should adopt the Iraqi approach and invest in a clandestine nuclear programme. His argument is based on the assumption that dependence on international conventions banning weapons of mass destruction will endanger Iran's national interest. Adopting a deterrence strategy, Iran should produce WMD, the scholar argues, but it is advisable not to reject international treaties and conventions in order to avoid further restrictions on the transfer of nuclear technology.[22] Since Iran's cooperation with the IAEA has not led to easy access to nuclear technology, others have argued that Iran must not ratify the CTBT,[23] and must withdraw from the NPT.[24] In September 2003, the Secretary of the Guardian Council, Ayatollah Ahmad Jannati, called for Iran's withdrawal from the NPT. However, he emphasized that the right to make the final decision belongs to the Supreme Leader, Ayatollah Khameneh'i.[25] More extensively, Hossein Shari'atmadari, the editor of the leading conservative newspaper, *Keyhan*, and a well-known conservative figure in Iran's political circles, proposed that the Iranian government should issue an ultimatum of no longer than three months to the IAEA. If the Iranian case is not taken off the agenda, Iran should resume reprocessing and even start the process of formal withdrawal from the NPT. He added that if the IAEA decided to send Iran's case to the UN Security Council, Iran should stop its association with the Agency.[26] Ala'eddin Borujerdi, a conservative Majlis deputy, stated that 'we shall certainly support policies based on our national interest and the peaceful use of nuclear energy in the seventh Majlis. We shall not permit international pressures to violate our rights under international law'.[27] According to the 77th Article of Iran's Constitution, international treaties, accords, and agreements must be ratified by the Majlis. Despite the signing of the Additional Protocol to the NPT based on Tehran Declaration, the final approval of the Protocol will be debated in the 7th Majlis.[28] The conservative-dominated Majlis has opted for a more hard-line position on the nuclear issue, and has passed a bill supporting the resumption of a uranium enrichment programme.[29] More recently, the majority of the lawmakers voted in favour of the resumption of Iran's nuclear fuel cycle programme, which was suspended in November 2004 as a result of Iran's talks with the EU-3.[30] However, it is unlikely that the Majlis deputies would go against the wishes of the Supreme Leader, Ayatollah Khameneh'i.

Fourth, the Iranian defence hawks argue that Iran should continue developing and producing missiles. When asked why Iran needs long-range missiles if its enemies were Iraq under Saddam and the Taliban-controlled Afghanistan, the most common response is that the Shahab-3 missiles are intended for deterrence. Arms can be used as political tools and not simply as military tools. Nuclear weapons can be used as bargaining chips to change the behaviour of one's opponents. Because the level of damage they can inflict on the enemies is intolerable, these weapons can be valuable assets in negotiations. Furthermore, these weapons can provide Iran with an effective retaliatory capability to counter the Israeli threat to destroy the Bushehr reactor and other Iranian nuclear installations. The proponents of this policy say that the same question could be put to Israel: Why does Israel need long-range missiles and satellites, if most of its enemies are in the Middle East? As long as Israel remains a source of military or political threat, so goes the argument, Iran should continue its nuclear power programme, and the development of its short- and medium-range missiles.

Fifth, there are official statements that Iran must promote non-military uses of nuclear power (e.g. in medicine, agriculture, etc). It would be irresponsible for Iran to ignore nuclear technology for peaceful purposes. Supporters of the nuclear programme consider access to advanced technology important for successful economic development, particularly the need to combat unemployment. Moreover, they argue that there is nothing in the NPT which makes it unlawful for Iran to pursue an enrichment programme. On 19 August 2003, key Iranian leaders again criticized the US government's efforts to obstruct the enhancement of Iran's nuclear power programme and declared that 'the positions of the United States and certain Western countries, which require Iran to give up nuclear technology, are unsuitable, unjust and oppressive, and the Islamic Republic of Iran will never accept these requests ... Iranian nuclear science is indigenous and peaceful, and the Islamic Republic of Iran, based on religious principles, will never use weapons of mass destruction'.[31]

## The anti-nuclear faction

On the opposite side, there are those who have argued against the nuclear option, believing that it would undermine Iran's national interest. They advocate careful evaluation of Iran's need for nuclear power, and nuclear military technology. To deal with Iranian vulnerability in the face of mounting American and Israeli pressures, they believe that Iran must continue relying on arms control and disarmament agreements. The main points raised in their arguments are as follows: First, the opponents argue that the weapons of mass destruction are inhumane and cannot be used in wars. Iran should not invest in a weapon system that cannot be used. Investment in nuclear weapons will be wasteful and unwise. In August 2003, Ayatollah Khameneh'i reportedly rejected the use of weapons of mass destruction, stating that 'contrary to the enemy's propaganda and racket, we are not seeking nuclear weapons. And we are fundamentally and morally opposed to WMD – in the same way that we considered chemical and biological weapons as forbidden, even at the time of the imposed war'[32] (referring to the 8-year Iran–Iraq war). On the same occasion, President Khatami had expressed his views on the morality of the use of such weapons by declaring that 'nuclear weapons have no place in the military and defence policies of the Islamic Republic [of Iran]'s, because this regime cannot use these weapons due to [Iran's] Islamic and ethical principles'. However, he added that 'the Islamic Republic of Iran will not abandon nuclear science and technology as the legitimate power base of the people and the regime'. [33] The reason he gave for this determination is that Iranians will never forgive the authorities if they decide to forgo nuclear technology.[34]

Vice President and Head of Iran's Atomic Energy Organization, Gholamreza Aghazadeh, stated in a general conference of the IAEA that 'Iran is fully committed to its NPT responsibilities, not only because of its contractual obligations, but also because of its religious and ethical considerations'.[35] In a Majlis session devoted to the question of Iran's nuclear programme, the then Foreign Minister Kamal Kharrazi stressed that the use of the WMDs is *haram* or strictly forbidden by Islam. 'We consider using biological, chemical and nuclear weapons as an act of *haram*', he said.[36] Others have also said that Iran is against the use and production of nuclear weapons because the Holy Qur'an has emphatically forbidden Muslims to kill women, children and old men during the wars and troop advancements. Islam has also instructed against seeking retribution. Because of our religious beliefs, nuclear weapons have no value, no utility and no effectiveness.[37]

Second, they argue, there is a visible technological gap between Iran and the nuclear club members. The political and economic costs of setting up the infrastructure needed to develop and produce new generations of nuclear weapons are exorbitant. Since Iran cannot compete in the nuclear arms race, it will become a sitting duck for the United States and the other nuclear-weapons states. It is not in Iran's national interest to develop a nuclear arsenal.

Third, the opponents say the Iranian government must examine fatal flaws, problems and costs that must be faced in adopting a nuclear approach. Iran cannot ignore the fact that its human and material resources are needed to deal with its immediate socio-economic problems such as inadequate non-oil export revenues, restricted access to advanced technology, rampant unemployment, drug addiction, water shortages, air pollution in major cities and so forth. The government should concentrate on economic development and encourage trade and investment.

If Iran were to pursue the nuclear path, it might not have sufficient resources for the development of the non-military sector of its economy. The majority of Iranians are not worried about the military aspect of national security at peacetime, but they are deeply concerned about job security, improving their standard of living and political freedom.[38] Environmentally conscious Iranians may regard Bushehr or other nuclear plants as the sources of low-cost energy without producing greenhouse gases, but are the power reactors secure? Can they withstand earthquakes and other natural disasters? An environmental-impact assessment of the Bushehr plant was conducted in June-September 1997 by F. Moattar and his colleagues from the Nuclear Research Centre of Iran's Atomic Energy Organization and School of Technology and Public Health in Tehran. They concluded that the most positive impact could be 'on socio-economic and cultural environment, and the most negative impact on natural environment'. They also indicated that the construction of the Bushehr reactor has been in compliance with the rules and regulations of the Environmental Protection Agency of Iran.[39]

The pro-nuclear group argues that atomic power is relatively cheap and cost-efficient, and 'nuclear energy is the world's largest source of emission-free energy. Nuclear power plants produce no controlled air pollutants, such as sulphur and particulates, or greenhouse gases. The use of nuclear energy in place of other energy sources helps to keep the air clean, preserve the earth's climate, avoid ground level ozone formation and prevent acid rain'.[40] Thus, it makes sense for countries like Iran to be interested in nuclear power production. However, the counter-argument is that Iran does not need nuclear power because it is one of the most oil-rich countries in the world. Brenda Shaffer, the pro-Israel research director of the Caspian Studies Program at Harvard's Kennedy School of Government, argues that 'Given that Iran is awash with oil and gas reserves and regularly flares off vast quantities of natural gas, Tehran's decision to allocate a major portion of its infrastructure involvement to develop nuclear power plants has been puzzling'.[41] Similarly, Carolyn James, an American political scientist, declares that it does not make economic sense for Iran to seriously consider nuclear power as an alternative to oil and natural gas or any other energy sources. She rationalizes that 'Iran is energy-rich. It is very expensive to create a nuclear energy programme. The cost of using its existing electrical power based on natural gas would be less than 10 per cent of nuclear generated power, yet Iran wants as much as 20 per cent of its energy to come from nuclear power plants. The desire to create nuclear power facilities simply does not make financial sense'.[42]

This narrow focus on whether a country is oil-rich can result in a one-dimensional conception of energy security. Iranians want to know why nuclear power is economically viable in the United States and other Western countries, but is viewed inefficient in their country.[43] During his January 2004 trip to Japan, the US Secretary of Energy, Spencer Abraham, said: 'You and I [United States and Japan] know that nuclear power is safe. It is reliable, it is efficient, it is affordable, and it is good for the environment'. He called for securing nuclear energy's future for environmental and economic reasons, and asserted that 'There is a very clear need for both of us [Japan and United States] to have a diverse fuel mix.

Our nations both must work to ensure that nuclear power continues to play a key role in our respective energy mixes. It is critical to dealing with global issues of climate changes, the environment, and energy and economic security'.[44]

At international level, there were 440 nuclear power plants in operation and 25 nuclear power plants under construction as of 21 October 2004. Of 30 countries relying on nuclear power for electricity generation, only 7 were developing countries. These countries with the nuclear share of electricity generations shown in the parentheses include South Korea (40 per cent), Argentina (8.6 per cent), South Africa (6 per cent), Mexico (5.2 per cent), Brazil (3.6 per cent), India (3.3 per cent), and Pakistan (2.4 per cent).[45] Khalil Musavi, the spokesman for the Iranian Atomic Energy Organisation (IAEO), said, given that many developed countries are using nuclear power, it is within Iran's rights to embark on peaceful use of nuclear energy.[46] Nuclear power reactors produced about 16 per cent of the world's energy in 2002. In 2003, 19 countries depended on nuclear power for at least 20 per cent of their electricity generations. For Lithuania and France, nuclear shares in electricity generation were respectively about 80 per cent and 78 per cent. Nuclear power plants represent 19.9 per cent of the US electricity generation capacity.[47] President Bush is an advocate of nuclear energy, and has called on Congress to promote research into the next generations of nuclear plants and encourage investment in existing nuclear plants.[48] Perhaps this is the reason why the director of the Atomic Energy Organization of Iran (AEOI), Gholamreza Aqazadeh, has announced that Iran wants to get 20 per cent of its electricity from nuclear power. If it makes sense for the US as a major economic power to rely on nuclear energy to supply at least one-fifth of its total electricity, it should be wise for Iran to maintain the reliability of its electric power systems by doing the same. It is also a matter of pride for Iranians not to fall behind regional powers such as Argentina, Brazil, Mexico, India, Pakistan and South Korea.

The principal problems of nuclear energy are economic ones because it is no longer competitive with other forms of power generation.[49] Many European countries are debating how fast to shut down their nuclear plants. Six plants were closed down in Japan, Germany and the UK during 2003.[50] The Swedish government is committed to shut down 'its nuclear power industry entirely by the time the youngest of its nuclear power reactors reaches the end its expected lifespan – which was generally assumed to be around the year 2010'.[51] Since its ratification of the Kyoto Protocol to the UN Framework Convention on Climate Change in March 2002, Sweden is committed to reduce greenhouse gases. The combination of phasing out its nuclear power reactors and fulfilling its climate change treaty commitment could prove to be costly for Sweden.[52] Even France which is viewed as the most pro-nuclear country is cautious about plans for new nuclear plant construction.

Nuclear power is not proven to be economically viable for some countries. The question is whether nuclear power is needed for Iran to meet sustainable development goals. Obviously, all energy options need to be examined and discussed as the essential policies of sustainable energy development in Iran. But is it viable? Do we create social, political, and environmental problems while growing our economies at a rapid rate? We must consider the fact that nuclear power is economically favourable in countries where other sources of energy are mostly imported. For Iran, nuclear power might be a relatively expensive option for electricity generation compared with oil and natural gas. Until future energy technologies improve the cost-effectiveness and the safety of nuclear power plants, Iran should avoid hasty expansion of its nuclear power industry. The money spent on constructing more reactors based on older Russian technologies is at the expense of the development of newer and safer renewable sources of electricity such as solar and wind power. There have been indications that Iran plans to build new nuclear power plants. Reportedly, 11 nuclear reactors are to be added to Iran's energy network by 2021. According to the Deputy Head of Iran's Atomic Energy Organization, Asadollah Saburi, the new plants will be built near the site of the first reactor in Bushehr. Iran has started initial negotiations with Russia and two unnamed European countries for building these reactors.[53] There must be careful assessment of Iran's energy mix before more expensive reactor projects are undertaken. The policy dilemma is that the amount of energy production has increased significantly to meet Iran's domestic needs. Iran's annual investment in the electricity sector is about $2 billion, which may go up to $4 billion by 2010. Given the current consumption rate, the country's gasoline imports bill may exceed $7 billion by the end of the fourth 5-year Development Plan, 2005–2010.

However, given the high foreign exchange requirements of imported technology for power reactors, the lack of a truly indigenous industry, and the growing demand on the government to develop other sectors of the economy, it is unlikely for Iran to be able to bear the cost of building more plants. Iran must consider the total cost of an expanded nuclear power programme, including costs such as the health effects of radiation, accidents and future waste disposal. The likely environmental effects of the daily operation of power plants on public health are not known. It has been argued that one year of operation of the current atomic industry results in thousands of deaths per year resulting from uranium mining alone. We do not know exactly how much the power to be generated by the Bushehr reactor is going to cost. What should be included in our cost estimates? To what degree are environmental, social and political considerations factored into the cost? The costs involved are related not only to the costs of investment for the construction of Bushehr nuclear power plant, but also to the costs of operating and decommissioning the reactor. No one knows how adversely the delays and cost overruns on the Bushehr reactor project have affected Iran's economy.[54] If Iran's oil and gas resources were put to better use, there would be no need for expensive nuclear power and resources could be used to develop other sectors of the economy.

If nuclear power is not the most efficient method of meeting Iran's energy needs economically, as well as ecologically, and in terms of social effects, what is to be done to meet the growing energy demands? First, Iranians must learn to use their available oil and natural gas more efficiently. Iran is faced with a shortage of vehicle fuel because of the unbridled domestic consumption of heavily-subsidized gasoline, reaching 70 million litres daily.[55] According to Petroagency Information

Network, Iran's electricity consumption will increase by 9 per cent in 2004.[56] Iranians have to learn to conserve energy and try to stop substantial smuggling of their relatively cheap fuel to Pakistan and other neighbouring countries. Iran has a network of natural gas lines, for example, Iran delivers gas to Turkey. With good maintenance, there will be no natural gas lost through leakages in the pipelines. Second, Iran must invest in renewable energy sources such as wind and solar power. A larger budget should be allocated to the Solar Energy Association of Iran which has complained that its annual budget is not adequate to cover its research in the proper use of solar energy.[57]

Nuclear power might be the most eco-efficient of all energy sources, but it is not the safest. Environmentalists pose important questions such as how safely could we store the nuclear waste, which will consist mostly of spent fuel. In the case of Iran's reactor programme, the questions are:

1   How to ensure the physical safety of power plants?
2   How to dispose of the dangerous waste provided by Bushehr reactor or future plants? Since there is no final repository for high-level radioactive waste, no one knows how much its disposal costs.
3   How much will Russia charge Iran for final storage?

On 22 August 2005, the Deputy Head of the Atomic Energy Organization of Iran, Asadollah Saburi, announced a further delay in the completion of the 1,000 MW Bushehr power plant which is now due to start in 2008. Among the stated reasons for the hold-up of the project were Iran's demand that Russia follow international safety standards, and the difficulty of reaching a mutually satisfactory agreement on the cost and procedures for returning the spent fuel to Russia. Under a 10-year supply agreement, Russia would provide fuel for the first Bushehr reactor, but Iran wanted to produce its own nuclear fuel in time for the second reactor at Bushehr.[58] In response to the Iranian announcement that the reactor would not be operational until 2006, Nikolai Shingaryov, a spokesman for the Russian Atomic Energy Agency said: 'I don't know what that is all about. We have not been officially notified of any delays. In fact, there are no delays. We intend to start it up in 2005. And we will do so', he added. The Head of the Russian Atomic Energy Agency, Alexander Rumyantsev, was due to visit Iran in early 2005 to sign the contract to return all the fuel to Russia after a decade of use.[59] On 26 February 2005, Iran and Russia reached an agreement on the transfer of radioactive fuel waste from Bushehr to alleviate international concern that the low-grade spent fuel could be used to make the so-called dirty bombs, or the radioactive dispersion weapons.[60] Iran plans to achieve self-sufficiency in the nuclear fuel cycle by mining for uranium ore in Saghand, central Iran, and enriching uranium at its nuclear facilities.[61] The director of mining operations at the AEOI, Qasem Soleymani, revealed Iran's plan to extract uranium ore in the first half of 2006 from the Saghand mine. Approximately 220 Iranian engineers and workers were involved in the mine, which was visited by the IAEA inspectors in 1992. Initially, Chinese experts were helping Iranians with the digging process. Since their departure in

2002, the mining operatives has been indigenous.[62] Apparently, Iran is seeking the means to produce nuclear fuel without reliance on Russia or other states. According to the AEOI, a total of 700 Iranian nuclear scientists and nuclear power plant operators have been trained at Russian nuclear sites.[63] In 2002, it was announced that over 100 Iranian engineers would be trained by Russia to work at the Bushehr power plant.[64] In September 2003, Iran's influential former President, Akbar Hashemi-Rafsanjani was asked by the Arab satellite news network, *Al-Jazeerah*, how he evaluated 'the EU's stance toward the Iranian nuclear programme'. 'We have always been subjected to such threats and we are not afraid of them', Mr. Rafsanjani said. 'What can they do? We continue our [nuclear] work and we are not dependent on them. Our scientists are busy working and one day we will be able to produce nuclear fuel within the country and make our power plants operational'.[65]

There is always the possibility of terrorist attacks and accidents. There should be more security around nuclear power plants than any other energy-related facility, such as dams. The cost of ensuring security may be very high. One hopes that nuclear accidents will never happen, but clearly they have occurred in the past, even in the most advanced countries. What is the likelihood of an accident involving transport planes or trains carrying the Bushehr spent fuel to Russia? How much will the clean-ups cost? A train accident in Iran involved the derailing and colli-sion of a string of 51 wagons loaded with chemicals, fuel and fertilizers at Khayyam station near Neyshabur, in the north-east of the country, close to Mashhad. 289 people were killed in the ensuing explosion. The then Transport Minister, Ahmad Khorram, blamed either human error or the actions of a disgruntled employee for the disaster.[66] Accidents due to earthquakes can also happen. After the 1989 earthquake, Armenia had to close down its Soviet-built Metsamor I and II nuclear power reactors that had been damaged. Metsamor II restarted its operation in 1995, but many European countries have tried to persuade Armenia to close it. Armenia, which depends on Metsamor II nuclear power plant for almost one third of its electricity, reached an agreement with the EU in 1999 to shut down the reactor in 2004, on the condition that the EU help Armenia with the operating costs during the interim. In 2001, the EU and Armenia agreed to postpone the closure of the reactor until 2006–2007.[67]

Fourth, we must support the establishment of a nuclear weapons-free zone (NWFZ) in the Middle East by persuading all the regional states to sign all the major arms control agreements. We could propose to place nuclear disarmament on the agenda of the Organization of Islamic Countries (OIC), and hold an annual conference on the issue of disarmament. The editor of *Entekhab* newspaper, Taaha Hashemi, said that we must avoid any move, for example, withdrawal from the NPT, which might prove the absurd US allegations about Iran's efforts to produce nuclear weapons.[68] The supporters of the establishment of a NWFZ in the region say that the Iranian government must start a defensive campaign to raise international public awareness about the fact that Iran, as a victim of the weapons of mass destruction used by Iraq in its war with Iran, can never be an advocate of the production and use of nuclear weapons. Iran must fight back to defuse the crisis, because a lie which is repeated frequently generally becomes accepted as truth.

## Options for Iran and their implications

### *Expansion of Iran's nuclear programme*

Iran could continue investing in civilian nuclear infrastructure like the Bushehr reactor, gradually moving to a near-nuclear status. Given the exorbitant financial cost, this option must be justifiable and acceptable to all the major political groups. A strong argument is that Iran can save its oil and natural gas for export if it substitutes nuclear power for oil as the principal source of energy for domestic consumption. This policy option might achieve its stated economic objectives of energy security, but we must consider the policy's side effects, namely, political outcomes. Iran's adoption of a pro-nuclear policy will have four major political side effects:

1   It will lead to a non-conventional arms race in the region.
2   It might have negative implications for Iran's political control of national security affairs.
3   It might lead to Iran's international isolation.
4   It might invite US or Israeli military responses. The presence of nuclear facilities may be a cause of armed attacks, or pre-emptive strikes against Iranian territory, with a potential for escalation.

Of the four potential outcomes, the last one has generated more debate among the Iranian public and policymakers. Iranian leaders have been watching the US reactions to their nuclear programme very carefully. In Iran's military establishment, the United States is viewed as an arrogant power seeking global hegemony. Therefore, a US military move against Iran will not come as a total surprise to Iranian military planners who are now getting ready for a likely US attack against the Bushehr reactor or other nuclear facilities inside Iranian territory. As to the reaction of Iranian forces to such an attack, the Commander of the Islamic Revolutionary Guards Corps (IRGC), Rahim Safavi, said 'the US ought to realize that our nation has the capacity to deal with any American attack. This propensity is shown by a high number of casualties (213,000 death and 320,000 war-related injuries) sustained by Iranians in the eight-year war with Iraq.'[69]

Because of occasional US military threats, some pro-nuclear Iranians have called for developing a nuclear insurance policy in order to prevent an all-out US attack. In the post-Cold War nuclear weapons policy and doctrine of the United States, Iran has been added to the United States' Single Integrated Operational Plan (SIOP), the main nuclear war plan, the highly-classified nuclear blueprint of targets and targeting assignments for US strategic nuclear weapons arsenal which is based on guidance given to the Department of Defense by the President.[70]

The announcement of a new nuclear targeting policy and the naming of non-nuclear weapons states (such as Iran) that are potential targets of US nuclear weapons are contrary to US obligations under the NPT.

The former Iran's Defence Minister, Ali Shamkhani, warned Israel and other nations that might have hostile intentions against Iran that such military actions would compel Iran to retaliate. He has left open the possibility for Israel or other hostile powers to conclude for themselves what to expect. The reason why Iranian military leaders have opted to publicize Iran's deterrent strategy is to avoid any major confrontation. Iran's declaratory policy is to unleash an all-out attack against Israel aimed at threatening the survival of its leadership. The ambiguity of such declarations should not be interpreted as signs of the weakness of key Iranian decision makers who are understandably interested in their own continued existence and well-being. The test of an upgraded version of Shahab-3 ballistic missile shows that this is not just an idle boast or a bluff on the part of Iran's leadership to confuse any potential aggressor. The continuing tests of Shahab-3 are in response to Israel's development of the Arrow missile defence system with the help of the United States.

The Iranian government has also concentrated on preparations for a hypothetical situation where deterrence fails and Iranian targets come under attack. Mr. Shamkhani emphasized Iran's need for 'protective nuclear defence equipment' in case of a nuclear crisis in the region. 'If our nuclear power plants are targeted', he said, 'there will be radioactive releases. You need special equipment to control it. Also some countries in our neighbourhood have achieved nuclear technology. We have to be prepared if there is an accident there'.[71] The nature of the US-Iran relationship will determine whether this high level of mutual distrust will change over time, given the uncertainties of each side's behaviour towards the other. To launch the process of the normalization of relations between these two adversaries, it is important to start from a realistic and scaled-down expectation that draws on historical precedents for non-military techniques of conflict resolution.

### Freezing Iran's nuclear programme

Iran could enter into negotiations with the EU for shutting down its nuclear power industry, with the following conditions:

1   All sanctions against Iran should be removed, particularly sanctions restricting foreign investment in its oil and gas sectors;
2   Iran would be admitted to the WTO; and
3   Iran would be a beneficiary of foreign technical aid to find substitute sources of electric power.
4   Iran would be given positive guarantees to ensure its national security in the absence of its nuclear deterrence capability. Eventually, Iran should be included in a viable regional security system in the Persian Gulf.

### Temporary suspension of Iran's plan for nuclear fuel cycle

Under the NPT, Iran can continue its cooperation with Russia and other willing states to train nuclear scientists and experts. Iran still lacks the technical expertise to develop a truly independent military nuclear capability. At the same time, with the help of the regional states, Iran could refocus its nuclear policy to explore ways to bring regional agreement on a WMD-free zone in the Middle East. A major obstacle to the success of arms control efforts in the Middle East is that Israel has stated that major arms control talks especially those related to nuclear arms control should not take place until peace treaties are implemented and tested by all major regional players including Iran, Iraq, Syria and Libya. The Arab countries, notably Egypt, would like the issue of the Israeli nuclear capability to be dealt with earlier. Egypt and Iran are displeased that Israel enjoys a nuclear monopoly. They want to force Israel's declaration by criticizing publicly and vigorously the fact that Israel is not constrained, while the other Middle Eastern states have closed their nuclear option by signing the NPT.

In an effort to persuade the Iranian government to sign the Additional Protocol to the NPT, the Foreign Ministers of Britain, France and Germany visited Tehran to ensure Iran's continued cooperation with the IAEA prior to the 31 October deadline. As a confidence-building measure, Iran announced on 21 October 2003 that it would cooperate with the IAEA with full transparency, and suspend its enrichment and reprocessing activities. And finally, on 18 December 2003, Iran signed the Additional Protocol, thus allowing short-notice inspections of its nuclear facilities by the IAEA's nuclear weapon teams.[72] Apparently convinced of Iran's willingness to honour its treaty commitments, the IAEA Director, Mohamed El Baradei, said, 'If you look at the big picture, we are clearly moving in the right direction. If you compare where we were a year ago and where we are today, that's a sea change'.[73] In a move which caused a setback, the Head of Iran's Atomic Energy Organization, Gholamreza Aqazadeh, announced on 31 March 2004 that 'Iran will test uranium producing in Isfahan for the next fortnight'. The Isfahan-based facility will produce the raw material for the fuel cycle.[74] Furthermore, the Majlis deputies passed a bill in May 2005 in support of the resumption of uranium enrichment activities. The move, which is in contradiction of a November 2004 agreement with Britain, France and Germany, shows Iran's dissatisfaction with the EU's package of incentives offered to the Iranian government in return for a nuclear freeze.

As long as the United States does not soften its stance against Iran, we should not expect a significant change in Iran's nuclear policy. Iranian leaders watch every move by the United States and react accordingly. For example, after the IAEA Board of Governors gave Iran until October 2003 to sign the Additional Protocol, the former President and Head of Iran's Expediency Council, Akbar Hashemi Rafsanjani, said that 'Iran's conditions for signing this document may be the same as those of the United States. If the United States has reserved its right to set conditions to safeguard its national security, Iran will follow suit by its conditional acceptance of the Protocol'. Consequently, Iran set several conditions including the exclusion of certain non-nuclear military sites and religious places from the IAEA inspections.[75]

Since the United States itself shows a reluctance to rely on multilateral arms control agreements, such as the CTBT and NPT, it will be difficult to strengthen the non-proliferation and disarmament regime. If the nuclear-weapons states are concerned about verification and the likelihood of cheating, they should work more closely with the UN to strengthen agreements such as the NPT and to deal with its discriminatory character. The nuclear-weapons states' unwillingness to eliminate their nuclear arsenals and the push to modernize their nuclear weapons are seen by Iran and other non-nuclear weapon state signatories to the NPT as a weakness of the non-proliferation regime. Instead of a drastic cut in its nuclear arsenal, the Bush administration is investing in a new nuclear weapons programme with an estimated cost of $485 million over the next five years if it is approved.[76] The failure of the United States and the other nuclear-weapons states to disarm rapidly is as inconsistent with the NPT as the non-nuclear- weapons states' suspected nuclear ambitions.

## Conclusion

It seems more likely for the Iranian government to continue insisting on the universality of the NPT before ratifying the Additional Protocol to the treaty that would allow persistent, unannounced or short-notice inspections of its suspected sites. By opting for more transparency, the Iranians tried to show their willingness to support non-proliferation. Iran cannot afford to develop a military nuclear capability for a number of reasons, including mounting US and international pressure, the prohibitive financial cost of nuclearization combined with the need for investment in the civilian sector of Iran's economy, and its dependence on Russia and other states for nuclear technology. However, Iranians are not likely to abandon the option of building a civilian nuclear infrastructure. The prospect of a US pre-emptive attack has not been viewed as an immediate threat by the Iranian leaders who believe the United States will not risk antagonizing Russia. They believe that their compliance with the NPT, proven by the IAEA inspections, will deter a US military strike against the Bushehr reactor.

Political expediency, disorganization and the lack of public debate on major foreign policy issues has often got in the way of objective and effective decision-making in Iran in recent years. Therefore, it is a good sign that Iranian policymakers have been publicly debating the pros and cons of developing a nuclear weapons programme. As we see, opposing Iranian views on nuclear policy exist not only across the political spectrum, for example, reformists versus traditionalists, but also within the same political grouping, for example, the self-declared moderate *Khordad* 2nd *Front*.[77] We can even observe drastic changes in the policy statements expressed by a key political leader over time. Before the 1997 presidential elections, the leftist daily, *Salam*, published articles criticizing the then president Akbar Hashemi-Rafsanjani's government for mismanaging national resources allocated for the Bushehr reactor project. When the former President Mohammad Khatami came into office, several energy policy statements of his government suggested that certain leftists/reformists had softened their previous opposition to nuclear power. Not surprisingly, Mr. Aqazadeh, as the Head of the AEOI, has repeatedly taken a pro-nuclear energy policy position in his annual reports to the IAEA. It is now clear that the conservative-dominated

7th Majlis is more favourably inclined to a nuclear option. A change in its orientation will be indicated by the decision of the new Majlis deputies to approve additional financial support for the construction of more nuclear plants or other nuclear facilities. In sum, the dominant view is that the non-proliferation regime must be supported and immediate collective measures should be taken to enhance its effectiveness. The international community should avoid any action that could make Iran react either by withdrawing from the NPT or by speeding up the pace of its military modernization. This author's personal anti-nuclear bias forces her to advocate the acceptance of international treaties that ban nuclear weapons in the hope of gradually achieving the goal of complete elimination of all destructive biological, chemical, nuclear and radiological weapons being stockpiled by states in their persistent search for security.

## Notes

1 For US attitude towards Iran's nuclear policy, see Jacqueline Simon, 'United States Non-Proliferation Policy and Iran: Constraints and Opportunities', *Contemporary Security Policy*, 17, 3 (December 1996): 365–394; Chen Zak, *The IAEA and Iran's Nuclear Program* (Washington DC, 2002); David Albright, *Iran at a Nuclear Crossroad* (Washington DC, February 2003); and U.S. Department of State, International Information Program, 'State's Bolton Says Iran "Dead Set" on Building Nuclear Weapons', *Washington File* (25 June 2004). Available at http://usinfo.state.gov/mena/Archive/2004/Jun/27–360963.html

2 On the policy of pre-emption, chapter 5 of the document indicates that 'The United States has long maintained the option of pre-emptive actions to counter a sufficient threat to our national security. The greater the threat, the greater is the risk of inaction – and the more compelling the case for taking anticipatory action to defend ourselves, even if uncertainty remains as to the time and place of the enemy's attack. To forestall or prevent such hostile acts by our adversaries, the United States will, if necessary, act pre-emptively.' See 'Prevent Our Enemies from Threatening Us, Our Allies, and Our Friends with Weapons of Mass Destruction', *The National Security Strategy of the United States of America* (Washington DC, 17 September 2002): 15. Available at www.whitehouse.gov/nsc/nss.pdf

3 IAEA Board Members for 2003–2004 were as follows: Argentina, Australia, Brazil, Belgium, Canada, China, Cuba, Czech Republic, Denmark, Egypt, France, Germany, Hungary, India, Italy, Japan, Republic of Korea, Malaysia, Mexico, Netherlands, New Zealand, Nigeria, Pakistan, Panama, Peru, Poland, Russian Federation, Saudi Arabia, South Africa, Spain, Sudan, Tunisia, United Kingdom of Great Britain and Northern Ireland, United States of America and Vietnam.

4 Daniel Poneman, *Nuclear Power in the Developing World* (London, 1982): 86.

5 Akbar Etemad, 'Iran', in Harald Muller, ed., *A European Non-Proliferation Policy* (Oxford, 1987) 212.

6 Paul Michaud, 'Iran opted for N-bomb under Shah: ex-official', *Dawn* (23 September 2003). Available at http://dawn.com/2003/09/23/int10.htm

7 Ibid.

8 Ibid.

9 'Mosahebeh ba Doktor Akbar Etemad, mo'asses va avallin ra'is-e sazman-e enerzhi-ye atomi-ye Iran' (An Interview with Dr Akbar Etemad, the Founder and First Director of Iran's Atomic Energy Organization), Khabargozari-ye Mehr, Internet Edition (14 January 2005). Available at www.mehrnews.com/fa/NewsPrint.aspx?NewsID=148499

10 Russian diplomats have said that Russia will continue its nuclear cooperation with Iran despite US pressures to stop the Bushehr reactor project. See 'Russia will continue to collaborate with Iran in Nuclear Energy despite US Pressure', *Russia Journal* (18 February 2004). Available at www.russiajournal.com/news/cnewswire.shtml?nw= 42588; see also 'Russia, Iran continue Nuclear Cooperation', Islamic Republic of Iran Broadcasting (IRIB) News (18 March 2004). Available at http://www.iribnews.ir/Full_en. asp?news_id=200611

11 See recent studies on Iran's nuclear programme, for example, Shahram Chubin, 'Does Iran Want Nuclear Weapon?' *Survival*, 37, 1 (Spring 1995): 86–104; Michael Eisenstadt, 'Living with a Nuclear Iran?' *Survival*, 41, 3 (Fall 1999): 124–148; Greg J. Gerardi and Maryam Aharinejad, 'Report: An Assessment of Iran's Nuclear Facilities', *Nonproliferation Review*, 2, 3 (Spring–Summer 1995): 207–213; 'Iran's Nuclear Ambitions, Full Steam Ahead?' *IISS Strategic Comments*, 9, 2 (March 2003): 1–2; and Nasser Saghafi-Ameri, 'Iran Nuclear Programme: The Question of Non-Proliferation', *Discourse: An Iranian Quarterly*, 5, 2 (Fall 2003): 63–82.

12 Iran has signed and ratified the following major multilateral arms regulation and disarmament agreements and international arms control treaties: 1. Outer Space Treaty (signed on 27 January 1967); 2. Convention on the Prohibition of the Development, Production and Stockpiling of Bacteriological (Biological) and Toxin Weapons and on their Destruction or BWC (signed on 10 April 1972, deposited on 22 August 1973); 3. Non-Proliferation Treaty (NPT) (signed on 1 July 1968, and deposited on 2 February 1970); 4. Partial Test Ban (signed on 8 August 1963, deposited on 5 May 1964); 5. Convention on the Prohibition of Military or Any Other Hostile Use of Environmental Modification Techniques or ENMOD, signed on 18 May 1977); 6. Sea Bed Treaty (signed on 11 February 1971, deposited on 6 September 1971); 7. Comprehensive Test Ban Treaty (CTBT) (signed on 24 September 1996); 8. Convention on the Prohibition of the Development, Production, Stockpiling and Use of Chemical Weapons and on Their Destruction or CWC (signed on 13 January 1993, deposited on 3 November 1997) and 9. Geneva Protocol of 1925 (deposited on 5 November 1929). Sources: The IAEA, *Status of Multilateral Arms Regulation and Disarmament Agreements*. Available at http://disarmament.un.org:8080/TreatyStatus.nsf and Nenne Bodell and Connie Wall, 'Annex A-Arms Control and Disarmament Agreements', *SIPRI Yearbook 2003 Armaments, Disarmament and International Security* (Oxford, 2003): 765–788.

13 Initially, the US presidents were sensitive to the misuse of Dimona as a nuclear power reactor to produce weapons-grade materials. In December 1960, the Dimona issue was raised by President Eisenhower. Later, the Kennedy and Johnson administrations tried unsuccessfully to pressurize the Israelis to stop using Dimona for military purposes. For a discussion of the controversy between the United States and Israel over the Dimona issue, see: Avner Cohen, 'Israel Nuclear History: The Untold Kennedy-Eskhol Dimona Correspondence', *Journal of Israeli History*, 16, 2 (1995): 176; 'Israel and the Evolution of US Non-proliferation Policy: The Critical Decade (1958–1968)', *The Non-Proliferation Review* (Winter 1998): 8, quoted in Gazit Mordechai, 'The Genesis of the US-Israeli Military-Strategic Relationship and the Dimona Issue', *Journal of Contemporary History*, 35, 3 (2000): 413–422.

14 For Iran's security policy and threat perceptions, see, for example, Daniel Byman, Shahram Chubin, Anoushiravan Ehteshami, and Jerrold Green, *Iran's Security Policy in the Post-Revolutionary Era* (Santa Monica, 2001); and Saideh Lotfian, 'Threat Perception and Military Planning in Iran: Credible Scenarios of Conflict and Opportunities for Confidence Building', in Eric Arnett, ed., *Military Capacity and the Risk of War: China, India, Pakistan and Iran* (Oxford, 1997): 195–215.

15 Seymour Hersh, 'The Deal, Why is Washington going easy on Pakistan's Nuclear Black Marketers?', *The New Yorker* (1 March 2004). Available at www.newyorker.com/ fact/content/?040308fa_fact

16 Pervez Musharraf, who came into power in a military coup in 1999, pardoned Abdul Qadeer Khan, the father of Pakistan's nuclear bomb, who was accused of having sold nuclear secrets to foreign powers. Pakistan, which is not a member of the IAEA and has refused to sign the NPT, has stated that it 'would never allow foreign inspectors to monitor its nuclear facilities and has no intention of freezing its nuclear or missile programmes'. See 'Pakistan Rejects Nuclear Inspections', *IRIB News* (18 February 2004). Available at www.iribnews.ir/Full_en.asp?news_id=198727

17 The pro-nuclear group includes conservative politicians and activists who publicly opposed the unconditional acceptance of the Additional Protocol which the Iranian government signed under the diplomatic pressure exerted by the EU-3. See, for example, '*Asgar-Owladi, dabir koll-e Mo'talefeh-ye Islami: Emza'-e protokol-e elhaqi rah-e jadidi bara-ye ferestadan-e jasusan beh keshvar ast*' (Asgar-Owladi, the Secretary General of Mo'talefeh-ye Islami: The Signing of the Additional Protocol Is a New Way of Sending Spies to the Country), *Resalat* (9 August 2003).

18 See the explanation of other instances of this doctrine in *The National Security Strategy of United States of America* (Washington DC 17 September 2002). Available at www.whitehouse.gov

19 'No Place for Nuclear Arms in Iran', *IRIB News* (23 July 2003). Available at www.iribnews.ir/Full_en.asp?news_id=184305

20 'AP: Iran to Extract Uranium in Early 2006', *USA Today* (5 September 2006). Available at www.usatoday.com/news/world/2004–09–05-iran – uranium_x.htm

21 Since 1997, this centre has become the research arm of the Expediency Council. The Chairman of the centre is the former president Hashemi Rafsanjani, and the vice-chairman of the CSR is Hasan Rowhani, who is also the Secretary of the Supreme National Security Council, and had been the senior Iranian official charged with nuclear negotiations with Britain, France and Germany to reach an agreement on suspension of Iran's uranium enrichment efforts.

22 Kamran Taremi, '*Selah-ha-ye koshtar-e jam'i dar khavar-e miyaneh va naqsh-e konvansion-ha*' (WMD in the Middle East and the Role of the Conventions), *Rahbord*, 19 (Spring 2001): 110.

23 Asqar Haqiqi, '*Ta'aroz bein-e si-ti-bi-ti va amniyat-e melli-ye Iran*' (Inconsistency between CTBT and IRI's National Security), *Majalleh-ye Pazhuhesh-e Hoquq va Siyasat* (Law and Politics Research Journal), 4, 6 (Spring and Summer 2002): 131–153.

24 '*Edameh-ye mozakerat ba azhans manfe'ati bara-ye Iran nadarad*' (Continued Negotiations with the IAEA has no Benefit for Iran), *Jomhuri-ye Islami* (14 March 2004): 3. The main cause of the growing disapproval of the IAEA was the Director General's report derestricted on 13 March 2004. See The IAEA, Board of Governors, *Implementation of the NPT Safeguards Agreement in the Islamic Republic of Iran* (Vienna, 24 February 2004).

25 Ayatollah Jannati said that 'The treaty has been denounced by a number of countries. Although Iran has inked the NPT, it is free to withdraw from it anytime'. See 'Friday Prayer Leader Calls for Withdrawal from NPT', *Tehran Times* (20 September 2003).

26 Hossein Shari'atmadari, 'Why Should we Commit Suicide for the Fear of Death?' *Keyhan* (14 March 2004): 2. Moreover, others have declared that Iran has no option but to withdraw from the NPT in order to protest the international double standard of putting pressure on a non-nuclear NPT signatory (i.e. Iran), and ignoring the case of a nuclear hold-out state (i.e. Israel). See '*Ejbar, Na Ejma*' (Compulsion, Not Consensus), *Jomhuri-ye Islami* (14 March 2004): 3.

27 '*Gozaresh-e Keyhan az barkhord-e faribandeh-ye azhans ba Iran*' (Keyhan's Report of the IAEA's Deceitful Treatment of Iran), *Keyhan* (9 March 2004): 14.

28 '*Majlis-e haftom va protokol-e elhaqi*' (The 7th Majlis and the Additional Protocol), *Saba* (14 March 2004): 2.

29 Ali Akbar Dareini. 'Iranian Lawmakers ok Uranium Enrichment', *Associated Press* (31 October 2004).

30 'Majlis Forces Gov't to Develop Atomic Fuel', *Iran News* (16 May 2005): 1 and 15.

31 *AFP* (Tehran), 19 August 2003; quoted in Naser Saqafi-Ameri, 'Iran's Nuclear Programme: The Question of Non-Proliferation', *Discourse*, 5, 2 (Fall 2003): 81.

32 *Keyhan* (in Persian) (7 August 2003): 14; quoted in Ali Mohammad Besharati, '*Estefadeh-ye solhamiz az enerzhi-ye hasteh'i*' (The Peaceful Use of Nuclear Energy), *Rahbord*, 29 (Fall 2003): 312–313.

33 *Iran* (in Persian) (7 August 2003); cited in Besharati, 'Estefadeh-ye solhamiz az enerzhi-ye hasteh'i', 313.

34 Ibid.

35 'Iran Rejects EU Stance on Linking Cooperation to Nuclear Pact', *Tehran Times* (20 September 2003).

36 'Use of Nukes Forbidden by Islam, Iran's FM Says in Rejecting US Charges', *AFP* (8 June 2003).

37 Besharati, 'Estefadeh-ye solhamiz az enerzhi-ye hasteh'i', 315.

38 The findings of a study based on a series of interviews conducted in Iran showed that 'Whereas few Iranians are opposed to the development of a nuclear energy facility, most do not see it as a solution to their primary concerns: economic malaise and political and social repression'. Karim Sadjadpour, 'Iranians Don't Want To Go Nuclear', *The Washington Post* (3 February 2004). Available at www.crisisweb.org/home/index. cfm?id=2504&l

39 F. Moattar et al. 'Environmental Impact Assessment of Bushehr Nuclear Power Plant', *Journal of Environmental Science and Technology*, 3 (Winter 2000).

40 Available at www.nei.org

41 Brenda Shaffer, 'Iran at the Nuclear Threshold', *Insight Turkey*, 6, 1 (January–March 2004): 78–89.

42 Carolyn C. James. 'Iran and Iraq as Rational Crisis Actors: Dangers and Dynamics of Survivable Nuclear War', in Eric Herring, ed., *Preventing the Use of Weapons of Mass Destruction* (London, 2000): 57.

43 A conservative political analyst, Hossein Sheikholeslami accused the United States of a hidden agenda of preventing Iran from developing alternative sources of energy. Washington, he said, 'wants Iran's oil reserves to be quickly depleted and this is why it is putting Iran under pressure and trying to prevent the country from acquiring or developing nuclear technology which would allow Iran to preserve its oil reserves for many years'. See 'US Accusations about Iran's Nuclear Programme Politically Motivated: Analyst', *Tehran Times* (9 March 2004): 2.

44 Available at www.nei.org/Speech_Abraham_1–9–04.pdf; and 'US Proposes to Budget Boost to Encourage "New Generations" N-Plants', *NucNet News* (6 February 2002).

45 International Atomic Energy Agency, 'Latest News Related to PRIS and the Status of Nuclear Power Plants', *WorldAtom*. Available at www.iaea.org/programmes/a2

46 *IranMania* (27 January 2003).

47 International Atomic Energy Agency, 'Latest News Related to PRIS and the Status of Nuclear Power Plants'.

48 'US National Energy Policy and Global Energy Security', *Economic Perspective* (9 May 2004). Available at http://usinfo.state.gov/journals/journals.htm

49 Energy is no longer cheap. It 'now cost some $5 billion per 1000 megawatt reactor. This cost has priced nuclear reactors out of competitiveness in the United States, despite government subsidies.' David Krieger, *Nuclearism and Its Remedies*, Nuclear Age Peace Foundation. Available at www.toda.org/conferences/hugg_hon/ hugg_hon_papers/d_kreiger.html

50 International Atomic Energy Agency, 'Latest News Related to PRIS and the Status of Nuclear Power Plants'.

51 W. Nordhaus, *The Swedish Nuclear Dilemma: Energy and the Environment*, (Baltimore, 1997): 3; quoted in Energy Information Administration, *International Energy Outlook 2003* (Washington DC, May 2003): 104.

52  W. Nordhaus, *The Swedish Nuclear Dilemma*, 151–152 and 157, quoted in *International Energy Outlook 2003*: 105.

53  '11 Nuclear Reactors Needed by 2021', *Iran Mania* (28 August 2004).

54  In early 2004, the head of Iran's Atomic Agency Organization, Gholamreza Aqazadeh, in a visit to Moscow expressed Iran's uneasiness about the delays in the construction of Bushehr plant, and emphasized the Iranian request about 'the timely completion of the reactor'. He expressed the hope that 'the effort by the Russian Nuclear Energy Ministry will be helpful in setting a definite date for completion.' 'Bushehr Nuclear Plan Process Lagging', *IRIB News* (26 February 2004). Available at www. iribnews.ir/Full_en.asp?news_id=199286

55  'Oil Giant Iran Runs out of Cash for Imported Petrol', *Associated Press* (25 August 2004).

56  'Electricity Consumption to Increase by 3000MW', *Iran Mania* (21 August 2004).

57  'Solar Energy Association Short of Budget', *Iran Mania* (9 August 2004).

58  'Bushehr Power Plant to Start Up in 2006', *Iran News* (23 August 2004).

59  'Russia Denies Delay in Bushehr Nuclear Plant', *Iran News* (26 August 2004).

60  For a discussion of risks of nuclear waste-shipping programme in the United States, see Fred Dilger and Robert Halstead, 'The Next Species of Trouble', *American Behavioral Scientist*, 46 (6 February 2003): 796–811.

61  Major new nuclear facilities are located in Arak (for the production of heavy water), and Natanz (for uranium enrichment).

62  Ali Akbar Dareini, 'AP: Iran to Extract Uranium in Early 2006', *Associated Press*, (5 September 2004).

63  'Russia Train Iranian Nuclear Experts', *IRIB News* (2 July 2003). Available at www.iribnews.ir/Full_en.asp?news_id=182938

64  'Russia to Train 100 Iranian Engineers for Nuclear Power Plant', *Iran News* (29 May 2002): 15.

65  *Iran News* (September 2003).

66  'Error caused Iran Train Blast', *BBC News* (25 February 2003). Available at news.bbc. co.uk/2/hi/middle_east/3487290.stm

67  'Armenia Says Energy Independence "must not be Interrupted"', *NucNet News* (28 October 2002).

68  *Taha Hashemi: 'Khoruj az en-pi-ti mosave ba ta'sir-e bishtar-e propagand-ha-ye Amrika ast'* (Taha Hashemi: Withdrawal from the NPT is Equal to Increased Effectiveness of US Propaganda), *Aftab* (30 September 2003): 11.

69  Faslnameh-ye Joghrafia-ye Nezami va Amniyati (Quarterly Journal of Military and Security Geography) (in Persian), 2, 1 (Spring 2003): 13.

70  *William M. Arkin*, 'The Last Word: Iran in the Crosshairs, Soon enough, even more Countries will Join the Target List', *The Bulletin of the Atomic Scientists, 51, 5* (July/ August 1995); and Bruce Blair, 'Cold War Era Assumptions Drive US Nuclear Force Levels' *(Washington, DC)*. Available at www.banthebomb.org/news/ 000522b.html

71  Ali Akbar Dareini, 'Iran Producing Nuclear Defence Equipment', *AP* (Tehran) (24 August 2004).

72  'Iran Signs Additional Protocol', *Global Security Newswire* (18 December 2003). Available at www .nti.org/d_newswire/issues/2003_12_18.html#C836A786, and 'CNN Interview with Mohamed ElBaradei', *CNN* (26 November 2003). Available at http://edition.cnn.com/TRANSCRIPTS/0311/26/i_qaa.01.html

73  'U.N. Nuclear Chief Sees "Sea Change" in Iran', *Reuters* (1 March 2004). Available at http://story.news.yahoo.com/news?tmpl=story&u=/nm/20040302/ts_nm/nuclear_ira n_elbaradei_dc_3

74  'Aqazadeh on Iran's Nuke Activities', IRIB World Service, English Radio (31 March 2004). Available at www.irib.ir/worldservice/englishRADIO/default.htm

75  Ali Akbar Salehi, the former Iran's representative at the IAEA, had stressed that the signing of the Additional Protocol should not be an infringement on Iran's sovereignty;

inspections should not threaten Iran's national security; Iran should retain the right to expand its peaceful use of nuclear technology; places which threaten the positions of national leaders should not be inspected; Iran's secret intelligence gathering sites should be considered off-limit by the IAEA inspectors. See *Aftab* (in Persian) (5 October 2003).

76  Walter Pincus, '$27 Million Sought for Nuclear Arms Study', *Washington Post* (20 March 2004). Available at www.washingtonpost.com/wp-dyn/articles/ A9359–2004Mar19.html

77  Named after Khordad 2, 1376 (12 June 1997), the day on which President Mohammad Khatami was first elected.

# 11 A case for sustainable development of nuclear energy and a brief account of Iran's nuclear programme

*Mehdi Askarieh*

## Introduction

Stimulated by the urgency of the Second World War, nuclear science progressed rapidly from the discovery of the neutron by Sir James Chadwick in 1932. Out of this basic knowledge came the discovery in 1939 that when atoms fission (i.e. are split), energy is released. This led in turn to the first controlled chain reaction (1943), the first atomic weapon (1945), and the first production of electricity using nuclear energy (1951). Thus, within a span of twenty years, nuclear energy developed from first principles to practical demonstration.

Following its first application for generating electricity in the United States, nuclear energy began to be applied to the production of electricity in the United Kingdom (1953), Russia (1954), France (1956), and Germany (1961) – five countries within the first decade. Ten more countries began nuclear-based generation in the 1960s followed by another ten in the 1970s. The oil crisis of the early 1970s provoked a surge in nuclear power plant orders and construction. Later that decade, the world economic slowdown, combined with the declining price of fossil fuels, curtailed the growth of nuclear energy demand. As this took effect, two accidents, at Three Mile Island in the United States (1979), and at Chernobyl in the former Soviet Union (1986), raised serious questions in the public mind about nuclear safety. The overall effect was a significant slowing down of the growth of nuclear energy in the 1990s. Nevertheless, some countries continued to push ahead strongly with reactor construction, thus contributing to small increases in nuclear electricity production.[1]

Altogether, 32 countries have so far produced electricity from nuclear reactors, amounting to over 10,000 reactor-years of operating experience, and generating by the end of the first 'nuclear century' over 40,000 Terawatt-hours (TWh) net of electricity. As of 1 January 2003, there were 441 commercially-operating nuclear reactors representing an installed generating capacity of about 357 Gigawatts (GW) net, supplying about 7 per cent of the world's total energy, and about 17 per cent of the world's electricity.[2] Within the OECD area there were 356 nuclear reactors in commercial operation in 17 countries, representing an installed capacity of some 306 GW net, and producing about 11 per cent of the energy supply (about 24 per cent of the electricity supply). Additionally, 34 reactors were under construction worldwide that will add a further 27 GW of net capacity.

This illustrates the high worldwide reliance on fossil fuels in supplying primary energy and producing electricity. The consequent production of greenhouse gases, which cause changes in the world's climate, is a main cause of the growing emphasis on 'decarbonising' the world's economies. Concern for the security of an energy supply arising from the concentration of oil and natural gas resources among relatively few suppliers is also a factor in national energy policies. Nuclear energy's lack of carbon emissions, and the relatively uniform availability of fuel resources worldwide, are focusing attention on its ability to meet these energy policy objectives.

Over the last decade, there has been a trend of improving nuclear plant performance measured by energy availability. This has led, in recent years, to many countries generating record amounts of electricity. For example, the countries experiencing record generation performance during 2001 include Argentina, Brazil, Bulgaria, Finland, France, Germany, India, the Republic of Korea, Russia, Spain, Switzerland and the United States.[3]

Yet, despite its maturity, widespread usage and steady progress, nuclear energy, when compared to other energy sources, has a level of governmental involvement and public concern that makes it unique among energy sources. Many factors contribute to this, including its military origins and its potential to be applied to weapons purposes; its technical complexity; the long-term implications of nuclear waste; its complicated safety, legal and insurance requirements; the consequences associated with potential accidents, the health effects of exposure to ionising radiation; and the large-scale investments required for its exploitation.[4] Understanding these issues is important, then, in understanding nuclear energy today.

## Nuclear energy and sustainable development

The world's demand for energy will continue to increase as a result of economic development and population growth. The overwhelming share of this growth is likely to take place in the developing countries, as they strive to raise the living standards of their growing populations. In 1998, the International Institute for Applied Systems Analysis (IIASA) and the World Energy Council concluded that by 2050, global energy demand would probably grow by a factor between 1.5 and 3.0 with demand for electricity at least doubling. In 1999 the British Royal Society and the Royal Academy of Engineering concluded that the consumption of energy would:[5]

> at least double in the next 50 years and ... grow by a factor of up to five in the next 100 years as the world population increases and as people seek to improve their standard of living.

The challenge will be one of responding to these demands in a way that supports society's growing desire to meet current needs without unduly impacting on future generations.

Energy is an important component of any policy for sustainable development because it is vital to human activity and economic growth. The fact that current technologies for providing energy are now increasingly viewed as unsustainable provides both opportunity and challenge. The extent to which nuclear energy can be shown to be sustainable will, to a significant extent, determine its place in the energy supply spectrum.

The sustainability of any development is customarily discussed under three dimensions: economic, environmental and social.[6,7]

## Economics aspects of nuclear energy

The costs of generating electricity are usually broken down into three major categories, the costs of investment (capital); operation and maintenance; and fuel.[8]

Investment costs include those of design and construction, major refurbishing, and decommissioning. The last comprises all the costs incurred from the shut-down of the plant until the site is released in accordance with national policy, and includes the costs to manage the radioactive and other waste generated during decommissioning until they are disposed of.

Operation and maintenance costs include all costs that are not considered investment or fuel costs, the main elements being the costs of operating and support staff, training, security, health and safety, and management and disposal of operational waste.

Fuel costs include costs related to the fuel cycle, including the costs of purchasing; converting and enriching uranium; fuel fabrication; spent fuel conditioning; reprocessing; disposal of the spent fuel or the high-level radioactive waste resulting from reprocessing; and transport. Fuel costs make up only about 20 per cent of the costs of nuclear-generated electricity, which is therefore relatively insensitive to fuel price fluctuations – in contrast to the position of fossil fuels.[9]

## Comparative costs of generating electricity

Compared with nuclear energy, natural gas-fired plants are characterized by low capital investment costs and significant fuel costs. Coal-fired plants are characterized by mid-range investment and fuel costs. In general, fuel costs represent a relatively large proportion of fossil-fuel-based generating costs that are, as a result, sensitive to fuel price variations. Renewable sources of energy, for example, wind and hydropower, are similar to nuclear power in having high investment and low production costs per unit of power produced.

A difference between nuclear energy and other forms of electricity production is that nuclear energy bears some costs that are not included in (are external to) the costs of other sources of electricity. Some of the costs associated with nuclear electricity generation included in the prices at which the resulting electricity is sold on the open market, include radioactive waste management and disposal.

Fossil fuel energy bears certain costs for reducing its emissions to air and water, as does nuclear energy, but a considerable part of the waste is disposed of into the atmosphere, imposing costs on the community that are not reflected in the price of its electricity.[10]

The economic competitiveness of nuclear power might be dramatically shifted if the external costs of fossil fuel generation were to be internalized. For example, if the external costs for carbon emissions alone were internalized through the imposition of a 'carbon tax', the effect on levelized generation costs would be significant.[11]

The ability to provide reliable, low-cost electricity is an important aspect of sustainable development. Nuclear energy can become cost-competitive with other major forms of electricity generation in the long term, possibly supplemented by political action to internalize environmental costs, engender social acceptance, and ensure security of fuel supplies. In the short run, its competitiveness is different in each country, depending primarily on the prices of fossil fuel, which tend to fluctuate.

Oil and gas have a fairly limited geographical availability, with Middle Eastern countries and the Russian Federation controlling over 70 per cent of world crude oil reserves and about two-thirds of natural gas reserves. Quite aside from the political instability that has sometimes characterized the supplier regions, the long supply routes to major markets are also vulnerable to disruption by political action.

As a nation's dependency on foreign sources for its energy increases, so do the costs and economic consequences of any disruption. Any energy source that reduced dependence on external fuel sources could be said to enhance the security of energy supplies and ultimately the security of the nation. Security has always been one of the main aims of energy policy.

Fuel costs are a major component in the price of fossil fuel electricity. Hence, the tendency towards fluctuations in fossil fuel prices translates itself into variations in the price of electricity, especially in a competitive market. The low share of fuel costs and high share of fixed costs in the case of nuclear electricity generation have, by contrast, a potentially stabilizing effect on electricity costs and prices.

Generally, the availability and use of as wide a range as possible of alternative energy sources tend to reduce demand pressure on any one fuel source and so contributes potentially to price stability overall.

## Environmental aspects of nuclear energy

The environmental sustainability of a particular material is usually discussed in terms of its availability, for example, the adequacy of reserves, and its direct impact on the environment.[12]

Uranium is widely dispersed in the earth's crust and in the oceans, being more abundant than silver. At the beginning of 2001, estimated conventional uranium resources (known and undiscovered) totalled above 16 million tonnes or nearly 250 years of supply at the prevailing rate of usage.[13] There are, in addition, unconventional resources in which uranium exists at very low grades, or is recovered as a by-product. These amount to about a further 22 million tonnes that exist in phosphate deposits, and up to 4,000 million tonnes of uranium contained in seawater. Research has hinted that it is possible to tap the vast seawater resources although, at present, only on a laboratory-scale. The cost of doing so is also estimated to be very high, approximately 5–10 times the current cost of conventionally mined uranium.

## Direct environmental impact

Nuclear power is one of the few energy sources that emits virtually no air-polluting or greenhouse gases. The entire nuclear fuel cycle, including mining of ore and the construction of power plants, has been estimated to emit between 2.5 and 6 grams of carbon equivalent per kWh of energy produced. This is roughly equivalent to the estimated releases from the use of renewable sources (wind, hydro and solar power), and about 20–75 times less than the emissions from natural gas power sources, the cleanest fossil fuel.[14]

Nuclear power is thus one of the prime means available for limiting the emission of carbon into the environment. In the developed countries alone, nuclear power plants avoid some 1,200 million tonnes of carbon dioxide ($CO_2$) emissions annually. Assuming that all nuclear power plants in the world were replaced by modern fossil-fuelled power plants, $CO_2$ emissions from the world energy sector would rise by some 8 per cent.[15]

Nuclear power avoids the emission of local air-polluting gases and particulates such as the sulphur and nitrogen oxides that have been linked to acid rain and respiratory diseases. The quantity of solid waste generated per unit of electricity is much lower for nuclear than for any fossil fuel source. It is essentially equivalent to that of renewable energy sources such as solar energy.

However, for nuclear power to make a very large contribution to precluding undue global warming, a large expansion in nuclear generating capacity would be necessary. At present, nuclear power is applied only in the production of electricity, one sector of energy use. Under current estimates, even if installed nuclear power capacity were to increase by a factor of 10 by 2100, its proportion of primary energy use would rise from the current 7 per cent to no more than 25 per cent, thereby avoiding some 15 per cent of the expected cumulative carbon emission during the period. However, if this expansion in nuclear capacity were to take place on the basis of current technology, there would be a considerable addition to the accumulated volume (and also the activity) of radioactive waste.

Nuclear energy is one of the options which could contribute to meeting the projected increases in the world's energy demand, essentially without adding to carbon emissions. But, to be effective and acceptable at this level, advanced reactor technologies and recycling fuel strategies would be required. In essence, as the century unfolds, the current fleet of thermal, light water reactors would need to be replaced by advanced technologies, such as fast-breeder reactors with fuel recycling. Such a change would require considerable investment, though not one likely to exceed the investment demands of other strategies for meeting increased energy demand while limiting global warming.[16]

## Waste longevity

High-level radioactive waste, although small in volume, remains radioactive for very long period. Deep geological repositories have been investigated for several decades, and the expert judgement is that there are no technical barriers to their construction to very high standards of integrity. Although there has been recent progress in Finland and the United States, no repository is yet operational. So the disposal of high-level radioactive waste remains, at present, a challenge to the sustainable development of nuclear energy.

Research and development on advanced fuel cycles and for the treatment of waste promise to reduce the volume of waste requiring isolation and the time this waste must remain isolated. Yet, the results of these investigations will not likely be available for several decades.

## Social aspects of nuclear energy

It is people who create and maintain any technology. In this respect, nuclear energy has certain special characteristics, based as it is on major 20th century scientific and technological developments. Much of the high cost of nuclear facilities is embodied in science and technology, essential for their continued safety and future development. The nuclear industry also employs a high proportion of skilled, graduate staff relative to most other major energy and manufacturing industries. They are important, though vulnerable, social capital, as well as a base for continuous improvement in performance within the industry (and in certain respects beyond it).

Maintaining and improving the technical and intellectual infrastructure to support nuclear energy provides numerous spin-off benefits for a society. As with other very advanced technologies, nuclear energy has historically played a very important part in the development of new materials, techniques and skills, which have been utilised by other sectors, for example, medicine, manufacturing, public health and agriculture, with consequent economic benefit.

All energy technologies have a tendency to create social concern, even conflict. In the case of nuclear energy, concern has focused on questions of safety, proliferation and waste- disposal. Coal has its own profound history of conflict and social division, as, on an international scale, has oil. The exploitation of even renewable energies has come under scrutiny and opposition arising from their visual intrusiveness and large-scale demands on land area. Large hydro projects have raised opposition on a global scale because of the social and environmental impacts of the massive flooding involved.

As with any other major industrial installation, and despite taking all precautions, nuclear power plants present risks to workers, to people living in the immediate vicinity, and, in the case of a very severe accident such as that at Chernobyl, to people living very far away. Usually, these risks are analysed in terms of radiological consequences as a result of (1) normal operation, and (2) from accidents. Given the highly qualified personnel, sound operational practices, and strict regulatory oversight, nuclear energy, from an industrial safety viewpoint, is relatively safe. For example, data from the United States for 2000 reveals an accident rate at nuclear power plants of 0.26 accidents per 200,000 worker-hours compared with a country-wide workplace average of 3.0.[17]

The risks from accidents are much harder to estimate, partly because nuclear accidents of all kinds have been very rare, and partly because the consequences could vary over so wide a range.

Studies have been conducted to estimate the chances of the protective barriers built into modern power plants failing in the course of an accident, causing radioactive releases of various hypothetical sizes. The calculations typically show that the chances of any such accident at the modern reactor, one that has been upgraded in keeping with the lessons of Three Mile Island and Chernobyl, are less than 1 in 100,000 per annum.

In considering the potential risks of nuclear energy it is necessary to regard it in the context of meeting increasing societal energy demands. An examination of the potential risks from different energy sources shows that the potential environmental and public health burdens from nuclear energy are smaller than those associated with fossil fuels.

The social element in sustainable development can only be met by addressing public concerns and gaining public confidence. It will be important to enable the public to put the social, ethnical and political issues raised by nuclear power into perspective with the different, but not altogether dissimilar, issues raised by the alternative sources of electricity generation.

Generally, when viewed by applying the three dimensions of sustainable development, nuclear energy can be seen to have the potential to meet a significant part of the world's future energy needs while meeting many of the objectives of sustainable development. The overall political trade-offs between the three dimensions of sustainability will differ from country to country, and will affect both the decisions taken and the means of addressing public concerns and securing public confidence.

## Non-proliferation

The incredible destructive potential of nuclear weapons has driven the international community to prevent their proliferation, or to 'keep the genie in the bottle'. Yet, the peaceful uses of nuclear energy are seen to provide much benefit. Because a good deal of knowledge relevant to nuclear weapon is intrinsically acquired in the course of the preparation for, and actual use of, nuclear energy and/or nuclear research facilities, preventing weapons proliferation while allowing civil nuclear development to go on is a difficult task. Consequently, the risk of weapons proliferation will remain an issue for nuclear energy and an important concern for the public as long as the link between civilian and military use of nuclear energy cannot be effectively and permanently cut.

Obtaining nuclear weapons is a complex undertaking, requiring not just specialized fissile material, but also the necessary knowledge and technology to be able to design, build, handle and deliver them. Physical testing of a nuclear weapon may also be sought to ensure its reliability and effectiveness.

Beginning in 1946, the international community targeted each of these 'essentials' with the objective of preventing access to the materials and critical technologies, preventing testing, and also seeking to control access to the technologies needed to deliver a weapon. These efforts culminated in a series of treaties, notably the *Treaty on the Non-proliferation of Nuclear Weapons* (NPT, in force since 1970),[18] and the *Comprehensive Nuclear-Test-Ban Treaty* (CTBT, not brought into force), which continue to form the basis of all efforts to prevent proliferation.[19]

The NPT divides the world into two groups – states that had nuclear weapons when the Treaty came into place, or the 'nuclear-weapons states' which included China, France, Russia, the United Kingdom and the United States; and the remainder of the signatories called the 'non-nuclear-weapons states'. As of the beginning of 2003 there were 188 signatories of the treaty, the most recent being Cuba, which acceded to the treaty in November 2002. Each nuclear-weapons state pledged not to transfer nuclear weapons, not to assist any non-nuclear-weapon state to develop nuclear weapons, and to work to achieve nuclear disarmament. India, Israel and Pakistan have so far refused to sign the NPT.[20]

## Controls on nuclear materials and testing of nuclear weapons

IAEA safeguards are the key means of detecting and deterring the diversion of nuclear material by a state. All non-nuclear-weapons states party to the NPT must agree to the application of IAEA safeguards to all of their nuclear material. Such comprehensive or full-scope safeguards agreement are intended to provide confidence that a non-nuclear-weapons state is complying with its commitment not to manufacture nuclear weapons. Furthermore, while not obligated to do so, each of the nuclear-weapons states has concluded safeguards agreements (so-called voluntary offers) that permit the IAEA to verify some or all of its civil nuclear activities. IAEA safeguards are also applied in states that have not signed the NPT (India, Israel and Pakistan), but only on selected facilities when required by the suppliers of the facilities or the nuclear material involved. In 1997, an additional safeguards protocol, which includes measures to improve the capability to detect possibly undeclared nuclear activities, was agreed. About 70 states have already signed it and the ratification process has been completed for 30 of them.

Negotiations for a 'comprehensive test ban' were initiated in January 1994 and the CTBT was concluded in September 1996, although it will not enter into force until all of the 44 states with nuclear power or research reactors have ratified it. It prohibits all nuclear explosions, either for military or civilian purposes. Its signatories (numbering 166 countries by October 2002) agree to prohibit or prevent nuclear explosions at any place within their jurisdiction or control, and not to encourage in any way participation in any nuclear explosion. The Treaty establishes a comprehensive verification regime, including the conduct of on-site inspections, provisions for consultation and clarification, and mutual confidence-building measures.

## Iran's nuclear programme

The Iranian nuclear programme was initiated in 1974 as one of the components of an ambitious energy plan based on optimum utilisation of energy resources: oil, gas, hydro and nuclear. The basic philosophy was a large diversification of sources of energy to reach an optimal energy mix with the aim of having a more flexible system of energy supply and of preserving national hydrocarbon reserves as long as possible.

There was a second reason for launching a nuclear programme. The country was in the process of rapid industrialization and all technological developments in the world were of great interest to Iran. Iran needed to have access to the nuclear technology not only for power generation, but also to enhance her level of technological development and to take advantage of various applications of this technology in her scientific and industrial activities. This is why research and development enjoyed a high priority in her nuclear programme.

Dr Akbar Etemad, the president of the of Atomic Energy Organization of Iran (AEOI) was given unprecedented authority of decision making and autonomy of action by statute of the organisation passed by the parliament. Etemad enjoyed the full trust and confidence of the Shah and the government.

In 1974, the German contractor Siemens began construction of two 1,200–1,300 MW pressurized water nuclear reactors near Bushehr. The German programme included 2,100 German workers and roughly 7,000 Iranian workers. The Shah of Iran intended that this programme would provide Iran with the infrastructure essential for industrializing the country.

The Siemens subsidiary, Kraftwerk Union AG (KWU), had been designing and building nuclear power plants since the mid-1950s. Experience gained in the early years with different reactor types soon led to the emergence of the light water reactor as the most economical technology. From the very beginning, Siemens pursued the development of both pressurized water reactor (PWR) and boiling water reactor (BWR) plants. Beginning in the early 1970s the German government supported efforts by Siemens/KWU to secure key nuclear reactor contracts in foreign markets.

The Bushehr I reactor was 85 per cent complete and the Bushehr II reactor was partially complete prior to the 1979 Iranian Revolution. The Bushehr I was due to be completed in 1981 as pressure testing of the containment for the first unit had been completed. After the fall of the Shah, construction of both reactors were halted. Ayatollah Khomeini declared this project 'anti-Islamic', and the government of Mehdi Bazargan soon abandoned it. Interestingly enough, just prior to the Iranian Revolution, the construction of a French-built reactor at a Karun River site had been cancelled, and Prime Minister Shahpur Bakhtiar had decided not to cancel the Bushehr reactors because they were to far along in the construction process. The construction of the nuclear power plant in Bushehr ceased in 1982 as a result of a fire in the plant.

During the Iran–Iraq War, Iraqi strike aircraft partially damaged both reactors. Iraqi warplanes first struck the Bushehr reactor on 24 March 1984, inflicting light damage. More Iraqi air strikes took place; two in 1985; one in 1986; two in 1987; and a final raid occurred in 1988. One of the reactors was severely damaged, with the structure sealed and the containment dome covered in sheet metal. The damage to the facilities was estimated at $2.9–4.6 billion.

In 1987, an Argentine–Spanish firm was negotiating to finish construction of the nuclear power plant. Designed to have two 1,200 MW reactors, it was expected to take 3 years to complete. However, nothing came of these negotiations.

Iran sought to rebuild the Bushehr reactor, and asked the Germans to resume work on the facility. In the face of diplomatic pressure applied by the United States, Iran was unable to persuade Siemens to resume work. Kraftwerk Union [KWU] proposed a new design, replacing the nuclear reactors with natural gas-operated turbines, but Iran was not interested in this alternative. The legal dispute between Siemens and Iran remained unresolved as of 1998. Iran claimed billions of dollars in damages, based on the fact that Iran had paid for a nuclear plant which was never finished. Siemens tried to resolve the dispute, which has been supported by the International Commerce Commission in Paris.

According to Russia's former atomic energy minister, Alexander Rumyantsev, the Bushehr reactor will be completed and ready for use in 2005. As agreed in an $800 million contract signed in 1995, Russia is providing Iran with the material and technical assistance to complete the VVER-1000 reactor. Russia will also be providing Iran with the reactor fuel to power the facility.

It appears that an agreement has been reached between Moscow and Tehran requiring that all spent fuel from the Bushehr reactor be returned to Russia (but only through the first decade of the plant's operation). In June 2003, Rumyantsev stated that Russia will withhold fresh fuel from Iran until such an agreement is formalized. However this deal has not been sealed, and the media is reporting that there has been some debate between the two sides regarding the specifics of the agreement.

The deal also called for the possible supply of two modern 465 megawatt VVER-440 reactor units, along with a centrifuge plant to enrich uranium, a 30–50 megawatt research reactor, 2000 tons of natural uranium, and technical training. The centrifuge plant was cancelled under American pressure; as of 2002 the status of the research reactor and the uranium was unclear, though the training had been initiated.

Based on estimates of plutonium output from typical pressurised light water power reactors, the Bushehr facility will produce enough weapons-grade plutonium in spent reactor fuel to provide Iran with means to construct roughly 35 nuclear weapons annually. However, in order for Iran to use the plutonium from Bushehr for weapons production, it must first construct a facility to extract plutonium from the spent reactor fuel. Thus far, there are no reports of Iran building such a facility.

In May 2003, Iran declared its intention to construct a 40 MW thermal heavy water reactor in Arak. Soon after, Iranian authorities provided the IAEA with the technical dimensions of the Iran Nuclear Research Reactor (IR-40), which is purportedly based on an indigenous design using natural $UO_2$ fuel and heavy water as both coolant and moderator. Although the reactor will be capable of producing weapons-grade plutonium, Iran claims that it is intended for use in research and in the production of radio-isotopes for medical and industrial applications. While visiting Iran in July 2003, IAEA inspectors discovered that despite the declared radio-isotope production purposes of the facility, no provisions had been made for the inclusion of hot cells. On 1 November 2003, Iran confirmed that it planned to construct an additional building at the Arak site to house hot cells for radio-isotope production.

On 3 October 2000, the Head of Iran's Atomic Energy Agency (Gholamreza Aqazadeh, the former Oil Minister), announced that Iran would pursue a plan aimed at meeting 20 per cent of the country's electricity demand through nuclear power. Aqazadeh said that the government had decided to build a second 1,000 MW unit at the Bushehr nuclear power complex as soon as work is completed on the current unit being built by the Russians. Aqazadeh further said that Iran was discussing further nuclear power plant deals with Russia and China.

Recent reports indicate that Iran is facing significant risk of severe power shortages by 2004 if 13,000 MW of additional electricity is not available. It is believed that this is a result of state-owned utilities converting their thermal power plants from oil to gas. The Iranian government hopes that the introduction of the Bushehr facility into the power grid will help prevent shortages.

## Conclusions

Nuclear energy is a technically complex source of energy that remains unique among energy sources as a result of a number of factors. In relation to nuclear energy in its current form, it has been shown that:

- Nuclear energy is a major source of energy in the world, producing about 17 per cent of the world's electricity.
- The disposal of high-level waste is not yet carried out; public opposition is the main constraint although progress towards implementing solutions is beginning to be made.
- Very high levels of safety are essential to nuclear energy deployment, although some degree of risk remains.
- Existing power plants are generally economically competitive, even in deregulated markets, but decisions to build new power plants may depend on public policy factors.
- Nuclear energy has certain advantages over other energy sources: carbon-free and air-pollution-free generation of electricity as well as security of supply.

In light of these factors and others not discussed here, nuclear energy is at something of a crossroads at the beginning of the second nuclear century as it undergoes a thorough review by governments, the public and industry. Decision-makers are faced with the difficulty of how to meet the continued growth in world energy demand while minimizing the environmental impacts of energy production. They must do so while accounting for public attitudes, the cost and competitiveness of the various energy sources, and public policy objectives such as security of supply and non-proliferation. How they resolve the tension between these sometimes-conflicting factors will ultimately define the extent of nuclear energy's use worldwide. How soon promising advances in state-of-the-art technology can influence these decisions will also play a significant role.

If a case cannot be satisfactorily made that nuclear energy is economically competitive, safe, and that there are acceptable solutions for its waste, then nuclear energy is likely to decline, at first slowly, in importance. Yet, if it can be demonstrated to the satisfaction of the public that nuclear energy does address these concerns, it is likely that there will be strong new growth in nuclear power.

The potential links between peaceful uses of nuclear energy and the proliferation of nuclear weapons merit special attention. Diversion from peaceful nuclear energy programmes is one possible route, although not the most likely one, for the acquisition of essential technology, equipment, or fissile material for making weapons by countries or groups who seek them. Since proliferation is essentially a political problem, governments should seek political solutions, including confidence-building between countries and enhancing regional security.

An international non-proliferation and safeguards regime has been put in place to address this risk. This regime is regularly reviewed and adapted to keep pace with a wider access to nuclear technologies throughout the world. National export controls should be consistent with the aims of international agreements in this area. Non-proliferation concerns should be integrated into the development of new nuclear facilities and processes.

A brief account of Iran's nuclear programme is given with particular emphasis on construction of the two pressurized water reactors at Bushehr. It is noted that Iran is facing significant risk of severe power shortages by 2004 if 13,000 MW of additional electricity is not available. The introduction of the Bushehr facility into the power grid will help prevent shortages.

## Notes

1  NEA Nuclear Energy Data 'Brown Book', Paris: Organization for Economic Co-operation and Development (OECD), 2002 (annual publication).
2  Nuclear power reactors in the world, Reference Data Series 2, Vienna: International Atomic Energy Agency (IAEA), 2002 (Annual Publication). See also the online Power Reactor Information System (PRIS) at www.iaea.org/programmes/a2
3  International Energy Agency (IEA), Key World Energy Statistics, Paris: OECD/IEA, 2002.
4  IEA, World Energy Outlook, Paris: OECD/IEA, 2001.
5  Royal Academy of Engineering, Nuclear Energy: The Future Climate, London: The Royal Society, 1999. Available online at www.royalsco.ac.uk/policy/nuclearreport.htm
6  NEA, nuclear Energy in Sustainable Development Perspective, Paris: OECD, 2000. NEA Issue Brief available online at www.nea.fr/html/pub/webpubs

7  IAEA, 'Sustainable Energy Development', *IAEA Bulletin*, Vol. 42, No. 2, 2000.

8  NEA, The Economics of the Nuclear Fuel Cycle, Paris: OECD, 1994. Available online at www.nea.fr/html/pub/webpubs

9  NEA, Projected Costs of Generating Electricity: 1998 Update, Paris: OECD, 1998.

10  NEA, Nuclear Power in Competitive Electricity Markets, Paris: OECD, 2000. Available online at www.nea.fr/html/pub/webpubs

11  NEA, Externalities and Energy Policy: The Life-cycle Analysis Approach, Workshop Proceedings, Paris, France, 15–16 November 2001. Paris: OECD, 2002. Available online at www.nea.fr/html/pub/webpubs

12  NEA, Nuclear Energy in a Sustainable Development Perspective, Paris: OECD, 2000. NEA Issue Brief available online at www.nea.fr/html/pub/webpubs

13  NEA, Uranium 2001: Resources, Production and Demand, Paris: OECD, 2002.

14  NEA, Broad Impact of Nuclear Power, Paris: OECD, 1993. NEA Issue Brief available online at www.nea.fr/html/pub/webpubs

15  NEA, Nuclear Energy and Kyoto Protocol, Paris: OECD, 2002.

16  NEA, Nuclear Power and Climate Change, Paris: OECD, 1998. Available online at www.nea.fr/html/pub/webpubs

17  NEA, Nuclear Education and Training: Cause for Concern? Paris: OECD, 2000. NEA Issue Brief available online at www.nea.fr/html/pub/webpubs

18  Laura Rockwood, 'The Nuclear Non-proliferation Treaty: A Permanent Commitment to Disarmament and Non-proliferation', *Nuclear Law Bulletin*, No. 56, December 1995. See www.nea.fr/html/law/nlb/NiB-56-en.pdf

19  Comprehensive Nuclear-Test-Ban Treaty. Available online at www.ctbto.org

20  IAEA, The Structure and Content of Agreements Between the Agency and States Required in Connection with the Treaty on the Non-proliferation of Nuclear Weapons (IAEA INFCIRC/153), Vienna: IAEA, 1972. Available online at www.iaea.org/worldatom/Documents/Infeires/Others/inf153.shtml

# 12 Managing oil resources and economic diversification in Iran

*Massoud Karshenas and Hassan Hakimian*

## Introduction

Since 1979, Iran has witnessed important socio-economic and institutional changes and has been affected by significant economic and political upheavals. These years have witnessed a succession of oil booms and busts, external war, trade sanctions and, more recently, heightened internal strife within the state. After nearly three decades, however, Iran's political outlook seems unclear to most observers, and the economic record is equally lacklustre with many Iranians experiencing a considerable retrogression in their living standards by regional and international standards.[1]

Since the second half of the 1990s, and with the surfacing of a reformist faction within the ruling hierarchy, the Iranian state has been beset by a divisive political struggle with different political factions openly competing for political and legislative supremacy. Partly as a consequence of this, and partly because of Iran's ability to live off its oil revenue, the agenda for economic reform has often been put on the back-burner, postponing the largely overdue modernization of Iran's ailing economy.[2]

In this chapter we argue that without fundamental economic and political reform the long term prospects of the Iranian economy will not be bright. First, we offer a broad overview of Iran's economic performance over the last two decades and characterize its structural features and continued weaknesses. Next, we turn to a discussion of possible models of oil revenue utilization and their economic and political implications. Our aim is to highlight ways in which structural reforms can lead to a diversification of the economic structure away from a dependency on the oil sector in the long term. We argue that the way to do so is to restructure the utilization of the oil industry to achieve true decentralization of economic decision-making and thereby pave the way for political reform.

## Iran's economic performance in perspective

That Iran has experienced a remarkable deterioration in its growth performance since the late 1970s is well established.[3] Comparisons with Turkey, Malaysia and Korea highlight this sharp trend reversal in the Iranian economy since the mid-1970s. Figure 12.1 demonstrates that Iran's per capita income grew faster than Turkey, Malaysia and South Korea between 1955 and 1975. Since the late

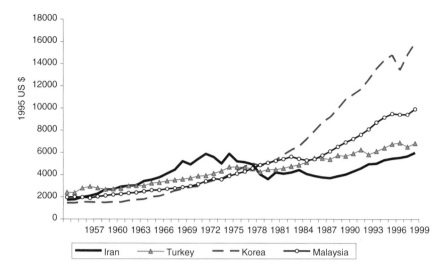

*Figure 12.1* Per capita GDP trends in Iran, Malaysia, Korea and Turkey, 1955–2000.

Source: Heston A., R. Summers and B. Aten, *Penn World Table Version 6.1*, Center for International Comparisons at the University of Pennsylvania (CICUP), October 2002.

Note: Figures refer to real GDP per capita in constant dollars expressed in international prices (base 1995).

1970s, however, Iran's growth rate has fallen behind with a widening gap emerging especially with South Korea and Malaysia who have managed to increase their per capita GDP consistently in this period and more than doubled it since the late 1970s. The same Figure demonstrates that Malaysia – another oil economy – has performed spectacularly better then Iran in this period, highlighting the fact that being an oil economy in itself is not a cause of lagging behind the other countries as has been the case of Iran.

Figure 12.2 highlights the comparison of economic performances between Iran and Turkey between 1960 and 2000. Starting from similar per capita income levels, Turkey shows a more steady growth rate and, following the collapse of growth in Iran in the 1980s, has overtaken Iran. Although much of the catching up by Turkey took place during the disastrous war years in Iran in the 1980s, from which Turkey and other neighbouring countries benefited economically, sustained economic growth in Turkey would not have been possible without fundamental economic reforms embarked upon by that country from the early 1980s. What is remarkable is that Turkey has achieved this with a generally lower investment ratio, which is an indication of the lower efficiency of investment in Iran.[4] As to the degree of diversification of the two economies, Figure 12.3 shows the share of manufacturing exports in total merchandise exports, which indicates that while Turkey has managed to increase its manufacturing share from negligible levels in the 1960s to over 80 per cent in 2002, Iran has barely managed to exceed the 10 per cent level.[5]

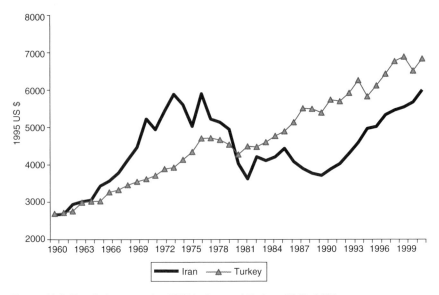

*Figure 12.2* Trends in per capita GDP in Iran and Turkey, 1960–2000.

Source: Heston A., R. Summers and B. Aten, *Penn World Table Version 6.1*, Center for International Comparisons at the University of Pennsylvania (CICUP), October 2002.

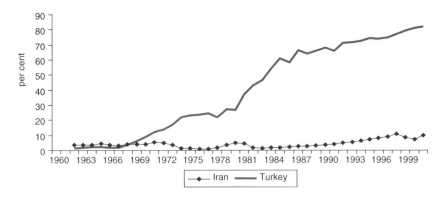

*Figure 12.3* Trends in share of manufacturing exports in Iran and Turkey, 1960–2000.

Source: World Development Indicators, World Bank, 2002.

Low and volatile economic growth rate has been part of the predicament of Iran's performance since the Revolution. Prior to 1979, Iran's average growth rate was nearly four times higher than growth in the first two decades after the Revolution (9 per cent p.a. against 2.5 per cent). Inevitably, the Iranian economy suffered the most in the 1980s during the war with Iraq, but even during the Second Five Year Economic Development Plan phase (1994–8), per capita income was rather stagnant. The most significant episode of growth in this period came in the early 1990s, during a brief period of post-war economic reconstruction and economic reforms, which abruptly ended amidst the debt crisis of the mid-1990s.[6] Even a resurgence of growth rate during the Third Five Year Plan years can be explained by buoyant international oil prices and it is not clear whether it can be sustainable.

Iran's poor comparative economic performance has not been limited to faltering growth alone. A combination of high inflation and high unemployment rates has also beset much of this period. Between 1993 and 2001, the Islamic Republic's inflation rate fluctuated in the range 11 per cent – 49 per cent with an average figure of over 23 per cent. In more recent years, it has averaged about 15 per cent per annum.[7]

Official estimates put unemployment at about 16 per cent, with much higher rates among the educated young Iranians.[8] The Third Five Year Plan anticipated job creation in the order of three-quarters of a million a year just to keep unemployment rate steady at 16 per cent. Even allowing for the fact that the tailing off of the population growth rate since the 1990s may ease off the supply-side pressure on the labour market,[9] two further considerations still lead to a fairly bleak outlook for the job market in Iran in the years to come. One of these is low womens' Labour Force Participation Rates, which is likely to rise (currently LFPR is around 15 per cent); another issue is labour productivity which is again likely to rise. According to the World Bank, Iran will need growth rates comparable to those attained by China (i.e. above 7.5 per cent) to be able to reduce unemployment rate to 10 per cent by 2010.[10] Unsurprisingly, persistent high unemployment is seen as the Achilles' Heel of the economy and one that is potentially capable of causing considerable social and political instability.

Another notable area of weakness has been Iran's inability to attract Foreign Direct Investment (FDI). Iran's current FDI inflows are abysmal both in absolute size and by any comparative measure. Total net FDI amounted to $32 million only in 2001, amounting to only 0.34 per cent of all FDI inflows into the MENA region. Since this region is severely underrepresented in its share of global FDI flows (accounting only for 1.3 per cent of the total), it is not surprising that Iran's share in the global FDI inflows is also a paltry 0.003 per cent.[11]

Figure 12.4 shows Iran's FDI flows in 2001 in comparison with her MENA peers: most notably, Turkey and Morocco, which are both relatively more open economies and each accounts for between one-quarter and one-third of all inflows into the region.

## The problem of oil-dependency

Although Iran has a longer history of industrial development and capital accumulation compared to most other oil-producing countries, its economic structure is still very much dominated by oil. For instance, this is seen in the dominance of oil exports in both the balance of payments and the government's fiscal revenues. Although non-traditional exports have risen in recent years, there are as yet few signs of a major breakthrough in terms of real economic diversification away from reliance on the oil sector. For instance, as mentioned earlier, Turkey and Tunisia

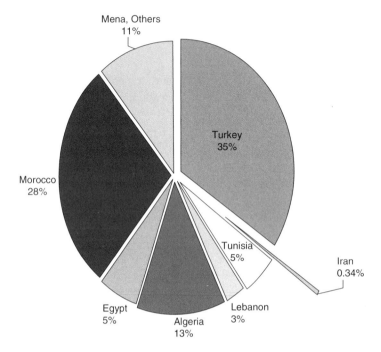

*Figure 12.4* Iran's FDI inflows as a proportion of MENA's FDI inflows, 2001.
Source: UNCTAD.

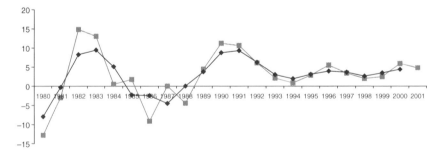

*Figure 12.5* Cycles of economic growth and oil exports income in Iran, 1980–2001.
Source: Based on Data from Bank Markazi Iran, *Economic Trends* (Tehran, various issues).
Note: Oil exports are measured in current US$, three year moving averages.

have managed to raise their share of manufactured exports to about three-quarters of their total exports. Egypt and Morocco also had a higher comparable share (over one-third in contrast to Iran's only 9 per cent) in the late 1990s.

Lack of sufficient diversification and continued high oil-dependency highlight Iran's economic problems in the last two decades. Figure 12.5 underscores the interlinked cycles of oil exports income and real GDP in Iran, suggesting a remarkable fit between the two.

This is further supported by an examination of the nature of economic cycles in Iran and their correlation with the oil boom and bust periods. Table 12.1 shows a strong relationship between changes in Iran's oil exports earnings and real GDP growth rate during both boom and bust phases in the past two decades. It can be seen that there is a striking association between these two variables both on the up and down phases of the growth cycle. For instance, the strongest relative recovery in economic activity after the Revolution (during the two-year period 1982–3) was helped by a strong recovery in oil revenues in the same period (exceeding 51 per cent on an average annual basis). Similar peaks occurred during 1989–91 (the initial stages of the First Five Year Plan) and in 1996. In both these instances, buoyant oil revenues aided recovery.

Similar strong associations can be observed on the down swing, too, when a decline in economic activity was accentuated or brought about by a contraction of oil income. Prominent examples of these periods are:

a   Early days of the Revolution and breakout of war (1978–81);
b   The OPEC oil crisis of mid-1980s (1984–6);
c   Last year of war with Iraq (1988);
d   Austerity package associated with the debt crisis (1994); and finally,
e   The oil price slump of 1997/8 and the subsequent recession in 1998.[12]

Contrary to most expectations perhaps, there is further evidence to suggest that oil-dependency has in fact increased during the Islamic Republic years. There is no doubt that there has been a strong long-term relationship between oil export revenues and economic growth in both pre- and post-Revolution periods. Here we define oil dependency in terms of the short to medium term relationship between oil export revenues and economic growth. Table 12.2 shows the results of regression

*Table 12.1* Boom and bust cycles: percentage of change in GDP

|  | *Per cent change in GDP* | *Per cent change in non-oil GDP* | *Per cent change in oil revenues* |
|---|---|---|---|
| **Boom phases:** | | | |
| **1982–1983** | 12.9 | 8.2 | 51.2 |
| **1989–1991** | 8.6 | 7.7 | 21.0 |
| **1996** | 6.1 | 7.1 | 27.6 |
| **1999–2002** | 4.3 | 5.3 | 27.9 |
| **Bust phases:** | | | |
| **1978–1981** | −3.7 | −9.0 | −9.9 |
| **1984–1986** | −2.3 | −0.6 | −31.1 |
| **1988** | −3.5 | −5.8 | −10.1 |
| **1994** | 0.5 | 1.8 | 1.9 |
| **1998** | 2.9 | 3.0 | −35.8 |

Source: Based on Data from Bank Markazi Iran, *Economic Trends* (Tehran, various issues).

Table 12.2 Short-term dynamics between oil exports and GDP growth

Dependent variable annual GDP growth

| | Pre-Revolution period | | | Post-Revolution period | | | |
|---|---|---|---|---|---|---|---|
| | 1 | 2 | 3 | 1 | 2 | 3 | 4 |
| $GOIL_t$ | 0.15 (1.81) | 0.14 (1.56) | 0.163 (1.52) | 0.193 (3.45) | 0.207 (3.61) | 0.239 (4.22) | 0.243 (4.13) |
| $GOIL_{t-1}$ | | −0.04 (−.46) | −0.029 (−0.28) | | 0.061 (1.06) | 0.094 (1.65) | 0.102 (1.65) |
| $GOIL_{t-2}$ | | | 0.052 (0.49) | | | 0.108 (1.89) | 0.116 (1.88) |
| $GOIL_{t-3}$ | | | | | | | 0.024 (0.41) |
| Constant | 0.08 (2.64) | 0.086 (2.35) | 0.076 (1.53) | 0.001 (0.06) | −0.002 (−0.11) | −0.011 (−0.51) | −0.012 (−0.56) |
| Adjusted $R^2$ | 0.113 | 0.062 | 0.009 | 0.331 | 0.335 | 0.411 | 0.383 |

Source: Based on Data from Bank Markazi Iran, *Economic Trends* (Tehran, various issues).

Note: The independent variable is annual growth of oil export revenues in current dollars. t-Ratios in parentheses.

estimates of annual GDP growth on annual growth of oil export revenues with various lag structures. As the table shows, the relationship in the pre-Revolution period (1959–79) is rather weak, but in the period after the Revolution (1980–2002) there is a significant relationship between the two variables, with much higher coefficient values than in the earlier period. The sum of coefficients in regression 3 in the post-Revolution period is 0.44, which is close to three-times higher than the value for the same regression in the pre-Revolution period. These results also corroborate the close association between oil export revenues and growth cycles in the Iranian economy in the post-Revolution period shown in Figure 12.5 and Table 12.1. But more significantly, they also show the increased dependence of the economy on oil in the post-Revolution period. It is not unlikely that with the setting up of the special Oil Stabilization Fund in recent years, this relationship has somewhat weakened. However, the root causes of this phenomenon are to be found in deeper structural features of the post-Revolution economy – predominantly associated with the lack of economic diversification and competitiveness of the non-oil economy – which cannot be remedied without fundamental policy reform.

## Policy challenges

The foregoing discussion has focused on the persistence of structural weaknesses – as manifested in increased oil-dependency in Iran's economy. These have combined with inadequate or ambivalent policy responses in the post-Revolutionary period, highlighting Iran's continued economic fragility despite its renowned mineral riches. These have, in turn, compounded oil-dependency, leading to a weak and uncertain investment climate, fragile public finances, and an inward-orientated economy for much of the last two decades.

Some observers have characterized Iran's failure to achieve structural transformation since 1980 as a state of 'structural trap'. This is defined as the situation 'in which political and economic obstacles avert the reallocation of capital from low-productivity firms and sectors to high-productivity ones'.[13] Accordingly, Iran's economy remains dominated by inefficient, subsidized and loss-making state-owned enterprises (SOEs), as well as the unregulated and unclear para-governmental organizations (*bonyad*s or foundations): conglomerates which benefit substantially from both implicit and explicit government subsidies.[14]

The introduction of the Third Five Year Plan in March 2000 ushered in a new direction in official policy-making. After several years of hesitancy, this Plan finally seemed to address the overarching question of economic reform by increasing the role and diversity of the private sector, reducing obstacles to foreign and domestic investment, initiating privatization, supporting export-led growth, and developing the non-oil sectors. The Plan set out a series of ambitious targets, including an average GDP growth of 6 per cent per year, average annual non-oil GDP growth of 6.8 per cent, and an average annual inflation of 15.9 per cent. Job creation was also targeted to reach three-quarters of a million new jobs annually. Moreover, external debt was to be kept at below $25 billion in order to ensure the attainment of a debt service ratio of 30 per cent by the end of the five years.

In recent years, there have been notable improvements in short-term macroeconomic indictors: aided by the rise in oil prices since 2000, the current account, trade balance and external debt obligations have all been stabilized; foreign exchange reserves too have been substantially strengthened.[15] Of more long-term significance, non-oil exports, which had dipped worryingly after 1997, have climbed back up to achieve a 6.3 per cent year-on-year growth rate in 2002.[16] Inflation has fallen back to 15 per cent. The most glaring failure in an improving economic environment is the high unemployment rate, still stubbornly fixed above 16 per cent.

Despite these recent improvements, political deadlock continues to affect economic performance adversely. Thus, some of the toughest structural changes that could transform the competitiveness of the economy have yet to be tackled. Effective reform of SOEs through privatization has not yet materialized, even though the legislative and regulatory environment governing the process has been established. So far, privatization has been confined to sales of government equity shares to private investors and *bonyad*s, with the majority control retained by the government. Given that SOEs are politicized institutions in which both workers and managers strive to prolong subsidies and perpetuate their redistributive function, this was perhaps largely predictable.[17] Moreover, large-scale privatization would inevitably entail mass redundancies, which are not politically feasible, particularly in an era of high unemployment.

Other areas for concern include the lack of labour market reform and banking sector reform. The former is highly contentious in Iran, and the latter critical for the success of the overall reform effort. In the past two decades, state-owned banks have taken on the role of satisfying the credit requirements of loss-making SOEs and para-governmental institutions that have access to rationed bank credits with substantial interest subsidies. Moreover, they lack adequate regulatory and prudential oversight and suffer from progressively deteriorating loan portfolios. Overall, these make the reform of the financial sector more of a priority – not least for encouraging and improving the general investment climate.

One of the most significant areas of reform was the successful unification of the exchange-rate system in March 2002. Although the new system still entails significant budgetary costs for the government, because these implicit costs have had to be replaced with explicit subsidies, the new system is more transparent, and has signalled to international investors the seriousness of Iran's reform effort.[18]

Other reforms have complemented the foreign exchange rate reform. Encouragingly, the Third Plan's launch coincided with a sustained rise in oil prices, which reversed declining oil revenues and closed the trade deficit. Contrary to previous oil price booms, this time the government has diverted excess revenue from the windfall to a newly established account (the so-called Oil Stabilization Fund), which is managed by Bank Markazi (Central Bank of Iran), and some of this has been used to pay back foreign debt.

However, without more fundamental economic reforms directed towards the creation of a diversified and competitive national economy, these recent reforms remain superficial and will be easily reversed under less favourable conditions in the international oil market. The rapid increase in oil prices since 2000 has created a semblance of economic success with relatively rapid growth and apparent internal and external balance. This type of oil-driven growth, however, is by its very nature, not sustainable in the long run. Each episode of oil price increases moves the economy to a higher plateau in terms of foreign exchange requirements to sustain the pattern of oil-dependent economic growth. Oil prices are subject to sharp fluctuations, and even if the country can smoothen the impact of such fluctuations through the operation of the Oil Stabilization Fund, without a continuous upward trend in oil prices the oil- dependent growth process will have to come to an end. Without fundamental structural reform to substantially improve export diversification, the recent reforms, as in the past, will sooner or later be reversed.

Export-diversification is not only a prerequisite for sustained growth in the long run, but also, critically, shapes employment-generation in the economy. As pointed out above, the fast rates of growth of supply of labour has meant that even the current rates of growth, which are high by the post-Revolutionary standards, cannot prevent unemployment from rising. The government has recently resorted to the ultimate weapon used in oil economies, that is, creating jobs in the private sector by giving subsidies to firms to create employment. This practice, however, is inefficient and unsustainable, and it further intensifies oil dependence of the economy.[19] The pre-requisite for reducing unemployment is a more diversified economy, building on job-creation in competitive, export-oriented activities by the private sector. This should be the main objective of economic reform in Iran, and the current reforms are far from adequate in addressing this issue.

It is sometimes argued that the high value of oil exports can itself crowd out other exports and become an obstacle to further diversification of exports. This argument is more likely to be true in the case of mature economies close to full employment of labour and with full integration into the world economy using the state-of-the-art technologies. However, in a developing economy like Iran with a young and rapidly growing labour force and with a huge technological gap and an ageing capital stock, oil exports can, under the right economic policies, be a complement to diversification into other export activities. A comparison with the case of Malaysia can shed light on this issue. As pointed out above, Malaysia, another oil economy, has maintained a robust growth performance over the past three decades, so that its per capita GDP, which was 40 per cent below Iran in the early 1970s, is now double Iran's per capita income (see, Figure 12.1). The sustained growth of the Malaysian economy has been made possible by building up a competitive non-oil export base, driven by both domestic and foreign private investment. As shown in Figure 12.6, in contrast to the case of Iran, being an oil economy has not prevented Malaysia from increasing its manufacturing export share from low levels in the mid-1960s to over 80 per cent in recent years. Whereas in the case of Iran in the post-Revolution period the contribution of foreign direct investment to capital formation has fallen to negligible levels, Malaysia in the same period has attracted foreign direct investment to the tune of 10 to over 25 per cent of its gross capital formation (Figure 12.7). More

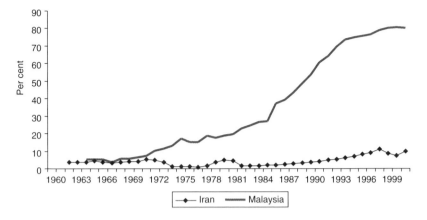

*Figure 12.6* Share of manufacturing in total exports in Iran and Malaysia, 1963–2001.
Source: World Development Indicators, World Bank, 2003.

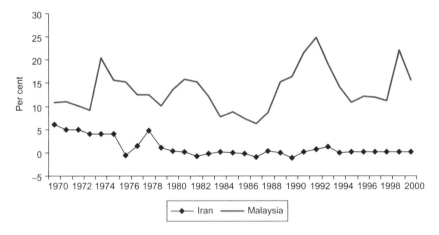

*Figure 12.7* Foreign direct investment in Iran and Malaysia, 1970–2001 (net inflows, percentage of gross capital formation).
Source: World Development Indicators, World Bank, 2003.

importantly, in addition to its financial contribution, foreign investment in the case of Malaysia has been instrumental in the transfer of modern technology, and in building up a competitive edge in export-oriented activities.

Lack of attention to the political economy aspects of reform can render apparently sound economic policies ineffective, even when due to force of circumstances the policies are rigorously implemented. In a comprehensive document articulating the case for economic reform in Iran, the World Bank has recently called for the abolition of the energy price subsidies in Iran.[20] Apart from reducing inefficiencies resulting from distorted energy prices, the proposed energy price reforms are estimated to increase the share of oil revenues accruing to the government by 10 per cent of the GDP. According to the World Bank report, such redistribution of income will increase national savings, which the report assumes will be used by the government to provide credits to boost private sector investment. This assumption is, in our opinion, rather simplistic. To begin with, the problem of lack of private investment in productive activities in Iran is not caused by the savings constraint. It is rather due to the lack of incentives in committing long-term investment in viable productive activities by the private sector. Some of the obstacles are related to the price distortions highlighted by the World Bank. But more serious problems relate to a lack of credibility in government policies, and the capture of the state by particular interests, which undermine competition and divert energies to unproductive, rent-seeking activities, and the arbitrary interventions by different branches of the government in safeguarding the interests of particular groups at the helm of power.

The World Bank cites the example of China in implying that in Iran a similar lack of democratic and transparent government may not be essential for the growth of the market economy. A small detail which is missing in this analysis is that Iran is not quite China. Given the huge oil surpluses in the hands of government, which with the new price reform policies will be substantially increased, the driving force of the Iranian economy will be state-centred, oil-financed activities. As long as the state remains undemocratic, and hence non-transparent, in an oil economy such as Iran, government policy will be dominated by particular rent-seeking interests that will inhibit the growth of an independent and competitive private sector-based economy. In the next section we discuss a number of possible structural reforms aimed at altering the nature of the state and oil-dependency in Iran.

## Utilization of oil revenues and democracy

Almost all oil economies have been grappling with the issues relating to the modes and mechanisms of utilization of oil revenues for a long time. A key question relates to the appropriate institutions in developing oil economies that can reconcile a democratic and transparent polity with oil rents being a sizable source of income in the economy. This is likely to be at the heart of any discussion on the democratization process in Iran and other oil economies in the Middle East in the coming years. Below we discuss a number of proposals put forward in recent publications, which are meant to reconcile the accrual of oil rents to the government with less centralized and more democratic modes of government, and more diversified economic outcomes. None of these proposals has been given adequate attention, particularly in the context of the Middle Eastern oil economies, as far as we are aware. The main concern of these proposals seems to be the relationship between oil and politics, and hence they have focused on ownership and the mechanisms of distribution of oil revenues rather than their optimum mode of *utilization*. As we argue below, separating the discussion of the mechanisms of distribution from utilization can in some cases be very problematic. We briefly discuss two proposals often referred to in the recent publications, and will proceed to discussing a third – and our preferred – proposal.

### The privatization proposal

We start with the privatization proposal, because this allows us to underline some of the basic concepts regarding the ownership, control, and modes of operation of the oil industry, as well as highlighting some of the basis facts regarding the Middle Eastern oil industry in general, and Iranian oil in particular. This proposal argues for privatizing the oil industry either by selling the assets of the industry and production rights to private companies, or by distributing marketable shares to the population.[21] It is argued that privatization helps invigorate the private sector and civil society, and turns the state into a tax state which will be more accountable.[22] It is argued that the combined result of these two tendencies would be conducive to the emergence of more democratic forms of government.

This proposal has been criticised on grounds of oil industry assets either becoming ultimately monopolized by a few domestic magnates, similar to the emergence of Russian oligarchs following its privatization programme, or falling into the hands of international oil companies.[23] Others have argued that this is the way capitalism works, and in any event, this would be a better outcome, both economically and politically, than the oil industry being monopolized by the state.[24] However, the main problem with this proposal, in our view, is that it does not pay due attention to the characteristics of the oil industry and the nature of oil reserves in the Middle East. In order to discuss the question of ownership in an orderly fashion, it will be helpful to distinguish between the ownership of oil reserves and the ownership of capital assets involved in the operational activities of the industry. This can help highlight the fact that the ownership of oil industry and the ownership of oil reserves are separate issues. Ownership of oil reserves entitles the owners to economic rent, while the ownership of industry by firms entitles them to a return on their capital and expertise. The rights and obligations of these two types of asset holding, and the nature of the relationship between the two, have been historically regulated by various types of oil contracts. The question of utilization of oil revenues, in the context of the Middle East oil, is mainly related to the issue of the ownership of oil reserves. We shall discuss the implications of privatization in relation to these two aspects of ownership in turn.

### Ownership of the oil industry and the national oil companies

The discussion of oil industry ownership, which is very different from the ownership of reserves and control of oil rents, involves a set of issues which are, at least in principle, more straightforward than the question of oil rents and democratization.

A brief look at the basic characteristics of the oil industry and the development of national oil companies in the Middle East would help the discussion.

Large sunk costs and high capital intensity, high risk, and substantial economies of scale, particularly in transportation and marketing, are well known characteristics of the oil industry. As a consequence the oil industry from its early days has been dominated by a few large, vertically integrated companies. The recent bout of mergers and acquisitions in the industry indicates that this tendency remains unabated – although the oil giants are increasingly diversifying into other energy sources, and are also involved in increasingly subcontracting to smaller service providers. The national oil companies, which have been developed since the 1950s in most Middle Eastern countries, were originally set up as both knowledge banks facilitating the negotiations with giant foreign oil companies, and as agents to facilitate joint partnerships with smaller, independent oil companies in developing fields in areas not covered by oil concessions to the major companies. Over time, the national oil companies developed into vertically integrated companies which came to dominate the oil industry in all Middle Eastern oil-exporting countries. This process particularly intensified after the 1970s when the old concessionary agreements were annulled and new riches allowed the governments to pursue their oil industry ambitions, perhaps trying to emulate the historical experience of British Petroleum. The outcome, however, has been in general the creation of very wasteful, inefficient and complicated entities, which can only survive by dint of huge subsidies, by earmarking relatively large parts of the oil export revenues for the upkeep of these companies, and by having access to cheap, subsidized oil. The mushrooming of job creation in these companies, and rampant corruption at higher levels, also play an important part in the clientelistic political relations in non-democratic states in these countries. Vertical integration in this case has less to do with the economic logic of the industry than with political patronage.

Since we are discussing the issue of ownership here, it should be kept in mind that the National Iranian Oil Company (NIOC), or any other national oil company in the region, does not have the ownership of oil reserves. These companies develop the oil reserves on behalf of the state, and their budgets normally comprise a share of oil export revenues in return for their services. The question of the future of these companies and their ownership types should be therefore confined to their capital, technology, expertise and other productive assets. There may be plausible arguments for privatization of these companies, but what is more important is that whatever their legal ownership type, these companies are not protected from competition. As integrated oil companies, the national oil companies should be given the same level playing field as foreign oil companies. That is, they have to be able to survive, in whatever legal or structural form, without resort to state subsidies. Ending political patronage in oil economies in the Middle East, and the construction of viable balanced economies in these countries, is not possible without the removal of such state subsidies. This is one of the preconditions for the emergence of a diversified economy along the comparative advantages of the country. This, however, does not solve the problem of control and distribution of oil rents. If anything, a more efficient oil industry is likely to increase the value of oil rents accruing to the state. Nor does this mean that the strategic decisions regarding production and exports can be left to private investors or the market forces. These issues have more to do with the question of ownership and control of oil reserves to which we shall turn next.

### *Ownership of reserves and control of oil rents*

Iranian oil reserves, and Middle East oil reserves in general, have two important peculiarities – first, they come in huge fields, and second the cost of production is extremely low compared to other regions. This has two very important implications, one regarding the regulation of the Middle East oil in the international oil market, and the second regarding the nature of oil revenues and their implication for the domestic economy. We discuss these in turn.

The international oil market, and particularly the low-cost Middle East oil, has always been regulated. Prior to the formation of OPEC this was done by the international oil cartel, which ensured price stability in the face of increasing production in the low-cost Middle Eastern fields. Since the 1970s this has been done by a combination of oil-producing and oil-consuming associations, where OPEC has played a particularly important role in regulating the output of the low-cost, high reserve and capacity Middle Eastern producers, with varying degrees of success. Such regulation of the Middle East oil production is of the utmost importance, because of the low cost and high reserves in the region. Without such regulation, oil prices become very unstable to the disadvantage of both the producers and the consumers. It is therefore important to dispel the illusion, created by some media commentators, that Middle East oil should be produced and exported within a 'free market' framework.[25] This is neither to the advantage of the exporting country nor the consumers in the long run. Decisions regarding investment, output, and pricing of oil need to be made within a national strategy which ensures optimal extraction of the oil resources and maximum revenues in the long run. This means that any fragmentation of the industry so far as these strategic decisions are involved should be avoided. In the design and implementation of a unified national strategy the roles of the national oil companies and the oil ministry will remain critical. In particular, unified, powerful and well informed national oil institutions are necessary to protect the interests of the country in negotiations and bargaining with large foreign oil companies. Such optimal depletion of the Middle Eastern oil reserves in a long-term perspective, which cannot be ensured by fragmented and often short-term perspectives of private investors, also best serves the interests of the consumers in the long run.

The second implication of the low cost Middle Eastern reserves, which has a more direct effect on the issue of ownership of reserves, is that much of the oil revenues take the form of rents or super-profits which cannot be easily divested by the government. That is, even if one offers the Iranian oil reserves in a wholesale fashion to competitive bids by international oil companies, the offer price or rental which goes to the government will be still the bulk of the revenues. In theory, it may be possible to argue that by issuing marketable shares to all Iranians one can get rid of the public ownership of the reserves, but this is neither practical nor justifiable. Such shares are likely to be quickly concentrated in the hands of a few large shareholders whose interests may be at variance with the long term strategic considerations regarding investment, output and the pricing of oil as discussed above. There are various other problems associated with this option arising from, for example, problems related to safeguarding of the interests of the future generations; environmental issues; uncertainties about reserves; lack of incentive structures to discover new reserves; problems with conferring the right of eminent domain to private companies, etc. Of course, one way to deal with most of these problems is to distribute non-marketable shares to the population, which can change as the population grows and new reserves are discovered, and with the state in charge of strategic decisions regarding investment, production and pricing, on behalf of the population. This is, however, a special case of the second option, namely, distributing revenues to the people, discussed below.

### The 'oil-to-the-people' proposal

This proposal suggests the distribution of oil revenues equally across the whole of the population. Another version of this proposal could be the distribution of oil revenues randomly across the population by, say, dropping notes from a helicopter. The effects will be more or less the same, with the random distribution option administratively less demanding and perhaps better in terms of perceived social justice effects. One version of this proposal in the Iranian context has been advocated by Hossein Bagherzadeh.[26] A more recent version surfaced in the press in the context of recent discussions of the reconstruction of Iraq. Recently, Guy Standing (an economist at the ILO), has also tried to enumerate some of the advantages of this proposal in the context of post-Saddam Iraq.[27] Since the Americans seemed to favour at least a version of this at some stage, and it also echoed favourably amongst some of the Iraqi politicians as well as in the popular media, it is likely that this proposal may gain prominence in the context of other oil economies.[28]

The proposal is based on an equal distribution of oil money in the form of handouts as a way of building a liberalized free market economy by reducing the size of the public sector and letting the people decide as to how best they want to utilize the oil revenues within a liberalized market economy. A political argument may be also constructed along these lines. It may be argued that oil revenues in the past allowed the gargantuan growth of the state and led to the atrophy of the civil society. The direct distribution of the oil revenues to the citizens would therefore supposedly redress this balance, and create the conditions for a strong civil society and a democratic polity. In addition to these effects, Bagherzadeh also points out that by getting part of the oil revenues directly to the poorest sections of society, this option leads to faster poverty reduction. He also argues that the equal distribution of oil revenues across the population prevents the undue concentration of the revenues in the hands of a few, and leads to better income distribution and a more just distribution of the benefits of oil. These can be regarded as the long-term or systemic arguments in favour of the proposal. There may be more short-term or contingent motivations for this proposal in the context of Iraq, which may have implications for other oil economies as well. For example, the Americans may perceive this proposal as doubly beneficial as a means to winning the hearts and minds of Iraqis in the aftermath of the war. Or they may even think that they could also gain credit in terms of them being viewed as the upholders of social justice by giving the Iraqi public for the first time direct control over the utilization of their country's oil income.

In our opinion none of the above arguments stands the test of careful scrutiny. On the contrary, we think that there are robust arguments against this type of proposal. We will try to address the above points in turn, and in the process will build up a case for the third proposal discussed below.

Starting with the systemic or long-term economic arguments enumerated above, would the distribution of oil revenues across the population create the conditions for a liberalized market economy? There are a number of important preconditions for a well-functioning market economy in Iran, most of which have the character of public goods requiring collective action. A well-functioning public administrative system with adequately paid civil servants; long term investment in the infrastructure; the creation of a flexible labour market which will require well run social security and pensions systems; and an overhaul of the financial system and the banking sector are obvious examples. Added to this are the building up of the education infrastructure, public health and other minimally-required social services. In non-oil economies, these types of activities are normally financed by government taxation, which is also partially true in most oil economies. In the long-run it is also desirable that these activities are financed by taxation in Iran, but this requires the overhaul of the taxation system and improvements in the collection system. Once the required public expenditure is taken care of, the next best use of oil revenues to bolster the construction of a market economy, is to set up investment funds to bolster private sector investment in small sector enterprises which are barred from access to formal capital markets. Only the excess profits from such investment funds can be legitimately used for distribution across the population, but even then very selectively, and for worthy causes rather than blanket distribution to all the population.

Another argument against the distribution of oil revenues to individuals relates to savings. Distribution of oil revenues to the population can lead to savings rates which may be socially sub-optimal. Collectively the population may deem higher rates of national savings desirable, but uncoordinated individualistic decisions would create sub-optimal choices. In the long-run, even when the taxation system is overhauled to cater for the needs of basic public services, it would be more beneficial to deposit oil surpluses in investment funds to bolster private investment than to distribute them across the population. Apart from strengthening the private sector economy, this can also help finance a general social security and pensions system from the profits of the investment fund.

Will the distribution of the oil revenues to the population help strengthen civil society and democratic institutions? Again, the balance of argument in our view is negative. Civil society is not composed of the mass of people with some money in their pockets. It is the outcome of social and economic development, a strong market economy, independent associations of various interest groups, and a state which can uphold law and order. As discussed above, the distribution of oil revenues across the population does not help these developments. A prerequisite of a strong civil society, as the arena of the formation and expression of particular interests, is a strong democratic state as the upholder of law and order (the rules of the game so to speak), and the general interest. A weak state which can be captured by particular interests through bribery or other means, or too strong and self-serving a state which leads to the atrophy of the civil society, can both lead to undemocratic and dysfunctional outcomes. Lack of individual civil rights will result when the particular and the general are enmeshed in one way or another as, for example, in medieval societies or modern day authoritarian states. Individual civil rights in modern societies are the result of the separation and balance between the particular (civil society), and the general or universal (the state). The construction of this configuration of social forces in present-day Iran, or in other oil states, requires careful attention to institution-building and socio-economic development, which will not be achieved by the distribution of oil revenues across the population. The nature of the utilization of oil revenues will, of course, certainly affect the balance, and needs careful consideration.

Turning to the aspects of poverty, inequality, and social justice in the proposal, one can find more arguments against it than in its favour. In a country like Iran, with a young and rapidly growing labour force, the long-term solution to the question of poverty is the creation of productive jobs on a sustainable basis rather than oil hand-outs. To the extent that oil hand-outs reduce the development potential of the economy in the long-run they can be counter productive. The immediate impact of the distribution of an equal sum of money amongst the population, would, by definition, be a one-time reduction in relative income inequality. But if this arrangement is at the expense of investment in physical and human capital in the economy, such income distributional effects will be short-lived. For the same reasons, such an arrangement may not be perceived as socially just by lower income groups. For example, consider a working class sole-breadwinner family man, who ekes out a living and is concerned about the future of his children, and at the same time appreciating the receipt of the few dollars a month hand-outs from the government. At the same time he observes that his younger neighbour, who does not have a family, and is more affluent, prefers to spend his oil hand-outs on more frivolous activities. This arrangement clearly will not be perceived as a just arrangement by the family man, who would prefer the investment of the oil revenues in procuring a more productive job with better remuneration for himself, and a better education and future for his children.

At a more general and philosophical level, there is no moral justification for a person who happens to be born in a land called Iran to receive hand-outs simply because the country happens to have oil resources. On the other hand, if the same individual is prepared to make an effort for social and economic development of his community, there is moral justification for oil revenues to assist him/her in that effort. Even worse, if the oil hand-outs help to propagate a culture of dependence and parasitic existence, they can be perceived as doubly repugnant. It is with a view to such considerations that the third alternative regarding the utilization of oil revenues is proposed below.

### The decentralized or 'regional' option

It is clear that the oil sector will dominate the Iranian economy for a long time to come. Oil revenue utilization needs to comply with a set of requirements in order to avoid the repetition of the distorted economic and political developments as in the past.

The first requirement is that oil revenues should not inhibit the full development and utilization of all other resources, namely human resources and other natural resources. Oil revenues should, in fact, be made to provide a positive inducement for such development.

Secondly, such developments in the non-oil sector should be based on decentralized, market-based principles in line with the comparative advantages of the economy. A basic prerequisite for this is that the state should refrain from engaging in economic activities that can be conducted on a commercial basis by the private sector. In fact, oil revenues should be used to bolster such activities in a manner which does not confer competitive advantages or rents to special interest groups with political influence. By implication, the state should also cease being perceived as the creator and protector of jobs in the economy.

This in turn necessitates the third requirement, namely, an accountable government subject to democratic checks and balances. The availability of oil revenues will of course always create the tendency for the oil states to overstep these boundaries. There is always pressure from below to utilize oil revenues to create jobs. At the top there will be intense competition within the state to capture the helm and gain access to the immense oil rents. At the extreme, an authoritarian state may come to dominate the economy and society by having access to the substantial oil rents.

The regional option is meant to create a balance between the centralizing and centrifugal forces in order to resist these tendencies. A review of some of the main characteristics of the oil economies in the Middle East, including Iran, can help to highlight some of the problems that this proposal is meant to address.

One of the main features of the oil economies in the region is the extreme centralization of these economies. This is often manifested in one or a few densely populated urban centres, particularly the capital, which is the seat of political power, growing in a hothouse manner and being the main beneficiaries of the expenditure of oil rents. The attraction of the working-age population to these urban centres handicaps the social and economic development of the outlying regions, and militates against the first requirement for balanced development discussed above, namely, the full utilization and development of other resources in the economy.

One consequence of this is that the economy becomes increasingly dependent on oil revenues, and the state increasingly becomes perceived as the creator and guarantor of jobs. In such economies one can often see the most modern amenities of life and technologies of production in the oil-driven urban growth centres, side by side with vast and increasingly depopulated areas with backward economies and, in some countries, with the old tribal relations in outlaying regions still intact. Oil becomes the life-blood of the economy and the state its heart and centre of gravity.

Of course regional development has always been a concern of development plans in Iran, as in other Middle Eastern Countries. In particular, in the post-Revolution period in Iran, regional disparities have received particular attention and, with better availability of disaggregated regional data, the government plans have paid increasing attention to regional dimensions of economic planning. However, the centripetal forces in the oil-dominated economy are so strong that regional disparities have been on the rise. One of the aims of the regional option is to prevent the reconstitution of the highly centralized and distorted economic structure by a mandatory distribution of oil revenues across all the provinces.

Another aim is to create regional and local power centres to counter the centralization of political power in the capital. The balance between the regional and central political power centres would create the necessary breathing space for the private sector economy and civil society to grow and assert their political influence through democratic channels. The architecture of the regional option needs to be tailored to the specificities of the countries concerned. In this chapter we can only discuss the basic principles which should guide such architecture, with particular reference to the case of Iran.

The fundamental prerequisite for this proposal to be effective is the balance between the regional political powers and the central government, and the reciprocal overseeing by the two in order to prevent each overstepping its constitutional mandate. To reconstruct the local economies and to reconstitute the current total centralization of power, oil revenues will, in the first instance, be totally allocated to the local governments according to some pre-set formula. The formula can be devised with reference to the current land/population ratios (to remedy the current lopsided state of regional development) at the outset, to be gradually replaced over time by variables which can act as incentives for the development of local private sector economies (e.g. private sector employment, productivity, etc.).

Within this framework, the central government will decide on the strategic issues of the oil sector, for example, pricing, investment and output, through the oil ministry or a reconstituted national oil company. It also manages the macroeconomic side of the oil revenue management (e.g. through the operation of the oil stabilization fund). The local governments collectively decide on the share of their oil revenues divided between the central government budget and their own budget devoted to education, health, policing and other local infrastructures. The shortfall in the budget of the central government, as well as the local governments will be filled by taxation. Apart from being accountable to their electorates, the mutual oversight of each other's activities by the two layers of government will contribute to greater transparency and openness of government. The details of the constitutional arrangements can be worked out in a manner that ensures an efficient division of tasks and complementary roles by the local and central governments within the judicial, legislative, and executive layers of government.

The regional option, if implemented properly, would have all the advantages of the other proposals without the disadvantages associated with the alternatives. With the right political balance of power between the regional and the central governments, it will do away with the authoritarian and centralizing tendencies of the oil states, as desired by the other two proposals, without having their disadvantages – namely, a chaotic international oil market, and unstable and sub-optimal oil export revenues that will result from the privatization option, as well as the problems associated with distributing oil revenues across the population as discussed above. On the economics side, it will redistribute the oil revenue more towards deprived regions and hence improve poverty and income distribution without handicapping the developmental potential of oil revenue expenditures. Once the institutional prerequisites for this proposal are in place, the functional use of oil revenues to bolster private sector activity and to bring about export diversification becomes a technocratic issue, and will not be blocked by the interest groups at the centre, as is the case at present.

On the negative side, questions may be raised about the regional proposal in relation to the possibility of its leading to rising regional tensions and ethnic strife. In our opinion, such concerns are unfounded. Currently, the strongest element in ensuring the regional and ethnic cohesion of the country is, arguably, the force of the central state. With the implementation of the regional option, the strongest element of regional and ethnic cohesion will become economic interdependence and self-interest rather than the force of the central state, although the latter will certainly play its role as well. At the outset, it is the flow of oil revenues through the different regions which acts as a glue reinforcing regional cohesion – or acts as a blood vessel connecting the different parts or regions in the body of the nation, but without the central state being its centre of gravity. In the longer run, with economic diversification and reduction of dependence on oil, the interdependent and diversified regional economies will reinforce regional cohesion.

## Conclusion

In the immediate aftermath of the 1979 Revolution, when the new constitution was being devised, Iran had a unique chance to introduce a new form of oil revenue utilization in order to prevent the inevitable centralizing tendencies of the old mode of control of oil revenues by the government. Neglect of this opportunity, as we have argued in this chapter, has led to the reinforcement of the old tendencies on a magnified scale. The oil-dependence of the economy has increased. The technological gap between Iran and its peers, both in the region and beyond, has widened, and economic diversification has stalled. Regional disparities too have increased. Politics has become more authoritarian, and rampant rent-seeking by narrow interest groups at the helm of the state has stifled democratization and economic reform. As we have argued in this chapter, these trends do not paint a bright future for long-term economic growth and prosperity of the country.

We have reviewed various proposals put forward to reconcile the accrual of large oil rents to the state with a democratic polity and a diversified economy. In our view, the regional option proposed in this chapter, appears to be, on balance, a more favourable option than the other alternatives proposed so far, at least under the specific conditions of Iran. This is far from being the final word. Many details of the regional proposal need to be worked out, and there is no reason why yet even better alternatives cannot be identified. We hope that these issues will be taken up in serious future debates by policy makers as well as academics.

## Notes

1 For a discussion and analysis of Iran's economy in this period, see: H. Hakimian and M. Karshenas, 'Dilemmas and Prospects for Economic Reform and Reconstruction in Iran', in Parvin Alizadeh (ed.), *Iran's Economy: Dilemmas of an Islamic State* (London, 2000); M.H. Pesaran 'Economic Trends and Macroeconomic Policies in Post-revolutionary Iran', in Alizadeh, *Iran's Economy*; S. Behdad, 'The Post-Revolutionary Economic Crisis', in S. Rahnema and S. Behdad (eds), *Iran after the Revolution: Crisis of an Islamic State* (London, 1996); H. Hakimian, 'Institutional Change and Macroeconomic Performance in Iran Two Decades after the Revolution (1979–1999)' (ERF, Cairo, 1999), *Working Paper*, No 9909; M. Karshenas, 'Structural Adjustment and the Iranian Economy', in Nemat Shafik (ed.), *Economic Challenges facing Middle East and North African Countries* (London, 1997); and H. Salehi Esfahani, 'Political Economy of Growth in Iran, 1963–2002', *mimeo*, University of Illinois, Urbana, 2002.
2 See P. Alizadeh, 'Iran's Quandary: Economic Reforms and the "Structural Trap"', *The Brown Journal of World Affairs*, ix (2003).
3 See, for instance: Hakimian and Karshenas, 'Dilemmas and Prospects'.
4 For example during the 1980–2001 period investment ratio in Iran was on average 24.1 per cent while in Turkey the average for the same period was 21.8 per cent.
5 The recent increase in the share of manufacturing exports from Iran is mainly due to petrochemicals which benefit from subsidized energy and oil input. The growth of the Iranian economy is still geared to the growth of volatile oil revenues, as we shall see below.
6 See Hakimian and Karshenas, 'Dilemmas and Prospects'.
7 Based on Bank Markazi data (Tehran, Iran).
8 Bank Markazi data (Tehran, Iran).
9 On Iran's population, see H. Hakimian, 'From Demographic Transition to Fertility Boom and Bust: Iran in the 1980s and 1990s', *Development and Change*, 37(3), 571–597.
10 World Bank, 'Iran: Medium Term Framework for Transition – Converting Oil Wealth to Development', *Report No. 25848-IRN, A Country Economic Memorandum*, Social and Economic Development Group (Washington, 30 April 2003).
11 All figures based on data provided by UNCTAD (Geneva).
12 See also H. Hakimian, 'Institutional Change and Macroeconomic Performance in Iran'.
13 See P. Alizadeh, 'Iran's Quandary: Economic Reforms and the "Structural Trap"'.
14 See further, Ali A. Saeidi, 'The Accountability of Para-governmental Organizations (*bonyads*): The Case of Iranian Foundations, *Iranian Studies*, 37, 3 (September 2004).

15  See, International Monetary Fund, 'Islamic Republic of Iran: Staff Report for the 2003 Article IV Consultations', IMF 2003.

16  Bank Markazi Iran, *Economic Trends*.

17  See P. Alizadeh, 'Iran's Quandary: Economic Reforms and the "Structural Trap"'.

18  Increased confidence in the Iranian economy recently led to a successful Eurobond offering, Iran's first since 1979, in which EUR0 300 million worth of sovereign government debt was subscribed by regional and European investors (MEED *Quarterly Review*, 3 September 2002). Meanwhile, the Tehran Stock Exchange (TSE) rose by 30 per cent in 2003 and was one of 2002's best performing stock markets in the world (BBC, 14 November 2002).

19  Similar measures are employed by some industrialized countries, for example, the United Kingdom, where short-term subsidies are provided to the private firms for employment and training of the youth. But the systematic use of such measures in an oil economy such as Iran is unsustainable and counterproductive.

20  See Iran, Medium Term Framework for Transition: Converting Oil Wealth to Economic Development, The World Bank, 2003. For a discussion of various government subsidies and their impact, see, M. Karshenas and M.H. Pesaran, 'Economic Reform and the Reconstruction of the Iranian Economy', *The Middle East Journal*, 49, 1995.

21  The case where the distributed shares across the population are not marketable, is a special case of the second proposal which is discussed below.

22  See, for example, R.D. Rotunda, 'Iraq, Oil, and Democracy', Cato Institute, April 2004, http://www.cato.org/dailys/04–23–04.html

23  See, for example, T.I. Palley, 'Combating the Natural Resource "Curse" with Citizen Revenue Distribution Funds: Oil and the Case of Iraq', Foreign Policy in Focus, December 2003, http://www.fpif.org/papers/ordf2003.html

24  See, for example, R.D. Rotunda, 'Iraq, Oil, and Democracy'.

25  See, for example, Ariel Cohen, 'Oil Privatization key for Iraq', United Press International, 06/17/2003, web address: http://www.upi.com/view.cfm?StoryID=20030617–115909–7172r

26  See, H. Bagherzadeh, 'Tarhe Democratizeh Kardan e Sanat Naft dar Iran /Proposal for Democratization of oil Industry in Iran', Iran-e Emruz, March 2002 http://www.iran-emrooz.de/archiv/bagerzadeh/1380/bagerz801229.html

27  G. Standing, 'Oil and Iraq', Letter to the editor, *The Financial Times* (26 June 2003): 18.

28  In the popular media, this proposal is often confused with the operation of the Alaskan Fund. In Alaska because of the extremely low absorptive capacity of the local economy oil surpluses have been invested by the government in a diversified foreign investment fund. The accumulation of these funds and the relatively high flow of dividends from the investments has led the government to distribute the dividends amongst the population, which has the added benefit of attracting people to reside in that harsh and remote part of the world. This Alaskan practice is not different from the current practice in Iran or other oil-exporting economies, where the government invests oil revenues on behalf of the people. The main difference is that because of the high absorptive capacity of the Iranian economy, much of the oil rent is invested in the domestic economy. On the contrary, the 'oil-to-the-people' proposal here is aimed at removing the government from being in charge of investing the oil rents.

# 13 Capital accumulation, financial market reform and growth in Iran

## Past experience and future prospects

*Ahmad R. Jalali-Naini*

## Introduction

Attaining a sustainable and high economic growth rate is a big challenge facing all developing countries, including Iran. To accomplish this objective Iran needs to invest heavily in infrastructure, human capital, new equipment/technology and upgrade its aging capital equipment in both the oil and non-oil sectors. Equally important, Iran needs to develop the social and institutional foundations that support the economic process. Higher growth is a socially desirable objective since it raises per-capita income and it provides the material resources for reducing poverty and promoting sustainable human development. Maintaining this balance is quite crucial for compelling reasons. Due to demographic and gender factors, the rate of growth of labour supply in the next decade is expected to be fairly high and a relatively high rate of economic growth is necessary to boost the demand for labour. A rapid population growth at the rate of 2.6 per cent per annum increased the population from 26 million in 1966 to nearly 66 million in 2002. Population growth has recently slowed down and is estimated at 1.65 per cent for the next decade. Yet, the growth rate of the working-age population will be significantly higher, about 2.6 per cent. According to World Bank estimates, by 2010 total population will be 75.9 million. Working-age population will be 51 million – compared to an estimated 43 million at the end of 2002. Aside from the population factor, an expected rise in the female labour-force participation rate will significantly increase the number of people looking for work in the near future. Failure to achieve a reasonably robust growth rate can result in higher rates of unemployment and increased incidence of poverty, particularly amongst the younger population, with unpleasant social consequences.

While Iran has the economic resources for above-average economic growth rates and the potential to join the rank of high-income developing countries, it faces a number of major obstacles attaining this goal. A major lesson to be learnt from the history of economic development is: 'basic needs first'. In the context of a developing society aiming for long-term progress, this translates into the recognition that individuals have a set of basic social and economic rights which must be recognized and protected by a strong legal foundations upon which institutions should be created to facilitate voluntary economic interaction and the flow of information (including price signals). Therefore, the basic policy challenge is the implementation of measures for the development of socio-economic institutions, to encourage greater participation and effort by individuals (non-governmental entities) via reduction of uncertainty and transaction costs. Economic policies that foster efficiency and are friendly to growth have a much better probability of success once the above social infrastructure is in place. The government has a leading role in this process – as it has for the provision of public goods and basic infrastructure.

This chapter is about capital accumulation and growth in Iran. While acknowledging that other policy issues – such as economic justice, the proper working of the labour market, the educational system and trade policy – are important, the focus of the chapter will be on capital formation, growth and related issues. This chapter discusses the composition of the gross domestic fixed capital formation, the cost of capital, investment and growth, and policies that can improve the mobilization of resources and the efficiency of investments.

## Major economic challenges for maintaining high growth rates

### Maintaining higher saving and investment rates

The demographic and gender factors plus a higher educational attainment by the young entrants to the labour market are the major influences on the supply side of the labour market. A considerable number of the unemployed persons in Iran are the urban youth. International evidence also indicates a higher rate of unemployment for the youth; the ratio of youth to general unemployment rate for a large number of countries is around 2. However, this ratio is significantly higher in Iran, at around 2.3. To keep the unemployment rate at the current levels, the Iranian economy requires a growth rate of about 8 per cent per annum for the next two decades. This, in turn, requires high rates of saving and investment. Since the early 1970s, the government sector has financed a large proportion of fixed domestic capital investment through proceeds from oil revenue. However, while the government sector can provide for investment in infrastructure and public goods, it is not financially and administratively in a position to be the main provider of investment funds for the economy and to be able to absorb the growing supply of workers.[1] Moreover, the unsuccessful experience of state-managed economies in the developing countries, including Iran, has given currency to the idea that, on efficiency grounds, the government should limit its direct involvement in enterprise management and focus more on 'governance'.[2] All this implies that the private sector needs to assume a much greater role in the investment process. However, this requires development of institutions, including money and capital markets, for greater mobilization of savings, and more efficient allocation of capital. Obviously, this improvement requires legal protection for the market participant and regulation and supervision for transparency and proper working of such institutions.

### Raising economic efficiency

The use of inputs (including energy) is relatively high per every rial of GDP in the Iranian economy. Better utilization of inputs and capital to deliver output requires higher efficiency standards in both government and private sectors. With a huge increase in the scale and scope of the government after the Revolution, administrative mechanisms, as opposed to price signals, were set to both allocate and divert resources to the government sector (including public enterprises). Under these conditions rent-seeking not only undermines allocative efficiency but also social equity. If the private sector is to assume a greater role, the state–market relationship must be redefined to allow for recognition of property rights, a more efficient price system and reduction of transaction costs through observance and enforcement of contracts. These measures can accelerate the development of private institutions, particularly in the financial markets which can potentially enhance efficiency of the capital-allocation process in the economy.

### Balanced macroeconomic policies

The traditional expansionary fiscal and monetary policies have frequently been used in Iran to deliver higher economic growth and employment. However, the experience has shown that these policies make little contribution to sustainable growth. Moreover, these policies exacerbate inflation and exchange rate uncertainty (particularly during low-oil export revenue periods) and are detrimental to growth.[3] Design and implementation of a balanced and credible macroeconomic policy package, based on the realities of the Iranian economy, and consistency in maintaining growth-friendly policies can pave the way for a higher and more sustainable, and potentially more equitable, growth.

### Rethinking industrial policies and promoting non-oil exports

Long-run growth of output and employment in the industrial sector faces the problem that the import-substituting industries may not be able to expand their output and employment at a high rate and on a sustained basis because of the limits of the domestic market. Re-evaluation of sectoral and industrial policies, supported and complemented with a credible and concerted macroeconomic/commercial policy package is in order. Capturing export markets and more specialization both at the regional and global levels may be the only option in the long run for employment creation in the industrial sector.

### Economic growth and the structure of production: 1950–2002

We can distinguish three different growth episodes in Iran over the last four decades: 1959–1977 (corresponding to Persian calendar years 1338–1356), 1978–1987 and 1988–2002. The average growth rates and growth fluctuations (measured by the standard deviation of growth rates in each period) are shown in Table 13.1. The average growth rate of non-oil GDP in constant prices during the first period was 10.2 per cent per annum. The average annual growth rate in the third period is 4.5 per cent per annum. On a per-worker basis, the distinctions between the three different periods are starker. The time trends in GDP, non-oil GDP and per-capita GDP are

*Table 13.1* Average growth rate and volatility (at constant 1997 prices, in per cent)

|  | GDP (% per annum) | | Non-oil GDP (% per annum) | |
|---|---|---|---|---|
|  | Mean | Standard deviation | Mean | Standard deviation |
| 1959–77 | 9.91 | 4.8 | 10.2 | 6.65 |
| 1978–87 | −1.77 | 8.5 | 0.34 | 5.78 |
| 1988–2002 | 4.31 | 4.67 | 4.5 | 4.8 |

Source: The Central Bank of Iran, National Accounts, 2003, Tehran, Iran, and Economic Trends, No. 33, 1382, 2nd Quarter.

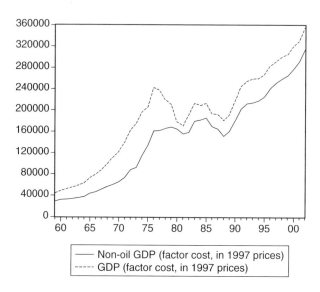

*Figure 13.1* GDP and non-oil GDP, constant 1997 prices.

shown in Figure 13.1. A clear break in growth trend can be observed during the second period. In the third period, there is another break in the growth trend, as economic growth resumes following the end of the war with Iraq.

During the above periods, the structure of production in Iran has changed significantly. The oil sector (as measured by its valued-added) grew at a rate close to the value-added generated in the non-oil GDP during the 1960–1972 period. With a rapid jump in crude oil prices during 1972–1974, the oil sector significantly outgrew non-oil GDP, consequently the ratio of value added in the oil sector relative to the non-oil GDP rose very sharply in a short period during the mid-1970s but declined rapidly in 1977 and the decline continued until 1986 – see Figure 13.2. In the 1990s, the share of non-oil GDP rose and reached the levels that had existed in the mid-1960s.

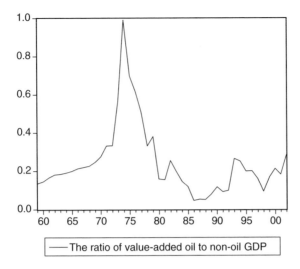

*Figure 13.2* The ratio of value-added oil to non-oil GDP.

*Table 13.2* Distribution of value-added in GDP at current prices (in per cent)

| Sectors | 1959 | 1971 | 1976 | 1988 | 2001 |
|---|---|---|---|---|---|
| Agriculture | 38.3 | 19.5 | 9.9 | 23.5 | 13.4 |
| Oil and gas | 12.0 | 25.0 | 38.2 | 7.3 | 15.2 |
| Industries and mines | 9.2 | 15.9 | 16.7 | 14.8 | 19.7 |
| Mining | 0.4 | 0.4 | 0.4 | 0.4 | 0.6 |
| Manufacturing | 6.0 | 9.7 | 7.6 | 8.7 | 14.3 |
| Electricity, gas & water | 0.3 | 1.2 | 0.6 | 0.9 | 1.2 |
| Construction | 2.5 | 4.6 | 8.1 | 4.7 | 4 |
| Services | 41.3 | 41.7 | 38.1 | 54.8 | 53.2 |
| Trade, restaurants & hotels | 13.5 | 8.7 | 6.6 | 18.3 | 14.3 |
| Transport & communication | 8.2 | 4.7 | 5.1 | 7.1 | 9.1 |
| Financial services | 1.1 | 2.5 | 3.8 | 0.9 | 2.2 |
| Real estate & professional services | 4.4 | 5.6 | 7.4 | 13.8 | 13.8 |
| Public services | 12.1 | 17.6 | 13.7 | 12.2 | 11.4 |
| Social, personal and domestic services | 2.1 | 2.6 | 1.5 | 2.5 | 2.5 |
| Less: Imputed bank service charge | 0.8 | 2.1 | 2.9 | 0.3 | |
| Gross Domestic Product | 100.0 | 100.0 | 100.0 | 100.0 | 100.0 |
| GDP (excluding oil) | 88.0 | 75.0 | 61.8 | 92.7 | 84.8 |

Table 13.2 shows the distribution of value added amongst different sectors or the structure of GDP in current prices. Differences in sectoral growth rates and changes in the inter-sectoral relative prices are the main causes of the significant fluctuations in the sectoral distribution of GDP. Agriculture's share in total value

added has shrunk since the early 1960s and the shares of manufacturing and services have increased. However, the share of the manufacturing sector in Iran's GDP is low when compared with that for middle-income countries.[4] The service, industry and mines, and agriculture sectors have the largest shares in GDP, in that order. In terms of the share in total employment, the picture is somewhat different. Service and agriculture rank first and second, respectively, in terms of their shares in total employment followed by industry and mines. The oil sector employment creation effect is very limited, considering its share of GDP, compared to agriculture, industry and services. Keller and Nabli's (2002) estimate of employment elasticity of non-oil GDP for Iran during the 1992–2000 period is 0.6, significantly below the estimated elasticity for the Middle East and North Africa (MENA) region, at about 1.1.

### Investment rate and growth performance

Figures 13.3 and 13.4 show aggregate investment/GDP, private investment/GDP and government investment/GDP ratios in the Iranian economy during the 1959–2002 period. The aggregate investment rate has fluctuated considerably in the short-run and has three distinct intermediate-run trends. Fluctuation in the investment rate is significantly correlated with oil revenues. During the 1970s, the investment rate rose substantially, in the 1980s the average investment rate fell to very low levels, partly due to the detrimental effects of the Iran–Iraq war (1980–1988). The investment rate rebounded after the war but declined in the late 1990s as lower oil prices and foreign debt repayment did not leave sufficient foreign exchange resources to finance capital investment on a large scale. With the

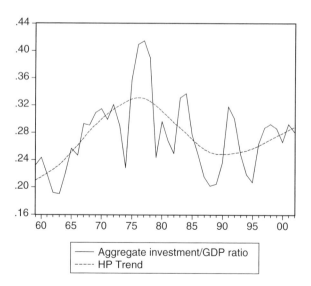

*Figure 13.3* Aggregate investment rate, 1959–2002.

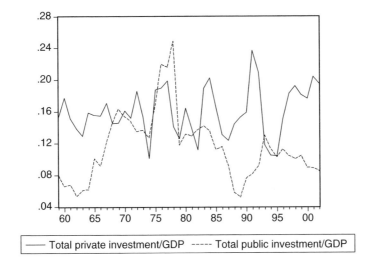

*Figure 13.4* Private and public investment ratios, 1959–2002.

recovery in the price of oil, the investment rate rose to nearly 30 per cent in the 2000–2002 period.

The period with the highest average growth rate in Iran (1959–1977) corresponds to the period with the highest ratio of aggregate investment to GDP or the highest growth rate of physical capital. Since capital/output ratio is a pro-cyclical variable, we expect it to be higher during expansion phases. In the period with the lowest growth performance, 1978–1987, the investment rate had a sharp downward trend. The growth rate of the educational attainment of the work force, as a proxy for human capital, does not seem to be strongly correlated with output growth. Therefore, based on the above we should expect that capital accumulation and employment to have been the main driver of growth, an issue to which we will return later.

Assuming a capital/output ratio of 3.5, a growth rate of 6.0 per cent converts into an investment rate of 30 per cent of GDP (World Bank 2003). An incremental capital/output ratio (ICOR) of 3.0 seems to be a more appropriate estimate for the Iranian economy.[5] Using the same assumptions as in the above study,[6] with an ICOR of 3.0 and a 6 per cent growth rate, the required investment/output ratio is 27 per cent. The required investment rate for a growth rate consistent with a constant rate of unemployment (8 per cent) is more than 33 per cent of GDP, which is significantly higher than the average rate over the last 15 years.

The ICOR estimate tends to be higher, the lower the investment efficiency. It should be noted that the mean investment/GDP ratio in Iran for the 1975–2000 period was around 25 per cent. This is about 2.5 per cent above the world average, 6 per cent below that in East Asia and the Pacific, and 3.5 per cent above the Latin American countries. The investment/GDP ratio in Iran is slightly higher than that for the MENA region, 4 per cent higher than in Turkey, 3.5 per cent less than Tunis, about the same as in Egypt and a tad higher than in Morocco for the same period. However, the Iranian growth performance does not rank as high as its investment ratio within this group for the 1975–2000 period.[7] This indicates problems with the efficiency of investments.

### Taxes and the cost of capital

The share of corporate tax in GDP in Iran is low compared to industrial countries and other regions of the world economy. In spite of this, the share of corporate tax in total revenue has traditionally been higher compared to the share of personal income tax in Iran. The primary reason for taxing corporations is to raise money. In the absence of an accounting/information system that can be used for measuring the income of tax units accurately and comprehensively, and with 'mixed' tax systems,[8] taxation of corporations becomes more practical. The major advantage of taxing corporations is that taxation of retained earnings at source can reduce the cost of identification and collection for tax administrators. The disadvantage is that corporate tax discourages the supply of capital, a factor relatively scarce in developing countries.

In recent decades Iran, like most other developing and MENA countries, raised more corporate taxes than individual income taxes due to difficulties in the identification of individual tax bases. The basic corporate tax rate was 54 per cent plus 10 per cent tax on companies. Additional non-tax charges had raised the effective tax to higher levels, making capital very costly, thus raising incentives for extensive tax evasion. Due to the high rate of corporate taxes, low investment rates and the need for a higher private investment rate in the economy to boost economic growth, the corporate tax structure was significantly modified and simplified in the first year of the Third Plan.[9] The new corporate tax law fixes the tax rate on non-public corporations at 25 per cent and on public corporations at 22.5 per cent.

Currently, there is no tax on bank deposits. Therefore, this particular tax does not enter the cost of capital. Table 13.3 shows the nominal 'profit' (or 'interest') rates on loans in the large government-owned commercial banks in different sectors of the economy. Additionally, there is limited credit available at subsidized rates in different sectors and the government pays the difference between the administered rates reported in Table 13.3 and the subsidized rates. The newly created non-bank credit institutions and the private banks charge on average about 4–5 per cent more for their loans compared to the interest rates charged by the government-owned banks.[10]

The prevailing 'profit' (interest) rates on agricultural, industrial and construction loans in the commercial banks were below the average inflation rate during the 1990s. The cost of loan has been lower for the firms that have access to the government owned banks' line of credit. There are, however, hidden costs of obtaining a loan and they include a fairly long waiting time, high transaction cost and informal charges. The cost of capital is substantially higher for the firms rationed in the credit market. Most of the rationed firms are small firms with low collateral. These firms have to borrow a part of or all their credit needs in the curb market. The curb-market rates can range from as low as 25–30 per cent to a high

*Table 13.3* Expected rate of profit on facilities, selected years (%)

| Year | Manufacturing | Agriculture | Trade & services | Export | Housing savings | Other |
|------|---------------|-------------|------------------|--------|-----------------|-------|
| 1963–69 | NA | NA | 8–10* | 8 | NA | NA |
| 1975–77 | 10** | 6–7** | 11–14* | 11 | NA | NA |
| 1984 | 6–12 | 4–8 | 8–12 | | 8–12 | NA |
| 1990 | 11–13 | 6–9 | 17–19 | | 12–13 | NA |
| 1991 | 11–13 | 6–9 | 18+ | | 12–16 | NA |
| 1992 | 13 | 9 | 18+ | | 12–16 | NA |
| 1993 | 16–18 | 12–16 | 18–23 | | 12–16 | NA |
| 1994 | 16–18 | 13–15 | 18–24 | 18 | 15 | NA |
| 1995 | 17–19 | 13–16 | 22–25 | 18 | 15–16 | NA |
| 1996 | 17–19 | 13–16 | 22–25 | 18 | 15–16 | NA |
| 1997 | 17–19 | 13–16 | 22–25 | 18 | 15–16 | 15–16 |
| 1998 | 17–19 | 13–16 | 22–25 | 18 | 15–16 | 18–19 |
| 1999 | 17–19 | 13–16 | 22–25 | 18 | 15–16 | 18–19 |
| 2000 | 17–19 | 13–16 | 22–25 | 18 | 15–16 | 18–19 |
| 2001 | 16–18 | 14–15 | 23 minimum | 18 | 15–16 | 18–19 |
| 2002 | 15–17 | 13–14 | 22 minimum | 17 | 14–15 | 16–18 |
| 2003 | 16 | 13.5 | 21 minimum | 16 | 15 | 18 |

Source: Bank Markazi Iran.

rate of 70–75 per cent per year. Note that much of employment creation in most countries including Iran takes place in small enterprises, and the adoption of measures to increase the access of these firms to credit and reducing the transaction costs of obtaining loans should be a policy priority.[11]

Over the last four years, measures like a reduction in the corporate tax, a very substantial reduction in the cost of import registration deposit, and a lower nominal exchange rate (brought about by higher oil revenue) have reduced the costs of acquiring capital goods. Consequently, the ratio of private investment in machinery and equipment (at constant 1997 prices) to non-oil GDP has risen significantly (Figure 13.5), which compares to a rising cost of capital in the 1993–1997 period during which the private investment rate fell to historically low levels.

### Capital, total factor productivity (TFP) and growth

A recurring theme in the recent literature on the sources of economic growth and 'convergence' is the relative importance of capital accumulation and TFP to economic growth. Some cross-country studies show that capital formation is the main driver of growth. Easterly and Levine are amongst those who identify productivity growth as the major source of differences in per-capita incomes. It appears that the bulk of East Asia's growth 'miracle' is, at the very least, as much due to rapid capital accumulation as it is due to TFP growth. Senhadji shows that in the MENA region, capital accumulation contribution to growth has been significant, while TFP contribution to growth, like in Latin America, particularly in the 1980s, was either negligible or negative.[12]

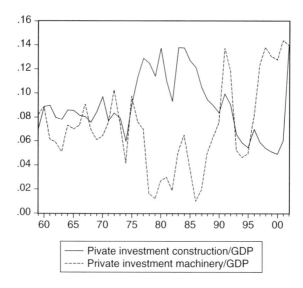

*Figure 13.5* Private investment/non-oil GDP.

In the Solow-Swan, Ramsey-Cass-Koopmans and Samuelson-Diamond class of models, saving rates and population growth determine the steady-state level of per-worker (for simplicity, per-capita) income. Finite growth is due to diminishing returns to private capital. Any growth in per-capita income in the long-run equilibrium is due to *exogenous* technical progress. Endogenous models allow different mechanisms to counteract this, hence the possibility of unbounded growth. For instance, some growth models (e.g. Lucas 1988; Romer 1986)[13] rely on knowledge accumulation or on human capital to deliver growth in equilibrium. In the Arrow scheme, 'learning' does this job without R&D expenditure, as a side effect of economic activity. Learning and knowledge accumulation can also occur as a result of R&D expenditure. Investment in human capital (HC) can also deliver social externalities to offset diminishing returns to private capital. In contrast to 'knowledge', which is a public good accessible to other producers, HC is a rival good. Macroeconomic treatment of human capital either focuses on the growth rate of HC (Lucas 1988)[14] or its level (Nelson and Phelps 1966).[15] In the Nelson-Phelps approach, the *level* (stock) of human capital generates growth, and differences in growth rates across countries are due to differences in the HC level.[16] A number of writers using growth-accounting approach (Benhabib and Speigel 1994)[17] suggest that HC as a separate factor of production has either zero or negative effect on growth and the main channel through which education influences growth is through its effect on TFP.[18]

Microeconomic studies show that individuals with more education earn more. The implication is that higher-education attainment rates should raise average incomes, particularly if one considers the positive externalities presumed to be associated with it. However, many empirical studies, particularly in MENA, show that human capital does not have a significant impact on economic growth or on the growth rate of output per worker.[19]

Empirical tests based on several forms of aggregate production functions with slightly different factor specifications have been attempted for Iran.[20] The estimation method includes OLS and Phillips-Hansen.[21] Different specifications and estimations result in different estimates for TFP.[22] Overall, the estimates indicate that while capital significantly contributed to economic growth for the 1959–2000 period, TFP was not a contributing element to economic growth in Iran. Human capital as a separate factor was not significant. If human capital is removed from the production function, leaving simple labour and capital, TFP contribution becomes positive though very limited. In this case, the only periods when TFP contributed to growth were 1961–1972 and 1989–2000, and human capital explained about 30 per cent of TFP. The oil-boom of the early- to mid-1970s resulted in a huge increase in public and private investment and a short period of capital-intensive growth. TFP growth during the 1973–1977 period was negative. TFP contribution to output growth was negative during the 1978–1988 period. This combined with a decline in the rate of capital accumulation resulted in a negative per-capita, non-oil GDP growth rate in this period. TFP is negative when human capital enters the production function as a weight factor for labour. In this case, TFP becomes negative when the growth rate of human capital is also taken into calculations.

## Public investment and economic growth

The main features of the fiscal system in Iran are the very high share of oil revenue in total government revenue and the very significant amount of off-budget fiscal and quasi-fiscal operations. These operations have included implicit energy and foreign exchange subsidies. Table 13.4 shows the ratio of government revenues and expenditures to GDP according to the official budget data and the same ratios calculated with adjusted data. As indicated by this Table, official data understate the magnitude of fiscal operations as a percentage of GDP. The average size of government expenditure as a percentage of GDP with official data is 23.7 per cent, compared to 42.4 per cent using the adjusted data. With unification of the exchange rate as of the beginning of fiscal year 1381 (2002), one major source of off-budget fiscal operations has been removed. Energy subsidies represent a fairly significant hidden economic value in the budget. Rationalization of energy subsidies will contribute to a more transparent fiscal package and a potentially significant increase in national savings.[23] The tax system in Iran finances a small fraction of government expenditures – for instance, in 2001, taxes comprised 30.9 per cent of total government revenue. As a consequence, inflation tax as a proportion of total revenue has been significant.[24]

In an endogenous growth setting, higher saving and, by extension, investment rates can generate higher growth rates. The same can be said about public investments. Given the fact that the Iranian government receives oil revenues

*Table 13.4* Term-investment deposit rates

| Year | Short term | Special short term | One year | Two year | Three year | Four year | Five year |
|------|-----------|--------------------|----------|----------|------------|-----------|-----------|
| 1991 | 6.5 | ... | 9 | 10.5 | 11.5 | ... | 14 |
| 1992 | 7.5 | ... | 10 | 11.5 | 13 | ... | 15 |
| 1993 | 8 | ... | 11.5 | 13.5 | 14.5 | ... | 16 |
| 1994 | 8 | ... | 11.5 | 13.5 | 14.5 | ... | 16 |
| 1995 | 8 | ... | 14 | 15 | 16 | ... | 18.5 |
| 1996 | 8 | ... | 14 | 15 | 16 | ... | 18.5 |
| 1997 | 8 | 10 | 14 | 15 | 16 | ... | 18.5 |
| 1998 | 8 | 10 | 14 | 15 | 16 | ... | 18.5 |
| 1999 | 8 | 10 | 14 | 15 | 16 | ... | 18.5 |
| 2000 | 8 | 10 | 14 | 15 | 16 | 17 | 18.5 |
| 2001 | 7 | 9 | 13 | 13–17 | 13–17 | 13–17 | 17 |
| 2002 | 7 | 9 | 13 | 13–17 | 13–17 | 13–17 | 17 |
| 2003 | 7 | 9 | 13 | 13–17 | 13–17 | 13–17 | 17 |

Source: Central Bank of I.R. Iran.

directly and invests a part of this income, the aggregate investment in the Iranian economy is highly influenced by the level of government investment and oil-export revenues. A number of endogenous growth models consider government expenditures on infrastructure and public goods to be complementary to private investment and hence growth-inducing (Barro 1990; 1995; Barro and Salai-Martin 1992).[25] This approach assumes that government expenditure (G) results in the provision of non-rivalrous and non-excludable public services to the economy and complementary to private sector inputs – investment in physical and social infrastructure. In this model, the rate of growth is positively related to the G to output (Y) ratio and negatively related to the tax rate. At low G/Y values, the positive effect of a higher G on the marginal product of capital dominates the negative distortionary effect of taxes. As G/Y increases, the distortive effect of taxes becomes larger. Thus, growth rate reaches a peak and then declines. Since public expenditure on physical and social infrastructure is assumed to be complementary to private investment, the marginal product of private capital increases and so does the rate of economic growth, up to a maximum. Thus growth is negatively influenced if G is relatively too large and has no effect when G is at the optimal level. The above class of models assumes a 'benevolent' government. Jalali-Naini and Karimi (2003) show that if the process of provision of public goods involves rent seeking, the growth effect of public expenditures declines with the degree of (budgetary) rent seeking.

The evidence from a number of large-sample cross-sectional international empirical studies points to a weak correlation between public investment and growth. This can be interpreted as either that the government investment is not a significant determinant of growth, or that governments are optimizing and invest up to the point where the marginal effect of such investments on growth is close to zero. The evidence obtained from growth regressions indicates that private investment has a positive effect on economic growth in Iran.[26] The effect of government expenditure on growth is positive but its coefficient is less than that of private investment.[27]

### Macroeconomic policy

Large-sample international empirical studies indicate that government policy does affect economic growth. High inflation rates and misaligned real exchange rates are not friendly to economic growth (Levine *et al.* 2000). Expansionary monetary and fiscal policies as a mechanism to boost output and employment have not been successful in Iran over the last three decades. Money-financed deficits often result in inflationary monetary expansion, particularly in those economies with shallow financial markets. Moreover, since they reflect resource imbalances in the loss-making government-owned enterprises, they have a very limited effect on output. Macroeconometric simulations of the Iranian economy show that money-financed deficits have very limited impact on output but are highly inflationary.[28]

A number of empirical studies show that a higher and more variable inflation rate increases instability and uncertainty and hence negatively influences growth. The level of threshold effect above which inflation significantly influences economic growth for industrial countries is estimated to be between 1 and 3 per cent and that for developing countries between 7 and 11 per cent (Khan and Senhadji).[29] The average annual inflation rate (measured by the consumer price index, CPI) in Iran during the 1974–2000 period was nearly 20 per cent per annum. The evidence shows that during periods when average inflation is higher, inflation–output trade-off becomes weaker.[30] There is evidence that higher inflation rates in Iran – while controlling for other variables that influence growth – are associated with lower rates of economic growth, hence a more stable macro environment can create conditions for higher growth and employment.[31] Empirical tests of models of money–output–inflation relationship with symmetric and asymmetric effects show that while expansionary monetary policies have a very limited positive effect on output, contractionary policies to control inflation have a significant negative influence on output in the Iranian economy.[32]

The essential elements of a macroeconomic policy package consistent with long-run growth in Iran are: fiscal discipline and the separation of monetary policy from the government budget complemented with a credible monetary policy. For an oil-exporting economy, the management of oil revenue fluctuations should also be part of the policy package. For smoothing the effect of fluctuations in oil-export revenues on government expenditures, the Third Plan instituted the Oil Stabilization Fund. The intention was to break the high correlation between the current oil revenues and current government expenditures, particularly government development expenditures. Even though the exchange rate unification and formation of the Oil Stabilization Fund have materialized during the Third Plan, there is a gap between policy and practice. The government has frequently drawn heavily from the Oil Stabilization Fund. Thus, as in the previous years, current oil-financed government expenditures are still highly correlated with current oil revenues. Experience shows that a high correlation is not satisfactory from a macro-policy perspective. Oil-price booms often result in unsustainable expansionary fiscal policy. Because of an inelastic domestic supply, sudden expansion of aggregate demand (due to oil-financed government expenditures) generates inflationary pressures within a relatively short period of time. With a cyclical increase in the price of oil, government expenditures, particularly development expenditures, increase. However, if government expenditures are not reined, once the price cycle turns around, the consequences are higher budget deficits and higher inflation rates.

## Financial policies and reform for mobilization of savings and improved investment allocation

Financial deepening requires a stable, low-inflation macroeconomic environment. The main objective of monetary policy is to promote price stability and reduce inflation risks by controlling monetary aggregates. Monetary policy reforms in the form of rationalization of price signals in the credit market and improved performance of the financial intermediaries are also necessary to induce more financial savings and better allocation of funds. Through higher and better investments, financial intermediaries can induce higher growth rates (Levine *et al.* 2000).[33] In this connection, not only financial development matters, but also the quality of financial intermediation, affected by institutions and economic policies, is of utmost importance. Although the scale of financial intermediation increased over the last three decades, one cannot say the same thing about its quality.

Commercial banks and insurance companies were nationalized and consolidated after the 1979 Islamic Revolution. Some of the consequences of a complete government control on the banking system – which until recently accounted for nearly all the official (excluding curb-market lending) intermediation activities in the financial sector – were administrative credit allocation and misaligned deposit and loan rates. Moreover, financial sector activity became dominated by bureaucratically directed credit allocation mainly to accommodate the credit needs of the public sector. The newly assumed role of the banking sector was different from what is generally presumed to be the function of the financial market: a mechanism for efficient allocation of financial resources to investment projects and sectors. Government control of the banking system increased the extent of quasi-fiscal activities during the 1979–1997 period and the banking system redirected a significant proportion of private saving to finance the government sector.

Figure 13.6 shows the net financial claims of the government and non-government sectors. It is shown that the net indebtedness of the government sector to the banking system rose sharply in the 1991–1999 period while the net claims of the private sector against the banking system grew, indicating a major reallocation of credit to the government sector. Since the early 1990s, the Currency and Credit Council sets annual targets for the allocation of credit to the private sector – monitored by the Central Bank – in different activities. These allocations are not based on any detailed or exact estimates of sectoral credit demand, but are more

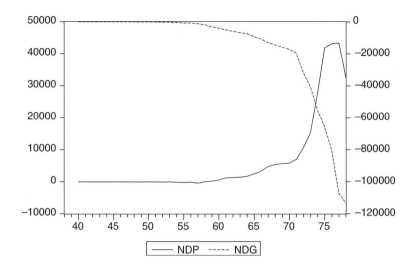

*Figure 13.6* Net financial claims of private and government sectors on the banking system.

like rules of thumb. In practice, the banks rarely observe the planned allocations in their lending practices.

Another aspect of government intervention in the credit market in Iran has been the provision of subsidized directed credit to favored sectors. It has been argued (Stiglitz 1994)[34] that due to market failures in the credit market, government intervention is warranted – directed credit programmes being an important instance. Directed credit programmes as a policy to promote industries and economic sectors have been in existence in Iran for a long time. However, there are limits to successful government interventions. Since bureaucrats have limited information, it is difficult to pick winners; also, this process involves rent seeking. Limited competition, bureaucratic structure and poor incentives can undermine the quality of financial intermediation. Inadequate management and supervision by government agencies that were given the responsibility to invest oil revenues contributed to waste and misallocation of resources, and the absence of a deep and efficient capital market exacerbated the problem.

In response to the above experience and to remedy some of the problems, the Central Bank since the mid-1990s began a rate-structure adjustment followed by a mini-privatization programme in the banking and insurance markets. In response to highly misaligned deposit and loan rates during the 1980s, a significant rate adjust-ment was introduced in the early 1990s. The deposit rates in the banking system that had been kept significantly below the rate of inflation for nearly 15 years were raised. Certificates of deposit with different maturities were introduced – Table 13.4 provides data on the structure of the term-investment deposit rates. These changes were meant to reduce 'financial repression' in the banking sector and, by raising financial savings, to increase the lending capacity of the banking system.

This policy was initially successful in reducing cash holdings relative to deposits, increasing non-sight deposits and 'term-investment' deposits in the banking system. However, fiscal/monetary policies were inconsistent with the new-deposit and loan-rate policies. With a big surge in the rate of inflation from 1993 until the late 1990s, the real rate on five-year deposits (the longest maturity deposit in Iran) began to decline quite substantially. The real return on five-year deposits has become positive again since 1999, though since the average gap between short-term, non-sight deposits and five-year certificates of deposit are nearly 10 per cent, short-term deposits have not seen a positive real return for decades. The magnitude of the inflation tax during the 1990s has been substantial and a reflection of a substantial degree of 'repression' in the financial sector. The sectoral loan rates, administratively set by the Currency and Credit Council, were also upwardly revised. As always, the priority sectors, such as agriculture, had the lowest loan rates (or 'expected profit') and those for domestic commerce had the highest rates. Table 13.3 shows the 'expected profit' rates in different spheres of economic activity for some selected years.

Since 1995, a number of private non-bank financial institutions – which are credit and saving institutions without the permission to issue checks – have begun business operations. Reducing the extent of private sector credit rationing, redirecting more credit to the private sector and limiting the control and share of the government in the banking system credit were the main elements of the credit policy in the Third Plan. As a strategy to achieve this objective, the Third Plan lifted the ban on private banks and credit institutions, in place since 1980. The empirical results reported by Jalali-Naini and Khalatbari (2003)[35] show that the rate of inflation during the 1960–2000 period was negatively correlated with growth, while bank credit to the private sector is positively correlated with growth. On the other hand, the growth in lending to the government did not significantly influence economic growth.

Until the late 1990s, the banks could not compete in rates as the Currency and Credit Council set the rates for all banks. With the re-introduction of the private banking system, the banks may now pay interest on a daily basis and private banks can set their deposit and lending rates, hence more flexibility in the interest rate structure. As part of the Third Plan reforms to allow more flexibility in lending practices and more resource flows to the private sector, the amount of directed credits set through budgetary allocations has declined gradually. The average margin between loan and deposit rates is estimated to be between 5 and 6.5 per cent. This spread is even larger for the newly created non-bank financial companies and the new private banks. If, as expected, more private banks enter the market, the margins should be squeezed to more competitive levels.

### The stock market

As part of the reform process and the creation of incentives for more private sector participation, the Tehran Stock Exchange began trading shares after a lull of about 10 years. There are different views regarding the effect of the stock market on the economy. Keynes regards stock market transactions as speculative and mainly resulting in changing the ownership of equity with no effect on the allocation of capital. As argued by Bencivenga *et al.* (1996) and Demirguc-Kunt and Levine (1996),[36] an important function of the equity markets is to provide liquidity to the owners of illiquid assets. This makes long-term investments less risky and with the rise in capital market efficiency, economic agents are induced to undertake more long-term, transaction-intensive investments – resulting in a higher return on savings. Thus, the growth of the equity market can positively influence saving and investment. In the Bencivenga *et al.* (1996) model, the same conclusion is obtained, if the above outcome does not result in changes in the composition of savings; in this case, the rate of capital accumulation increases.[37]

The number of companies accepted in the Tehran market rose to 334 by the end of 1381 (21 March 2002) with a market capitalization of 117,772.9 billion rials. The market capitalization ratio (capitalization value as a percentage of GDP) has increased significantly over the last five years. Market capitalization ratio is presumably correlated with the ability of an economy to mobilize capital and diversify risk. As suggested by Gurley and Shaw (1960) and empirically shown by Demirguc-Kunt and Levine (1996) at low levels of development, commercial banks are the dominant financial institutions, and in the process of economic growth, equity markets and specialized financial intermediaries develop. Stock market capitalization ratio also increases continuously from the average for low-income to middle-income and high-income countries. However, there are substantial variations across countries. The market capitalization ratio in Iran increased from less than 1 per cent in the early 1990s to around 12.7 per cent of GDP (at factor prices) by the end of 1381 (21 March 2002). This ratio is close to the average value for middle-income countries. The equity market's contribution to raise investment funds for private companies has been rather limited.[38] The share of new capital investments financed through the stock market in the gross domestic fixed capital formation during the last five years is nearly 2 per cent and has been rising rapidly since 1998. The equity cost of capital ranges in different sectors from 4 to 10 and for cement the P/E multiples are much higher.

Aside from generating liquidity and potentially reducing the risk of holding illiquid long-term assets in the economy, the growth of the stock market has had two additional potentially positive by-products. First, many of the public enterprises have been transferred and auctioned-off through the stock market. The recommended method of privatizing public enterprise in the Third Plan is through the equity market. Thus, a deeper, better functioning and more liquid stock market can facilitate and accelerate the privatization programme. Second, since the managers of publicly traded corporations must disclose their financial statements on a regular basis, they are under some pressure to show satisfactory results. Moreover, shareholders question corporate executives and examine financial reports in annual meetings; this process keeps the managers under some monitoring pressure.

### Oil and non-oil exports and exchange rate trends

Oil-export revenues have been the main source of foreign exchange in the Iranian economy during the last five decades. A perpetual objective of the economic plans in Iran, particularly after the 1979 Revolution, has been the growth of non-oil exports. But reaching this goal has proved difficult. Factors that have hindered growth of non-oil exports are: the availability of oil revenues, the posture of fiscal policy and the structure of the domestic economy/relative prices. Non-oil exports, while growing at moderate rates during the 1960–1973 period, fell sharply as a ratio of total exports during the early- to mid-1970s as oil exports grew rapidly (Figure 13.7a).

In real terms, non-oil exports had a peak in 1973 and a higher peak in 1994 in the post-Revolution period (Figure 13.7b).[39] The decline in non-oil exports in the 1980s was due to political uncertainties following the 1979 Revolution, the effect of the war with Iraq and a rising official real exchange rate (RER). With a sharp reduction in the RER and the removal of a number of restrictions on exporters, nominal non-oil exports rose after the termination of hostilities with Iraq, until 1994. However, after a change in the mix of economic policies in 1994, exports declined in both absolute and real terms. The devaluation of rial during 1998–1999 and a gradual removal of currency-surrender regulations for non-oil exporters helped non-oil export recovery during the past few years.

Broadly speaking, oil revenues have two distinct and compensatory effects on oil exports. In the short-run, higher oil revenues tend to increase the aggregate investment rate and decrease the real exchange rate. Business-cycle studies of the Iranian economy corroborate contemporaneous co-movement between oil revenues and investment expenditures – and more generally, real aggregate expenditure and oil revenues.[40] In other words, on the one hand, higher oil revenues allow the economy to have more investment and intermediate goods to increase production, including those for external markets. On the other hand, a significant increase in the level of oil revenue has been associated with a declining real exchange rate in Iran – the inter-mediate link being an expansionary oil-financed fiscal policy.[41] A booming natural

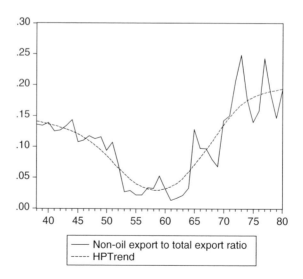

*Figure 13.7a* Ratio of non-oil to total exports.

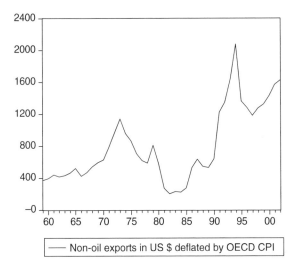

*Figure 13.7b* Price adjusted non-oil exports.

resource sector and an appreciation of the domestic currency, the 'Dutch Disease', tend to move resources out of tradables and into non-tradables.

Thus, whilst saving and investment resources increase as a result of higher oil revenues, price signals, the macroeconomic policy mix and the domestic economic structure do not allow the initial boom to turn into an export-led growth sequence. A policy mix containing expansionary fiscal and monetary policy along with a fixed exchange rate, and as a consequence, a lower real exchange rate (RER) is the 'stylized fact' of almost every oil-boom episode in Iran. To control for the relative price effect of higher oil revenues, the RER should be kept in an equilibrium zone. To achieve this, fiscal discipline and monetary restraint must be exercised to keep the domestic rate of inflation close to the world rate.

The RER influences both the level and the composition of output. Figures 13.8 and 13.9 show the trends in two different measures of the real exchange rate in Iran. In Figure 13.8, the RER is defined as the market exchange rate (domestic currency per unit of US dollar) adjusted by the ratio of the OECD CPI index and the domestic CPI index. Since the early 1990s, the RER has been moving around a stable trend line, in spite of several rounds of large nominal devaluation. A partial nominal devaluation was attempted in 1986 to form a multiple exchange rate system, raising the rates for exporters. In 1992, a partial devaluation was implemented to unify various exchange rates around the free-market rate. The fiscal and monetary package, however, was not consistent with the objective of achieving real depreciation via nominal devaluation as a means to stimulate exports and discourage imports.

The traditional view is that expenditure-switching policies should be backed with expenditure-reducing policies to achieve a real depreciation. Fiscal

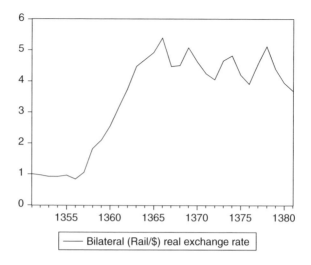

*Figure 13.8* The real exchange rate index (1351 = 1).

expansion, foreign exchange scarcity resulting from a reduction in oil prices and foreign debt repayment, and limited access to international financial markets turned inflation tax into the balancing variable in the system. The inflation rate picked up significant momentum in 1993 and reached its highest level in 1995. As a consequence, a real depreciation was not achieved by the exchange rate unification policy in 1992 and the Central Bank had to implement several rounds of devaluation. Using a simple macroeconometric model, Jalali-Naini and Khiabani (1997)[42] demonstrated that the negative effect of a money-fiscal expansion on the trade balance was greater than the positive effect of currency devaluation, resulting in lower levels of exports, higher levels of imports and deterioration of the trade balance. In the above circumstances, a nominal devaluation may not result in a real devaluation or stop an RER appreciation – as was experienced in the Iranian economy during the 1992–1995 period.

Figure 13.9 shows the ratio of the index price of exported goods to the index price for home goods, called the internal real exchange rate for 'exportables' (IREX). IREX is a signal for the allocation of domestic resources to domestic sectors that produce these two categories of goods and services. A higher level of IREX should create incentives to move resources to 'exportabales'. Conversely, an increase in the relative price of non-traded goods, a higher RER, increases the supply of non-traded goods and reduces the supply of traded goods. Consequently, employment shifts to the non-traded sector. IREX had a big jump in the mid-1980s followed by a reduction in that ratio since the late 1980s. The other measure of RER also experienced a large increase, reflecting a large real depreciation, between 1979 and the mid-1980s. A sustained appreciation of RER undermines economic expansion through non-oil export promotion.

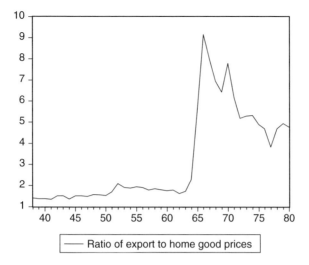

*Figure 13.9* Real exchange rate trend.

From a macroeconomic perspective a successful export-promotion policy could create a new growth engine. The positive externalities generated from more effective international competition can boost economic performance at the micro level and its aggregate effect can induce higher productivity and efficiency and higher real incomes. For the future, raising the growth rate of non-oil exports to generate growth and higher incomes will be a more compelling option for the Iranian economy than it has been in recent decades. Three distinct sets of policies must be implemented. The macroeconomic policy mix should be designed such that relative price signals do not disfavour the export sector, correcting the exchange rate misalignment in favour of tradables. Administrative restrictions and transaction costs for exports should be minimized. The domestic market structure should be reformed to induce more competition, limiting domestic protection and potential rent-seeking opportunities in the domestic market to send stronger signals to the local firms to seek more profits through innovation and efficiency and higher international competitiveness. The above reforms and a stronger policy commitment to exports will increase the amount of domestic and foreign investments, outside the energy and petrochemicals, for non-oil export industries.

### Summary and some policy recommendations

The hard economic facts facing Iran in the early 21st century are a rapid increase in the number of young and educated entrants to the labour market who want well-paid jobs, while the old want higher pensions and better health care. To generate higher incomes for the average household and to create a sufficient number of jobs to keep the rate of unemployment steady, the economy must grow at about 8 per cent per year, a feat that has not been achieved for a sustained period (three or more years) in the last 27 years. Given that the public sector is not able to significantly increase employment, policy makers need to implement macroeconomic policies friendly to growth and to greater private sector participation. The main challenges and policy recommendations are listed below. Note, as was stressed in the introduction to this chapter, 'appropriate' economic policies have a much higher probability of being effective when a social and economic environment conducive to economic transparency, stability, efficiency and wider participations by private individuals exists.

1.  To reach higher growth rates, the Iranian economy needs to save and invest a significant fraction of its GDP. For instance, to have a growth rate of 8 per cent, the investment rate should be between 32 per cent of GDP. To encourage investment on this scale, the legal and political uncertainties for non-government entities and the private sector should be reduced. Transparency in investment laws and regulations, legal protection to domestic private investors and reduction of bureaucratic impediments and transaction costs to encourage FDI are the type of non-price policies that should be implemented to encourage greater participation by non-government entities in the economy.

2.  High investment rate requires high saving rates. The government can raise its saving rate through fiscal discipline and more efficient tax collection. Control on the growth rate of government expenditures, more financial discipline on public enterprises, and overhauling the tax collection are the kinds of fiscal measures to boost government saving rate. In this connection, privatization of public enterprises in economic spheres, where the government has no special knowledge, expertise or advantage, should proceed at a speedier pace.

3.  The recent tax reforms have reduced the marginal tax rates on corporations and individuals, particularly individuals with below middle-income earnings. The lower tax rates must be compensated with a better tax administration/collection system; otherwise a persistently low tax/GDP ratio will give rise to a situation where either the oil revenues or the inflation tax will have to be relied upon to finance a higher proportion of current expenditures. This can potentially reduce investment in infrastructure and capacity creation in a number of economic sectors where the public sector has a large presence, and therefore result in a lower rate of economic growth and employment creation.

4.  Reform of the financial sector for mobilization of a greater volume of financial savings and a more efficient allocation of social capital should focus on terminating sustained financial repression and improve the quality of financial intermediation. Reducing the extent of private sector credit rationing, redirecting more credit to the private sector and limiting the control and share of government in the banking system credit should continue as the main elements of credit policy. Empirical studies show that higher credit flows to the private sector are positively correlated with growth. On the other hand, growth in lending to the government sector did not significantly influence economic growth.

5.  Policies in the banking sector should focus on increasing the quality of financial intermediation and a gradual reduction in the extent of the government's quasi-fiscal activities. Institutional development, greater specialization, increased competition and creation of transparency, improved supervision and regulation by monetary authorities, and implementation of better accounting and risk-control standards are the recommended policies to raise the quality of financial intermediation. These measures should improve credit allocation and result in a higher average efficiency of the investments financed by the banking system.

6.  Directed-lending programmes should focus more on small firms and sectors with high risk and high social rate of return (e.g. agriculture) and must find ways of linking lending to performance indices. Enhanced credit access by small firms and lower transaction costs of obtaining credit by small firms – whose growth is essential for significant employment creation – should be adopted. One way to achieve this is to lend to firms in sectors where competition disciplines borrowers (e.g. the export markets) or where subsidized loans are linked to indices of productivity and efficiency.

7.  Promotion of non-oil exports is one way of raising sustainable economic growth in Iran, particularly in light of the fact that it is expected that per-capita oil-export-revenue will decline in real terms in the future. To raise the growth rate of non-oil exports, exchange rate misalignment in favour of tradables should be avoided. Moreover, the domestic market structure should be more competitive. By limiting the extent of domestic protection and rent-seeking opportunities, the authorities can send stronger signals to the local firms to seek more profits through innovation, efficiency and higher international competitiveness.

## Notes

1   Sectors such as health and education where the government spent heavily and created large numbers of jobs during the 1980s and 1990s are now experiencing excess employment.

2   The government has had a privatization programme since the First Development Plan (1988–1992) that has been carried onto the Second and Third Development Plans. However, the actual number of companies privatized has fallen short of the quantitative targets set by the government in each of the above plans.

3   In recognition of the importance of a more friendly macroeconomic environment for economic growth, the Second and Third plans called for credible fiscal and monetary policies, but a significant gap exists between policies and practice.

4   The morphology of growth undertaken by Chenery and Syrquin studied structural changes for a large sample of countries. The rise in per-capita income was associated with 'normal patterns' of development and structural change, in particular a decline in the share of agriculture and an increase in the share of industry and services. There was initially a presumption that predicted changes in the sectoral composition of output were indicative of a more balanced growth path or that following the 'normal' pattern could generate some growth momentum on its own. Obviously, for primary commodity-oriented economies (also oil exporters), changes in the sectoral composition of output deviated from the 'normal' path. In the primary-oriented economies the service sector was found to be larger and the manufacturing sector smaller than the average for

non-primary developing countries. See H.B. Chenery, Moses Syrquin, *The Patterns of Development 1950–1970* (London , 1975).

5 The basic result in the theory of business investment is that the optimal stock of capital is a function of the rental or the real cost of capital. In the simplest version, we assume a representative competitive firm maximizes the present value of its profits (Π), with a discount rate equal to r. For more details see David Romer, Advanced Macroeconomics, New York, McGraw Hill, 1996, chapter 8.

$$\Pi = \int_{t=0}^{\infty} e^{-rt} [\pi(K(t)\kappa(t) - I(t) - C(I(t))] dt.$$

Where $K$ is the industry-wide capital stock, $\kappa$, is the firms' own capital stock, and $\kappa_{t+1} = \kappa_t + I_t$, and $C(I)$ is investment adjusted cost. It is possible to form a Hamiltonian,

$$H(\kappa(t), I(t)) = \pi(K(t))\kappa(t) - I(t) - C(I(t))q(t)[I(t) - \dot{\kappa}(t)]$$

The first order conditions of interest is $\pi(K)(t)) = rq(t) - \dot{q}(t)$ which implies that demand for capital will rise until the marginal revenue product of capital (with $p = 1$ here) is equal to its marginal cost. In the above $q_t$ is equal to the purchase price of capital (assumed here to be 1) plus the marginal adjustment cost, and r is the interest rate. With a fixed real cost of capital, the amount of investment is proportionate to the increase in output and that proportion is given by ICOR. For a Cobb-Douglas production function, output ($Y$) is obtained from capital ($K$) and labour ($L$), the optimal capital stock is $K^* = \alpha Y/\psi$, where $\alpha$ is the elasticity of output with respect to capital and $\psi$ is the cost of capital. With a constant $\psi$ normalized to unity, $\Delta K = \alpha \Delta Y$, $\Delta K$ is net investment and is equal to $K_t - K_{t-1}$. Gross investment is $\Delta K + \delta K_t$.

6 An initial capital/output ratio of 1.8 and a depreciation rate of 5 per cent.

7 The MENA figures are based on World Development Index CD ROM, World Bank, 2001.

8 It is a tax system that combines features of a global and a schedular system. The former applies a unitary rate to income from all taxes and the latter taxes the principal sources of income flow at different rates.

9 Two major types of tax reforms, concerning corporate and value-added taxes, have been on the policy agenda in Iran in recent years.

10 Deposit and lending rates have been reduced since the writing of this chapter in November 2004.

11 A close substitute for bank and equity financing for large corporations, mostly government-owned entities and enterprises, is called 'Participation Shares'. The basic 'profit' rate charged on 'Participation Shares' is 17.5 per cent. This medium-term financial instrument is supposed to be a certificate-of-equity participation in specific projects between the issuer and the public. However, the financial market views them more like a medium-term bond with limited risks because they are usually backed by bank guarantees.

12 See A. Senhadji (1999) 'Sources of Economic Growth: An Extensive Growth Accounting Exercise', *IMF Working Papers*, WP/99/77, Washington, DC, 1999.

13 Roemer, Paul, (1986) 'Increasing Returns and Long-Run Growth', *Journal of Political Economy*, Vol. 94 (October): 1002–1037.

14 Lucas, Robert E. Jr (1988) 'On the Mechanics of Economic Development', *Journal of Monetary Economics*, Vol. 22 (January): 3–42.

15 Nelson, Richard R. and Edmund, S. Phelps (1966) 'Investment in Humans, Technological Diffusion, and Economic Growth', *American Economic Review: Papers and Proceedings*, Vol. 61(2): 69–75.

16 Aghion and Howitt draw a distinction between knowledge-based endogenous growth models and Schumpeterian interpretations of endogenous growth models. Empirical evidence has not been supportive of the first generation of endogenous growth models. See P. Aghion and P. Howitt, *Endogenous Growth Theory* (Cambridge, MA, 1998).

17 Benhabib, J. and M. Speigel (1994) 'The Role of Human Capital in Economic Development: Evidence for Aggregate Cross-Country Data', *Journal of Monetary Economics*, Vol. 34 (2), 1994: 143–173.

18 Mankiw, Romer and Weil argue that by adding HC, a better explanation of per-capita income differentials between industrial countries and DCs can be obtained from the traditional growth models. Their Solow-augmented model did in fact obtain much better empirical results than the earlier convergence tests. See N.G. Mankiw, D. Romer and D.N. Weil (1992) 'A Contribution to the Empirics of Economic Growth', *Quarterly Journal of Economics*, 107(1992): 407–437.

19 Pritchet (1996) raises a challenging question as to 'where all the education has gone in MENA?' This is an important policy issue, since a large fraction of the government resources in Iran (and also in MENA) is spent on publicly funded education. See L. Prichett (1999) *Has Education Had a Growth Payoff in the MENA Region?*, World Bank, 1999.

20 See A.R. Jalali-Naini (2003) *Economic Growth in Iran: 1950–2000* (Global Research Project, Global Development Network, 2003) and A.R. Jalali-Naini and H. Karimi, (2003) 'Budgetary Rent-Seeking and Economic Growth' (paper presented at the 10th Annual Conference, ERF, Marrakesh, 2003). The inputs in the production function were the physical capital stock and the employed workers weighted by their human capital, as measured by their average years of schooling. The homogeneity condition was not imposed but the estimated elasticities were very close, though less than unity. A time-dummy variable is included to capture the effects of the Revolution, the war and foreign exchange scarcity on the economy during the 1977–2000 period.

21 The Phillips-Hansen method is appropriate for estimation when a single co-integrating vector exists between a set of I(1) variables. A number of studies estimate the sources of growth using first difference form to account for the existence of a unit root in output, capital stock and labour-force variables. Differencing has the disadvantage of removing long-run information from the data. The issue of unit root can be handled on two different levels. First, if we impose *a theoretical* identification, the aggregate production function must have one co-integrating vector; hence we can confirm the existence of a long-run equilibrium relationship using the Engle–Granger method. Second, we can estimate a co-integration regression to deal with the issue of non-stationary variables using the Johanson–Juselius (1990) method and to estimate the sources of growth. If there is a single co-integrating vector, the two procedures are different in so far as the estimation methods are different. Moreover, in this case the use of the Phillips–Hansen estimation method is appropriate. See S. Johansen and K. Juselius, 'Maximum Likelihood Estimation and Inference on Co-Integration – with Applications to the Demand for Money', *Oxford Bulletin of Economics and Statistics*, 52(1990): 169–210.

22 The production function specification here is of the following form

$$Y_t = A_t[K^\alpha(H_t L_t)^{1-\alpha}]f(.)$$

where $f(.)$ measures the factors that cause a shift in the production function, aside from productivity shocks. It has a general functional form; the specific form is ascertained through empirical estimation.

23 The growth rate of energy consumption in Iran, particularly in the transportation sector, is very high and this is partly due to the low relative price of energy.

24 See A.R. Jalali-Naini (1999) 'The Sturcture and Volatility and Taxes in Selected MENA Countries' (www.world bank/mdf3, 1999).

25 Barro, Robert J. (1990) 'Government Spending in a Simple Model of Endogenous Growth', *Journal of Political Economy*, Vol. 98, 1995(supplement): 103–125, *Economic Growth*, New York: McGraw-Hill. R.J. Barro and Xavier Salai-Martin (1992) 'Public Finance in Models of Economic Growth', *Review of Economic Studies*, Vol. 59 (October): 223–251.

26 Easterly and Rebelo maintain that government expenditures do not affect growth in the same way and certain categories of government expenditures may have a stronger

effect on growth. They find that government investment, especially in transportation and communication, is positively correlated with growth. To capture the effect of different types of public investment on growth, government investment may be divided into strategic and non-strategic sectors. The former consists of government investments in transportation, communications, water, and electricity, and the latter includes all other types of government investments. Public spending on education may be used as a proxy for government investment in human capital. The estimated coefficient for this variable has the expected sign but is not statistically significant and therefore not reported here. Easterly and Sergio Rebelo (1993) 'Fiscal Policy and Economic Growth: An Empirical Investigation', *Journal of Monetary Economics*, Vol. 32(December): 417–458.

27 This result is slightly different from an earlier version of this chapter where the coefficient for government investment was found to be positive but not significant. In a later test which is reported here we had three extra observation years and a slightly modified regression equation.

28 See A.R. Jalali-Naini (2000) *Review and Reform of Monetary and Exchange Rate Policies*, Plan and Budget Organization (Tehran, 2000).

29 Mohsin S. Khan and Abdulhak S. Senhadji (2000) 'Threshold Effects between Inflation and Growth', Washington, DC: IMF Working Paper, WP/00/10.

30 For more details see, Jalali-Naini and Nazifi 2002.

31 For details see Jalali-Naini 2003.

32 See A.R. Jalali-Naini and F. Nazifi, 'Inflation–Output Tradeoff and Asymmetric Effects of Monetary Stocks', *Plan and Development Quarterly*, 3(2002).

33 Levine, Ross, Loayza, Norman, and Beck Thorsten (2000) 'Financial Intermediation and Growth: Causality and Causes', *Journal of Monetary Economics*, 46(2000): 31–77.

34 Joseph, Stiglitz (1994) 'The Role of the State in Financial Markets', Proceedings of the World Bank Annual Conference on Development Economics 1993, Washington, DC: the World Bank, pp. 19–52.

35 A.R. Jalali-Naini and F. Khalatbari, (2003) 'Financial Markets and Economic Growth in Iran'. www.gdnet.org/pdf2/gdn_library/global_research_projects/explaining_ growth/ Iran_financial_final.pdf

36 V.R. Bencivenga, B.D. Smith, and R.M. Starr (1996) 'Equity Markets, Transaction Costs, and Capital Accumulation: An Illustration', *World Bank Economic Review*, 10(2), May: 241–265. Demirguc-Kunt, Asli and Levine, Ross (1996) 'Stock Markets, Corporate Finance, and Economic Growth: An Overview', *World Bank Economic Review*, 10(2), May: 223–239.

37 However, a change in the composition of saving such as increasing holdings of the existing equity can have the opposite effect.

38 Since the mid-1990s, 'Participation Shares' have been used as a security for medium-term financing of investment projects. Although there have been instances where private companies have used these shares to raise investment funds, they are primarily issued by the government agencies and government corporations for investment finance. Since a couple of years ago the Central Bank has also occasionally issued these shares for conducting monetary policy. See A.R. Jalali-Naini and M. Toloo, 'Participation Shares and Monetary Policy', *Proceedings of the Ninth Annual Conference on Monetary and Exchange Rate Policies* (IRI Central Bank, 2001).

39 Data on non-oil exports are based on the figures for non-oil exports, Central Bank of Iran and the OECD CPI price index from the IMF data bank.

40 For details see A.R. Jalali-Naini 2003.

41 The real exchange rate is defined as EPw /P, where E is the nominal exchange rate, Pw is the world price level, P is the domestic price level. Alternatively, the real exchange rate can be defined as the ratio of tradable to non-tradable prices.

42 A.R. Jalali-Naini and N. Khiabani (1996) 'The Effect of Macroeconomic Variables on the Trade Balance in Iran, Iranian Journal of Trade Studies, No. 3, Summer 1997.

# 14  Human resources in Iran*

## Potentials and challenges

*Djavad Salehi-Isfahani*

## Constraints and opportunities

Critics of the economic development strategies followed by most Middle Eastern countries often point to their lagging human development indicators as a sign of failure.[1] While it is true that the growth performance of these countries has been generally quite poor since the 1980s – only sub-Saharan Africa has had a worse experience – it is not true that they have failed to expand education. In fact, the rate of growth of years of schooling in the Middle East and North Africa (MENA) has been the fastest of any region in the last 40 years.

The difficulty for economic growth appears to lie in translating this rising education into rising productivity. Doing so is not just a matter of restoring growth, though that is an essential task, but in alleviating acute social pressures arising from youth unemployment fuelled by rapid population growth. For quite a while these employment problems were solved by the accumulation of physical capital bought with oil. With that option no longer viable, solutions for human resource problems must be found elsewhere, particularly in the markets for labour and human capital.

This regional problem summarizes well the diffculties that Iran faces in the new century. Per person oil revenues, though relatively high in recent years, are still one-fourth of their peak in the mid-1970s. Despite a significant decline in the rate of population growth (halved from 3 per cent, per year, in the 1970s, to 1.5 per cent in 2004), growth of the labour force is still quite high (about 3 per cent, per year), and employment problems for the rising number of young workers loom large. The youngest group of 15–24-year-olds is growing at 3.9 per cent annually, making it very difficult to reduce unemployment despite relatively buoyant growth in recent years.

Even if the oil resources that financed Iran's ambitious investment plans in the 1970s had kept apace, Iran would still be facing diffculties because in the last 30 years the global economy has come to depend more on human than physical capital. For a state-dominated economy such as Iran's, creating human capital is much harder than creating physical capital. Human capital is widely distributed among individuals and is therefore less responsive to planning and government directives. It is much easier to identify, direct and persuade large public and private firms to invest in development projects than to persuade families and individuals to invest in education, for which (indirect) incentives must be offered through the labour market where rewards to human capital are realized. One can more easily imagine railroads being built by decree in an economy that does not need or reward rail transportation, than imagine individuals being persuaded to invest in learning to write where employers do not reward writing skills. This then leads me to identify Iran's rigid labour markets as the largest obstacle to the development of its human resources, and reforming it as a principal challenge facing Iran in the new century. The main task would be to shift rewards from unproductive skills, such as rote memorization and test taking skills, to productive but hard-to-test skills ranging from a specific skill, such as writing, to more general skills such as creativity and the ability to work in teams.[2]

Turning to potentials, there have been favourable developments on the demographic front that bode well for the long-run economic growth. The decline in fertility which started in the mid 1980s, and was in part brought about by a decline in infant mortality, reduced the average number of births per woman by more than half. Lower fertility not only helps reduce the future growth of the labour force, but, more importantly, it provides a tremendous opportunity for economic growth by allowing the ratio of adults to children to rise dramatically for the next 20 years. Population projections show that the ratio of adults aged 20–54 to children aged 0–14, which is an important indicator of resources available for education, will increase by as much as threefold from its low historic level of one. This is the well-known demographic gift that the rapid reduction in fertility makes available,[3] whose actual value depends on the extent to which the economy is able to translate the age structure advantage into productive human capital and long-term growth. Whether or not the gift is used wisely depends very much on what sort of signals the labour market is giving to individuals and families about returns to investment in human capital.[4]

The key to improving these signals is institutional reform focused on the market for labour. Iran's labour markets offer a high degree of protection to employed workers in the form of job security and fixed remuneration unrelated to productivity. Ironically, the protection is offered most to those who need it least, the better-educated in the public sector and the formal economy, shielding them from competition with young job seekers who are entering the labour market in large numbers. In Iran's formal sector, hiring, firing, and wage setting policies, are less dependent on productivity than on connections and credentials, neither of which is a sound basis for human capital development. Iran's labour laws are written to protect jobs, not to promote human capital accumulation. Increasing competition in the market for labour, especially between the employed and the unemployed, is the key to institutional reform in the human resource sector.

The prognosis for institutional reform may seem quite dim at this particular time (Spring 2004) as 'reformists' prepare to exit the legislature, this exit very likely to be followed by their departure from the executive branch. But market reform in general, and labour market reform in particular, may well be on the agenda of those who succeed them. The Fourth Five Year Plan (2005–2009), which is subtitled 'A Knowledge-based Economy in Interaction with the World Economy', was supported by the reformist Parliament and has now passed with its essentials intact by the conservative-dominated Parliament. The public and political debate over market reform in Iran, which started in the early 1990s and flourished during the populist 'reform' period, appears to have swayed the public opinion away from state control of the economy and toward a market-based economy. The public now appears to have least confidence in the public sector than at any other time in recent history, and are therefore most willing to support privatization, foreign investment and more competition in the markets for capital and labour. The reformists in Parliament and the conservatives in the Guardian Council succeeded in reaching an agreement in one specific case: the sixth Parliament was able to amend the Labour Law to exempt firms with five or fewer workers from some of its provisions. This gives small entrepreneurs more say in their manpower decisions, and removes one obstacle that they face in creating jobs. More significantly, reformists and conservatives do not appear to be far apart on the need to put in place a comprehensive social security system that would reduce the country's dependence on its labour markets for provision of social insurance. Politically, such a system is a prerequisite for the success of any labour market reform.

The plan of this paper is as follows. The next section provides the conceptual framework to understand Iran's human resource potentials and constraints. Section 3 analyzes population trends, focusing on the demographic transition and its consequences for economic growth. Section 4 reviews the successes and failures of Iran's education system. Section 5 describes the structure of employment and shows how the uncompetitive nature of Iran's labour market influences education. Section 6 outlines the broad framework for a growth-oriented human capital policy in Iran, and section 7 provides concluding remarks.

## Human capital in theories of growth and development

Recent theories of economic growth and development have emphasized the role of human capital in growth and thus placed the behaviour of the family, which plays the crucial role in the accumulation of human capital, at the centre of the growth process. These theories show how family decisions with respect to fertility and child education determine whether or not a country is able to break away from the pressures of population and underdevelopment and enter the phase of modern economic growth. The centrality of family decisions in growth derives from the simple fact that they determine the rates of growth of population and human capital, which in turn influence economic growth. At the core of these theories lies the economic theory of fertility first stated by Gary Becker.[5]

The influence of family decision on growth can be demonstrated by the correlation across countries and over time between the levels of fertility and years of schooling on the one hand, and development status on the other. Figure 14.1 tries to capture this idea by depicting the place of all developing countries in the fertility-education space.[6] Fertility is measured by the total fertility rate (TFR) and education by the average years of schooling. The countries in the sample are tightly placed around a negatively sloped curve fitted to the data.[7] This line

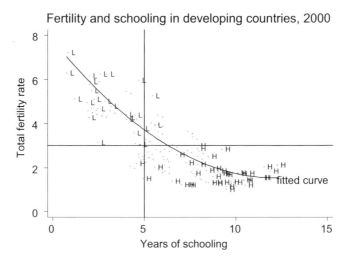

*Figure 14.1* Household choice and economic development: comparing poor and rich developing countries, 1960–2000.

Source: Penn World Tables, version 6.1, Barro and Lee (2002).

summarizes the pattern of development with respect to fertility and education which is implied by the experience of the sample of 104 developing countries in the last 40 years. I divide the fertility-education space into four quadrants, using the rather arbitrary but defensible critical values of 5 years of schooling for the completion of the primary level, and 3 births for a firm sign of the average family being in control of its fertility. There is also a strong correlation between the location of the countries in the graph and their level of development as captured by their per capita income (indicated by 'L' for low income and 'H' for high income countries; middle income countries are not marked). The upper left quadrant represents the underdeveloped state, with uncontrolled high fertility and low education. The lower-right quadrant represents its opposite, the developed state, known as the modern economic growth regime,[8] in which families have only a few children and invest heavily in their education. In 1960, before the East Asian miracle, all developing countries were situated in the top left quadrant. Forty years later, in 2000, some had succeeded in moving down to the fourth quadrant while others stayed behind. Two contrasting experiences emerge, both of which are now well known. In the last forty years, sub-Saharan African families have on average stayed with a high fertility-low education regime, whereas East Asian countries have for the most part experienced the transition to low fertility-high education regime. Those that have entered quadrant four have experienced steady growth and rising incomes as if they have taken off on a growth path, never to look back.

Figure 14.2 locates the position of MENA countries in the year 2000 in the same TFR-education space. They form an in-between case, with Iran at the very intersection of the two lines.[9] There has been considerable success for most MENA countries in lowering fertility and increasing education, but none have shown signs

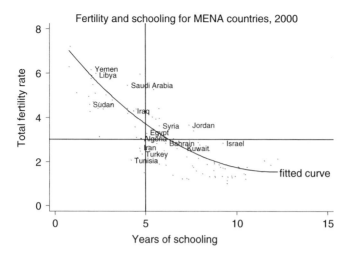

*Figure 14.2* Household choice and economic development: comparing MENA with other developing countries, 1960–2000.

Source: Penn World Tables, version 6.1, Barro and Lee (2002).

of steady growth. Their growth has been more in the form of boom and bust than steady rise in income.[10] The link between education and growth appears different for these countries. Education at all levels is more heavily subsidized, reducing the cost to individual families. There is also the lack of a close relationship between education and skill needs of the economy, which is itself related to a divergence between private and social returns to education in the Middle East.[11] I will explore the fall in fertility and increase in education in Iran in more detail in sections 3 and 4 below and return to the issue of productivity in section 5.

## Demographic transition and the potential for economic growth

The most important economic event of the last century in Iran, including the discovery of oil, is the transition from high to low fertility. The top half of Figure 14.3 tells almost the entire story: improvement in health and lower child mortality followed by lower fertility, from nearly 7 births to fewer than 3. The visible bump in the fertility graph around the time of the revolution, which at the time created doubt as to whether the anaemic demographic transition that started in the 1960s would continue at all in the pro-natal Islamic Republic,[12] proved significant for the age structure effect known as the demographic gift.[13] The temporary rise in fertility distinguishes Iran's transition from that of other countries, such as Turkey, depicted in the bottom half of the figure, for which the demographic gift is spread over a longer period.

The effect of the rise and fall in fertility on the age structure, which is the force behind the demographic gift, can be seen from Figure 14.4, which depicts age

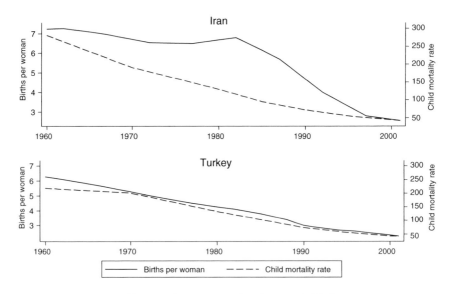

*Figure 14.3* Demographic transition in Iran and Turkey, 1960–2000.

Source: Author calculation's, World Bank (2003).

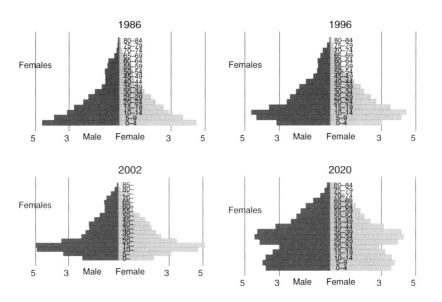

*Figure 14.4* Changes in age structure are already evident in 1996.

Source: Statistical Center of Iran, Censuses of population, 1986 and 1996; HEIS 2002 (see Appendix); and United Nations, *World Population Prospects: The 2002 Revision.*

Note: The age structure pyramid for 2002 is constructed using survey data. Sample weights are used to inflate sample numbers to population levels.

pyramids using census and survey data (for description of survey data used in this study see the Appendix). In 1986 the age structure was the youngest, when Iran had the largest number of children relative to adults following the baby boom of 1979–1981. By 1996, fertility decline is already evident in the age structure and by 2002 the age pyramid probably has its narrowest base for the next 20 years (as the larger cohort of mothers enters child bearing age even lower fertility may mean more children in total).[14]

The effect of changes in the age structure on human resources for education are depicted in Figure 14.5 which uses United Nations projections to show the rise in the ratio of adults (aged 20–54) to children (aged 0–14) in the coming decades. This ratio, which has been historically below one, is seen to be rising to 2 or even 3, depending on assumptions about fertility. The medium projection, which assumes fertility will decline slowly to replacement level (already achieved for most urban areas) by 2025, shows the adult–child ratio to reach 2 in 15 years. This implies that in 2020 there will be twice as many adults (parents and teachers) per child as there were as recently as 1995. This presents Iran with a tremendous opportunity for growth of human capital and economic growth in the next 25 years.

A dramatic manifestation of the effect of these changes in age structure on the education of the young is the large swings since the revolution in the size of the primary school age population (6–10 years). The primary school age population doubled from about 5 million at the time of revolution to about 10 million in the early 1990s, causing a huge problem with shortage of schools and teachers. Schools increased the number of shifts, sometimes to three, in order to cope with demand. In the 2003 school year, thanks to lower fertility, there were only 6.7 million

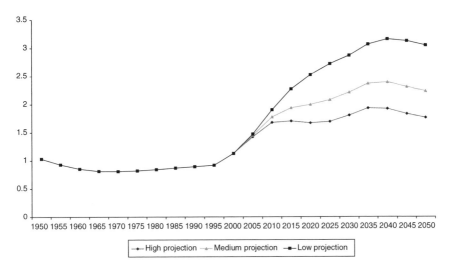

*Figure 14.5* Rising adult–child ratio, 1950–2050.

Source: Author's calculations, and United Nations, World Population Prospects.

Note: The ratio of adults 20–54-years-old to children 0–14-years-old.

students at the primary level. As a result of the dramatic change in the ratio of adults to children, there were many primary teachers without a job who volunteered to teach pre-school. Despite the fact that public schools lacked the formal authority to teach 5 year-old children, the ministry allowed schools to use their classrooms for free and hire former primary school teachers with funds contributed by parents and private sources to set up pre-school. As a consequence, Iran now has the highest level of pre-school enrolment in the Middle East: about 50 per cent of 5 year-old children are enrolled in some form of pre-school. In view of the importance of early childhood education, in this particular case, the demographic gift is being put to good use.

## Expansion of education

Despite the adverse demographic trends in the 1980s, in recent years Iran has seen an impressive and widely distributed increase in educational attainment for men and women in rural and urban areas. These gains are illustrated in enrolment rates (Table 14.1) and average years of schooling (Table 14.2) by cohort. Table 14.1 shows near-universal schooling for boys in lower secondary (middle school) age and for

*Table 14.1* Enrolment rates by gender and level of education, 1995–2002

| Year | Primary | | | Lower secondary | | | Upper secondary | | |
|------|------|-------|-------|------|-------|-------|------|-------|-------|
|      | Boys | Girls | Total | Boys | Girls | Total | Boys | Girls | Total |
| 1995 | 108.6 | 101.4 | 105.1 | 100.1 | 81.6 | 93.1 | 72.7 | 66.7 | 69.8 |
| 1998 | 108.9 | 102.9 | 106.0 | 102.2 | 85.1 | 95.9 | 79.9 | 81.2 | 80.5 |
| 1999 | 107.7 | 102.4 | 105.1 | 102.6 | 85.0 | 96.0 | 78.0 | 81.5 | 79.7 |
| 2000 | 107.2 | 102.2 | 104.8 | 102.6 | 85.0 | 96.1 | 77.1 | 81.7 | 79.3 |
| 2001 | 103.7 | 99.5 | 101.6 | 102.8 | 85.9 | 96.6 | 77.9 | 83.8 | 80.8 |
| 2002 | 101.8 | 98.1 | 100.0 | 103.6 | 87.5 | 97.8 | 76.6 | 82.6 | 79.5 |

Source: Ministry of Education, Tehran, Iran.

*Table 14.2* Educational attainment by gender and cohort (average years of schooling)

| Cohort | Rural | | | Urban | | |
|--------|------|--------|-------|------|--------|-------|
|        | Male | Female | Total | Male | Female | Total |
| 1940 | 1.40 | 0.10 | 0.70 | 5.80 | 2.80 | 4.40 |
| 1950 | 3.20 | 0.70 | 1.90 | 7.70 | 5.10 | 6.40 |
| 1960 | 4.90 | 1.70 | 3.30 | 8.80 | 6.50 | 7.70 |
| 1965 | 5.50 | 2.80 | 4.10 | 9.10 | 7.50 | 8.30 |
| 1970 | 6.80 | 4.20 | 5.40 | 9.50 | 8.40 | 8.90 |
| 1975 | 8.00 | 5.90 | 6.90 | 10.10 | 10.10 | 10.10 |
| 1980 | 8.60 | 7.50 | 8.00 | 10.70 | 11.00 | 10.90 |

Source: Author's calculations, HEIS 2002.

girls in primary age for the entire period 1995–2002, and increasing enrolments at higher levels over time. Enrolment of boys in upper secondary peaked in 1998 at 80 per cent and fell slightly to 77 per cent in 2002. Enrolment rates for girls has continued to increase over the period and surpassed those for boys in 1997. In recent years, girls have made up for their lower enrolment in lower secondary by greater persistence to high school and beyond, thus enabling them to raise their share in the university-entering class in 2003 to nearly two-thirds.

Table 14.2 shows the remarkable narrowing of the gaps in average years of schooling between rural and urban, and between men and women. For those born during 1940–1949 both gaps are large; they narrow considerably over time, and practically disappear for urban men and women. Women born in the 1940s had on average less than half the education of men, whereas those born after the Revolution (1980–1984) had on average 0.3 years *more* schooling. Similarly, rural individuals born in the 1940s attained on average about 10 per cent of the schooling of urban individuals, compared to 80 per cent for the 1980–1984 cohort. Changes in the gender gap are also seen from Figure 14.6, which depicts the fitted values of years of schooling, indicating a clear narrowing starting with those born after 1970.

The narrowing of the gender and rural–urban gaps in education, along with the equally widely distributed phenomenon of fertility decline, is evidence of significant change in the role of the Iranian family in the economy, from the traditional units of survival and procreation to agents of growth. The narrowing of the gender gap

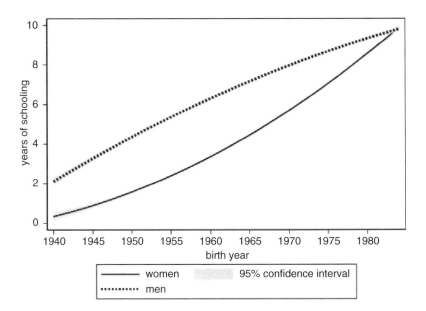

*Figure 14.6* The narrowing of the gender gap (fitted values of years of schooling by birth cohort, 1940–1980).

Source: Author's calculations from HEIS data files for 2002.

is of great significance because the education of the future generation of Iranian youth depends more on the education of women than men.

The narrowing of the gender gap in education and, more specifically, girls surpassing boys in high school and university enrolment, is observed in many developing countries, including in some of the more conservative MENA countries such as Kuwait and Saudi Arabia.[15] From a human resource perspective the question is whether the increase in girl education is the result of increased demand for educated female labour or whether it is supply driven. In all MENA countries men outnumber women in the work force by three to one, so the demand explanation is probably not pertinent. As we will see below, Iranian women's participation in market work has not appreciably increased over time and their unemployment rate is the highest. Girl education is more likely driven by supply side factors. One reason why women persist in high school and university may be that white collar jobs considered suitable for women (and mainly located in the public sector) require high school or college education. Another possible explanation is the current imbalance in the marriage market may have induced women to stay in school longer and improve their chance of marriage. This imbalance is caused by the larger cohort of women born during the baby boom of the 1979–1984 who reached marriage age in the late 1990s and sought mates in the older and smaller cohort of men of marriage age. Finally, enforcement of gender separation in schools after the Revolution may have induced the more traditionally minded parents to invest more in the education of their daughters.

## Education, labour market and economic growth

Rising education is a necessary condition for growth, but it is by no means sufficient. Indeed, somewhat surprisingly, empirical evidence is at best mixed on whether more education leads to rising per capita income.[16] The experience of MENA countries is one of the more stark cases of rising education with no growth.[17] A casual look at the paths of per capita income (declining and fluctuating) and years of schooling (rising monotonically) reveals the same for Iran: per capita growth appears more closely associated with the ups and downs of oil prices than with rising education. But if education is not contributing to higher output why more is of it being produced? It would seem that individuals benefit from education (i.e. private returns to education are high) while the economy does not (social returns are low). High private returns to formal education are evident from the correlation between wages and schooling in Table 14.3. The most important wage premium, the one which drives incentives for formal schooling, is that of the university-educated over high school. This premium increased from 23 per cent in 1992 to 36 per cent in 2001. In addition, the unemployment rate for those with tertiary education is about half of those with secondary education.[18] Low social returns are more difficult to demonstrate for Iran, but evidence of a lack of correlation between output and education in the aggregate economy is well documented for the countries of the Middle East and for all developing countries.[19] Iran fits the bill better than most developing countries in having driven a wedge between private and social returns to education, that is, wages increase with

*Table 14.3* Average hourly real wage of urban men aged 25–34 (2001 rials)

| Education level | Survey year | |
|---|---|---|
| | 1992 | 2001 |
| Illiterate | 4613 | 3007 |
| Read/write | 4368 | 4265 |
| Primary | 3896 | 3609 |
| Lower secondary | 3756 | 4340 |
| Upper secondary | 5113 | 5108 |
| Tertiary | 6301 | 6963 |
| Total | 4511 | 5000 |
| Number of observations | 724 | 761 |

Source: SECH 1992 and 2001.

education while productivity does not. Thus individuals and families have the incentive to invest in education even though such investments do not lead to greater social output. Economists have demonstrated that the reason for a divergence between private and social returns is often market failures of one kind or another. In this case, it is the failure of the labour market to provide individuals with better signals of which skills are productive and which are not.

The divergence between private and social returns in Iran is evident in the weak connection between what students learn in secondary schools and what they need when they are hired later. Schools (and parents) emphasize rote memorization of facts to prepare students for national tests at the expense of learning of skills that employers find useful. Since we can safely assume that by itself rote memorization is not productive, we may conclude that it pays to teach and learn mere facts as opposed to real skills.

The question, then, is what sort of a system would encourage its young to learn the wrong stuff? The answer is, inevitably, a well-meaning system. Iran's labour markets are not able to induce investment in productive human capital because they are burdened with the task of providing insurance and security to those employed. The usual labour market task of matching workers with jobs, which ensures economic efficiency and signals what skills employers need and reward, has become secondary.

Provision of insurance happens to be in great need in developing countries like Iran where individuals have recently left traditional communities with kinship-based mutual support networks, for an urban capitalist life that has yet to develop the type of social insurance system that now exists in social democracies of the Western world. Thanks to a less than abundant terrain and variable rainfall, social insurance has been historically necessary for survival in Iran. It may therefore not have been accidental that the development of capitalism in Iran brought with it a good dose of socialist thinking and state regulations which protected individuals against risks inherent in the operation of markets in general and the market for labour in particular. Iranians have sought and received protection from markets of all kinds. Subsidies and other interventions in markets for essential goods such as food, medicine, and energy, protect them from the vagaries of nature, health, and international energy markets. Public provision of jobs and regulation of private sector employment protect them from the most essential uncertainties of capitalism–competition for jobs with its attendant job insecurity. This is not to say that Iranians are having it all too easy. A sizeable section of the society is poor and vulnerable to income and consumption risks. In a relatively poor and unproductive country such as Iran, offering social protection comes at a cost, and offering it ineffciently, at a huge cost.

### The heavy burden of public sector employment

The labour market is the place where rewards to skills of all types are determined. These rewards are the signals that guide the actions of the young and their parents in allocating time and effort to acquiring skills.[20] Labour markets differ in their efficiency of signalling. Labour markets with open entry and exit – that is, employers decide on whom to hire, fire, and how much to pay – provide more accurate signals of what employers need. Rigid labour markets – those that restrict employers' action regarding who stays on the job and who leaves, and how much each worker is paid – are not able to reveal accurately how employers value different skills. Their signals are thus distorted, often signalling high values for diplomas and thereby encouraging investment of time and effort in activities which are not inherently productive.

As I have argued elsewhere,[21] Iran's labour market falls into the second category. Labour market rigidities are usually a consequence of government interventions which take two forms: government acting as the largest employer, and regulating private sector employment. In Iran both forms are in effect. The public sector has shrunk somewhat but it is still the main employer of educated workers. Figure 14.7 shows the changing pattern of public and private sector employment. Since the mid-1990s the share of public sector in employment has declined (from 20 to 16 per cent), while that of the salaried private sector has increased (from 21 to 31 per cent). Whereas in the 1984–1995 period there were an equal number of salaried jobs in the public and private sectors, by 2002 there were nearly twice as many wage workers in the private sector as in the public sector. The share of the self-employed has declined a bit since the mid-1990s, thus the share of all private jobs has increased only moderately.

Iran's labour market has indeed attracted more educated workers but perhaps not to the jobs in which they are most productive. Changes in the education of the labour force (defined as persons aged 15–64 not in school) since the Revolution are seen from Household Expenditure and Income Surveys (HEIS) data for 1984–2002 depicted in Figure 14.8. Table 14.4 shows in more detail the increase in educational attainment of the work force during 1992–2001 using Social and Economic Characteristics of Households (SECH) data (tabulations from the 2000 employment survey and HEIS are very similar). Public sector workers are on average much more educated than private sector workers, and among public

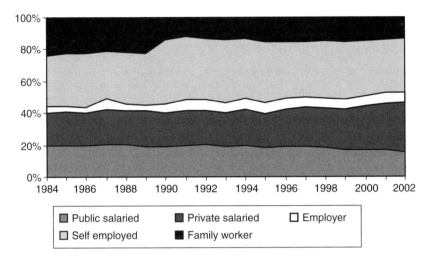

*Figure 14.7* The declining pre-eminence of the public sector: structure of employment by type of job, 1984–2002.

Source: Author's calculation, Household Expenditure and Income Survey, various years.

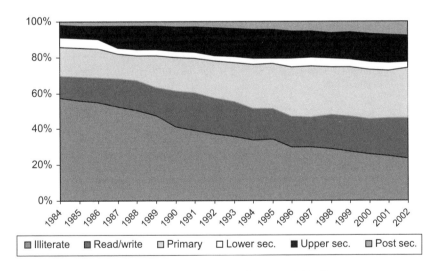

*Figure 14.8* Educational attainment of the labour force, aged 20–65.

Source: Author's calculation, Household Expenditure and Income Survey, various years.

*Table 14.4* The education of workers employed in public and private sectors

| Education | Men | | | | Women | | | |
|---|---|---|---|---|---|---|---|---|
| | Public | | Private | | Public | | Private | |
| | 1992 | 2001 | 1992 | 2001 | 1992 | 2001 | 1992 | 2001 |
| Illiterate | 22.60 | 14.31 | 5.82 | 3.73 | 25.46 | 21.51 | 1.90 | 0.51 |
| Read/write | 20.38 | 12.54 | 12.00 | 4.90 | 25.93 | 13.62 | 2.66 | 2.81 |
| Primary | 35.43 | 29.98 | 23.53 | 14.80 | 27.31 | 19.00 | 4.56 | 2.05 |
| Lower secondary | 12.70 | 22.61 | 21.43 | 19.14 | 8.33 | 10.04 | 8.37 | 6.57 |
| Upper secondary | 7.75 | 13.66 | 23.12 | 25.14 | 10.65 | 22.94 | 42.97 | 34.10 |
| Tertiary | 1.14 | 6.91 | 14.09 | 32.58 | 2.31 | 12.90 | 39.54 | 61.13 |
| Total | 100.00 | 100.00 | 100.00 | 100.00 | 100.00 | 100.00 | 100.00 | 100.00 |

Source: Author's calculations, SECH surveys, 1992 and 2001, Statistical Center of Iran.

*Table 14.5* Types of jobs for university-educated workers

| Job type | Men | | Women | |
|---|---|---|---|---|
| | 1992 | 2001 | 1992 | 2001 |
| Employer | 3.27 | 5.35 | 0.00 | 0.35 |
| Self-employed | 10.78 | 9.22 | 9.92 | 3.15 |
| Public wage worker | 79.08 | 63.59 | 85.95 | 83.57 |
| Private wage worker | 5.88 | 20.36 | 4.13 | 12.59 |
| Unpaid family worker | 0.98 | 1.48 | 0.00 | 0.35 |
| Total | 100.00 | 100.00 | 100.00 | 100.00 |

Source: Author's calculations, SECH surveys, 1992 and 2001, Statistical Center of Iran.

sector workers women are more educated than men. In 2001, 58 per cent of men in the public sector had upper secondary education or more, compared to 20 per cent in the private sector; for women, 75 per cent in the public sector compared to 35 per cent in the private sector.

The influence of public sector employment policies on education in Iran derives in part from the fact that public sector is increasingly the main destination for the university-educated. The share of university-educated workers in public sector employment has more than doubled in the last 10 years, from 17.6 per cent in 1992 to 38.0 per cent in 2001.[22] More importantly, as Table 14.5 shows, educated workers, especially women, are still primarily employed in the public sector. In 2001, 84 per cent of women and 55 per cent of men with secondary schooling or above were in government employment. In contrast, the sectors with greater potential for growth – private wage sector and self-employment – accounted for 29 per cent of male and 15 per cent of female employment. Differences between the public and private sectors are especially noticeable among younger workers, aged 20–34, as shown in Figures 14.9 and 14.10.

Schooling of public sector workers, aged 20–34

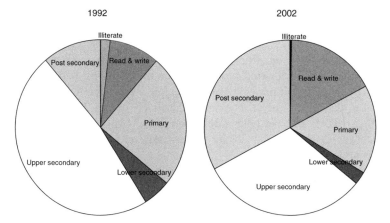

*Figure 14.9* The young and educated have been attracted to the public sector.

Source: Author's calculation, Household Expenditure and Income Surveys, 1992, 2002.

Schooling of private sector workers, aged 20–34

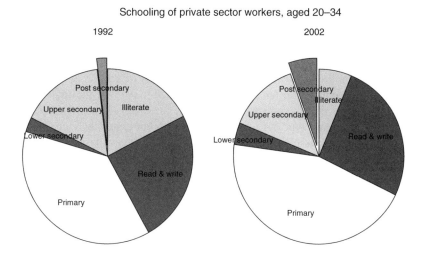

*Figure 14.10* Private sector employees are mostly the less educated.

Source: Author's calculation, Household Expenditure and Income Surveys, 1992, 2002.

The role of the private sector in employment is increasing, but it will be sometime before it can be said that students and their parents look primarily to private employers for signals of what pays to learn. The distribution of job types for the university-educated men has changed in favour of the private sector, from 6 per cent in 1992 to 20 per cent in 2001. This trend is more obvious when we consider younger workers aged 20–29 years, of whom 27 per cent worked in the private sector in 2001, up from 6 per cent in 1992. While this trend weakens the power of public sector employment rules on the education market, it does not necessarily imply higher productivity in these jobs. Wages for university-educated workers in the private sector have in fact declined sharply from an average of more than 10,000 rials per hour to less than 8000.[23] This could be the result of graduates increasingly taking jobs for which a university education is not required (such as taxi driving).

What do people learn from the signals coming from a dominant public sector about what is good to learn in schools and at home? Consider just two aspects of the public sector's employment policies; a rigid wage structure (diploma based salary scale), and life time employment (hardly anyone is laid off for lack of productivity), and then imagine a young student watching the behaviour of her most likely employer: virtually all new public jobs require a university degree, once employed she will be paid according to the level of her formal schooling, and promotion and layoff are not directly related to her productivity. The signal is loud and clear: learn and study what you will but above all get a university degree! Unfortunately, the problem does not end here. Getting a degree can be accomplished with a fairly narrow set of skills – test taking – and requires little by way of investment in skills that are hard to test, such as ambition, confidence, creativity, ability to work in teams and writing, as well as good physical health. Iran's test-based education system amplifies many times the distorted signals from the public sector to affect learning at all levels of schooling. Parents and students are encouraged to focus on what is needed to pass the multitude of tests that lead to entry into the university, especially the much feared *concour*, to the detriment of all other types of investments that do not appreciably contribute to this goal. Investments in non-testable skills therefore receive less attention from teachers and parents in Iran than they do in countries in which employers are able to reward such skills. Encouraging individuals to seek higher education is a good thing, but only if it does not result in a distorted portfolio of investment in human capital. In flexible labour markets, where employers can, subsequent to a period of employment during which they learn about the workers' non-testable skills, decide on pay or even lay off those revealed as unproductive, individuals invest in their human capital in a more balanced way, resulting in higher productivity.[24]

### Regulation of private sector employment

Rigidity of employment in Iran is not confined to the public sector. Iran's 1990 Labour Law, which regulates various aspects of private employment, compels private employers to behave in much the same way as public sector managers.[25]

The Law's intention is, of course, very noble: to increase job security and worker welfare by reducing the impact of arbitrary employer decisions to lay off workers and set their wages. But its effect goes way beyond worker protection. First, as with the public sector employment practices, in rewarding education it favours formal schooling and thereby promotes credentialism.[26] Second, because it limits competition between those who currently hold the jobs and those who seek them, it reduces the incentive of both groups to continually invest in their skills. Third, all laws restricting employer ability to pay according to individual productivity or to lay off unproductive workers raise labour costs and discourage employment.

It is not clear to what extent the regulations are enforced or would succeed in their goals if enforced. The sharp parliamentary debate in 2003 to exempt establishments with five or fewer workers from the Law indicates that it may have been binding even for small enterprises. Enforcement at larger enterprises is considerably easier, of course.

### *Demand for educated labour*

The sluggish nature of labour demand (and the economy) is evident in the changes in the distribution of employment. Figure 14.12 (and Figure 14.11 in more detail) show that the share of agriculture has declined steadily during 1984–2002, from 38 per cent to 23 per cent. Construction and services have gained while manufacturing has basically remained unchanged. The most dynamic sector is construction, whose share in employment nearly doubled, but, as we saw earlier, this sector employs very little educated labour, so an increase in its activity does not imply an increase in private sector demand for educated labour. The stagnant nature of manufacturing employment is at odds with rising wages. Figure 14.12

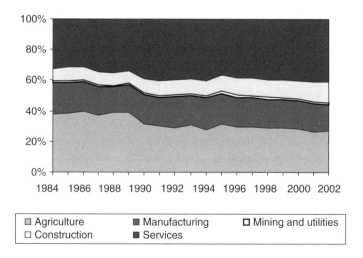

*Figure 14.11* Sectoral composition of employment, 1984–2002.

Source: Author's calculation, Household Expenditure and Income Survey, various years.

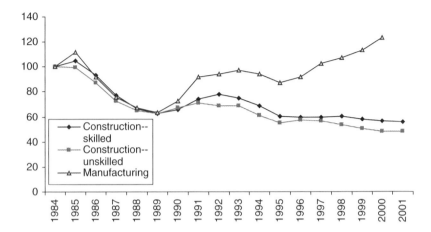

*Figure 14.12* The real wage indices for construction and manufacturing, 1984–2001.

Source: The Central Bank of the Islamic Republic of Iran, *Annual Reports*, various years.

shows a remarkable growing gap in the paths of real wages for construction and manufacturing workers. The former, dominated by private sector and less educated, have experienced a steady decline in real wages despite economic growth in recent years and increase in demand for construction labour. By contrast, workers in manufacturing, which is still dominated by publicly owned enterprises, have enjoyed rising real wages despite falling employment. Rising wages is consistent with reduction in overstaffing and rising productivity, but is most likely the result of administrative wage setting in the formal manufacturing sector.

A possible reason for the expansion of construction relative to manufacturing evident in Figure 14.11 is the fact that employment in the construction sector is generally exempt from the Labour Law due to the temporary nature of construction activity, whereas manufacturing is not. In addition, the construction sector has benefited from the influx of refugees from Afghanistan who work for much lower wages than Iranian nationals and are less likely to invoke the Law in case of labour disputes. Since there is no implied tenure for workers in a construction crew, demand for workers in construction does not suffer from the regulations to the same extent. Unfortunately, as noted earlier, returns to education are rather low in construction, so its expansion will not have a material effect on human resource development in Iran.

Figure 14.12 provides implicit evidence for a widening gap between wages of the less and more educated workers, as captured by those in construction and manufacturing. The widening gap is the other side of the coin from rising returns to education. Since private returns to education are important incentives for schooling, it is worth looking for more direct evidence for the magnitude and the direction of change in returns to education from micro data. Fortunately, such evidence can be gleaned from SECH data which reports hours worked and wages for all employed individuals in the survey, as reported in Table 14.3, which shows hourly wages for 1992 and 2001 for workers with different levels of education. As noted earlier, private returns to schooling are inferred from comparing average wages for different levels of schooling. Between 1992 and 2001 the average college premium (excess of the average wage for workers with university relative to high school education) increased from 23 percent to 36 per cent.

## *Labour supply of women*

Because of its close relation to fertility and investment in child education, the labour supply of women is viewed as a key development indicator. Economic development entails changing time allocation of women, with less time allotted to childrearing and more to education and market work.[27] Iran presents an anomaly to this generalization. Iranian women are relatively well educated, have low fertility, but so far have stayed away from market work. An increase in women's labour supply can change the human resource situation in Iran substantially. If Iranian women were to participate according to the international norm, given their fertility and education, three times as many women would be seeking work outside the home and unemployment would rise substantially.[28] It is therefore important to know how many women will be actually doing so, but this is difficult to estimate because we do not know enough about their labour supply behaviour and the factors that keep it low. Several key economic factors have been identified by labour and development economists.[29]

Economic factors include potential wage, which is related to demand conditions as well as women's education, assets and other (primarily husband's) income, and value of her time at home, which is mainly influenced by her fertility decision. In addition, there are social factors which are difficult to pin down. The literature on women in Iran (and the Middle East) makes frequent references to paternalistic gender norms as a factor that inhibits women's market work.[30] Tradition and patriarchy seem reasonable explanations for low rates of market work of Iranian women, but then they are equally good explanations of why women are prevented from going to school or from lowering their fertility, two big changes that have already taken place. If tradition and patriarchy were indeed obstacles to rising female education and lower fertility, how were they overcome, and can the same happen for women's market work?

Social norms, whether culturally or politically enforced, have been offered as explanations of a decline in labour force participation of women after the Islamic Revolution. Participation rates dropped between the 1976 and 1986 censuses, from 12.9 per cent to 8.6 per cent. However, the decrease in the aggregate participation rate hides much interesting detail. First, rural work has not been defined consistently in all censuses, resulting in a variation that is unrelated to actual economic conditions.[31] So, explaining changing participation of urban women is less prone to this type of error. Second, disaggregating the census data by age reveals a more complex pattern, as is demonstrated in Figure 14.13.

Participation of younger age groups has declined after the Revolution more sharply for men and women in rural and urban areas. This is most likely due to increased schooling rather than to any change in employment policies. The decline in participation for older age groups is less noticeable. For women, the drop in participation during 1976–1986 is serious only for those in rural areas, perhaps due to a difference in the definition of market work in rural areas, as noted earlier. For urban women, participation stay the same during 1976–1986 for those aged 25–34, and actually *increased* slightly for the 35–44 year old women. If adverse social norms affected participation after the Revolution, their effect is not evident from the experience of 25–44 year old urban women.

A more likely explanation for low participation of urban women in market work is the lack of suitable jobs. A parallel explanation for rising female education is greater availability of schools for girls with female teachers and a separation of the sexes in the public sphere. Women have taken advantage of one type of suitable jobs, those in the public sector, so very likely the same could happen when suitable private sector jobs become available.

Figures 14.14 and 14.15 use HEIS data (see Appendix for description of data) to provide more detail on participation of urban women in market work by age

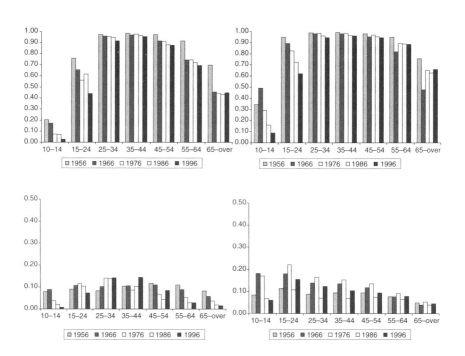

*Figure 14.13* Participation rates of men and women according to census data.

Source: Statistical Centre of Iran, *Statistical Yearbook*, various years.

Note: The scale for women's participation is drawn to 0.5 only.

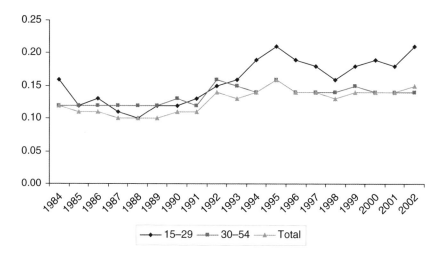

*Figure 14.14* Participation rates of urban women have stayed relatively constant since 1992.

Source: Author's calculations from HEIS surveys, various years.

Note: Participating are those employed or unemployed and not in school.

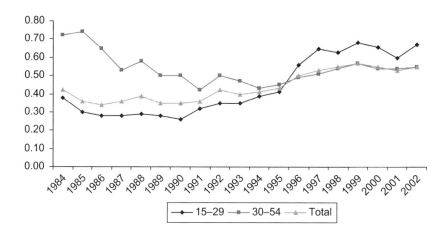

*Figure 14.15* Participation rates for urban women with a high school education or higher have increased slightly.

Source: Author's calculations from HEIS surveys, various years.

and education over time. First, there is no evidence of increasing participation in recent years; participation rates are flat for 1995–2002, which does not speak well for any demand explanation since the economy has been growing in these years. However, rising participation for urban women with at least a high school education (Figure 14.15) indicates that educated women, especially the younger group, have been able to find more white-collar jobs in the growing economy. Another interesting aspect of this graph is the decline in participation of educated women aged 30–54 during 1984–1994. This graph suggests that women would be seeking work in increasing numbers if the rising trend of younger women seen during 1990s continues and older women resume their activity rates of the 1980s. The result would be much higher unemployment rates in the future.

### Unemployment

Even with an unchanging rate of women's labour force participation, Iran's labour force is growing at a rapid pace. The rising size of the cohorts entering the labour market has been sufficient to keep labour force growth at over 3 per cent. At this rate, even a well functioning labour market would have a difficult time absorbing all who enter the market in search of a job. For the next few years, each year between 800,000 to 1.1 million new workers will be entering the labour market (depending on the assumption about the labour force participation of women).[32] To keep unemployment constant, the economy would have to grow by about 8 per cent annually, which is a formidable task. To appreciate the enormity of the employment problem facing Iran, consider the fact that if women were to participate at the same rate as men, as many as 1.6 million would be entering the market each year, which is about the same as the number of workers entering the US labour market annually, with more than 25 times the GDP!

So far unemployment has been rising in urban areas, especially among the young and women (Table 14.6). Urban women had the highest unemployment rate in 2002, followed by urban men. Unemployment rates for the 20–29 year age group and for the more educated (high school education and above) are extremely high, indicating very low turnover in the labour market.

## Human capital policy for growth

The government of Iran considers providing jobs as one of its most important tasks. Accordingly, in the Third Five Year Plan (2000–2004) it directed its fiscal and credit policies toward job creation.[33] But job creation programmes constitute a short-run solution to a much larger problem, namely, the poor functioning of the markets for labour and education. A better approach would be to focus on 'human capital policy', a set of policies that aim to improve the efficiency of these markets.[34] The Fourth Five Year Plan (2005–2009) which is focused on human capital and labour market reform, promises to do more in this direction. In this section I argue that education reform on its own is not good human capital policy, and for it to be so, it must be jointly implemented with labour market reform.

*Table 14.6* Unemployment: the young and educated are hardest hit (percentages)

|  | 1992 | 1997 | 2002 | 1992 | 1997 | 2002 |
|---|---|---|---|---|---|---|
| Age 20–64 | | | | | | |
| Male | 7.5 | 8.5 | 11.0 | 10.0 | 11.6 | 12.7 |
| Female | 4.6 | 3.5 | 11.4 | 12.1 | 19.5 | 28.1 |
| Age 20–29 | | | | | | |
| Male | 11.9 | 13.5 | 18.3 | 18.7 | 21.8 | 23.2 |
| Female | 4.0 | 5.5 | 21.1 | 22.0 | 29.5 | 46.0 |
| Age 20–29 with upper secondary education and above | | | | | | |
| Male | 24.1 | 26.7 | 28.9 | 26.6 | 28.6 | 24.4 |
| Female | 45.1 | 31.5 | 52.3 | 28.3 | 32.9 | 45.5 |

Source: Author's calculations from HEIS, various years.

Iran's highly centralized education system could, of course, benefit from reform. The Ministry of Education defines the curriculum for both public and private schools, and controls quality through its monopoly on textbooks, teacher training, and, most importantly, nationwide testing at high school and university entrance levels. The most valuable aspect of the system is its objectivity. It is meritocratic to a fault. Students are put through a series of multiple choice, machine-read tests, which culminate in the much feared university entrance examination (*concour*). The unintended but logical consequence of this system is low student interest in the subjects they study, emphasis on rote memorization, and less attention to activities that promote creativity and other non-testable skills. The latter are not only not emphasized, they are often sacrificed for the good of the students themselves who must pass one test after another in order to rise up through the educational ladder and have a shot at the big prize of entering university.

Many observers of Iran's education system have identified closing the huge gap between what students learn in schools and what they need to learn to be productive in their jobs as the system's most pressing need for reform. The gap often manifests itself in too much focus on the part of students and employers on diplomas and too little attention paid to the content of the diplomas, a problem that is well known in many developing countries as *credentialism*. Because *credentialism* is not a problem caused by the education system alone, and happens because markets reward diplomas better than productive skills, it cannot be solved by education reform alone. Similarly, curricular reform to close the gap between what schools teach and what employers need is diffcult without changing incentives originating from the labour market.[35] As long as the labour market sends signals that diplomas and high test scores are rewarded, curricular reform will have limited impact.

Two examples should make this point clear. A major reform of the educational system, introduced in 1992/93, was to deal with the skills issue by designing a type of vocational training in high schools, known as *Kar-o-danesh* (work and knowledge), which made it easy for less academically able students to obtain a high school degree doing what they could do best, earning high school credit even while working in a workshop outside school. The aim was a noble one, to direct lower ability students who were deemed unsuitable for theoretical studies to learn practical skills. The option proved less desirable than its proponents had hoped. By 1996 about 7 per cent of all high school students had taken *Kar-o-danesh* as their option. *Kar-o-danesh* was not popular because students who entered it were prevented from going on to university (it became known to students and parents as the 'blocked path'). To make it popular, the government changed the rules so *Kar-o-danesh* students could sit for the entrance examinations for *Kardani* (specialisation), a two-year post-secondary programme intended for those who were in Technical and Vocational branch (one step above *Kar-o-danesh*). If they pass the *Kardani* course, they become eligible to take the university entrance examinations, the *concour*, or sit for yet another entrance exam into a higher two-year *Kardani* program which offers a university degree.

Almost immediately demand for *Kar-o-danesh* increased, even though the chances of entering a university through this roundabout way are extremely small. *Kar-o-danesh* accounted for 20 per cent of all high school enrolment in 2002. Evidently private returns to technical education were too low to induce students to enrol in *Kar-o-danesh*, but even a negligible shot at university education raised the expected returns enough to increase enrolments. The low private return to technical education is not evidence of low social productivity, but the result of rigid labour market policies. Signalling technical skills is more difficult than knowledge, so employers in a rigid labour market who cannot terminate the employment of unproductive workers may still favour diplomas over skills when making the initial employment decisions.

Another example is an unsuccessful attempt to enforce the public school curriculum in physical education.[36] A few years ago, the Ministry of Education, correctly believing that physical education is important for human resource development, asked schools not to substitute maths quizzes during phys-ed hours. To its surprise, parents opted to pull their students during those hours to take them to personal tutors, and in some cases to private schools, many of which specialize in test taking, and many lacking even the physical space for any kind of play. In what appears to be an interesting caveat to privatization, public schools, which are less sensitive to the distorted signals, try to offer a more rounded education than private schools that are supposed to be more responsive to parental demand and market signals.

Globalization has begun to put pressure on local education systems around the world. In China, increased awareness of the skill needs of the global market has been vividly demonstrated by the success of a how-to-do manual for family education.[37] In Iran, where pressures to study abroad are as strong as in China, parents with the prospects to send their children abroad for education may care more about character building than test taking, and therefore invest in a more balanced set of skills, which includes art, music and sports. If signals from Iran's labour markets were more like those coming from the United States or Canada, the vast majority of Iranian parents who do not intend, nor can afford, to send their children abroad, would also opt for a more varied curriculum, making the reform of school curriculum much easier to implement. Given the distorted incentives created by the labour market, rational parents would not take advantage of any enlightened education reform that risks their child's chance of entering a university, because in Iran a university degree is still the best way to land a job with secure pay. The message is rather simple: labour market reform before education reform, and the time is now, while the demographic gift is for the taking.

To improve the incentives that the labour market creates for human capital accumulation, reform should aim at increasing its flexibility. Higher flexibility would increase employer discretion in wage setting and the decision to terminate employment. This would then allow the employers to more accurately signal the type of skills they need and how these skills are rewarded. But before steps are taken to increase flexibility, the government should first proceed with the implementation of a comprehensive social insurance scheme that combines income protection (rather than job protection) with incentives to remain economically active. This would then be closely followed by legislation to amend the Labour Law to reduce its restrictions on employer actions. The Fourth Five Year Plan, approved in Fall 2004, contains legislation to move forward with respect to social protection. It rationalizes the existing variety of programmes into a unified system under a new Ministry of Social Welfare. As part of a comprehensive social protection plan, the government should also offer unemployment insurance that encourages active job seeking and retraining at the same time as it offers some income protection for those laid off. It is only with credible moves in this direction that political obstacles for increased flexibility of the labour market and revision of the Labour Law can be overcome.

Education reform aimed at improving human capital accumulation should move in step with changes in employment policies and focus in the two areas of curriculum reform and reducing the impact of testing on student incentives. While some of the necessary changes would have to be initiated by the government and in public schools, as the educators of the vast majority of children, others would follow gradually from changed incentives of parents. Reducing the role of testing, especially the computerized system in operation for national tests, would be the most difficult to implement. Change to a more subjective system of testing would be resisted because of fears of favouritism. However, with labour market reform and reduced emphasis on diplomas, the objectivity that is most important would be that of employers, whose interest (profits) are best served by an objective evaluation of an individual's productivity. Including the evaluation of writing ability in testing throughout the school years is both important and costly to implement. Such a change has been recently implemented by the Scholastic Aptitude Test (SAT) used for college entrance and the Graduate Record Examinations (GRE) used for entry into graduate schools in the United States. Other desirable changes would be to permit other inputs to be used in admission into universities, such as recommendation letters. While retaining objectivity would be difficult, most university admission officers and employers in advanced countries have come to rely on them extensively. Finally, more strict evaluation of students after entering the university, with the intention of dismissing those who fail a broader definition of capability, would also help reduce the negative impact of the university entrance examinations.

## Conclusion

John Caldwell offered a definition of economic development that foresaw the new approach by economists described in section 2 and depicted in Figures 14.1 and 14.2.[38] He notes that in traditional, less developed countries, the transfer of resources is from children to parents (in terms of old age security and farm labour), whereas in developed countries it is from parents to children (in terms of investment in education and bequest). In Figure 14.1, being in the lower right quadrant implies that intergenerational transfers are from parents to children, and the top left quadrant the other way round. According to this criterion, Iran may have just entered the new phase, well before other manifestations of a developed status, such as high per capita income, political and judicial development, are visible. It also suggests that, contrary to popular belief, in the good old days of the 1970s Iran was not on the verge of entering the developed state.

Having said this, there is no theory that suggests that passing the crucial barrier from high to low fertility implies a one-way ticket to development, but there is enough empirical support to make one cautiously optimistic. For one thing, there are no poor countries that meet both criteria of low fertility and high education, at least none that have grown for a long period. Equally comforting is the observation that none have reverted to the upper-left quadrant having secured a place in the developed (bottom-right) quadrant. As for Iran, its citizens having come so far in the 'modernization' process and passed important thresholds in fertility and education, one can only hope that the country would be able to find its way through a diffcult period of reform to economic and social development.

Iran is aided in this big push by the unusual size of its demographic gift, as represented by the rising adult–child ratio seen in Figure 14.5, and by its vast oil and gas resources. The key to its success in moving along the path to development is to expand human capital rather than mere formal schooling. Iran faces serious obstacles in taking full advantage of its good luck to increase its stock of human capital.

Masses of educated workers remain unemployed, and perhaps even unemployable due to lack of proper training. With unemployment rates as high as 40 per cent, and with long spells of joblessness after 12–16 years of studying, and for some even succeeding at it, young graduates face a labour market which does not offer them the chance to prove their worth. Designed for low turnover, the labour market gives a huge advantage to those who already hold a job and thus, in effect, prevents the young from competing for those jobs. Everywhere young people need hope as they step into the so-called real world. In Iran, they step into a labour market which is optimized to offer job security but not much hope.

Loosening restriction on employers to allow a reasonable rate of turnover is a good economic and social policy, especially if implemented along with welfare and social protection reform. It is an essential step in undoing the equilibrium created by high private returns to formal schooling and *credentialism*. Delay in reform can be very costly because of the limited time – about 20 years – during which the demographic window of opportunity is open. Managing the large inflow of young and educated workers so it will not become socially explosive, and taking advantage of the demographic opportunity, are the two main reasons why reform of the labour market cannot wait for the arrival of social democracy or a resolution of the political rivalries which have absorbed the public's attention in Iran for the past several years.

On both sides of the political spectrum, policymakers increasingly realize that more flexibility for private employers is good for attracting domestic and foreign investment. If they were also to realize its importance for investment in human capital, they would be so much more likely to do something about it. Though their positions on labour market reform are not far apart, reform may be far off. Politics in Iran may have to mature further before it can produce agreements where common ground exists. Only then can a more competitive labour market emerge, one which is as friendly to those who enter the market as to those who are already in it.

### APPENDIX: MICRO DATA

The data used in this study come from two types of household surveys: Household Expenditure and Income Surveys (HEIS) which are regular annual surveys, and Social and Economic Characteristics of Households (SECH), which are multi-round, integrated household surveys collected from time to time. Both surveys are conducted by the Statistical Centre of Iran and are nationally representative. HEIS are generally larger in size, ranging from about 5,000 in 1986 to 36,000 house-holds in 1995 (or about 30,000 to 193,000 individuals). SECH surveys contain more detailed information on births and deaths and employment conditions, but from the point of view of this study their main advantage is the availability of data on individual and household earnings.[39] I have relied on HEIS when a longer time series was needed and on the SECH when comparison of two years (1992 and 2001) was sufficient or when it was the only source for a certain variable such as wage.

### Notes

* I wish to thank for comments Homa Katouzian, Andrea Kavanaugh, Hossein Shahidi, Hassanali Mehran and participants in the Conference on Iran Facing the New Century, University of Oxford, 5–7 April 2004. I also wish to thank the Statistical Centre of Iran, and in particular Mr N. M. Nassiri, for making available to me the micro data used in

this study. However, they are not responsible for any errors or views expressed in this paper.

1  United Nation, *Arab human development report 2002: creating opportunities for future generations* (New York: United Nations Development Programme, 2002).

2  Djavad Salehi-Isfahani, 'Population, Human Capital, and Economic Growth in Iran', in Ismael Sirageldin, editor, *Human Capital and Population in the Middle East* (I. B. Tauris, 2002); Djavad Salehi-Isfahani and Russell D. Murphy, 'Labour market flexibility and investment in human capital', unpublished, Department of Economics, 2004.

3  Robin Barlow, 'Population Growth and Economic Growth: Some More Correlations', *Population and Development Review*, 20 (1994): 1; David E. Bloom and Jefferey Williamson, 'Demographic Transitions and Economic Miracles in Emerging Asia', *World Bank Economic Review*, 12 (1997): 3.

4  Salehi-Isfahani, 'Population, Human Capital, and Economic Growth in Iran'.

5  For a survey of his work see Gary S. Becker, 'Fertility and Economy', *Journal of Population Economics*, 5 (1992): 3.

6  I have used similar graphs to discuss the global trade off between quantity and quality of children in Sergei Guriev and Djavad Salehi-Isfahani, 'Microeconomics of growth around the world', in: Gary McMahon and Lyn Squire, editors, *Explaining growth, a global research project* (New York: Palgrave/MacMillan, 2003), and Djavad Salehi-Isfahani, 'Microeconomics of growth in MENA: the role of households', in J. Nugent and M.H. Pesaran (editors), *Explaining Growth in Middle East,* Contributions to Economic Analysis, volume 278, London: Elsevier, 2006.

7  The estimated equation for the curve is $y = 7.11 - 1.1x + 0.046x^2$, where $y$ is fertility (TFR) and $x$ the average years of schooling for the population 25 years and older. All coefficients are significant at one percent level and $R2 = 0.73$.

8  Oded Galor and David N. Weil, 'Population, Technology, and Growth: From Malthusian Stagnation to the Demographic Transition and Beyond', *American Economic Review*, 90 (2000): 4.

9  Among MENA countries for which data were available, only Sudan and Yemen are low income according to the above definition; Persian Gulf exporters are high income and the rest are middle income.

10 Nemat Shafiq, 'Rents, Reform and Economic Malaise in Middle East and North Africa', *Research in Middle East Economics*, 2 (1997).

11 Lant Pritchett, 'Has education had a growth payoff in the MENA region?', unpublished World Bank Working Paper, 1999.

12 Akbar Aghjanian, 'Population Change in Iran, 1966–86: A Stalled Demographic Transition', *Population and Development Review*, 17 (1991): 4.

13 For a general discussion of how the demographic gift can help economic growth, see Barlow; Bloom and Williamson; David E. Bloom, David Canning and Jaysee Sevilla, *Economic Growth and the Demographic Transition* (National Bureau of Economic Research, 2001) (W8685) – Technical report; David E. Bloom, David Canning and Jaysee Sevilla, *Demographic Dividend: A new perspective on the economic conse-quences of population growth* (Santa Monica, CA: Rand, 2002) (MR-1274). Technical report; for an application to Iran, see Djavad Salehi-Isfahani, 'Demographic aspects of economic development in Iran', *Social Research*, 67(2000): 2; Salehi-Isfahani, 'Population'.

14 Unlike the other two, the age structure for 2002 is derived from survey rather than census data. As such it is not strictly comparable with them. However, the survey numbers have been scaled up to the country as a whole, using sampling weights.

15 United Nation, *Arab Human Development Report 2003: Building a Knowledge Society* (New York, NY: United Nations Development Programme, 2003).

16 Robert Topel, 'Labor Markets and Economic Growth', in Orley Ashenfelter and David Card, editors, *Handbook of Labour Economics*, volume 3 (Elsevier Science B.V.,

1999): chapter 44; Lant Pritchett, 'Where has all the education gone?' *World Bank Economic Review*, 15(2001): 3.

17 Pritchett, 'Has education had a growth payoff in the MENA region?'.

18 According to the 2000 Employment Survey, unemployment rates for men with secondary education was 22 per cent and with tertiary education 10 per cent; for women 44 and 18 per cent, respectively.

19 Christopher Pissarides, 'Labour markets and economic growth in the MENA Region: The role and relationship between human capital and growth', ERF, Cairo, 2000; Pritchett, 'Where has all the education gone?', and Pritchett, 'Has education had a growth payoff in the MENA region?'.

20 The discussion of the interaction between the labour market and education draws from D. Salehi-Isfahani and Russell D. Murphy, 'Labour market flexibility'.

21 Djavad Salehi-Isfahani, 'Labour and the Challenge of Restructuring in Iran', *Middle East Report*, 28(1999): 210; Salehi-Isfahani, 'Population, Human Capital, and Economic Growth in Iran.

22 Author's calculations, SECH data, 1992 and 2001.

23 Author's calculations, 1992 and 2001 SECH surveys.

24 See Salehi-Isfahani and Murphy, 'Labour market flexibility', for a comparison of investment outcomes in labour markets with different institutions.

25 The text of the Law is available in English from the International Labour Office website http://www.ilo.org, and in Persian from Nasser Resainia, *Majmoue ghavanin kar Joumhouri Eslami Iran* (The Complete Labour Law of the Islamic Republic of Iran) (Tehran, Iran: Saman, 1996). For a discussion of its main features see Salehi-Isfahani, 'Labour and the Challenge of Restructuring' and Hamid Tabatabai and Djavad Salehi-Isfahani, 'Population, labour, and employment in Iran', in Djavad Salehi-Isfahani, editor, *Labour and Human Capital in the Middle East: Studies of Markets and Household Behaviour* (London: Ithaca Press, 2001).

26 Salehi-Isfahani and Murphy, 'Labour market flexibility' show how, when unable to lay off workers hired by mistake, rational private employers emphasize objective test results and formal schooling rather than take a chance with weaker signals of productivity.

27 Kristin Mammen and Christina Paxson, 'Womens Work and Economic Development', *Journal of Economic Perspectives*, 14(2000): 4.

28 World Bank, *Iran: Medium Term Framework for Transition, Converting Oil Wealth to Development* (Washington, DC: World Bank, Social and Economic Development Group, Middle East and North Africa Region, 2003): 18.

29 Mammen and Paxson, 'Women's work'. For determinants of women's market work in Iran, see D. Salehi-Isfahani, 'Market work of women in Iran', paper presented in the 10th Annual Conference of the ERF, Sharja, 2002.

30 Valentine M. Moghadam, 'Women, work, and ideology in the Islamic Republic of Iran', *International Journal of Middle Eastern Studies*, 20(1988).

31 Valentine M. Moghadam, 'Women's Employment Issues in Contemporary Iran: Problems and Prospects in the 1990s', *Iranian Studies*, 28(1995): 3–4; Tabatabai and Salehi-Isfahani, 'Population'.

32 Mehdi Shafaeddin, *Diversification, Employment and Development: Towards A Long-Term Strategy for an Oil-Exporting Country; The Case of Iran* (2001) – ERF Working, number 2001–2013, Cairo, Egypt; World Bank, 'Iran: Medium Term Framework'.

33 Central Bank of the Islamic Republic of Iran, *Annual Report, 1381 (2002/03)* (Tehran, Iran, 2003): 13.

34 James Heckman has used the term human capital policy to discuss education and labour market linkages in the United States in J. Heckman and P. Klenow, 'Human Capital Policy', in: M. Boskin, editor, *Policies to Promote Capital Formation* (Stanford, CA: Hoover Institution), and Pedro Manuel Carneiro and James J. Heckman,

*Human Capital Policy* (Institute for the Study of Labor (IZA), Discussion Paper number 821, 2003).

35  Salehi-Isfahani, 'Population, Human Capital, and Economic Growth in Iran'.

36  Reported in an interview with the Deputy Minster of Education, Hamshahri, *Interview with Rahim Ebadi, Deputy Minister of Education*, 10 January 2000.

37  The book *Harvard Girl* has sold 1.6 million copies in China (Harvard Magazine, July–August 2002).

38  John C. Caldwell, 'Toward a Restatement of Demographic Transition Theory', *Population and Development Review*, 2(1976): 3–4.

39  In addition to these, there are employment surveys which only span the more recent years but are more specialized on employment. They are not used in this paper.

# 15 The significance of economic history, and the fundamental features of the economic history of Iran*

*Homa Katouzian*

Just as Natural History is the mother of the biological sciences, Social History is the mother of the social sciences. Classical political economy was developed in a dynamic era, a period of European history where a series of long-term social developments were approaching their peak in the French Revolution and the Industrial Revolution of England. It is not at all surprising that Adam Smith and David Hume spent time with the French Physiocrats, notably Quesnay and Turgot, and with the French philosophers, especially, though not exclusively, Voltaire and Rousseau.[1]

It was precisely the dynamic quality of the era that led economic and social and political theorists alike to look into the nature and causes of change, and therefore regard history as a principal source of the foundations of their knowledge. A similar process was taking place, but more slowly, among biologists who were trying to discover the nature of life and the origin of species, and the causes of long-term biological changes through time. Darwinism was in fact the end, not the beginning, of this process. It was through the historical as well as empirical approach that Adam Smith formulated his critique of feudal society and structures and attacked protectionist policies which he described as 'the policy of Europe'.[2] Throughout the century or so in which classical political economy or economics developed – roughly from 1770 to the 1870 – history was in evidence, either explicitly or tacitly as the background to contemporary economic analysis. Even Ricardo who evidently was not much in command of historical knowledge, used historical concepts and categories created by others – but particularly Adam Smith – before him. Not only James Mill, close friend of both Jeremy Bentham and David Ricardo, but the less well-known, though not less intelligent, Richard Jones made comparative studies of Indian economy and society and helped to clarify the social and historical features which had been known before them as Oriental Despotism, and which Marx and Engels after them defined as the Asiatic Mode of Production.[3] The process of mixing history and analysis, or rather, theorizing with a firm grasp of history and historical evidence, reached its peak in the work of Marx, who my be regarded as the last of the great classical economists.

It is not surprising that in the late 19th century neo-classical economic theory and method emerged as a more-or-less alternative approach to classical political economy. For by then a new era had been established, the era of democracy, industry and empire. The new era presented fresh problems that needed to be sorted out, now that the process of long-term accumulation of capital and the role of social classes in economic change had been studied, and a satisfactory solution for the transformation of values into prices had not been found. There was need for a modern theory of the firm, of price and wage determination, of interaction of markets, of international trade. In other words the time had come for the static conditions of the mature industrial capitalist system – rather than the dynamics of its emergence – to be studied in detail. Both the magnificent dynamics and the aggregate economic analysis of classical economics were thus pushed aside, and with them history began to fade out of sight.

But the neo-classical system was not quite established without an argument, especially as regarded the significance of history in general and economic history in particular. In a formal debate on the general methodological problems and issues of economic and social theories, for example, Cunningham, the English historian, pointed out that:

> Economic 'generalizations' must necessarily be relative to a given form of civilization and a given stage of historical development. This according to Mr. John Stuart Mill 'is what no political economist would deny' ... we have to thank the Comtist criticism for forcing us to remember that the material truth of economic principles depends on complicated social conditions, and that they have no independent validity.'[4]

The debate continued but, outside of the Marxist framework, it became more focussed on the abstract nature of neo-classical theory, and less on the question of social and economic dynamics or on the view that any social and economic theory was valid only for the stage of history to which it referred. Thus, a leading economic historian of the early twentieth century criticized the 'empty economic boxes', meaning models and theories which had little correspondence with empirical reality.

Yet this was long before economic theory became almost the same as mathematical economics. Leon Walras was an early neoclassical economist who virtually founded mathematical economics by presenting his general equilibrium model based on simultaneous equations. But it was the partial-equilibrium approach which was most influential from its foundation until after World War II. This was the product of the Austrian school – of Menger, Böhm-Bawerk and Wiesser – and especially the Cambridge school – led by Alfred Marshall. Marshall and his pupil Keynes were both trained mathematicians but neither of them set much store by general equilibrium analysis and both of them explicitly rejected extensive use of mathematics in economic theory, explaining that it would divert attention from problems of the real world.[5]

Nevertheless, after the Second World War mathematical economics rapidly expanded and became fashionable, so much so that by 1980 it had become virtually identical with economic theory itself. That is to say, in most cases, mathematical economics began to mean economic theory, and economic theory, mathematical economics. A common complaint of the critics against modern mathematical economics was that it was too abstract. The defenders used to counter the argument by saying that no definition of 'too much abstraction' was ever put forward by the critics. In other words, they wondered how much abstraction would be acceptable and how 'too much abstraction' was defined. Or putting it another way yet again: at what point and under what circumstances may it be said that there has been *too much* abstraction?

To this question I suggested an answer. There can of course be no doubt that abstraction and generalization is necessary for any body of scientific, including social-scientific, theory. Abstract theories in any science necessarily refer to simplified problems which nevertheless may become the foundation of solving complex scientific questions. Any scientific theory necessarily refers to a simplified version of the real world, focussing on the most important variables, in the hope of shedding light on the complex problem or problems which it means to solve.

My solution to the question 'How much abstraction is too much' was that if an abstract theory has a counterpart in the world of reality – i.e. if it corresponds to a real-world problem which needs to be solved – then it is legitimate. Therefore, any theory which does not have a counterpart in the real world is not scientifically legitimate, and is a product of too much abstraction.[6] I compared the activities of some mathematical economists (or for that matter some mathematical physicists) to those of the medieval scholastics, who, since the triumph of the Renaissance and of modern science have often been objects of ridicule, normally cited as symbols of intellectual obscurantism and social irrelevance. Now, the scholastics are laughed at (it would be too mild to say 'criticized') for trying to answer questions such as 'How many angles can stand on top of a pin?' This is an abstract question but, putting aside its purely metaphysical quality, it is a question to which there is no counterpart in the world of reality. In other words, not only does the question not exist outside the minds of those preoccupied with it, but far worse, there is not a single problem in the world of reality of which that may be regarded as a simple and abstract version.

I have not been looking at journals of economic theory and new economic models and theories for twenty years. But I can say with complete justice that, before then, many, if nor most, theoretical economic models that were put on the market resembled the old scholastic question about the assembly of the angles, such that I even described the whole of our era as the age of New Scholasticism. That however was with respect not just to the practice of academic economics but to modern scientific establishments in general, a discussion of which is beyond the scope of this article.[7]

It is of course possible, perhaps even necessary, to tolerate the pursuit of such irrelevant questions, whether now or in the medieval past, as being useful to the development of sheer analytical rigour. The point however is that if it becomes the most widespread and most rewarded scientific pursuit within an academic discipline, it would be a gross waste of scientific resources; it would leave unanswered many a real question which could otherwise have been tackled, and it would result in little if any real advancement of science. Unfortunately it takes much more time to study the historical background and social setting of an economic problem, than to simply set up a little mathematical model which can be solved to its owner's satisfaction; and much more difficult to be rewarded for the former pursuit than for the demonstration of some mathematical skill.

History then provides the background, points to the social dynamics and defines the social framework in which economic and social problems emerge and demand solution. This does not mean that every economist must be an economic historian or a sociologist. It means that economic studies, whether theoretical or empirical, whether as an academic pursuit or as a policy prescription, must have in the background the history and social framework to which they refer. If this had not been the case, knowledge of economics would have stayed at the medieval level and against the social and economic background of feudal Europe, or perhaps at the age of mercantilism. Indeed, classical economists and later neo-classical economists after them were successful to the extent that they had the historical background as well as the changing social framework more-or-less firmly behind their general approaches to economic questions.

There can be endless examples of the uses of economic history and of historical approaches to economics. Here let me present two examples from my own experience the first one of which – my theory of the nature and causes of the growth of service industries – is completely apart from my studies of Iranian history and political economy. The German Historical School of the latter half of the 19th century – Roscher, List, Schmöller, Hilderbrand, Bücher, etc. – led an attack both on classical political economy and on the contemporary neo-classical economics such that may be summarized as follows. First, they argued that economics was by its very nature incapable of formulating abstract and general hypotheses. Second, that the correct procedure for the study of economic phenomena and problems was by the use of historical investigation. Third, that such historical investigation would in time lead to the formulation of historical 'general laws' nevertheless specific to certain stages of history, precisely because the data on which they are based would be different from one stage to another. Finally, it is implicit in the foregoing that there can be differences in policy conclusions according to the various socio-cultural frameworks or stages of history in which the subject is being studied; for example, they regarded *laissez faire* and free trade of possible – perhaps even beneficial – relevance to England but not to Germany, which was at a lower stage of economic development.[8]

The German Historical School had the better of the argument over neo-classical economics in three ways. First, their nationalist instinct proved right and the German economy succeeded in economic development not by the application of free trade but through interventionist as well as protectionist policies. This was later reaffirmed by Japan and there are now neo-classical theories which explain why such policies aided rather than hindered economic growth and development in those countries. Second, their emphasis on the relevance and usefulness of historical knowledge and the role of cultural and institutional factors was well-founded and their attack on the purely logical method of Ricardian and some neo-classical theorists was justified. Third, the German criticism implied the ultimate indivisibility of the socio-economic problems and the usefulness of a multi-disciplinary approach to their solution.

However, the defects of the German Historical School were no less than their merits. The biggest mistake of this School was their belief in socio-economic studies by *direct* observation – involving a detailed study of historical facts and much else besides – and the inference of 'general laws' through this procedure. To put their strength and weakness in one sentence, the Germans were wrong in general and right in particular: they were wrong to advocate direct generalizations from historical knowledge, but right in indicating the relevance of historical knowledge to economic and social theory, and pointing out the limits to generalization whether by deductive or inductive methods.

The theories of stages of economic progress formulated by Bücher, Schmöller, Sombart, etc., were of some value, and as a matter of fact economic analysis has since explained – i.e. established the causal relations for – these 'empirical laws'. For example Freidrich List's descriptive scheme of Agricultural, Agricultural-and-Manufacturing and Agricultural-Manufacturing-and-Commercial stages of economic development was later analysed in terms of the Primary, Secondary and Tertiary Stages of growth.

The personal experience I mentioned above is related to this. In the 1950s and 1960s this theory was all but forgotten. Not only that. Virtually all the mainstream social and economic theories were describing the service industries as unproductive according to one or another analytical proposition. The leading Cambridge economist Nicholas Kaldor was firmly convinced that the greatest obstacle to British economic growth was the size of the service sector in the economy,[9] to the extent that, in his capacity as economic adviser to the then British government, he had advised them to impose a special tax on service activities so as to encourage a shift of resources from service activities to manufacturing industry, an advice which they had accepted. The tax imposed was known as Selective Employment Tax, or SET.

Many sociologists, many of them not Marxist, misunderstood Adam Smith's and following him Marx's attack on 'unproductive labour' and firmly believed that all service activities were unproductive, and based their teaching and research on this assumption. Even Raymond Aron, the leading anti-Marxist French Sociologist, claimed that productivity was 'frequently non-existent' among services. Putting all that aside, taking a historical view of stages of economic development was totally unacceptable to mainstream economics, because it smacked of either nationalist or Marxist economic theories which they rejected. It was also justified on the basis of a misunderstanding of the meaning and methodological implications of Popper's attack on historicism.

When, in 1968, I came to write my dissertation of Master of Science in Economics – M.Sc. (Econ.) – for the University of London, I decided to take a fresh look at this unfashionable historical theory. First, I wished to explain why the shares of services in output and employment were increasing despite the belief that they were unproductive or at least hindered growth. And second, why the share of this sector was also large in many, if not most, developing countries, whereas the original theory had anticipated that services in poorer countries would have a small share in output and labour force. It would be too lengthy a diversion to try even to present a summery of my study and analysis here. Very briefly, I explained both the problems by pointing out the unusual heterogeneity of services as compared to both agriculture and manufacturing, and proposed three analytically distinct categories of them: 'old services', 'complementary services' and 'new services'. I explained that the income-elasticity of demand differed for these groups of services both among themselves and through time, such that on balance the service sector would steadily expand in advanced countries. I also pointed out that productivity and productivity growth was significantly different among the three categories of services which I had identified, and this made the impact of each of the categories on the overall productivity growth of the economy different. Not only did I predict that services would grow steadily in advanced counties, but I even predicted – in 1968 – that the use of computer technology would help greatly enhance the productivity performance of service activities such as banking, finance and commerce.

Regarding the apparently odd case of large services in many developing countries, I pointed to the impact of the rise of international tourism, and the application of 'new services', the origin of both of which were in advanced, not in developing countries: on the one hand the income-elasticity of demand for tourism in *advanced countries* is high and it leads to the growth of demand for the services of *developing countries*; on the other hand, new services are products of scientific and technological progress in advanced countries which create demand in (especially the not so poor) developing counties. In addition, I analysed the impact of oil revenues on the growth of services in oil-exporting countries.

This was 1968 and the year in which I submitted an article based on this study, entitled 'The Development of the Service Sector: A New Approach', to *The Economic Journal*, which had originally published Kaldror's article and was then still edited at Cambridge. It was turned down without argument: they even doubted my figures, apparently simply because they showed that the mainstream view of the performance of the service sector was invalid. It was subsequently published in *Oxford Economic Papers* in 1970[10] and made hardly any impact at the time, but not for long. In 1978, when I was invited by Germany's Institute of World Economics to a conference to comment on their staff's study of the service sector I realized that my theory was becoming fast fashionable because real economic events were demonstrating its relevance and usefulness.[11] In 1982 I was invited by the United Nations in Geneva as economic consultant to write a chapter on the service sector in the world context for the annual *Trade and Development Report* by the UN's Conference on Trade and Development, UNCTAD. This I did and it was subsequently published in *TDR* 1982 under the title of 'Services and the World Economy'. It was there that I fully saw the extent to which recent studies of services worldwide had been subsequently based on my theory, for example, Eves Sabolo's book-length study for the International Labour Organization – entitled

*The Service Industries* (Geneva, 1976) – which had successfully applied my concepts and categories to a large number of countries, both advanced and developing.

That was a general theoretical study without specific reference to any specific country or group of countries, although it did distinguish between the cases of the advanced and developing worlds. My other main resort to historical study to make sense of a political and economic problem had already begun in the mid-1960s. This was the question of the logic of Iranian history, society and economy.

For reasons that I have explained elsewhere it became clear to me that the existing models of social and economic analysis – be they Marxist, neo-classical or other – certainly in regard to the problems and strategies of economic development, did not render realistic results in the case of Iran.[12] All such theories and models – regardless of their ideological origins and differences – had been developed against the background of European history and society and then supposed, both by them and by developing countries themselves, that they were universally valid. I have demonstrated in another context that while all scientific theories are general, no scientific theory can enjoy universal validity.[13] Let me emphasize that the problem was not due to the existing tools and methods of the social sciences which have universal validity, but of social and economic theories and models developed against the European background, which – if correct – are generally valid in the case of European societies alone. The question then was to discover, by means of the appropriate application of the same methods that have resulted in European social and economic theories, the logic and sociology of Iranian history as the relevant and realistic background to the current problems and efforts at their solution. This I did through a long and continuous – and, I might add, extremely lonely – process of a comparative study of Iranian and European society and history, while at the same time I was trying to develop realistic models for the political and economic development of Iran. The result was very briefly as follows.

Iran was a **short-term society** in contrast to Europe's **long-term society**.[14] It was a society in which change – even important and fundamental change – tended to be a short-term phenomenon. And this was precisely due to the absence of an established and inviolable legal framework which would guarantee long term continuity. Over any short period of time, there could be notable military, administrative and property-owning classes, but their composition would not remain the same beyond one or two generations, unlike traditional European aristocracies, or even merchant classes. In Iran, property and social positions were short-term, precisely because they were regarded as personal privileges rather than inherited and inviolable social rights. The situation of those who possessed rank and property – except in very rare examples – was not the result of long-term inheritance (say, beyond two generations before) and they did not expect their heirs to continue in the same positions as a matter of course. The heirs could do so only if they managed to establish themselves on their own merits – merits being the personal traits necessary for success within the given social context. There thus was a high degree of social mobility, unthinkable in medieval and much of the modern European history. This did not exclude the position of the Shah himself, since legitimacy and the right of succession was nearly always subject to serious challenge, even rebellion.[15]

The most visible example of the short-term nature of Iranian society is the habit of declaring a building – especially a residential building – as *kolangi*, a 'pick-axe building'. Most of these buildings are no more than thirty (even twenty) years old, and they are normally sound in foundation and structure. In a few cases they may be run-down and in need of renovation, but the feature that results in their condemnation as such, and incidentally wipes off the value of the structure and only leaves the price of their site, is that their architecture and /or interior design is unfashionable, according to the latest forms, concepts or whims. Therefore, rather than building a new house or whatever, thus adding to the stock of existing physical capital, it is demolished by the owner or purchaser, and a new building is erected on its site. That is how I have come to describe the short-term Iranian society alternatively as *jame'h-ye kolangi*, 'the pick-axe society', a society many of whose features – political, social, educational, literary, etc. – are constantly in danger of receiving the pick-axe treatment by short-term whims of fashion.[16]

Lack of long-term continuity, by definition, resulted in significant change from one short period to the next, such that *history became a series of connected short runs*. In this sense, therefore, change was more frequent – usually also more drastic – and as noted, social mobility across various classes considerably higher than in traditional European societies. But, also by definition, it rendered very difficult *cumulative* change in the long term, including the long-term accumulation of property, wealth, capital, social and private institutions, even the institutions of learning. These did normally proceed or exist in every short term, but they had to be reconstructed or drastically altered in the subsequent short terms.

Evidence of the short-term nature of the Iranian society as described above is to be found virtually in all of its aspects almost throughout Iran's long history, both pre- and post-Islamic. Here we shall present a brief analysis of three of its main features closely related to one another:

- Problems of legitimacy and succession, and the toll that this took of rulers, other royal persons, and ministers and military commanders
- The tenuous nature of 'life and possessions' (*jan o mal*)
- Problems of accumulation and development

Here I shall just take up the third feature, that is problems of accumulation and development. If there is one point on which all the major theories of economic development are agreed it is that the Industrial Revolution occurred as a result of long-term accumulation of, first commercial, then industrial capital. Long-term accumulation of capital was a necessary, even though not sufficient, condition for modern industrial development. Without it, neither the necessary investment would have taken place in the commercial sphere, resulting in the unification of the internal market and virtually continuous expansion of foreign trade, nor would there have been sufficient investment in the goods which made the innovation and application of modern techniques and processes possible in agriculture and industry. In a particularly clear and convincing historical generalization, Alexander Gerschenkron described the process of European industrialization until the 20th century in three stages, from the countries such as England which started first, through those such as Germany and Austria to Russia and Eastern Europe. In the first group of countries it was the firm which led the process of accumulation for a long time. In the second, banks played a crucial role and financing industrialization, and in the third group, the state.[17]

The simple but highly acute point about the necessity of long-term accumulation of capital was discovered by early classical economists, who observed that in order for the firm to expand it needed to accumulate, and in order for it to accumulate, it had to save first. This was what they sometimes described as the process of 'ploughing back capital'. Turgot described the process more clearly than any one before him. But it was Adam Smith who put forward a memorable argument for the necessity of prior saving for the expansion of the firm, hence the industry and therefore the whole economy. He said with a certainty – perhaps even dogmatism – uncharacteristic of his even tempered approach to most matters of theory and policy that it was not so much technical progress, but saving and investment, making its innovation and application possible, that was the principal cause of industrial development. He therefore concluded that every saver was a friend, and every spender, an enemy of the society. Thus he wrote in Book II of his renowned treatise:

> Whatever a person saves from his revenue he adds to his capital [and] as the capital of an individual can be increased only by what he saves from his annual revenue or his annual gains, so the capital of the society which is the same with that of the individuals who compose it can be increased in the same manner.[18]

In other words, aggregate saving is the sum of the savings of all firms and individuals. Furthermore, he said, it is saving, not production, which is the initial cause of investment, of capital accumulation.

> Parsimony and not industry is the immediate cause of the increase in capital. Industry indeed provides the subject which parsimony accumulates. But whatever industry might acquire, if parsimony did not save and store up, the capital would never be the greater.[19]

It follows that savers compensate for the habits of the spendthrift in preventing economic decline. Savers therefore help the society, while spendthrifts hinder it:

> If the prodigality of some was not compensated by the frugality of others, the conduct of every prodigal...tends not only to beggar himself but to impoverish his country...Every prodigal appears to be a public enemy and every frugal man a public benefactor.[20]

Later, Malthus, Marx, Hobson, Tugan-Baranovsky and Keynes – using different approaches, and putting forward more or less strong arguments – showed that this theory was valid so long as aggregate demand would match aggregate supply at full employment in general. And in particular, so long as money is not hoarded, that is, so long as saving does not remain passive but is turned into investment by the saver or others who borrow from him. Yet the Keynesian criticism – at least insofar as it affected policies of achieving and maintaining full employment – was so successful that, in the practice of macro-economic policy, virtually all distinction between investment expenditure and consumption expenditure ceased. This had disastrous consequences for – certainly the British – economy between 1950 and 1980, when not only new investment but even renewal of stock was neglected so long as aggregate consumption was adequate to maintain full employment.[21] Indeed, Keynes himself might have said 'And Keynes conquered England as completely as the Holy Inquisition conquered Spain.'[22] There can be no doubt that long-term economic growth would require a significant rate of saving and investment (from domestic or foreign sources) even for developed industrial societies.

To sum up the fundamental points made above, capital accumulation required significant and continuous saving for long-term investment. Finance for investment was supplied directly by the savings of propertied classes, by banks, the state or – in the last century and a half – by all of them. Since the 20th century, development finance has also been supplied by advanced industrial countries for investment in third world economies. Its classic and earliest example was the long-term accumulation of – first commercial then industrial – capital in England, mainly by the bourgeoisie, the commercial classes, although 'enlightened landlords' also participated in the process from mid-17th century onwards.

Yet, to save continuously and at a significant rate would be *rational* only in a social framework where there was no endemic fear of plunder and confiscation. Even in Europe, long-term capital accumulation was greatly encouraged, first by the emergence of free towns – burgs and so forth – which afforded protection from feudal encroachments; and, secondly, by the rise of the Renaissance and absolutist monarchies, with the full blessing of the commercial and middle classes, which gave them protection vis-à-vis the great aristocratic magnates. It was the accumulation of financial capital which made possible the financing of technical innovations, and, through time, this led to modern technological development and industrial expansion – that is, what used to be generally known as 'the industrial revolution'.

There used to be a puzzle posed by classical economists, and later economic historians and development economists, to which apparently no solution satisfactory to themselves and others has been offered. It was this: Why did the process of capital accumulation not begin in societies like Iran in their rich and technologically advanced times, say in the 9th to 12th centuries. The clearest answer to that question is that it was not safe to engage in long-term saving for fear of plunder and confiscation; and that in a small number of cases where such attempts were made, or for other reasons a very large commercial fortune was amassed, later plunder and confiscation put an end to the process.

Max Weber's solution to that old puzzle was that the other, non-accumulating, societies lacked something corresponding to Protestant ethics. Weber's theory of the crucial role played by these ethics in shaping 'the spirit of capitalism' in Europe is intelligent, though it has also been subjected to serious criticism.[23] Notwithstanding that, the question in the context of our inquiry is whether such ethics could have become widespread in societies where, at least in practice, there was no right of long-term property ownership; and, if they did, and even lasted, for reasons which are difficult to envisage, they would have resulted in long-term accumulation of capital.

Because even if significant saving *had* taken place in such highly discouraging circumstances, it would not have resulted in long-term accumulation when it was perennially plundered. There can be little doubt that Protestantism, and especially its more radical sects, actively encouraged frugality and hard work (even in spite of Luther's emphasis on salvation by faith, and Calvin's doctrine of pre-destination).[24] But, from a scientific point of view, it is virtually impossible to know whether this was primarily a cause or consequence of the growth of the bourgeoisie and rise of commercial capitalism in Western Europe, that is the familiar scientific problem of determining the direction of causation – what in simple parlance they call 'the chicken or the egg problem'. However, even assuming – as does Weber, virtually – that it was a cause, it is unlikely to have been such, if the European bourgeoisie had not had legal protection for their property, a protection which was much enhanced by the emergence of the Renaissance absolutist states with their blessing and support.

Thus in answering the fundamental historical question as to why the Industrial Revolution did not take place in countries like Iran, I wrote – in 1978 in *The Political Economy of Modern Iran* – in an attempt to explain the chief reason for lack of long-term capital accumulation in Iranian history:

> The Iranian landlord...enjoyed no...right to his title, or security of his income. If European capitalist property involved an inviolable ('natural') *freedom*, and feudal property involved an inviolable ('natural') *right*, Iranian landed income and wealth were an alienable (arbitrary) *privilege*...the same state of insecurity of income and wealth applied to merchant capital, both in the merchant's lifetime and after.
>
> Capital accumulation requires postponement of present consumption, i.e. saving; and saving necessitates a minimum degree of security and certainty concerning the future. In a country in which money itself – let alone financial and physical assets – has been under the threat of confiscation and expropriation...it is impressive that financial capital *was* accumulated and trade *was* carried out to the extent that they were...The entire course of Iranian history and the existing chronicles of its events are crowded with examples of this state of insecurity and unpredictability [25]

Long-term accumulation of capital was indeed one necessary condition for industrial development. But there were other conditions, other coincidental changes that made the emergence of modern state and society possible, not least the rise of the absolutist state in Europe which made capitalist property freer than before from the encroachment of the old aristocratic magnates. This factor both helped and was helped by the 'spirit of capitalism' which sought to please God by low consumption, high saving and hard work.

It might have been a commonplace if the fundamental point had not been constantly in danger of being missed about long-term development; that it is a process which marks a total transformation of the society from one state into another, and not just one which merely results in an increase in the share of industrial goods and services in the national output, or in secularization of the law, politics and social relations, or simply in the emergence of the mass society. It is total transformations of this kind – changes which required a long and continuous process, in some cases taking a few centuries to transform the society – that seldom took place in Iran, and on the few occasions that they did for some time, the basic norms of arbitrary state and society led to their disruption, sometimes followed even by decline and retrogression, thus turning history into a series of 'connected short terms'.[26] And that is why, despite such commercial, cultural, and technical achievements in certain periods, traditional Iranian society did not reach stages of development corresponding to post-Renaissance Europe.[27]

Between the two Iranian revolutions in the 20th century, arbitrary and unsystematic copying from Europe – that is what I have described elsewhere as 'pseudo-modernism'[28] – did produce new institutions, organizations, goods and services.[29] This was achieved most noticeably through the 1960s and 1970s with the help of large and increasing oil revenues which virtually descended like manna (*ma'edeh*) from heaven[30] into the coffers of the state, and which it disbursed in an arbitrary fashion. But the relationship between state and society remained essentially the same, such that in the second Iranian Revolution of the 20th century (1977–1979) the propertied classes either supported the Revolution or remained neutral, much as they had done in the first one (1905–1909).[31]

Development requires not only *acquisition and innovation*, but also, and especially, *accumulation and preservation*, whether of wealth, of rights and privileges, or of knowledge and science. European society was a 'long-term society'. Major change, whether the fall of feudalism, the rise of capitalism and the emergence of the liberal state, whether the rejection of Aristotelian physics, Ptolemic cosmography and the Greco-Roman political thought, or the Roman Catholic hegemony – all of these took a long time and a great deal of effort and struggle to occur, but when they finally did, the change was irreversible, and a new social framework, a new law, a new science, even a new religion was established that would once again take much time and effort to change, even to reform.[32]

The long-term society makes possible long-term accumulation, precisely because the law and traditions that govern it, and its institutions, afford a certain amount of security by making the future reasonably predictable. At the same time, and for the same reason, it makes major change in the short-run very difficult. In the long-term society, revolution, whether in law, politics or science is a rare and extraordinary occurrence, but when it does happen it is non-reversible and therefore has long-term effects.

For as long as the peasants lived on the most meager subsistence, and the state as well as property-owning classes spent virtually all their income on consumption, and the saving and accumulation of the very few was lost in the long run through confiscation, plunder, division in inheritance, etc., there could never have been long-term economic development in Iran of the kind that is associated with European history and society in the past few centuries. Foreign aid and international borrowing could have been used, and were to a very limited extent used, but they could not have resulted in long-term industrialization.

This then was the logic and sociology of Iran's history. But in studying the political economy of Iran in the 20th century there was another new and important factor which needed careful and precise consideration, not just to understand and predict the relationship between state and society but, as part of it, also make sense of the economic and political events. This new factor was oil.

Oil revenues accrued to the state directly and were an important source of both income and – especially – foreign exchange to it. Much of the development of the economic infrastructures that took place under Reza Shah and from the mid-1950s under the Second Economic Plan would not have been possible without the oil revenues, not to mention the cost of military and civil administration. But it was from the early to mid-1960s that the oil revenues began to grow steadily and at substantial rates, and from 1973 onwards when, in consequence of the quadrupling of crude oil prices, they virtually exploded.

In order to study the special characteristics of Iran as an oil-exporting country it became necessary to develop a general model of the political economy of oil-exporting countries. The model thus developed had the following as its fundamental features: Oil revenues are in the nature of an economic rent, because the participation of domestic factors in the production of crude oil and the return to them by way of factor payment is a tiny proportion of the annual oil revenues, which are directly received by the state, virtually like manna from heaven. They are not just an important source of income but make up a very high proportion of the country's foreign exchange earnings. They thus become the independent variable of the economic system. And in countries such as Iran where the power of the state tends to be absolute and arbitrary, they would enhance and reinforce that tendency, and afford the state the independent means by which to extend its bureaucracy, military networks and means of coercion as well as pursue its goals of economic development. In the case of agricultural, oil countries like Iran the strategy of development would tend to be biased against agriculture, especially as there seems to be no need for its contribution to foreign exchange earnings, and petrodollars can be used to import food and other agricultural necessities and luxuries.

To the extent that the oil revenues make the state independent of the domestic means of production and the social classes, the latter become dependent on the state for employment, direct hand-outs and privileges, borrowed capital for investment, as well as general welfare schemes ranging from education and health to food subsidies. Therefore, as the fount of economic and political power, state expenditure affects the fortunes of various social classes. In a larger, agricultural oil economy, where oil revenues per head of the population are not large enough to ensure a reasonable living standard for all members of the society, this type of relationship gives rise to a new, petrolic, system of social stratification: the state has to be selective in affording even the minimum standard of comfort to individual members of the society, and those who benefit significantly from it constitute only a small percentage.

The expanding military-bureaucratic complex, the professional and other educated groups and even the business classes together make up the *clientele of the state*. Next in line are the masses of the urban population, who will look to the state for actual employment opportunities, a guaranteed minimum wage, food subsidies, health and educational schemes, etc., as well as the chance of rising to join the clientele, although both the actual and the potential aspirations of many of them are likely to be frustrated. Last come members of the rural society, the peasantry who are too poor, too numerous and politically too weak to pose the danger of direct retaliation. They are more likely to vote with their feet by marching on the cities and at their gates swelling the ranks of those urban masses whom the state would like to keep reasonably happy.

The entire system would depend on the size and strategy of state expenditure. The state's *consumption* expenditure expands its own military-bureaucratic network. The effectively unearned increases in the clientele's income lead to a high rate of private consumption expenditure. State *investment* expenditure would tend to place great emphasis on urban expansion, emphasizing construction, modern service activities and heavy industries, and employing the latest, capital-intensive, technologies. This would face the country with serious shortages of highly skilled labour, both mechanical and managerial, and also result in technological unemployment.

Whether or not monetary expansion is a 'cause' of inflation, in a society where ostentation is a most important determinant of social status (even recognition as a *person*), people would tend to spend their excess liquidity on goods and services. And when for this and other reasons inflation becomes a feature of everyday life, even those with a great deal of cash to dispose of would buy a lot of durable goods, especially urban land and property – in order both to defend and improve the value of their liquid assets. And because of the insecure and short-term nature of the society and political economy, they would tend to spend on speculative assets and activities, whether urban property or forward purchase and sale of everyday commodities. Regarding saving and investment, precisely because of the short-term nature of the society and the state of insecurity and unpredictability, private investment in manufacturing and services, whether large or small, tends to be limited to short horizons, often being limited to two or so years and seldom going beyond five years and more. In any case, net aggregate saving out of *non-oil* output and income tends to be much too small for a developing economy – consisting of 2 to 3 rather 10 to 12 per cent of the national income – most of the aggregate 'saving' being in fact due to the unseen hand of the oil revenues.

Such are the rudiments of an elaborate model which I developed for the study of the oil-exporting economies in the 1970s.[33] And it was on the basis of that as well as the historical short-termness and arbitrary nature of state and society that I was pessimistic about prospects for the long-term development of the Iranian economy, compared to predictions based on existing European models, if not all of which predicted the imminent emergence of 'the Japan of the Middle East', they were nevertheless highly optimistic about the outcome of the oil price revolution for the Iranian economy.

And it was on that basis that, while the Revolution of 1977–1979 was still proceeding, I described it not as a class war combined with a related struggle against imperialism, but as the revolt of the entire society against an arbitrary state which happened to be a client state of Western powers, emphasizing that despite many differences between that and the Constitutional Revolution, they were similar inasmuch as both of them were revolts of the society against the state, much as it has been the case in Iranian revolutions since time immemorial.[34]

To conclude briefly, economic history and the history of political economy are useful and respectable academic pursuits in their own right, just as history itself is one of the most important fields of learning and scholarship in every civilized country. But they are and can be even more important than that especially when they are conducted not just in a descriptive but also in an analytical framework. Their contribution is necessary for studies of the logic and sociology of the history of the society or societies to which they refer, and therefore in helping to provide the relevant perspectives for the study of economy and society. Not every economist, sociologist or political scientist has to be a historian, but their work is meaningful, realistic and relevant to the extent that it is conducted against the appropriate social background and reality, which history, its logic and its sociology can provide, on the condition that these too are constructed on a realistic and relevant plain.

Theories of European economy and society differ insofar as they may be Marxist, liberal and other. Yet despite serious conflicts among them it is clear that they are based on the fundamental characteristics of European society, and that the historical background to all such systems and ideologies is unmistakably European history, from the Greeks to modern times. Models based on such theories can also be of some use in Iran but so long as their assumptions do not contradict the basic features of Iranian history and society where these are different from the corresponding features of Europe. Iran has been an arbitrary state and society, with an embedded and persistent antagonism between the state and society, absence of an independent legal framework, tendency towards chaos and disorder, an unusual degree of insecurity and unpredictability, high social mobility, etc., which may be summarized in the concept of 'the short-term society'. And the rules of social and economic behaviour, public and private economic decision making, etc. can be, and often are, very different from the assumptions of models which are based on theories of European society and economy, irrespective of the ideology or paradigm to which they refer.

## Notes

* Keynote address communicated to the conference of the Iranian Economic Association on Economic History and Iranian Economic History held in early December 2004 in Tehran.
1 See Homa Katouzian, *Adam Smith va Servat-e Melal*, second edition (Tehran, 2003). See further, *The Life of Adam Smith*, Jacob Viner (ed.) (Fairfield, NJ, 1977).
2 See Katouzian, *Adam Smith* and Adam Smith, *A Study in the Nature and Causes of the Wealth of Nations*, Edwin Cannan (ed.) (London, 1961).
3 See, for example, Homa Katouzian, *Iranian History and Politics* (London and New York, 2003), chapter 1; Katouzian *Ideology and Method in Economics* (London and New York, 1980), chapter 2; Katouzian, *The Political Economy of Modern Iran*, chapter 2; James Mill, *The History of India* (London, 1977). Richard Jones later received a round of applause from Marx (in contrast to Ricardo) for his emphasis on the significance of historical evidence for economic analysis. See Karl Marx, *Theories of Surplus Value* (Moscow, 1968) 2: 399–403.
4 Quoted in Katouzian, *Ideology and Method*: 34, and cited in R. L. Smyth, ed., *Essays in Economic Method* (London, 1962). The idea was of course not very novel. In particular it had been anticipated by Vico, Herder and Michelet. See Isaiah Berlin, 'Historical Inevitability' in his *Four Essays on Liberty* (London, 1969). See also Berlin's *Vico and Herder* (London, 1975) and *The Hedgehog and the Fox* (London, 1988). See further, J.A. Schumpeter, *Economic Doctrine and Method* (London, 1954).
5 Numerous sources may be cited for this but it is clearly argued both in Marshall's *Principles of Economics* and Keynes's *General Theory of Employment, Interest and Money*. For a summary discussion of the history of this debate, see Katouzian *Ideology and Method*.
6 See Katouzian, *Ideology and Method*, 7.
7 See in particular Homa Katouzian, 'The Hallmarks of Science and Scholasticism: A Historical Analysis', *The Yearbook of the Sociology of the Sciences*, 1982 (Reidel, 1982).
8 This is my own comprehensive formulation, in *Ideology and Method*, of the theses of the German Historical School of economists who were numerous and came in two generations. But for a more detailed account of their ideas see, for example, Joseph A. Schumpeter, *Historian of Economics: Perspectives on the History of Economic Thought*, ed. Laurence S. Moss (London, 1996). Eric Roll, *A History of Economic Thought*, (London, 1974). Colin Clark, *The Conditions of Economic Progress* (London and New York, 1957). Simon Kuznets, *Modern Economic Growth: Rate, Structure and Spread* (London, 1996); Simon Kuznets, *Economic Growth and Structure* (London, 1966).
9 See Nicholas Kaldor, 'Causes of the Slow Growth of the British Economy', *Economic Journal* (1966).
10 See Homa Katouzian, 'The Development of the Service Sector: A New Approach', *Oxford Economic Papers* (November 1970).
11 See for my comments, Homa Katouzian, 'Services in International Trade: A Theoretical Interpretation' in Herbert Giersch, ed., *International Economic Development and Resource Transfer* ( Tübingen, Institute of World Economics, 1979).
12 See Homa Katouzian, *Iranian History and Politics: The Dialectic of State and Society* (London and New York, 2003) Preface and Introduction.
13 See Katouzian, *Ideology and Method*, 7.
14 See, for example, Homa Katouzian, 'Problems of Democracy and the Public Sphere in Modern Iran', *Comparative Studies of South Asia, Africa and the Middle East*, 18, 2, 1998, reprinted *in Iranian History and Politics*, and '*Dar Ta'assob va Khami, va Tajjali-ye an dar Jame'eh-ye Kolangi*' in *Kiyan*, reprinted in *Tazadd-e Dawlat va Mellat, Nazariyeh-ye Tarikh va Siyasat dar Iran* (Tehran, 2001).

15 See Homa Katouzian, *State and Society in Iran, The Eclipse of the Qajars and the Emergence of the Pahlavis* (London and New York, 2000) 1–3; *Iranian History and Politics*, '*Farrah-ye Izadi va Haqq-e Elahi-ye Padshahan*' in *Ettela'at Siyasi-Eqtesadi*, 129–130, 1998; 'Legitimacy and Succession In Iranian History', *Comparative Studies of South Asia, Africa and the Middle East*, 23, 1&2, 2003.

16 See Katouzian, 'Problems of Democracy' and '*Dar Ta'ssob va Kham*i'.

17 See Alexander Gerschenkron, 'The Approach to European Industrialization' in *Economic Backwardness in Historical Perspectives* (Cambridge, MA, 1962).

18 See Adam Smith, The *Wealth of Nations*, ed. Edwin Cannan 1, 2, 3 'Of the Accumulation of Capital, or of productive and unproductive labour': 320.

19 Ibid.

20 Ibid.: 321–323. See further, Katouzian, *Adam Smith va Servat-e Melal*: 95–97 and 153–157.

21 For an extensive account and discussion of this subject, see Katouzian, *Ideology and Mehtod*. See also, Katouzian, *Adam Smith va Servat-e Melal*.

22 Keynes said this about Ricardo, whose theory (which was directly based on Smith's) he was attacking. See his *The General Theory of Employment, Interest and Money*, 2.

23 See Max Weber, *Protestant Ethics and the Spirit of Capitalism* (London, 1930); R. H. Tawney, *Religion and the Rise of Capitalism* (London, 1937). For a short but poignant critique of Werner Sombart (as well as Weber, in whose spirit he wrote his *The Jews and Modern Capitalism*), see Hugh Trevor-Roper, 'The Jews And Modern Capitalism', in *Historical Essays* (London, 1957). See also his 'The Medieval Italian Capitalists', ibid.

24 See further, Dickens, *The Age of Humanism and Reformation* (London, 1977); Joel Hurstfield, The Reformation Crisis (London, 1965); V.H.H. Green, Luther and the Reformation (London and New York, 1954); Mann Phillips, Erasmus and the Northern Renaissance (London, 1949).

25 See Katouzian, *The Political Economy of Modern Iran*, 18–20.

26 See, for example, Homa Katouzian, 'Arbitrary Rule, A Comparative Theory of State, Politics and Society in Iran', *British Journal of Middle Eastern Studies*, 1, 24, 1997, and *State and Society in Iran*, 1.

27 See further, Katouzian, *Iranian History and Politics*.

28 For the latest version of this author's concept of 'pseudo-modernism', see *State and Society in Iran*, 11.

29 See further Homa Katouzian, 'The Pahlavi Regime in Iran' in H.E. Chehabi and Juan Linz (eds), *Sultanistic Regimes* (Baltimore, 1997) and *The Political Economy of Modern Iran*.

30 As Rumi has it: 'Ma'edeh az asmen shod 'a'deh / Chon keh goft 'Inzil 'alaina Ma'ideh''.

31 See Homa Katouzian, 'Towards a General Theory of Iranian Revolutions', *Journal of Iranian Research and Analysis*, 15, 2, 1999, reprinted in *Iranian History and Politics*.

32 This discreet and long-term process of change in science as well as society had been well known. In the case of society it had been well documented and subjected to much theorizing. In the case of knowledge and science, it had once been discussed in the original sense of Hegelian and Marxian concepts of ideology (i.e. 'ideology' as consciousness bound by the limits of moral and/or material development in its various 'stages'). Thomas Kuhn offered a new model in the case of 'scientific revolutions', though he overlooked the fact that it was equally valid for the history of all (not just scientific) knowledge, and implied that it was necessarily the best procedure for the advancement of science. See his *The Structure of Scientific Revolutions* (Chicago: The University of Chicago Press, 1970); Homa Katouzian, 'T. S. Kuhn, Functionalism and Sociology of Knowledge', *British Journal for the Philosophy of Science* (June 1984), 'The Hallmarks of Science and Scholasticism' and *Ideology and Method in Economics*, 4.

33 Cast in more technical and comprehensive terms than the above brief, it took a long time for it to be accepted for publication, and that by an unorthodox journal, the others not being convinced for academic or other reasons. See Homa Katouzian, 'The Political Economy of Oil Exporting Countries', *Peuples Mediterraneans* (1979). See also 'Oil *versus* Agriculture, A Case of Dual Resource Depletion in Iran', *Journal of Peasant Studies* (April 1978), and 'Oil and Economic Development in the Middle East', in *The Modern Economic History of the Middle East in its World Context*, Essays Presented to Charles Issawi, ed. George Sabagh (Cambridge, 1989).

34 See Katouzian, *The Political Economy of Modern Iran*, 18. Later I gave the question of the nature, causes and consequences of Iranian revolutions a general treatment in 'Towards a General Theory of Iranian Revolutions', *Iranian History and Politics*.

# Index